WELCOMING FINITUDE

ORTHODOX CHRISTIANITY AND CONTEMPORARY THOUGHT

SERIES EDITORS
Aristotle Papanikolaou and Ashley M. Purpura

This series consists of books that seek to bring Orthodox Christianity into an engagement with contemporary forms of thought. Its goal is to promote (1) historical studies in Orthodox Christianity that are interdisciplinary, employ a variety of methods, and speak to contemporary issues; and (2) constructive theological arguments in conversation with patristic sources and that focus on contemporary questions ranging from the traditional theological and philosophical themes of God and human identity to cultural, political, economic, and ethical concerns. The books in the series explore both the relevancy of Orthodox Christianity to contemporary challenges and the impact of contemporary modes of thought on Orthodox self-understandings.

WELCOMING FINITUDE

TOWARD A PHENOMENOLOGY OF ORTHODOX LITURGY

CHRISTINA M. GSCHWANDTNER

FORDHAM UNIVERSITY PRESS
New York • 2019

for Lisa Gassin and Tracy Gustilo

CONTENTS

PREFACE

This book attempts to open a space for a phenomenological account of Orthodox liturgy. It is thereby directed at three quite different audiences: first, liturgical theologians or scholars of ritual; second, philosophers (especially those who employ phenomenology—the study of experience—as their philosophical methodology); and third, Eastern Orthodox Christians or scholars of Orthodox Christianity, broadly conceived. The question of why one should bother thinking about liturgical experience philosophically can thus be raised in at least three different ways: First, why should liturgical experience be examined with philosophical tools? What sort of insight might philosophy provide for what is often an intensely personal religious experience? What can philosophy add to our understanding or especially our living of liturgical experience in a particular religious tradition? In short, what can a phenomenological exploration of liturgy add to the theological study of liturgy? Second, why should philosophy, even if it can examine religion, focus on liturgy? Why not deal with doctrine or belief statements or claims about the divine? Would these not be much more appropriate and congenial topics for philosophy to investigate? Of what interest could ritual—especially the ritual of a specific tradition—possibly be to the philosopher? And third, why bother with Orthodox liturgy specifically? How could a philosophical investigation of liturgy possibly have anything to say to Orthodox Christians involved in liturgical practice? How might it illuminate their experience? This preface gives a brief preliminary answer to each of these groups of potential readers. The introduction will provide fuller accounts of phenomenology and liturgical theology inasmuch as they are in the background of this more focused philosophical study of Eastern Orthodox liturgy.

First, why should the Eastern Orthodox religious tradition involve itself in a phenomenological investigation of its practices? One reason is that Orthodoxy has traditionally stressed the importance of experience. For example, Pavel Florensky, an important early twentieth-century Russian Orthodox philosopher, begins his *The Pillar and Ground of Truth* with the claim that "living religious experience" is at the very core of the Orthodox tradition: "Only by relying on immediate experience can one survey the spiritual treasures of the Church and come to see their value . . . The Orthodox taste, the Orthodox temper, is felt but is not subject to arithmetical calculation. Orthodoxy is shown, not proved. That is why there is only one way to understand Orthodoxy: through direct Orthodox experience."[1] Thus, "to become Orthodox, it is necessary to immerse oneself all at once in the very element of Orthodoxy, to begin living in an Orthodox way. There is no other way."[2] Similarly, Vladimir Lossky opens his popular *The Mystical Theology of the Eastern Church* by contrasting Orthodox "direct experience of the truth" to Western (Catholic) dogmatic and abstract theology. The "mystical theology of the Eastern Church" is about "lived experience."[3] Experience, especially liturgical experience, is consistently posited as not only absolutely essential for the Orthodox tradition, but as its most authentic marker.[4]

One should think, then, that Orthodoxy would be particularly well suited to make a contribution to religious phenomenology. Yet often this insistence on experience remains rather generic, used primarily to speak of Orthodoxy as a "living" faith rather than a dead scholasticism. Furthermore, "experience" can easily become a purely subjective category, referring to a personal, interior encounter, which cannot be shared or articulated. If the experience is so singular and intimate that nothing can be said about it, how would one determine that it functions as a broader characteristic of "Orthodoxy"? Does not the positing of such experience become a rather arbitrary exercise in which one sort of unarticulated experience is posited against another without any way of distinguishing between them or even knowing to what they refer? Is there a way to articulate the broader structures of such experience without destroying it as experience or imposing foreign and inappropriate categories upon it?

This book will suggest that phenomenology can provide such a method to think more carefully about religious experience, specifically liturgical experience, in a way that allows it to unfold from itself. Phenomenology seeks to depict experiences as they actually reveal and manifest themselves, to allow us to see them as they show or give themselves. It is a form of attention and depiction that has its own rigor. It gets beyond merely individual and empirical experience in order to examine broader structures and patterns in ways that would allow us to think more deeply about the character and meaning of such experience. The careful depiction of the phenomena tries to uncover their "truth" (*a-letheia* as uncovering of what has previously been covered up [*lēthē*]). It is therefore an eminently suitable method for examining religious experience as well.

This already begins to address the question of why such philosophical exploration might also be of interest to the liturgical theologian or the scholar of ritual. Alexander Rentel asks: "Do we need liturgy? Why do we Orthodox Christians do this? Celebrate our services like this? Do they have to be this way? What do they mean? Do we even have to do liturgy as Christians?"[5] While phenomenology cannot resolve the theological question of whether this is something Christians *have* to do, it certainly does grapple with the issue of meaning explicitly. This question about the meaning of liturgy is frequently raised by liturgical theologians. For example, Gordon Lathrop's main thesis in his magisterial three-volume theology of liturgy is: "To inquire into the structure of the *ordo* is to inquire about the way meaning occurs in Christian worship. The thesis here operative is this: Meaning occurs through structure, by one thing set next to another. The scheduling of the *ordo*, the setting of one liturgical thing next to another in the shape of the liturgy, evokes and replicates the deep structure of biblical language, the use of the old to say the new by means of juxtaposition."[6] His discussion of holy things, holy people, and holy ground seeks to explore these structures, but his continual appeal to paradox and the attempt to interpret everything through the lens of this juxtaposition of opposites at times could do with more nuanced analyses of the experiences to which he appeals. A phenomenological depiction of such structures might supplement the theological account he provides.

Often how liturgy means is either simply presupposed or remains unarticulated. Paul Janowiak repeatedly refers to an ability to feel liturgy deeply in one's bones: "In many ways, the real presence of Christ in the bread and wine seems so ingrained in our liturgical bones that further discussion hardly seems necessary."[7] While people who practice liturgy regularly may well resonate with this description, it does not really help either them or others to understand what happens in liturgy or to illuminate how it is experienced. The eminent liturgical theologian Robert Taft says quite bluntly: "We need a phenomenology and a philosophy of liturgical reform, and we need it badly."[8] Even when authors do engage in a deep exploration of the topic, phenomenology could nevertheless provide an added dimension. Graham Hughes laments: "Otherwise stated, no one of whom I am aware who writes explicitly on liturgical theology considers it necessary to attend equally seriously to the world in which late modern worshippers are set—the world, that is, from which such worshippers come *to* the meanings proposed in worship—as a constituent element in the achievement of liturgical meaning."[9] He draws primarily on deconstruction and semiotics in his investigation into the meaning of worship. A phenomenological analysis might help supplement such a focus on linguistic analyses with a broader exploration of the experiential dimensions of liturgy and the ways in which they connect to the world "outside" of liturgy. Phenomenology is well suited to investigate these dimensions of liturgy and ritual by providing a rigorous methodology for depicting the structures of the liturgical experience. In this way, a phenomenological examination of liturgy might enable a deeper exploration of the way in which time, space, body, affect, and other such elements function in liturgical experience or at least supplement the investigations already undertaken by liturgical theologians.

Third, why should philosophy turn to the investigation of liturgical experience? Here, a couple of answers are possible. On the most basic level, philosophy ought to examine religious ritual because it has been far too exclusively focused on doctrine or abstract faith statements.[10] Although religious people certainly hold beliefs, religion is at least as much about concrete practices as it is about abstract statements of doctrine.[11] If one wants to understand how a faith or a tradition functions, one must look at its habits, practices, and experiences. While philosophy has increasingly turned in this direction in recent years—especially in contemporary French phenomenology, as will be laid out in more detail in the introduction—such investigations have still primarily focused on individual religious experience. There is very little examination of broader communal patterns of religious experience such as liturgical experience or ritual practices. Furthermore, this contemporary phenomenology of religious experience is almost exclusively Roman Catholic in tenor and inspiration. In that respect, it has developed certain blind spots: aspects of religious experience that are never examined because they do not occur or are not of primary concern in that particular tradition. While some Protestant philosophers are beginning to contribute to this discussion, Eastern Orthodox voices are practically non-existent.[12] Engaging them more fully might not only add a wider range of perspectives to the phenomenological investigation of religious experience, but also help address some of its intense focus on exclusively individual experience.

For example, although Jean-Yves Lacoste employs the terminology of "liturgy" (but explicitly distinguishes it from "ritual" or "cult") and several of the French phenomenologists speak of the Eucharist, such analysis is not understood in terms of the larger liturgical context and the significance of concrete liturgical practices for the daily living of Christian life. Instead, it is treated as one isolated instance or moment of (often intensely personal) revelation, as a phenomenon that is given to a recipient, but in a way that is disconnected from its larger phenomenal horizon in liturgical experience. The analysis often focuses almost exclusively on the singular act of eucharistic participation or even on the contemplation of the blessed sacrament, a specifically Roman Catholic experience of the Eucharist.[13] At best it constitutes a phenomenology of the sacrament, but not a phenomenology of liturgy. Liturgical experience, in contrast, is not singular or individual, it is corporate and communal. It can uncover something about our "common" being in the world and the ways in which experience is manifested as shared. Here an Orthodox perspective may widen the field of study for the examination of liturgical and religious experience.

Why might liturgy specifically be an appropriate locus for an examination of religious experience? Paul Ricoeur not only raises the question of where we must start for a philosophical investigation of religious phenomena and how we might speak about them, but argues that the best place to begin to explore the meaning or truth of religious experience is to look at how it is articulated in language, by which he means the biblical texts, which he takes to convey the most primordial (or "originary"—both are translations of Heidegger's *ursprünglich*) experience of Christian faith. In an essay on "Philosophy and Religious Language," he discusses three assumptions or presuppositions that are important for investigating religious expression. The first is that "whatever ultimately may be the nature of the so-called religious experience, it comes to language, it is articulated in language, and the most appropriate place to interpret it on its own terms is to inquire into its linguistic expression." Secondly, this kind of religious discourse "is not senseless" but it is "worthwhile to analyze it, because something is said that is not said by other kinds of discourse." In other words, "it is meaningful at least for the community of faith that uses it either for the sake of self-understanding or for the sake of communication with others exterior to the faith community." Third, the religious discourse makes truth claims that "must be understood on its own terms" and hence must use its own "criteria of truth" instead of imposing foreign criteria on it. Consequently, "a hermeneutical philosophy . . . will try to get as close as possible to the most *originary* expressions of a community of faith, to those expressions through which the members of this community have interpreted their experience for the sake of themselves or for others' sake."[14] Ricoeur himself, presumably because of his Protestant Reformed background, always focuses exclusively on the biblical texts, which he takes to be the most "originary" or "primordial" expressions of faith.[15] Yet, it is not at all self-evident that the Christian Scriptures are really the sole or most "primordial" locus of religious experience in the Christian tradition. Indeed, it may well be argued that liturgy or at least the context of Christian worship is more primordial in several respects.

That is not necessarily to insist that the claim of primordiality is absolutely crucial. The idea that one could actually determine what is the most originary or primordial form of religion (or any other manifestation of human experience) or that to do so would be particularly productive in terms of insights one might not gain otherwise, has itself come under challenge. It is probably enough to affirm that liturgy has been an essential, widely prevalent, and determinative Christian religious practice to make it worth investigating, without having to claim some sort of originary character for it. The language is used here primarily because Heidegger repeatedly (although not always) excludes the possibility of an *ontological* analysis of religious experience (rather than a simply ontic one, this distinction will be clarified in the Introduction) on the basis of primordiality, which only philosophy investigates. Such language is also adopted to some extent by Lacoste and Falque in their insistence on a starting point in "ordinary" experience or the human "as such." Thus, what matters here is that we can start with liturgy as a "given" of religious experience and validly examine it on phenomenological terms and with phenomenological tools, rather than interpreting it as some sort of wellspring or sole *Ursprung* of all religion.

That being said, some discussion of how specifically "religious" experience relates to broader "human" experience will obviously be necessary. It will indeed show up in every chapter to some extent, but a brief survey of some of them may justify—at least in preliminary fashion—why an examination of liturgy might be an appropriate locus for an investigation of religious experience.

First, most, if not all, other forms of Christian spirituality, practices of prayer, and reading of biblical texts arose out of liturgy, were traditionally read and heard within liturgy, and often still are experienced in this way in the Eastern tradition: The creed is said in every liturgy, the decisions of the councils are celebrated within liturgy, Scripture is primarily read in liturgy, most "doctrinal" theology appears in liturgy, even personal prayer often grows out of and leads toward communal liturgy. Liturgy is the primary place where Christian adherence is visible and Christian faith is practiced, at least in the Eastern Orthodox tradition and, one might suspect, in some form also in other Christian denominations, where "going to church" or being a "practicing" Catholic or Protestant often remains the most visible link to the tradition.[16] Many liturgical theologians claim that liturgy is "primary theology," that is to say, as much a source for theology as the Scriptures or doctrinal formulations. For example, Aidan Kavanagh contends that "sacramental discourse is primary for understanding the Church, . . . it transcends and subordinates theological reflection on the Church just as the law of worship transcends and subordinates the law of belief."[17] This is an argument made by many Western liturgical theologians from various Christian traditions and indeed by some patristic scholars. It is also increasingly stressed by several contemporary Eastern Orthodox theologians, not all of them liturgical scholars, who are calling for recognizing liturgy as a primary source for theology in the Eastern tradition.[18]

Second, liturgy has been the primary expression of Christian faith from the earliest centuries. Although there is very little evidence for how the Christian communities of the first two centuries practiced their faith, it is fairly clear that it was liturgical inasmuch as it involved shared prayer (especially the evening prayer at the setting of the sun) and a communal meal (Eucharist or agape or a combination).[19] Early communal prayers may have been patterned on Jewish practices and many Christian communities may have continued celebrating Jewish liturgical feasts, while increasingly also gathering on Sundays to celebrate the resurrection. While the exact shape of these early "services" is unknown and the extent of its

reliance on Jewish patterns fairly tentative, due to the great diversity of
practice in and lack of evidence for both Jewish and Christian communities at the time, it is clear that the primary identifier of belonging to the
emerging Christian faith was a participation in its liturgical gatherings.[20]
Evidence for the shape of celebrations becomes much clearer in the third
and positively explodes in the fourth century. Not only does liturgy provide the primary pattern for Christian life at that time, but it now comes
to play a very important role in catechesis. All the early catechetical lectures
(Cyril of Jerusalem, Ambrose of Milan, John Chrysostom, Gregory of
Nyssa, Theodore of Mopsuestia) are liturgical in character and were held in
the context of liturgy (often after the dismissal of the catechumens from
the liturgy after the preaching of the word and before the start of the
eucharistic part of the liturgy). The catechumens are taught how to pray
(often via an explanation of the Lord's Prayer) and what to believe (usually
by learning the creed—or some creed—by heart), but these are not private
practices to be performed at home—they are public affirmations and
prayers to be said in the context of liturgy together with the other "people
of God."

Indeed, the term "liturgy" (*leitourgia*) means "work of the people." The
use of this word itself is telling. In the ancient (Greek) world, it referred to
the semi-obligatory gifts donated by rich citizens on behalf of the state.
The wealthier citizens were expected to give to "public works," to put on
games and theaters, to maintain religious houses and ceremonies, to contribute to the upkeep of public buildings, to intervene with charitable
donations in cases of famine caused by drought or flooding. This language
of public engagement or charity was adopted by the Christian tradition to
describe its communal ritual practices. According to Hemming, "to undertake *leitourgia* is to make a public manifestation, through visible works, of
the invisible (and so mystical) meaning and destiny of the *laos*."[21] Or, to
cite Kavanagh again: "Rather, this full public liturgy, this urban act, this
duty owed to God like taxes were owed to the state (the word *leitourgia* was
used in antiquity to designate both sorts of acts) was simply the Church
manifested in its deepest nature in the human *civitas* as the presence, the
embodiment in the world of the World to come, of the Kingdom, of the
new and final age."[22] While the term had already been used to refer to
certain forms of religious sacrifice (for example, in the translation of
the Septuagint), its form of gift-giving really constitutes a kind of taxa-
tion on the wealthy. Later Christian preachers are still quite aware of this

connotation when they exhort the richer members of their communities to practice liturgy by giving generously on behalf of the poor and starving.[23] Liturgy, then, is the work of the Christian people as the concrete manifestation of their participation in the Christian community.

Liturgy was "public" in several other ways. Many early Christian buildings for worship were basilicas, which were essentially public meeting houses.[24] They did not imitate religious temples (whether Jewish or pagan) but instead the main administrative building, which then became slowly transformed into a more deliberate sacred space. Liturgical ceremonies rivaled other public forms of entertainment (not always successfully), such as the games, horse races, and the theater. This is evident both in the rhetorical form of liturgy and preaching and in the reactions of the audiences as they are reported for congregations for centuries (applauding, yelling, sighing, complaining, and other loud responses).[25] Preachers repeatedly had to call congregations to silence and attention and often exhorted their communities to come to liturgy in explicit comparison with the attraction of the games or races (especially John Chrysostom for whom this is a constant theme). Christian liturgy also took over other popular public practices such as festival processions, sometimes in competition with "heretical" Christian groups, such as the Arians. Such processions must have been immensely popular; they still occurred several times a week in tenth- and eleventh-century Constantinople.[26] Christianity shaped the social and political culture of the late Roman empire through its liturgical transformation of public space, through seeking to create more or less deliberately (and more or less successfully) a Christian polis.

Besides the initial catechesis for Christian conversion, liturgy also became the primary locus for shaping Christian identity.[27] When Christianity increasingly became the dominant or even the main religion of the people, the central place for teaching and forming Christian identity was within liturgy. Although there certainly also always were private forms of devotion and presumably some level of catechesis in the home in the rearing of children into the faith,[28] the main opportunity for any sort of "official" instruction in the faith was in the liturgical context. One learned what it meant to be Christian within the context of participating in liturgy. And liturgy was extensive and pervasive, especially once there was a strong monastic presence in the cities, which shaped the liturgical life in the Eastern parts of Christianity in profound ways. Although certainly not all or even the majority of urban dwellers participated in the various daily offices in the monasteries, the participation of lay men and women in at least some of the daily morning or evening offices remained the case for centuries.[29] Identity continues to be shaped also in other ways through liturgical practices, especially through the liturgical cycles of fasting and feasting, which constantly exhort to repentance while always holding before us the hope of transformation and even resurrection. Life cycle practices were also deeply marked liturgically, especially once infant baptism became common and marriages and funerals were held in churches and defined by liturgical ceremonies (much later for marriages than for funerals, which became "Christian" early on, deeply influenced by the cult of saints and their relics, which emerged out of the commemoration and celebration of martyrs).

Liturgy, then, shaped Christian identity in profound ways and in many cultures continues to do so. Liturgy is the living out of Christian faith, the place and time where faith is demonstrated and practiced. It is only with the Protestant Reformation in the West that "faith" was increasingly defined in terms of personal belief or adherence to (mental agreement with) certain dogmatic statements.[30] In most other times and places (not only Christian, but maybe even more so for other traditions), religion was and is expressed in terms of practices. Just as being Jewish was as much about lighting Shabbos candles or keeping kosher, so being Christian was expressed in terms of fasting and feasting or lighting candles in front of icons. Personal and communal identity was shaped liturgically, by how one lived life together in community and what gave such life meaning and significance. "Orthodoxy" is as much about "right worship" (*doxa* in the sense of glory) as it is about "right doctrine" (*doxa* in the sense of opinion). Even the fierce rhetorical battles that were indeed fought over doctrine, especially in the fourth and fifth centuries (and which at times resulted in physical and not merely rhetorical violence), to a certain extent arose out of liturgical questions and practices about right worship: Is the Son divine or are we worshipping a creature? What does it mean to refer to Mary liturgically as the "Mother of God" (*theotokos*)? Are icons appropriate tools for prayer or are they idolatrous and should be removed from churches? And these controversies did not merely agitate a few ivory-tower theologians (almost all "theologians" at the time were clerics worried about their communities not academics worried about their CVs), but clearly moved average people, as not only the controversy over icons in the eighth and ninth centuries, but also Gregory of Nyssa's much earlier complaint demonstrates: "Every corner of Constantinople was full of their discussions: the streets, the market place, the shops of the money changers, the victuallers. Ask a tradesman how many obols he wants for some article in his shop, and he replies with a discourse on generated and ungenerated being. Ask the price of bread today and the baker tells you: 'The son is subordinate to the father.' Ask your servant if the bath is ready and he makes an answer: 'The son arose out of nothing.'"[31] These issues mattered to people because they touched their identity and that identity was shaped liturgically.

Finally, liturgy is seen as the primary locus in which God is encountered, as the place where "earth and heaven" meet. Maybe the best illustration of this is the famous account of the Kievan ambassadors who report their experience in Hagia Sophia to their chieftain Vladimir:

> Then we went to Greece, and the Greeks led us to the edifices where they worship their God, and we knew not whether we were in heaven or on earth. For on earth there is no such splendor or such beauty, and we are at a loss to describe it. We only know that God dwells there among men, and their service is fairer than the ceremonies of other nations. For we cannot forget that beauty.[32]

They witnessed a splendor at Hagia Sophia that left them wondering whether they were in heaven or on earth, and they were somehow certain of God's presence there. This report, frequently taken to be exemplary of the spirit of the Orthodox tradition, makes liturgy the primary "source" for deciding the "truth" of this faith: It was the experience of worship that convinced them that this was the true religion, not an account of doctrine, not a creed, not even the Scriptures (indeed, there is no reference to the Bible at all). The "Greeks" apparently did not argue with their visitors or explain their faith or otherwise seek to convince them. They took them to church. The visitors are overwhelmed by its beauty and it is this beauty that convinces them of the viability of the faith. This seems a God worth worshipping, a God who "lives there with people." Regardless of whether this is an actual (or accurate) report of a real event, it certainly conveys what is believed about liturgy: Here God is in some way manifested on earth. Orthodoxy is the "right" faith for them because of the beauty of its liturgy, which demonstrates that God dwells there. Within liturgy, believers expect to encounter the divine in some form and to have communion with God. Liturgy, then, is the place and time where religious faith is at its highest and most visible display; it is the locus where Christianity becomes "real," where it is practiced and lived, where one becomes and lives as a Christian by participating in the ecclesial community.

This means that liturgy is not only an eminently appropriate place for examining faith and religious identity, but that it conveys the very core of that identity as the primary locus for religious experience. Phenomenology, as the study of experience and its meaning, can start in no better place if it wishes to investigate the meaning of Christian religious experience, at least as it was practiced for most of Christian history and still profoundly shapes Christian identity in the Orthodox tradition.

ACKNOWLEDGMENTS

Although I have been interested in questions of liturgy and Eucharist from a theological perspective for a long time, I first explored the possibility of a phenomenology of liturgy at the invitation of Jim Faulconer in a talk to his students at Brigham Young University in April 2009, of Philipp Rosemann at the University of Dallas in November of the same year, and of B. Keith Putt at Samford University in April 2015. A preliminary version of the chapter on temporality was presented at the invitation of Mark Wrathall at a conference on phenomenology and religious life at Oxford University in April 2016. I have delivered papers on various aspects of the topic of liturgy and phenomenology in the context of meetings of the Society for Ricoeur Studies; the Society for Phenomenology and Existential Philosophy; the Postmodernism, Culture, and Religion Conference at Syracuse organized by John D. Caputo in 2011; the International Network for the Philosophy of Religion; and various other contexts. Many of these presentations resulted in published papers. Although none of that material is used explicitly in this book, the conversations at the conferences, the comments of reviewers, and various replies to published work have all informed my thinking about liturgy and all are hereby gratefully acknowledged.

The topic of liturgy found a quite different consideration in my Ph.D. thesis on the role of non-human creation in the major feasts of the Orthodox tradition, which was written at the intersection of ecological theology and liturgical theology under the supervision of Andrew Louth, from whom I learned an immense amount quite aside from the research undertaken in Durham, UK. The intense reading in liturgics and patristic theology I was able to undertake in the context of preparation for that thesis was made possible through a sabbatical year (2009–2010) from the University of Scranton. A preliminary draft of the present book was composed with the help of a faculty fellowship from Fordham University in the academic year 2015–2016. I am grateful to both universities for these occasions to research, think, and write more intensively. During the fellowship year, I spent several months in Paris in the Spring 2016, pursuing research at the Institut Catholique, which was made possible through the immense generosity and hospitality of Emmanuel Falque and the Institut. Without the use of the Byzantine library there, the benefit of Falque's lectures, and the time to think and write without distraction, this project certainly would not have come to fruition.

I also want to thank Telly Papanikolaou and George Demacopoulos for welcoming this book into their series in Contemporary Orthodox Studies at Fordham University and for their frequent encouragement of my work— on this topic and more broadly—along the way. It has been a pleasure to work again with Nancy Rapoport, whose patience and expertise as a copy editor are most appreciated.

I would like to thank especially all those who have read prior versions of this manuscript and provided valuable feedback: Gregory Tucker, John Behr, Bruce Morrill, Laurence Hemming, and Tracy Gustilo. Extended email conversations about parts of the project with Joe Calandrino (especially during the initial drafting in the spring of 2016) also helped clarify my thinking on several of its aspects. Their thoughtful questions, perceptive criticisms, and helpful corrections have made this a far better manuscript. Although I have not adopted every suggestion made (partly for reasons of space), I certainly considered all of them carefully. Gregory especially saved me from several howlers at the last minute and always responded promptly and graciously to my desperate inquiries on matters both liturgical and Greek. All remaining errors and inadequacies are obviously my own.

In the academic years 2015/2016 and 2016/2017, a liturgy discussion group met at St. Vladimir's Orthodox Theological Seminary, in which we read a variety of texts on liturgy and discussed them together. I want to thank all of the members of this group for the manifold suggestions of relevant sources and the vigorous and frank discussions: Tracy Gustilo, Gregory Tucker, Will Rettig, Evan Freeman, Harrison Russin, and Kyle

Parrott. I am also grateful to Leanne Parrott for allowing me to use one of her beautiful photos for the cover of this book. The extended community at St. Vladimir's and the vibrant liturgical life there have done much to nurture me and help me survive the past years in New York. In this respect, I am especially grateful for the friendship of Kate and John Behr, Nancy Rentel, Gabrielle and Harrison Russin, and Tracy Gustilo, as well as the many student families who over the years have made me feel part of the community.

This book is dedicated to two Orthodox friends who have been fellow "liturgy geeks" for years: Lisa Gassin and Tracy Gustilo. Lisa took me to my first Orthodox liturgies, patiently answered my countless questions, and engaged enthusiastically in every sort of theological discussion imaginable. She also generously served as my sponsor when I was received into the Orthodox Church many years later and has continued to listen to all of my gripes and complaints about institutions, theology, and life for far more years since. Tracy has not only done her share of such listening, but also read every word of the initial manuscript carefully and provided invaluable critique and advice. We have had more discussions about liturgy over the years than may well be healthy. On a more mundane level, she has graciously put up with my countless attempts at inflicting culinary experiments on her, pulled me out of various levels of depression an infinite number of times, listened to more complaining about ecclesial and academic life than anyone should have to stomach, and patiently tolerated my incorrigible cynicism, sharp tongue, and short temper. I am deeply grateful to both for their generous friendship, stimulating conversations, and kind prodding.

INTRODUCTION

As this book tries to address multiple audiences who may well not be familiar with the other disciplines that are engaged here, the Introduction tries to provide some background for phenomenology as a methodology and the ways in which this philosophical examination touches on liturgical theology. (Brief introductions are also provided in each chapter for what liturgical theology and phenomenology have to say to the respective topic under consideration for those readers not familiar with the material.) This may also be a good place to make clear that I claim no expertise in all of the multiple disciplines and bodies of research that are on some level relevant to the topic of liturgy: liturgics (as the historical study of liturgy), liturgical theology, ritual studies, patristics, Orthodox theology more broadly, art history and the study of religious architecture, iconography, and others. I have in all cases attempted to find the most up-to-date research and to inform myself as thoroughly as possible, but obviously could not possibly master that many disciplines and may well have missed some important recent information or disregarded crucial methodological parameters. I beg the indulgence of the experts in the various fields for this philosophical engagement with a variety of insights from their respective disciplines.

Phenomenology as a Method for Examining Religious Experience

Phenomenology is a rich and diverse philosophical approach that has developed as a tradition, in which various phenomenologists stress different

1

methodological aspects or carry the thought of previous thinkers in new directions. Phenomenology has also been appropriated by other fields, such as psychology, theology, literature, archaeology, art history, religious studies, and others, where it is often used in a quite different sense.[1] It is thus important to state clearly up front with what sort of definition and shape of phenomenology this study operates and to show how the methodology is employed in this specific project.

Maybe the most important thing to recognize about *philosophical* phenomenology is that it speaks of experience in a philosophical and not primarily in an empirical sense.[2] The first two major phenomenologists expressed this in a quite different way, but on the matter of methodology there is no fundamental disagreement between them.[3] Edmund Husserl, usually considered the "father" of phenomenology, speaks of the *epochē* or "reduction" as an essential and maybe the most basic phenomenological attitude.[4] It means that in order to depict phenomena as they appear to consciousness and to ascertain something about their meaning, we must set aside our preoccupation with the everyday world (or what he calls the "natural attitude") and especially the main preoccupation of previous philosophy: How does the thing "out there" get into my mental "in here"? This split between empirical object and mental image of it in understanding, which is expressed in various ways by all modern thinkers from Descartes onward and reaches its height in Kant's distinction between noumena ("things" or objects as they are "in themselves") and phenomena (how they appear to us), is seen by phenomenologists as a dead-end. Phenomenology seeks a new starting point that would be able to examine experience without this gap between a "world out there" and its representation in the mind ("in here"). Husserl sets it aside by "bracketing" the concern with empirical existence and instead focusing on phenomena as they actually appear to consciousness. Thus, instead of worrying about whether our mental "image" of the chair "corresponds" to a "real" chair "out there," the phenomenologist examines instead how the experience of the chair is given to us in consciousness as a real experience. Even if one may not be certain there really is a chair "out there" aside from its image in my mind, we certainly do experience seeing a chair and act as if the chair is real when we sit on it and experience it as solid or fragile, comfortable or hard. The question of its existence "in itself," apart from our experience of it, in some way misses the fundamental way in which experience is always already experienced *as* an existing reality. Husserl goes beyond this to stress that a genuinely philosophical phenomenology is interested not just in the individual experiences that appear to one particular consciousness, but rather in the very *structures* of experience for human beings, thus in the shared world of experience and its meaning beyond my particular empirical encounters. He even suggests in various places of his work that we can get at the "essence" of phenomena by such practice of reduction (and other investigative activities, such as imaginative variation).

Husserl's most important student, Martin Heidegger, no longer speaks of "reduction"—he rarely uses the term unlike some more recent phenomenological thinkers who return to Husserl on this point—nor does he seem primarily interested in consciousness per se. Rather, he seeks to understand being as a whole or as such, to which human being, as the one being that considers its own being (usually called "Dasein," the German word for existence, literally "being there"), provides special access. But Heidegger makes a similar distinction between what one might call "empirical" or concrete experience and its more strictly "philosophical" investigation, namely what he calls the "ontic" (or "positive") and the "ontological" (or "phenomenological"), respectively. He claims that all the other disciplines—psychology, anthropology, sociology, but also chemistry, biology, physics, and even theology—are "ontic" or "positive" sciences, inasmuch as they deal with particular aspects of human being or concrete instances of such being. Philosophy instead engages in a general analysis of human being per se, in its very existence. Philosophy, as phenomenology, deals with the fundamental structures of Dasein as such.[5]

Both Husserl and Heidegger (and indeed most subsequent phenomenologists) claim that the experience of consciousness or of human being in the world is so hard to examine precisely because it is both closest to us and furthest away. In everyday life, we take it as obvious and self-evident; we are so deeply and intimately wrapped up in it that it becomes difficult to see or even to focus on it more fully. Such a more deliberate focus requires a "step back," a kind of suspension or withdrawal, which may well be another way of describing the phenomenological "reduction." In order to see and depict how experience is manifested or given, one must temporarily suspend one's "participation" in it in order to see fully what appears there. This is not a denial of empirical or "actual" experience or an abstraction from the concretely lived reality in a way that would make it unrecognizable, but a particular focus or attitude that enables a better "view." We often see better when we take a step back or distance ourselves a bit; sometimes we are too close to an event or experience to have any sort of "perspective" on it or to see it clearly. Philosophy as phenomenology teaches us to see more fully what appears by shifting our viewpoint at least momentarily, by suspending certain presuppositions and involvements temporarily, not to reach an "objective" place that would speak from "nowhere" or a completely "neutral" or "scientific" point of view, but to focus on our very involvement and engagement with things differently, so that the mode of this engagement, the terms of our involvement, the manner of our "wrapped-up-ness" with the world, the "how" of our living and being in the reality of experience, can itself become the subject of investigation—because it usually does not, because we usually simply take it for granted and are unaware of it. Phenomenology, then, brings to awareness and attention the experience we actually live out—usually without such awareness—by taking a momentary step away from the living of the experience so as to examine and understand it more fully. The French phenomenologist Maurice Merleau-Ponty says that "true philosophy entails learning to see the world anew" and roots it in the primary philosophical impetus of wonder, which Aristotle already highlighted as the origin of philosophical thinking.[6]

The attitude of the reduction and its "bracketing" of questions of objectivity or existence, then, is not a separation from the world or a denial of its reality. Nor are the "ontic" and the "ontological" in Heidegger two completely different spheres or levels of thinking. Heidegger often points out that particular ontic examples can give us insight into ontological structures and that the ontic frequently has a pre-ontological sense or is even mixed up with the ontological (as he thinks it is in many prior philosophers). Especially after strong reactions to his "idealist" focus, Husserl also increasingly turned back to what he called the "lifeworld" (*Lebenswelt*) to consider how it presents itself phenomenologically and might reveal experience more fully and in a more engaged sense. This call to "return to the things themselves," which already guided Husserl and Heidegger, is heeded especially by the French phenomenologists who appropriated their thought subsequently. Phenomenology continues as a vibrant tradition in France today. And while in Husserl and Heidegger phenomenology remained rigorously agnostic (or possibly even atheist), partly because phenomenology's fundamental emphasis on the immanence of experience seemed to exclude *a priori* any consideration of "transcendence," such as that associated with a notion of God, French phenomenology has increasingly turned to an investigation of religious experience in a variety of ways. Providing some examples of how they investigate this may lead us beyond the fundamental presupposition about phenomenology as a philosophical exercise in order to work out this methodology more fully and illustrate how it might operate in the context of religious experience. This will remain here merely an introductory sense of such exploration of experience. We will return to various aspects of their work more fully in the treatment that follows.

Jean-Yves Lacoste shares Heidegger's starting point of an analytic of Dasein as being-in-the-world, as it is laid out in *Being and Time* [7] He argues explicitly that Heidegger's analysis of the structures of Dasein must be the base line for any phenomenological investigation, especially an investigation into religious being. Thus he accepts to some extent Heidegger's claim that phenomenology is more primordial and more basic than theology. Yet he goes on from there to examine what he calls human "being-before-God" [8] and shows that an investigation of such being "coram dei" or "before the Absolute" can also reveal ontological structures and is not purely ontic. While liturgical or religious being is always secondary, later, or even optional, it is not merely empirical or particular but can provide further insight into the human condition as such. In *Experience and the Absolute*, Lacoste's fullest exploration of "being-before-God," he calls such being faced with the Absolute, "liturgical" being. He defines his use of the term "liturgy" as referring to "the logic that governs the encounter between the human and God," regardless of where such an encounter might take place. [9] Although he acknowledges that this may well include concrete liturgical practices, he focuses instead on more fundamental religious structures or experiences. In these structures, such as monasticism or asceticism, being-before-God emerges as liminal, as essentially concerned with abnegation. Being before the Absolute is a rupture with ordinary being; it challenges us and dispossesses us of our preoccupation with being. It thus confronts us with another possible dimension of being, another mode of existence. Such being before the Absolute is always optional; it is a surplus. And, yet, to exist "kenotically," to exist "in the image of God" is to access a dimension of human existence that is closed to "ordinary" Dasein and reveals something about it, which it would not have discovered otherwise. [10] It gets at a deeper dimension of who we are and opens new possibilities. These possibilities undo our mundane or normal ways of being in the world and "break with the closure of being-toward-death." [11] The liturgical "figures" and experiences of abnegation, pilgrimage, all-night vigils, asceticism, holy foolishness, dispossession, parousia, and so forth are all instances of such kenotic liminality as it suspends and challenges ordinary ways of being. For Lacoste, although phenomenological language is eminently helpful for describing liturgical being, such being is always in radical discontinuity with the "world."

Jean-Luc Marion instead does not adopt a Heideggerian starting point, but argues that much of human experience (including religious experience) is not adequately understood in either Husserlian or Heideggerian terms.[12] In his view, Husserl focuses only on phenomena that appear as objects and Heidegger is only interested in the question of the manifestation of Being or beings. Yet many phenomena, so Marion suggests, do not appear or manifest themselves primarily as objects or beings. Important historical or cultural events, works of art, the face of the beloved other, or the revelation of Christ are not adequately described as either "objects" or "beings" and, in fact, even their mode of appearing is quite different from that described by Husserl or Heidegger.[13] Marion argues that instead such phenomena appear as "saturated," which is to say that no concepts can be imposed on them, but that they give themselves entirely from themselves. Instead of constituting such phenomena through the intentionality of consciousness, as was Husserl's aim, in the case of saturated phenomena we are given abundant intuition that we cannot fully grasp or contain.[14] Religious phenomena, that is, phenomena of revelation, are given to us and appear in our experience, but they do so in particularly overwhelming and bedazzling ways that require new phenomenological descriptions.

Michel Henry criticizes Husserl's and Heidegger's work for a quite different reason.[15] He thinks that their distinctions between phenomenon (as the intuitive given) and its mode of phenomenality (how it is constituted by consciousness) are still too strong and disregard the fact that experience actually manifests as itself in the very way in which it manifests itself. The phenomenon is its phenomenality; the two can never be separated. We experience directly and immanently within our very flesh, as this flesh feels itself feeling in its self-affectivity. Although Henry's early work articulates this notion of life as flesh and as the seat of auto-affection already in great detail, in his final works he argues that the most genuine insight about such phenomenality is found in Christianity, in the words of Christ.[16] Christ communicates the truth of life, which is the very life of God, to us as the sons of God who are generated out of and within the divine life. Henry contends that in Christ we have access to the very phenomenality of experience and that only in participating in this life of God through the flesh of Christ, we are truly ourselves and genuinely alive. In Henry's work, phenomenology is not merely appropriated to make sense of religious experience, instead Christianity itself is taken to be the only genuine phenomenology.

While Jean-Louis Chrétien makes no such overarching claims about all of phenomenology, he employs its language and tools in order to depict a variety of concrete experiences and aspects of human existence, many of which are either explicitly religious or have religious connotations and dimensions, such as the call and the response, the fragility of the voice, the vulnerability of the human body, the experiences of fatigue, breath, hope, creativity.[17] Whether he is speaking of the beauty of the world, the hospitality of speech, the commitments of responsibility, or the touch of the suffering body, Chrétien draws indiscriminately on poetic or religious, philosophical or mystical texts in a way that suggests that they are all equally valid sources of reflection on experience, whether such experience is identified as religious or not. Chrétien does not explicitly argue *for* the validity of an examination of religious experience, he simply engages in it as if it were the most obvious thing to do for a phenomenologist. His very practice of depicting religious phenomena in a phenomenologically sensitive fashion, which truly reveals something about how these phenomena show themselves, provides a justification for its appropriateness.

Even more recently, Emmanuel Falque has opened explicit dialogue between phenomenology and theology in a way that tries to get beyond some of the distinctions between them still evident in prior thinkers. He argues that it is time to "cross the Rubicon" and admit that we do better phenomenology as theologians and better theology as phenomenologists.[18] He has devoted a whole trilogy to the experience of the Triduum (Western Good Friday, Easter Sunday, and Maundy Thursday), examining the experiences of death and suffering, life and resurrection, body and Eucharist, in a way that begins with "ordinary" human experience but moves smoothly from there to more explicitly religious experience.[19] In all of his work, Falque argues that the starting point for phenomenology must be agnostic, "the human as such" (*l'homme tout court*) and that only from there we can proceed to more explicit theological reflection and the consideration of specifically religious experience. Even there he sees it as entirely in continuity with "ordinary" human experience, as a sacramentality of the world and an affirmation of creation. His spiritual sensitivities are hence quite

different than those of Marion or even Lacoste. While he is deeply influenced by Marion who directed his doctoral thesis on Bonaventure, Falque's
phenomenology is one of "ordinary" rather than "extraordinary" experience, one that affirms creation and corporeality rather than Marion's
strong leaning toward apophaticism. Heavily influenced by Merleau-
Ponty, he also stresses the elements of bodiliness in our human experience
(in the world and in religious experience) and seeks to overcome what
he perceives as a split between "body" and "flesh" in twentieth-century
phenomenology.

In that respect Falque agrees with Lacoste that we must begin any investigation of "religious" experience—even that of death, resurrection, or
Eucharist—with "l'homme tout court," the human as such, or with ordinary human existence as we all experience it in the world and in our daily
lives. We begin with a shared (agnostic) philosophical vocabulary and
broader philosophical presuppositions about the human. The "theological"
move to explicitly religious experiences or modes of being comes after and
arises from within its context, even when it can shed light on philosophy
or provide phenomenological insight. Although Falque wants to overcome
some of the strict divisions between philosophy and theology he sees especially in Marion and argues in the strongest terms that theology and phenomenology can mutually enrich each other, he is unequivocal that the
starting point for any (philosophical) investigation must be the shared
ordinary and most basic human experience.[20] He disagrees with Lacoste,
however, in regard to the relation between religious and ordinary being.[21]
For Falque, it does not constitute a rupture with the "world" or with
"ordinary" existence, but instead a continuation and affirmation of it in a
different mode. We do not break with our ordinary experience of birth,
life, death, or the body, but enrich our understanding of it, live it in a
fuller and more authentic mode that does not deny its "ordinariness."
Theology can draw on phenomenological language precisely because it
speaks of the same human experience and experiences it first of all as fully
finite and utterly human (even for Christ). A "transformation" or "metamorphosis" of our experiences of suffering, life, or the body by the crucifixion, the resurrection, or the Eucharist, does not constitute a denial of
ordinary experience or an erasure of it, but enables us to be fully human
here and now.

While this provides some preliminary examples of how religious experience enters into philosophical discussion today, it also already points to

some divergences and disagreements and to the need to clarify some methodological questions. Three of them are particularly important and must be briefly addressed here. One concerns the very possibility of a phenomenological analysis of religious experience, the second the philosophical starting point for such an examination, and the third the role texts and their interpretation play in this context, that is to say, the relation between phenomenology and hermeneutics.

Phenomenology and Theology

Both Husserl and Heidegger were quite clear that phenomenology must always practice "methodological atheism" and that an examination of religion has no place in phenomenology proper.[22] Husserl, in fact, repeatedly condemned the various attempts to appropriate his methodology for religious purposes and had several rather unkind things to say about the religiously inflected phenomenological work of Max Scheler, Edith Stein, and Rudolf Otto.[23] Phenomenology excludes any recourse to "God" or "transcendence" (in a religious sense) because it deals with the immanent phenomena of consciousness. Heidegger was similarly dismissive of any attempt to marry phenomenology with theology and he rigorously insisted that "Being" in his sense had nothing to do with "God" and that theology is a mere "ontic" or "positive" science, functioning just like history, anthropology, biology or chemistry, while only phenomenology can be truly "ontological."[24] While theology deals with "Christianness," with the empirical faith of a particular individual, phenomenology instead addresses the very structures of human existence. While there might be some correlation between the ontic, empirical experience of sin examined in theology and the ontological phenomenon of guilt explicated by phenomenology—and occasionally ontic phenomena can reveal something about ontological structures—the two projects are radically different in their thrust and methodology.

Even the French thinkers, despite all their religious interests, maintain some of these distinctions. Marion insists over and over again that he is investigating the mere "possibility" and structure of phenomena of religion and not providing any justification for the "actuality" of some empirical event, to which only theology would have access.[25] The saturated phenomenon provides the structure of how religious phenomena manifest themselves but makes no claims about concrete instances of revelation.

Lacoste and Falque both consider an examination of "religious experience" in the sense of Friedrich Schleiermacher, Rudolf Otto, or Mircea Eliade an exercise of anthropology or sociology of religion and not genuinely phenomenological.[26] This is precisely why Lacoste does not investigate actual liturgical practices or what he calls "the cult" but the basic structures of human being before the Absolute.[27] A concern with more concrete religious practices or experiences would no longer be phenomenological.

Yet it is hard to see how this neat division can be fully maintained. On the one hand, is it possible to speak about something like an experience of the "Absolute" without the religious structures and practices that give some content to what that might mean? Without some reference to how the Absolute actually has been or currently is encountered, how is this any more than a purely abstract thought experiment rather than the examination of "the thing itself as it shows itself"? The constant references to the parousia and the eschaton in Lacoste's work, which provide for him the means for positing "liturgical" being as complete rupture with "ordinary" being, pose a similar problem. How can we know anything about the nature of this parousia or eschaton apart from the religious texts that refer to it, albeit in very tentative and elusive fashion? Neither "absolute" nor "eschaton" seem accessible on purely phenomenological grounds. Why should we assume that an exposure before a "God" or an "Absolute" is an important dimension of humanity, unless such a phenomenon is manifested through mystical experience, spiritual affectivity, or religious practices? And indeed Lacoste has recourse to such experience by pointing to various sorts of monastic traditions (especially asceticism), to the tradition of the holy fool, and to recognizably "Christian" structures of prayer. Even his fairly abstract analysis of human being "coram dei" still implies, or even requires, recourse to concrete religious experiences, at least as examples or illustrations. And at times they go beyond mere illustration. He explicitly claims throughout his treatment that various aspects of monastic or ascetic experience "undo" or "challenge" Heidegger's descriptions of human being. These presumably "ontic" phenomena are thus taken to challenge ontological presuppositions, at least in certain contexts.

This actually points to another genuine problem in the contemporary accounts. By purporting to be about fundamental structures of human being instead of concrete religious practices, they are either unaware, or simply hide the fact, that their analyses are always heavily colored by their own religious background and that they draw on it for presenting these structures. All of the contemporary work is deeply and irrevocably Christian and it is also all recognizably Roman Catholic.[28] At the same time, it is not at all clear why an examination of the religious "lifeworld" should be *a priori* excluded from phenomenological investigation. Religious structures and practices have almost always been an important part of human societies and therefore can be validly examined as a significant dimension of human existence, just as much as aesthetic or economic or political practices, experiences, or structures. Anthony Steinbock even treats mystical experience as such a "phenomenon" open to phenomenological examination. He considers it representative of what he calls "vertical" experience—that is, our experience of relation to something or someone above and beyond us, rather than "horizontal" experience. Like Marion, he is trying to free (Husserlian) phenomenology from its remnants of Cartesian obsession with the object (in the sense of *Gegenstand*) and the need for a certain kind of evidence that follows the mode of "objectivity," even if it is not quite like that employed in the natural sciences. In his study of mystical experience and of the "moral emotions," he tries to open dimensions of human experiencing and knowing to phenomenological investigation that cannot be reduced to experiences of objects.[29] And although he speaks of this in terms of givenness, unlike the French thinkers he does not presuppose a distinctly Christian or Roman Catholic version of that experience, but treats mystical texts and the experiences they report as givens that can be unfolded phenomenologically without any hidden apologetic agenda. At the very least, his work shows that a serious phenomenological engagement with concrete religious practices is possible.

An examination of the particular practices of a tradition can address several of these concerns at the same time. On the one hand, it states up front what religious practices are under investigation without presenting itself as a neutral investigation that later turns out to be heavily colored by a particular tradition—which is not to say that a more particular investigation therefore can have no implications for other traditions or even other religions. On the other hand, it holds together the ontic and the ontological, the lifeworld and the "reduced" world of phenomena, in a way that neither simply collapses one into the other nor pretends that one can or should abstract a phenomenological realm entirely from the lifeworld from which it draws its phenomena.[30] This is not to say that such an analysis of a particular religious tradition and its practices therefore reduces phenomenology to the empirical or becomes a mere sociology or anthropology of religion. As long as it maintains the attitude of the reduction—allowing phenomena to unfold rather than imposing scientific parameters upon them—and investigates the structures and meaning of these practices rather than simply describing particular empirical instantiations, it remains phenomenological. Even here a range is possible: This particular project tries to focus as fully as possible on the structural or systematic end of the spectrum, drawing on examples primarily as illustrations for the phenomenological structures of liturgical experience as it is presented in liturgical practices in the Eastern tradition. A companion project lays out far more fully the concrete "lifeworld" of the liturgy, as it can be "read" from patristic sources.[31] Maybe both together provide a fuller picture of how ontic/ontological or lifeworld/world of phenomena might interact fruitfully.

Phenomenological Starting Points

The second methodological matter concerns the starting point for an examination of human existence before God. While there is broad agreement among the French thinkers on the first methodological matter (what constitutes a phenomenological investigation), there is disagreement about what might be the appropriate starting point. Both Lacoste and Falque argue that we must begin with "ordinary" human being or with "the human as such" before we can speak of "religious" being or human being-before-God. Although they differ significantly in how they deal with the religious dimension afterwards—Lacoste interpreting it almost entirely as radical rupture with and rejection of "ordinary" being, Falque proposing much greater continuity and affirmation of the human as such—both agree that phenomenology must start, as Heidegger insists, with the most fundamental human structures of existence, which are not religious and in regard to which the religious is a supplement or alteration or regional variation. Here the distinction between phenomenology and theology runs along "agnostic" lines. The practice of phenomenology is, philosophically speaking, always at first "atheist" and the human per se is more fundamental (more "ontological") than the human within religious experience. But why should an "atheist" or "neutral" position of the human necessarily be more "primordial" or "originary" than a religious one? Indeed, in his lectures on the phenomenology of religious life even Heidegger suggests otherwise and argues that the "primordial" experience of the Christian communities to whom Paul addresses his letters shows something about more fundamental ontological structures and his analysis there closely parallels his analysis of Dasein in *Being and Time*.[32]

Although neither Marion nor Chrétien confronts this question as clearly as Lacoste and Falque or puts it in precisely those terms, their practice of phenomenology implies a very different presupposition. Marion argues that we not only can but must begin from the "given" of revelation and allow it to unfold from itself.[33] He thinks of this as an essentially phenomenological approach: an unfolding of the manifestation or revelation of the phenomenon as it shows and gives itself. The implications of this proceeding from the "self" of the phenomenon imply a quite different starting point than Lacoste or Falque. Marion treats what he calls "phenomena of revelation" as a given from the start and assumes that phenomenology, which is concerned with what appears and manifests itself, has not only an ability but indeed an obligation to unfold the given of even the most excessive and revelatory phenomena, as long as they actually show or manifest themselves within experience. Thus, Marion does not start with prior assumptions about "ordinary" ways of being and move toward to the "religious" as their transformation or an experience that would be later and optional in relation to "normal" human being-in-the-world, but instead insists that we can start with the given of revelation as it comes to us. Indeed, in some way there can be no "prior" because such a "saturated" phenomenon comes in utterly unpredictable fashion; it surprises and overwhelms us; there is no way in which we could prepare for it or make sense of it from our prior experience. On the one hand, it does constitute a kind of rupture—it is utterly different from our experience of "objects"—yet on the other hand, it is not unlike our experience of other rich phenomena, such as the encounter with a dazzling work of art or an unpredictable and incomprehensible historical event. The "line" of liminality or paradox here does not run between "secular" and "sacred" or "worldly" and "religious," but rather between "poor" and "rich," between an experience of objects that can be constituted by intentionality and an experience of saturated phenomena that cannot be so constituted. There is thus no split for Marion between "ordinary" being or the human "as such" and the recipient of the saturated phenomenon. There is simply a distinction between poorer and richer phenomena as they appear within experience. The experience of an overwhelming historical or cultural event, the contemplation of a magnificent work of art, the intimate pleasure or pain felt by flesh touched erotically or cruelly, the encounter with the loving gaze of the other are not fundamentally or structurally different from an experience of revelation, although the latter may well be even more intense and combines elements or characteristics of the others. The fundamental distinction for Marion is not between "religious" and "ordinary" or "non-religious" ways of being, but between experiences of objects (the "poor" phenomena of math, science, and technology) and richer experiences (the "saturated" phenomena of culture, aesthetics, and religion). And Marion even repeatedly claims that the "rich" or "saturated" phenomenon, especially that of the gift of the Eucharist, must serve as the paradigm for all phenomenality, from the richest to the poorest. The saturated phenomenon that gives itself from itself and cannot be constituted by intentionality is also the paradigm for the object, which can be fully constituted by intentionality.[34]

Chrétien rarely deals with methodological questions explicitly, but his easy move from poetic to philosophical to religious texts and phenomena and his frequent practice of drawing from a multiplicity of sources without qualitative distinction between them seems to imply that he thinks of them as in continuity with each other. The phenomena he examines—the fragility of the voice, the vulnerability of the body, the beauty of the world offered as gift, the phenomena of hope and promise, among many others—are found and displayed as much in explicitly religious sources as in ones that do not speak about religion and are not rooted in such a tradition. All these are treated as a "given" open to phenomenological investigation. Richard Kearney goes even further by speaking of a "sacramentality of the everyday" or a "liturgy of the little things."[35] Instead of trying to sequester religious experience into a liturgical or cultic space, we should discover it at work everywhere around us, in a cup of water offered to "the least of these" or in the stories of Woolf and Joyce. Here, liturgy or sacramentality has been broadened to all of life and experience. This account does not ask us to think of religious experience as something separate, but instead to recognize and celebrate (maybe also shelter and increase) the sanctity already in the world. Both Chrétien and Kearney want us to extend our hospitality to a liturgy or spirituality of the world and to see its apparently ordinary experiences as already filled with grace or holiness. This clearly posits a quite different task not only for how to speak of religious experience, but even where to find it and what to identify as religious.

To some extent, the question of starting point may depend on the focus and goal of the investigation: If one is trying to reach the question of the meaning of Being as such (Heidegger) or to provide a more convincing account of human perception in general (Merleau-Ponty) or to analyze the very phenomenality of all phenomena as rooted in the self-affectivity of life per se (Henry) or to lay out how all phenomena appear as givens within givenness as such (Marion) or even to show human being before the Absolute (Lacoste), one may well need to start elsewhere than if one wants to unfold the meaning of concrete religious experiences and practices. A phenomenology of religious experience, or even specifically of liturgical experience, is a much less ambitious project focusing on a much narrower range of human experience, even if such particular experience is taken to have implications for broader religious and even wider human experience. In that case, it may even be necessary to begin—as Ricoeur does for the religious experience conveyed in the Jewish and Christian Scriptures or Marion for the encounter with the phenomenon of revelation—with the religious experience itself as an existential given and to investigate it as such a given.

It is important to stress, however, that a phenomenological investigation must begin with the human not the divine. Human religious experience is open to phenomenological investigation, God or the Absolute directly is not. Thus, we can treat religious experience as a given within human experience and must not assume it as something utterly exceptional, extraordinary, and inaccessible within the "world." Religious experience, if it means anything, is lived here and now, not in the parousia, to which we have no phenomenological access. That is not to say that such analysis or depiction of the "given" of religious experience as it is manifested in the experience ought to turn into an attempt to "prove" it in some fashion as "authentic" or to establish its explicit source in a "God" who is manifest within it in a particular way and in no other. While references to "God" are certainly part of this experience and the world in which it is lived, to describe this world and experience does not have as its goal either to validate divine initiative in the liturgical drama or to defend one liturgical approach as superior to another (especially if that is taken to mean that it is somehow closer to the divine "source"). That would no longer be a phenomenological or philosophical project.

Phenomenology is thus employed here to depict and investigate religious (specifically liturgical) experience as it occurs and to analyze its structures and the ways in which meaning emerges or is presupposed in it, to take a momentary step back from the concrete participation in the religious experience, not in order to suspend or deny it, but in order to perceive it more fully and see it more clearly. A careful depiction of such an experience can unfold its meaning and help us to see how it is manifested from itself. As noted previously, although phenomenologists tend to speak in the first person singular, this is not their personal, empirical, or purely subjective "I" but in some sense a "we," namely *human* experience per se. A phenomenology applied to religious experience seeks to depict and unfold how such experience occurs and is meaningful, not merely to uncover one personal, purely subjective and arbitrary instance of it.[36] Phenomenology provides a rigor to an examination of religious experience by unfolding its particular kind of rationality as it emerges from itself. Yet it does not really do anything radically new; it merely seeks to unfold what is already there as a given.[37] At the very least, hermeneutics provides a justification for beginning with the "given" of a "world" shaped by and encountered in texts and practices instead of searching for an entirely neutral or absolute starting point, including that of the "human as such."

Hermeneutics and Phenomenology

This brings us to the third issue, namely the role of hermeneutics in the analysis of religious experience or, more specifically, of liturgical experience. Can any examination of liturgical experience be "purely" phenomenological without always already having hermeneutic elements? Do we ever have access to unmediated experience and even if we did, can it be expressed without language, without filtering it through our ways of expressing and interpreting its experience? If not, how do these hermeneutic elements function within the phenomenological description or analysis? What is the relationship of this hermeneutic methodology to the phenomenological presuppositions and methods that situate the larger project of engaging with the meaning of liturgy?

Although the most important hermeneutic thinkers, Hans-Georg Gadamer and Paul Ricoeur, were deeply influenced by phenomenology and made frequent use of it in their work and even Heidegger spoke early on of his phenomenology as a "hermeneutics of facticity," hermeneutics and phenomenology have often been uneasy bedfellows, especially in the more recent phenomenological thinkers.[38] Michel Henry, for example, vigorously rejects hermeneutics as a lying and deceptive discipline, which only serves to introduce a false distance into the intimate and utterly immanent experience of self-affectivity.[39] Phenomenon and phenomenality are one; no hermeneutic distance between them can intervene. Lacoste does not make negative comments about hermeneutics, but in most of his work simply ignores it by relying almost entirely on Heidegger's phenomenology in his explication of "liturgy" as human "being-before-God." In one of his more recent books he addresses it briefly more explicitly and there folds it into phenomenology: "A phenomenology that does not interpret what it allows to and makes appear is an infirm phenomenology—luckily few have done so. A hermeneutics that forgets its phenomenological origins and rootedness in phenomenology has become a common undertaking, but one must wonder whether it is not destined to failure. . . . In any case, the field of interpretation is that of a phenomenology in its aleatory moment."[40] The rest of his extensive treatment of speech in this book is purely phenomenological and rarely refers to hermeneutic treatments. Marion is often quite dismissive of hermeneutics as a "mere" practice of interpretation, which he seems to interpret in fairly arbitrary terms, although he occasionally acknowledges that it might operate for the endless and multiple unfolding of the richness of the saturated phenomenon.[41] While he does not seem to think that hermeneutics could ever get at "truth," it can preserve or protect the excess of the phenomenon by showing the endless number of interpretations that are possible and by highlighting the fact that none of them are adequate.[42] At other times Marion explicitly exhorts theologians to abandon their preference for hermeneutics and to focus instead on phenomenology as a much more appropriate methodology for unfolding the givenness of the manifestation of revelation.[43]

This, however, already points to an important parallel between the two practices: Both hermeneutics and phenomenology seek to "unfold" or depict what is "given" in experience, what is manifested there. While hermeneutics focuses more heavily on interpreting such experience for its meaning and in order to "understand" it, phenomenology does not eschew all attempts at understanding, and even when it does not seek to "explain" but merely to "depict,"[44] it is still interested in uncovering meaning and significance. Here surely Lacoste is right that phenomenology always already interprets what it unfolds.[45] And while hermeneutics tends to focus more strongly on texts and phenomenology focuses more heavily on consciousness of objects or experiences, both have shifted in emphasis: Hermeneutics increasingly also examines actions and "life" (as in much of

Ricoeur's and Kearney's work), while phenomenology frequently has recourse to texts that depict experience (especially in Marion and Chrétien), sometimes relying almost exclusively upon them (as is also true, ironically, of Henry's use of the gospels in his *I Am the Truth* and *Words of Christ*). This is particularly evident in Falque, who explicitly calls for a wedding of phenomenology and hermeneutics and puts forth a "Catholic" hermeneutic proposal that would focus on the body and the voice and thereby go beyond Ricoeur's "Protestant" hermeneutics of "the meaning of the text" and Lévinas's "Jewish" hermeneutics of "the body of the text."[46] In the Anglophone thinkers who are interested in religion philosophically (especially Kevin Hart, Merold Westphal, John D. Caputo, and Richard Kearney), hermeneutics and phenomenology always interact and are rarely distinguished explicitly (this is particularly evident in Kearney's project of "carnal hermeneutics").[47] It is then less a matter of whether one must choose between hermeneutics and phenomenology, but more an issue of what one means by these terms, how their practices are taken to interact with each other, and how they are employed methodologically.

It might be useful to say something brief here, however, about how they are employed in this particular project. First, phenomenology and hermeneutics must function together for an interpretation of liturgical experience today. We have no direct access to the liturgical experience of the ancients; we really do not know how a person in fifth-century Constantinople might have "experienced" a particular liturgical occasion (indeed, neither hermeneutics nor phenomenology is going to give us access to that, despite the desire of historians to examine or recreate such experience[48]). Rather, the point is to try to understand the meaning of liturgical experience now and also to show that it is a coherent religious experience that is worth examining in its own right. At the most basic level, phenomenological categories are employed here for describing practices (whether observed or reported in texts) and hermeneutic ones for interpreting them, especially by setting them in relation to others or into their larger context, as the hermeneutic circle advocates. In that respect, the phenomenological description can often come first, while hermeneutics is employed to analyze its meaning. Yet, while we cannot rely solely on texts (but must also describe actions, emotions, affects, sensory impressions, and so forth) it would be silly to ignore the liturgical texts altogether. Hermeneutics hence also often functions in the background in terms of a guideline for the responsible handling of texts (not ripping them out of context or imposing entirely foreign horizons upon them arbitrarily, becoming aware of one's presuppositions as much as possible, being attentive to the language—including style and genre—within which experience is reported in a text, and so on). In that respect, hermeneutics often comes first by guiding the basic handling of texts, which can then become useful for phenomenological analysis.

One might also draw on hermeneutics and phenomenology to focus on or highlight different aspects of an experience or practice: While hermeneutics helps analyze its language and depict the sort of "world" it might set forth for us, phenomenology allows greater focus on elements of affectivity, corporeality, temporality, and other such topics, which have been examined by phenomenologists in great detail. Yet these two approaches or sides are obviously connected: How an action affects emotions or the body is obviously connected to its "language" (even without words) and functions within and as part of its proposed "world." When Heidegger analyzes space and time in *Being and Time*, he speaks of it as a hermeneutic exercise that seeks to unfold the ways in which Dasein is always already "understanding," while he later drops the hermeneutic language and appears to focus more fully on phenomenology (or to find new ways of thinking altogether). It may thus not be necessary to draw tight distinctions between the two approaches. Both hermeneutics and phenomenology depict and analyze, both seek to understand, both are concerned with meaning and significance, both are not a purely "scientific" approach to some "historical" incident or text, but instead grapple with the contemporary horizon and the ways in which texts, actions, and experiences mean here and now. Although this project is conceived primarily as a phenomenological one—a study of the experiences and meanings of liturgical life—hermeneutic tools are often used as well without treating them as opposed to the overall phenomenological thrust of the project.[49]

The "World" of Liturgy

Liturgical theologians have actually already engaged hermeneutics on various levels. Several investigations explicitly draw on Ricoeur's work to develop a hermeneutics of liturgy.[50] As mentioned in the preface, the question of how to interpret the meaning of liturgy also frequently comes up in theological treatments of liturgy. Yet even when the question is not raised in as obvious a fashion, the way in which liturgy is discussed has implications for how its texts and practices are taken to function, how what we say and do in liturgy "means" and has an "effect" on our lives and the world. The implication is that the language of liturgy is on some level mimetic: Liturgy is taken to configure certain aspects of prefigured "life" in some way that is assumed to refigure or transfigure it in turn.[51] This is obviously the quintessential hermeneutic question: How does the "world of the text"—in this case that of liturgy—relate to the "world of the reader"—to the person engaging with the liturgical world?

This notion of mimesis is probably worked out most fully in the writings of Ricoeur who speaks of poetic and symbolic language, including that of the biblical texts, as opening a "world of meaning." Biblical texts are "poetry" in the Greek sense of "poesis" as "making"; like literary texts, biblical texts create or open a world through their narratives.[52] This "world of the text" parallels what Gadamer calls the "horizon" of a text.[53] Both draw on Heidegger's analysis of Dasein as being-in-the-world for inspiration on this point. Thus, this is not simply a hermeneutic, but a phenomenological point; it is hermeneutics in the sense of Heidegger's "hermeneutics of facticity."[54] The texts enter our experience and themselves reflect human experience. They present ways of being in the world. We can enter this world in the way in which we enter into a narrative in sympathetic imagination. This is possible because the narrated world already is mimetically modeled on our experienced "life-world." In his three-volume work on *Time and Narrative*, Ricoeur develops this insight into three stages of mimesis: Narrative texts are "prefigured" in life; they are to some extent an "imitation" of life (mimesis$_1$). The narrative "configures" life; it "portrays" life (mimesis$_2$). Finally, the texts influence life by "refiguring" or even "transfiguring" it (mimesis$_3$).[55] We are influenced by texts, and our lives are shaped by them in important ways. When texts are meaningful they have an impact on us and transform us. Although Ricoeur applies his three-fold mimesis primarily to narrative texts, he also claims it to be true of the biblical texts.[56] The particular "world" opened by the biblical texts is shaped by their very multiplicity and abundance. Their exhortation to change and transformation is one of the ways in which their world functions mimetically.

The same questions can be asked about liturgy: First, does liturgy draw on life? Does it assume that our lives *prefigure* its world in some fashion? Does liturgy take up the concerns of life we bring to it? Second, does liturgy *configure* life within its texts or narrative structures? Does it represent or even enact life? Third, does liturgy *refigure* or transform our lives, does it have an impact on how we live, open new possibilities of being? In sum, is the "world" of liturgy internal to the texts, operative only within the liturgical space? Or is it a world that is prefigured by life, configures life, and refigures life? Furthermore, how might we negotiate the various worlds at work in liturgy, especially when the texts draw on previous texts of a different genre? For example, how does the world of the biblical texts so frequently employed enter the liturgical world and configure it? Does the liturgical world merely imitate or represent the biblical world? Certainly the biblical characters on which liturgy draws have at least partially a mimetic function: We are to imitate them, they give voice to our own struggles or serve as examples we are to follow. Yet although Christ and the Theotokos play a huge role in liturgical texts, it is far less clear that this is primarily a mimetic role. They are constantly addressed, celebrated, or petitioned in the texts, but more as interlocutors than as clear examples for imitation, although this is certainly assumed some of the time. Inasmuch as they are a central feature of the liturgical world—and not just verbally but also in prominent images via the iconography—some mimetic connection with their actual lives is presumably implied. Some of the patristic mystagogies also claim that liturgical language in both texts and actions functions mimetically, at least for the case of the eucharistic liturgy, which they interpret as mimetic recreation and representation of Christ's life and actions.[57]

In fact, there is some controversy in the contemporary literature over whether liturgy as a whole functions mimetically. Andrew Walker White claims that Byzantine liturgy contains no mimetic features and is not about performance.[58] In his view, theater was a "pagan cult activity" from which theologians and hymnographers separated themselves clearly and deliberately. In liturgical space, music, and performance of liturgy, the Byzantines deliberately turned against mimetic interpretations of liturgy and opted for purely "spiritual" ones. All parallels to theater in terms of architecture, iconographic display, or musical performance are purely incidental.[59] He puts this in the strongest possible terms: "Why not read the Divine Liturgy as a drama, when the Church Fathers seem to invite us to do just that? The answer, in a nutshell, is: because the Liturgy was not conceived as a drama, it was not performed as one, and the record shows clearly that the Fathers and their successors intended the laity to have a primarily spiritual experience through their work, not an aesthetic one." While he acknowledges that history "lay at the foundation of Christian dogma," he insists that "the Liturgy was not designed to enact that history so much as cite or indicate it, incorporating the narrative into a performance whose ultimate goal was purely spiritual."[60] Liturgy has nothing to do with mimetic representation or drama and to suggest otherwise is to detract from its spirituality.

Cuneo, in contrast, explicitly emphasizes the mimetic function of liturgical language.[61] Although he rejects a purely anamnetic or vividly dramatic account, he does consider liturgy to be a form of reenactment that immerses us in patterns of life via the roles we observe.[62] Liturgical "reenactment" enables the listener to "imaginatively identify . . . with characters in the core narrative," to imitate the roles presented by liturgy via identification with them, to "appropriate the riches of the narrative," and hence to "construct and revise their narrative identities."[63] Although this imitation is not merely fictive, it does involve engaging with narratives, identifying with their characters and imitating their actions in our lives. Mimetic reenactment, for Cuneo, is central to liturgy.

Derek Krueger similarly locates the mimetic dimension of liturgy in terms of the models portrayed within it but also in the performative nature of much hymnography. For example, he shows how for Romanos (maybe the most important Byzantine composer of liturgical hymns) biblical subjects become "models for and models of Christian typological thought: his exploration of their thoughts demonstrates how Christians should think within their own minds, at once present to the story, the characters, God, and themselves."[64] Romanos' strategy is mimetic: "His Christians come to knowledge of themselves through conformity to types."[65] Similarly, he says about another hymnographer: "Symeon subscribes to an indigenous, Byzantine Christian theory of the formation of the self in which rehearsing the scripted thoughts and physical postures produces an authentic subject."[66] The parallel to ancient mimesis is drawn explicitly: "In a manner analogous to theater, ritual activities involve playing and ultimately inhabiting the mythic roles of sacred narrative."[67]

In this regard, it is interesting—and problematic—that both liturgical scholars and philosophers often conceive of liturgy in terms of sacred "play." Krueger, in the final phrase just cited, refers to ritual as "playing" and this is a fairly common assumption in studies of liturgy or ritual.[68] These claims appear to originate with Romano Guardini's brief reflection on "The Playfulness of Liturgy" in his 1930 text *The Spirit of the Liturgy* and to have become popularized by Huizinga's 1938 analysis of the play element in human culture, in which he consistently identifies any form of ritual as play, often in fairly dismissive fashion.[69] Subsequent thinkers simply repeat this: Hans-Georg Gadamer, for example, speaks of ritual as play, which "represents a world wholly closed within itself," albeit "open toward the spectator."[70] The central characteristic of play for him is self-presentation, total absorption, a kind of "back-and-forth," and ultimately the representation of a "meaningful whole."[71] Although Gadamer's focus is not on liturgy (but on the aesthetic phenomenon), liturgy repeatedly serves as an example for the play-character of art in his treatment. Similarly, Lacoste often refers to liturgy as play. For example, in his essay on coaffection, he claims that "the liturgical play is a visible play, ranged along with every possible sort of 'communicative practice.'"[72] He especially appeals to the category of drama: "Now if one characteristic of liturgical experience is clear, it is that this experience, this play, does not require any actual representational consciousness, but actors in a spectacle without spectator. The category of drama has pride of place here, and it is as *dramatis persona* that one participates in liturgy—to participate in it otherwise, for the pleasure of seeing or hearing, would be the error par excellence, a pseudo-participation incapable of letting things be what they are."[73] He makes similar comments in other places.

Yet, phenomenologically speaking, liturgy is experienced quite differently than either a theatrical spectacle or a game. Although liturgy may appear as an elaborate performance or even a kind of "show" to the external observer, it is not experienced this way by the participant. We do not experience the performance of liturgy as play-acting in either the way in which children play "make-believe" or in the manner in which actors perform on a stage. Although there are certainly rules and patterns in liturgy and they are engaged with "seriousness," as is true of playing, the imitative dimension of liturgy is neither experienced as involvement in a game, as passive observation of a spectacle staged for an audience, nor even as the kind of play-acting that prepares children for "real" (that is, adult) life. Play—even when one becomes wholly absorbed in it—is always experienced as at least on some level "made up"; indeed, that is part of its very enjoyment. The mimesis of liturgy is not simply theatrical performance and its modes of participation—as we will see—are not akin to play-acting.

Ricoeur's account of mimesis as prefiguring, configuring, and refiguring life thus seems more appropriate to liturgy. For Ricoeur, the mimetic function of narrative is particularly useful for speaking of personal identity and the meaning of one's life.[74] Our lives are always characterized by struggle with the chaos of life, the events that come to us unpredictably and disrupt our comfortable ways of being. Narrative is an attempt to make sense of such discordance and to introduce meaning into the chaos of life by providing a narrative that seeks to give coherence or at least greater concordance to it. This does not mean that everything becomes harmonious or that the narrative is a neatly linear one. But narratives provide the counterbalance of concordance to the discordance experienced by the encounter with the diverse and unsettling interruptions of my plans that come to me from the outside, that are imposed upon me often against my will. Complex mythic narratives recreate this struggle mimetically and allow us to find some sort of *katharsis* through the narrative, which thereby provides a measure of meaning to our lives. Our lives are always "in quest of narrative," according to the title of one of his essays on this topic.[75] This mimetic relationship between narrative and life fits liturgy far better than the notion of play.

In fact, liturgical theologians (or really almost anyone writing about liturgy) explicitly assume that liturgy is supposed to have an impact on our lives and they actually often employ this language of "world" to speak of what liturgy does.[76] At times exorbitant claims are made for liturgy's relation to the world and for how its language and actions can impact all of human experience: Liturgy is, according to the (revised) title of Schmemann's most well-known book, "for the life of the world."[77] And he explicitly says that liturgy is "not an escape from the world, rather it is the arrival at a vantage point from which we can see more deeply into the reality of the world."[78] In Kavanagh's words, it is "nothing less than the way a redeemed world is, so to speak, done."[79] Lathrop claims: "In the Christian liturgy, it is the assembly itself, encountering Christ in word and sacrament, that becomes a hole in the fabric of things, through which life-giving power flows into the world. *But this hole is in this world and for this world.* Indeed, the structures of the world urgently need such hole."[80] David Fagerberg is maybe the one to reiterate this claim the most frequently and to put it in the strongest terms:

> The people do not assemble on Sunday to worship because God is confined to a sacred place on a sacred day. They do not assemble to do Church, *they assemble to do redeemed world.* The arena of the life of faith is not some kind of sacred precinct, *it is the world.* Then what

is the purpose of assembling on Sunday? Not because God is here and not there, but so that the assembly, in their individual mundane vocations, *can transform what is there* by what was ritualized here.[81]

These are strong assertions. What does it actually mean to be "doing the world" or to act "for the life of the world" or to operate in the world as the true "arena of the life of faith"? In what sense is the liturgical ascetic "simply a stunningly normal person who stands in constant witness to the normality of Christian *orthodoxia* in a world flawed into abnormality by human choice," as Kavanagh asserts and of which Fagerberg reminds us repeatedly?[82] Even Robert Taft, not usually given to the sort of exorbitant theological claims Schmemann or Fagerberg frequently make, ends his meticulous historical study of the liturgy of the hours with a question about the relation between liturgy and life: "In short, the touchstone of our liturgy is whether or not it is being lived out in our lives. Is the symbolic moment symbolizing what we really are? Is our shared celebration of life a sign that we truly live in this way?"[83] Irwin puts this even more explicitly in terms of a relation between text and action: "In accord with the dialectical thesis of this book, two things matter. That the *text* of the liturgy be interpreted in relation to the *context* of our communal and personal lives and that the *context* of all of life be lived in harmony with the *text* of enacted liturgy so that liturgy and life can be intrinsically and keenly related. It is the Christian's prayer that they might eventually become congruent."[84] Yet, Chan is right to ask: "If the liturgy forms the church, how does it do it?"[85]

What does it mean to speak of liturgy primarily in terms of a transformation of the "world"? If the final aim of worship is to transform the whole world, maybe even the entire universe, what does this mean for the relation between liturgical being and being-in-the-world? What are the presuppositions about the world and the human being within it implied in these highly rhetorical statements? How does the "world" of liturgy (of the "sacred"?) relate to the "ordinary" world of human experience? Although the claim seems to be that all of "world" should become "liturgy" and that to be a "liturgical being" is to be a fully human being, surely at least the former is not currently the case and the latter at the very least contentious.[86] Indeed, Rentel wonders about the "tragic feeling of disconnection" we often experience between Orthodox liturgy and our concrete lives.[87] How do particular signs, symbols, or rites express what liturgy does and how does it actually make this happen in our lives? In both Ricoeur, when he analyzes the biblical texts, and in the liturgical theologians, we rarely get beyond the assertion that religious language functions mimetically or creates a meaningful world. There is very little explicit unfolding or description of this world and our possible entry into it. Often the investigation simply stops with these assertions. Yet what happens in this world has to be read from the way in which it "functions," the way in which it negotiates time, organizes space, moves bodies, engages the senses, shapes affectivity, opens onto alterity, forms identity.

This also reveals again that an examination of liturgy, even of the language of liturgy, cannot just be about texts. Liturgy is far more than texts and we cannot fully understand its meaning by focusing solely on its texts. Although hermeneutics is often understood as the practice of the interpretation of texts, even the major hermeneutic thinkers themselves already go beyond texts. Ricoeur insists (albeit far less in his analysis of the biblical texts) that actions in many ways function like texts and can be "read" for meaning in a similar fashion.[88] Actions and practices, especially highly symbolic actions or practices like the liturgical ones, can be "read" and interpreted just like texts. They are an essential part of the liturgical "universe" of meaning and they often invite to participation far more vividly and more obviously than texts alone can do.[89] What is "done" in liturgy is as important as what is said, what texts are read or chanted, and the relation between them matters for ascertaining meaning. The actions and practices of liturgy in all their rich variety, then, must be interpreted as part of any exploration of liturgical "meaning," as part of the hermeneutic circle, which cycles not only between parts and wholes of texts, but also between texts and actions, as well as between specific actions and larger ceremonies. The fact that texts are often chanted or sung, rather than simply read, is also significant. Music engages us on a quite different emotional level and is far more easily remembered than simple words, especially when it has rhythm and is repeated frequently. Certain musical settings are associated with certain feast days and are an important element of how the occasion is experienced and what emotion it evokes. Meaning is not simply literal or theoretical, but affective and physical.

In terms of the "sources" for liturgy, then, we cannot draw merely on texts, but must investigate a wide variety of genres, including ritual actions and devotional practices.[90] Concretely, this means that the sources for an analysis of liturgy cannot be only the written liturgical texts employed now, but also a whole array of other sources, whether strictly textual or not: the earlier liturgical sources that shaped and influenced later practices and often continued to be used in private or monastic settings even when they dropped out of cathedral rites, the homilies for particular occasions that analyze their meaning or describe their experience for their audiences, devotional texts and items, mystagogical texts that seek to interpret or explain liturgy to their audiences, the art, music, and architecture that shapes the liturgical space, the biblical texts and the calendar that assigns them to specific occasions, the liturgical movements (especially in the back and forth between nave and sanctuary), sacred items (such as censors or chalices, even vestments), bodily movements and postures (standing, kneeling, prostrating), sensory experiences (incense, candles, water, bread, wine), and much more. When texts are examined, they must be investigated not merely for their "dogmatic character," such as claims about doctrine or belief, but also for the ways in which they describe or even prescribe moods or experiences. All these are important aspects of the liturgical world and shape its meaning. Thus, any discussion of liturgy must focus not just on texts, but on the actions and gestures of liturgy, on the ways in which it is embodied, on its lived reality and hence on experience.[91] Here also we can see the way in which hermeneutics and phenomenology must ultimately overlap and interact in order to provide an adequate account of liturgical experience.

One aspect of this discussion of the world of the text, however, is worth highlighting here already. Regardless of what is ultimately claimed or confirmed for the relationship between the world of liturgy and the world of lived everydayness, it is this "world" of liturgy that is the phenomenological and hermeneutic horizon for liturgical experience. Space and time, body and affect, communal and personal identity within liturgy are experienced within the "world" of liturgy, against the liturgical "horizon." Liturgical experience can be examined phenomenologically because its phenomena appear within liturgy and are undergone within its context. And although most of hermeneutics distinguishes between the "horizon" or "world" of the text and the contemporary horizon or the world of the reader and argues that these two come together in understanding (for Gadamer they even "fuse" or "melt together"), there is, at the same time, a recognition that we already share this world at least to some extent. Sympathetic imagination with even strange narratives and texts is possible because of a shared humanity that experiences and confronts the world in many similar ways despite all diversity of behaviors, practices, and modes of understanding.[92] Obviously, there is a range of such shared exposure; some texts are considerably more foreign to us than others and sometimes the effort of understanding must be much greater. But if a text and its horizon were entirely foreign and strange to us in every way, we would not be able to "enter" it and it would not be able to "mean" for us.

This is also why the attempt to understand texts and narratives is not of mere historical interest. These texts and practices can still speak to us and they are still able to transform us if we are capable of entering into their horizon. Thus, even if a particular liturgical horizon may seem strange at first glance (or even at second or third exposure), its rich symbolism and the world of its texts and actions is still a world worth exploring. Consequently, a phenomenological study of liturgy is not only for those who actively engage in it within a particular tradition, but can give us wider insight about religious experience and its meaning. It is not a mere analysis of antiquated texts or practices, but a living tradition that we can enter and encounter even from our contemporary horizon. An account of Eastern Orthodox liturgy can, then, also have implications for other liturgical traditions and, indeed, for human experience more broadly.

Thus, a phenomenology of liturgical experience can depict how liturgy opens a world, how space and time are experienced within it and shape its experience, how bodies move within liturgy and how they are affected by liturgy's appeal to the senses and the emotions, how personal and communal experience interact with and shape each other. While phenomenology has provided rich depictions of the body and affectivity, of our experience of alterity or encounter with the other, of temporality and spatiality, and so forth, these actually only rarely make an explicit appearance in the current analyses of religious being and at times are specifically distinguished from it. Thus, in Marion, the phenomenon of the flesh or of affectivity is treated as a different kind of saturated phenomenon than that of the other. The phenomenon of revelation, although it contains aspects of both, is yet again a quite distinct phenomenon. A fuller analysis of liturgical experience, however, shows that temporality, spatiality, corporeality, affectivity, and so forth, all play an important role in the experience. Liturgy is not just about eucharistic participation, but it is a fully embodied experience that engages the whole human being in a meaningful world. It thus practically offers itself to phenomenological investigation. All the main topics that have occupied phenomenologists (whether religious or not) are relevant to liturgy and part of its meaning: space, time, affectivity, corporeality, personal and communal identity, and so forth. Through its extensive examinations of such topics, phenomenology is well equipped to deal with the larger "life-world" of liturgy as fundamental human experience.

A much fuller phenomenological engagement with liturgy will thus be beneficial to philosophical phenomenology, liturgical theology, and Orthodox thought: by providing a more rigorous grounding for thinking about liturgical experience and by opening new paths for thinking about religious experience more broadly.[93] That is the contribution the present study seeks to make. In what follows, the phenomenological guidelines just mentioned are employed in broad brushstrokes, inasmuch as they describe and analyze the aspects of human being in the world, which phenomenology has examined extensively over the past century—time and place, body and flesh, senses and emotion, communal identity and encounter with the "other"—for what they tell us about the experience and meaning of liturgy. The concern, then, is with how liturgical experience is manifested, how liturgy appears or is "given" (in the broader Husserlian sense of *Gegeben-heit*). And if investigating the meaning of Christian liturgy is to investigate the meaning of Christian life, then, philosophically speaking, to investigate a particular instantiation of religious experience also has implications for the meaning of human religious living and experiencing in a broader sense. Throughout, the task is the *philosophical* exercise of ascertaining and understanding such meaning as fully as that is possible, not a more theological or confessional exercise of imposing particular meanings or making normative claims about how meaning *ought* to function in these or other contexts. While phenomenology may not be able to avoid making normative claims entirely, the primary goal here is description and analysis for the purpose of greater understanding—no more and no less.

1

TEMPORALITY

I n his introduction to Orthodoxy, Sergius Bulgakov describes the height of Orthodox liturgical experience:

Holy Week is the heart of Orthodox rites. It may be said that it is anticipated and prepared for during the whole year. Great are the joy and beauty of the services of the great feasts . . . but all the services pale before the beauty of the grandiose rites of Lent and above all of Holy Week. And the luminaries themselves pale, as stars before the light of the rising sun, before the light and joy of the night of Pascha. The resurrection of Christ is a high festival in the whole Christian world, but nowhere is it so luminous as in Orthodoxy, and nowhere—I dare add—is it celebrated as in Russia, just at the moment when spring begins with all its sweetness and transparence. Pascha night, its joy, its exaltation, transport us to the life to come, in new joy, the joy of joys, a joy without end.[1]

This description is full of references to time: the annual cycle of feasts, the periods of Lent and Holy Week, the night of Pascha, its connection to spring, and its anticipation of the "life to come."

The temporal dimension of liturgy is maybe its most obvious feature. Not only does liturgy take a lot of time, but much of it is concerned with time: remembering events in the life of Christ or of the Theotokos, especially in the great feasts. Yet these events are not "remembered" in purely chronological fashion; they are spread out over the entire liturgical year.

While there is obviously a logical temporal connection between the feasts of the Annunciation and of Christ's Nativity, separated by exactly nine months, the "dating" for others is considerably less obvious and often influenced more by the historical conditions for the emergence of the feast or by theological rationales, such as the placement of the feasts of Theophany or Dormition.[2] The temporality of liturgy is quite complicated: Although it involves remembering, such commemoration is not simply chronological or purely historical.

Indeed, not only is this temporality not strictly chronological, it is not even predominantly linear because it proceeds in cyclical fashion and actually involves several cycles: daily, weekly, and annual. The daily offices, today generally celebrated only in monasteries (although there is evidence that at least in Constantinople lay people attended various daily services for centuries and monastic spirituality profoundly marked the larger culture), organize the day into seven times for prayer: beginning with vespers in the evening (as in the Jewish tradition, the liturgical day begins at sundown),[3] then compline or nocturnes, matins, followed in the daytime by the first, third, sixth, and ninth hour. At the same time, these services also provided occasions for creativity when elaborate hymns were composed for these daily offices (especially matins), a process completed and confirmed by the Stoudite reforms in the ninth and tenth centuries. The daily cycle is complemented by the weekly cycle. Just like each hour, each day is devoted to a different theme, such as the crucifixion or the resurrection. Every moment of the day and every day of the week is hallowed with sacred memory, filled with holy examples to imitate, directed toward the ascetic struggle of patterning one's life upon Christ.

The week begins and culminates in the eighth day; according to Schmemann's popular interpretation, this is the day outside of days, the day that does not count in the chronological counting of days, the day that ushers us into the kingdom.[4] Although some of Schmemann's claims have been revised by further liturgical study, such as the supposed connection to Jewish practice and the point of emergence of a regular Sunday celebration, his interpretation is still assumed by many and Sunday certainly remains the most significant liturgical experience for the average churchgoer.[5] Already in the late first century, Wednesday and Friday are mentioned as fasting days, commemorating Christ's suffering and death.[6] While these daily and weekly cycles are most obvious to monastics and touch the lay person primarily in terms of the Sunday celebration of the liturgy and possibly the weekday fasting, the annual cycle deeply influences the liturgical lives of practicing Orthodox Christians. Spread out over the entire year, beginning in September, seasons of fasting and feasting alternate in a continuous succession that is neither linear nor progressive. It is often claimed in rather facile fashion that the Judeo-Christian tradition replaced a meaningless cyclical view of time with a much more meaningful linear account. While it is doubtful that linearity by itself is intrinsically more meaningful than circularity, this superficial account is also patently untrue.[7] In its liturgy, its cycles of fasts and feasts, Christianity (and also Judaism) remained cyclical, presumably precisely because the cyclical was indeed meaningful. The temporality of liturgy does not proceed neatly from past through present to future, accumulating a series of "now" moments like links on a chain. The liturgical organization of the day, the week, and the year takes into account experienced time: night and day, the seasons, even the months of the year inasmuch as they are associated with sowing and harvest. What happens in nature in some way is taken to represent or support the soteriological events or at least not to be utterly separate from them.[8] This melding of imagery taken from nature with the events of salvation is particularly obvious at Pascha, which is consistently read—from the earliest homilies via the Paschal letters announcing the date of Easter for a particular year to much of the later liturgical texts—through the imagery of spring and its new life.[9] It may not be coincidental that the most important and strictest fasting period falls into the time of year that food would have been scarcest in an agricultural environment that depended on the coming of spring to replenish its food sources. The alternation between fasting and feasting itself is significant and marks Orthodox liturgical experience—to some extent even Orthodox cultural experience—maybe more profoundly than any other liturgical feature.[10] It affects not just what happens in church, but what happens at home and in the marketplace, what foods are purchased, prepared, and eaten.

Liturgy thus not only remembers, but also cycles continually between fasting and feasting. The entire liturgical year is structured around this "back-and-forth" experience from penitence to celebration and back, over and over again. The liturgical year in the Orthodox Church begins on September 1st and is organized by a fixed and a movable cycle of a total of twelve major feasts (plus Pascha) and four fasting periods. The fixed cycle celebrates especially the incarnation via feasts of Christ and the Theotokos, such as his Annunciation (March 25), Nativity (December 25),

Theophany (January 6), and Transfiguration (August 6), and her Nativity (September 8), Entry into the temple (November 21), Meeting with Symeon and Anna (February 2), and her "falling asleep" or Dormition (August 15).[11] These are supplemented with various minor feasts, commemorations of saints on every day of the year, and three fasting periods, preceding the feast of Christ's Nativity (for 40 days), the feast of St. Peter and Paul,[12] and of the Dormition (for 14 days). The movable cycle depends on the date of Pascha, the "feast of feasts," the single-most important celebration in the liturgical year. Pascha is preceded by a forty-day fast, Great Lent, which is itself preceded by three preparatory weeks, but the feast is prepared even more immediately by Holy Week (not usually considered part of Lent), which is begun by Lazarus Saturday and the feast of Palms (the entry into Jerusalem) and culminates in Pascha. It is followed by the fifty days of celebration leading up to Pentecost, with the feast of the Ascension on the fortieth day.

These annual cycles, especially the alternation of fasts and feasts, most clearly mark Orthodox liturgical experience today. While not everyone may show up for one of the less dramatic feasts, especially when they fall in the middle of the week, such as the Entry of the Theotokos into the Temple or the feast of the Meeting/Presentation, the more important feasts and liturgical celebrations, such as Nativity, Theophany, Holy Week, and Pascha are usually well attended. Especially on Pascha churches are absolutely packed with people who never go near the place on any other day or night of the year. In Orthodox countries, this feast involves large celebrations that have significant cultural impact (similar to Western Christmas and with similar aberrations). And while not everyone keeps Great Lent strictly, according to what are still essentially monastic fasting rules, most people are at least aware of it and modify their diets to some extent—and they certainly "feast" on Pascha regardless of how haphazardly they may have fasted in the preceding forty days. Thus, time is marked into "fasting" and "feasting" in a continually revolving cycle. Orthodox cultures have been deeply shaped by this alternation and indeed some peculiar Western practices (such as eating pancakes on Shrove Tuesday) also go back to such Lenten habits, although the fasting schedule has long since been abandoned and few remember the origin of such habits (namely to use up any remaining eggs and dairy in the house).

The two "sides" to the liturgical experience, encapsulated in the practices of fasting and feasting, are not entirely separate, however, but often fold in on each other. The first week of Lent, for example, is characterized by an intense effort of penitence suffused by an emphasis on joy in all the liturgical texts.[13] Even more concretely, in many parishes the rite of forgiveness at the end of Forgiveness Vespers, which begins Great Lent, is accompanied by the singing of the Paschal canon, which constitutes the height of joy at the celebration of Pascha. Similarly, the "Kneeling Vespers" on the celebration of Pentecost reminds of the penitential dimension while the feast is still continued for another week. Fasting and feasting do not simply follow on each other in linear fashion, but are in continual tension with each other. This tension marks liturgical experience maybe more profoundly than any other pattern. The temporality of liturgy then does not fit into chronological, measurable, "calendar time," as we assume time to function based on our contemporary scientific and historicized worldview. We require a different approach for understanding the complex and multi-layered fashion in which liturgy handles time.

Liturgical Theology and Time

Liturgical theologians often grapple with the complicated ways in which past, present, and future intermingle within the liturgy. One of the strongest features they note about liturgical temporality is the paradox or tension evident in its texts and practices between anamnesis (memory) and eschaton (anticipation).[14] Liturgy not only stages the past; it also envisions the future. Anderson points out that liturgical practices maintain "a particular relation to time" inasmuch as they "work to manifest that which is past, to present or re-present that which is in and of the present, and to continue to develop or emerge in and from the future."[15] Irwin argues that in liturgical time, in some way past, present, and future come together: "the biblical and liturgical notion of remembering is always about an event that encapsulates the past, the present, and the future, and by its unique nature, it is something in which we can 'take part in' here and now."[16] Although most agree that liturgy has a relation to both past and future, the emphases are often different.

Many liturgical theologians stress the anamnetic dimensions of liturgy. Irwin insists that "all liturgy is an act of memorial." This does not mean that liturgy simply remembers, but through liturgical action "we are contemporary with the saving events of our redemption, which are never relegated to the past but always perdure and are perpetuated in and through the liturgy." Thus, "it is in and through the liturgy, celebrated in common in a covenanted people, that these saving events that happened once and for all in saving history are renewed and we are drawn into them by this very act of celebration."[17] Limouris similarly claims: "All the great events of Christ's sufferings and triumphs are happening again in a mysterious way, through the sacramental life of the church. Calvary and the resurrection are the church's daily experience. This is why in every liturgy we refer to these events not only as belonging to the past but as taking place really now, before us."[18] The idea that liturgy is an enactment in the sense of a performance is quite popular. Pfattreicher speaks of the liturgical year as "a work of symbolic memory, the process by which we not only repeat past experience but reconstruct it." It is "a kind of drama, an enactment of the history of salvation."[19] Liturgy accordingly is interpreted as relating primarily to the past but in such a way that the past is somehow recreated in the present. What does it mean to "perpetuate" or "reconstruct" the past in the present?

Other liturgical scholars focus more on the future. Schmemann strongly emphasizes the eschatological dimension and function of the eucharistic liturgy. In the liturgy, somehow the "coming kingdom" is said to break in and to become real. He claims that in liturgy we enter with the saints and the angels into the heavenly celebration; we anticipate it within our own liturgy, but this is not "mere" anticipation, it actually becomes "real" within the celebration.[20] The joy of the eschaton becomes present within the liturgical performance. This is not only true of the weekly celebration, but even more so for Pascha, the feast of feasts.[21] Other liturgical scholars have followed him in stressing the eschatological aspects of liturgy or have sought to combine anamnetic and eschatological functions. For example, Don Saliers says: "The central thesis of this book is simple: Christian liturgy as rite and as prayer is thoroughly eschatological."[22] Kavanagh also insists: "Thus when the liturgy of Christians deals with time, as it inevitably must, it does so not in the short term but *sub specie aeternitatis*, that is, eschatologically."[23] Irwin tries to hold both dimensions together: "Thus the *synaxis* of the Word is itself an eschatological experience—of salvation experienced here and now and of the fullness of salvation to be realized in the eternal kingdom. Thus all liturgy can be understood as the privileged, though provisional, encounter with saving events of the past experienced anew though the liturgy . . . The Liturgy of the Word, which manifests and is an epiphany of the kingdom, moves the Church toward the time of its completion and fulfillment in the eschaton."[24]

In contrast, Rouwhorst argues that the eschatological dimension of early Christian liturgy is overstated.[25] Some liturgical scholars have tried to resolve this tension by arguing that initially liturgy was primarily oriented eschatologically and that the more historical emphasis is a later adjustment when the parousia was no longer expected as urgently. Taft has shown this assumption to be without basis in the historical record and argues that anamnetic and eschatological features were always present simultaneously, albeit maybe one or the other stressed more strongly by certain "schools" of interpretation.[26] How do we make sense of this idea that the future comes "into" the present or that the past is in some way "perpetuated" by the present liturgy? It surely cannot mean that we are magically transported into the past or future during the liturgical service.[27]

Pfatteicher tries to resolve this question in terms of exemplarity. Liturgy serves as "a kind of template by which our lives are given a common shape and order to encourage the living of *our* life in the light of past events that are not past (memory) and in expectation of the future that is already in our possession (hope)."[28] Such shaping of life is possible through the repetition that occurs in worship, which instantiates an eternal present.[29] Actions become habitual through repetition.[30] Janowiak speaks of it as "a repeated, liturgical pattern that becomes engraved in the bones and marrow of the assembly."[31] Senn also stresses this dimension of repetition and links it to social ritual, which functions to unify the community that celebrates it.[32] Lathrop says, with even more rhetorical flourish: "The passage of the day, morning with its light and possibilities and night with its fears and comforts, is made to witness to God. The basic marking points of our experience of time become places to stand, open toward God as creator of time."[33] Yet how does ritual pull us into the meaning of the past? How does it become a "template" for our lives? What does it mean that an experience of time can become a "place to stand"? Can phenomenology help us investigate this complex experience of time more fully?

Phenomenology and Temporality

Various phenomenologists have thought deeply about our human experience of time. Husserl already complicates the linear, scientific account of time as a series of punctual "now" moments and instead shows how even the experience of a temporal sequence includes multiple layers of a flow of time with various moments or aspects held in memory and anticipation.[34] We are conscious not of individual moments that follow on each other in chronological fashion, but we experience a unity of perception within the flow of time, which has duration and extension. Merleau-Ponty also briefly discusses temporality, arguing that time is not in the things themselves, but always "presupposes a view upon time."[35] Time is neither a simple flow of sequences, nor is it a "succession of nows" in consciousness. He claims that time is "not an object of our knowledge, but rather a dimension of our being."[36] Merleau-Ponty is quite critical of Heidegger, however, and seeks to hold onto a sense of the continuity of time and on the present as primary.[37] He ultimately speaks of time as "the sense of our life" and as what enables a unification of subjectivity and objectivity.

Probably the most well-known phenomenological account of temporality is that of Heidegger. As the title of his most famous work, *Being and Time*, indicates, time is absolutely central in his thought, indeed he seeks to think the being of Dasein *as* temporality.[38] Heidegger distinguishes our phenomenological experience of time from scientific presuppositions. We do not first of all experience time in a linear or chronological fashion as calendar time; this arrangement ("calendar" or "clock" time) comes later. The past is not "back there" but "here" in memory, the future not "far away out there" but "here" in anticipation. Instead of merely sitting in time, we engage it much more actively. For example, if I "dwell" on something (a painful memory for example), I am far more "present" to it than anything that is happening to me at this moment. While pain has a way of riveting me to my body at this very moment, many other experiences actually take me out of the moment in some fashion and make me more "present" to other temporal modes: I worry about a particular event I anticipate, I regret a moment that has passed, and so forth. Heidegger stresses that time "concerns" me (*geht mich an*). Indeed, most fundamentally, for Heidegger temporality illustrates the structure of Dasein as care/worry (*Sorge*), as concerned engagement with one's existence, and enables its constitution. Our experience of time opens the world in a particular fashion: We project ourselves toward the future, live *as* our future possibilities. Human temporality, for Heidegger, is "ek-static" (that is, we "stand out" into it). All three modes of time are experienced in some sense simultaneously and ecstatically. Heidegger works this out in regard to the notions of understanding, affectivity, and fallenness, which he had examined earlier in the book (and to which we will return in other contexts).

For Heidegger, our experience as temporal is oriented by our existence as being "toward" our possibilities in the face of our existential angst over the end, namely our death as the very "possibility of impossibility" (§53). This is not a concrete fear of a specific event or accident that might cause our death, but it refers to the existential possibility of the nothing, the closing down of all human possibilities for me. At the same time, it is what enables the very possibility of my projects and my orientation toward possibilities I might choose or grasp. It is *my* death that uniquely individuates and singularizes me. While I may witness another's death and mourn his or her loss, I cannot "live" another's death. Even in sacrificing myself for another or for a cause, I do not save the other from the death that must still be undergone. Heidegger argues in an early lecture to the department of theology at the University of Marburg that Christianity or theology cannot have the same experience of being toward death or of temporality because the question of time is always foreclosed theologically by that of eternity. Theologians (so Heidegger claims) read time through and starting from eternity, while we need to read time through time and starting from it.[39]

Lacoste uses Heidegger's treatment of human being-in-the-world as a starting point and from there develops "being-before-God" as an exceptional and optional stance that goes beyond such basic human existing.[40] This being-before-God constitutes a radical rupture, a complete conversion or subversion, even a suspension or supererogation of human being-in-the-world. Lacoste stresses that "whoever says 'liturgy' says 'rupture,'" that "liturgy works rupture," and that "liturgy contests our being-in-the-world and subverts it."[41] The liturgy is not a "school of religious experience," but instead a radical non-experience and non-event.[42] He frames this primarily in terms of a challenge to Heidegger's account of Dasein as being-toward-death. Our being-before-God "denies that death has the last word on life." Instead, "the logic of the eschaton liturgically interferes with that of our being-toward-death."[43] Thus, the temporality of "liturgical" being-before-God is almost entirely characterized by such radical rupture and suspension of "ordinary" human temporality.

Although *Experience and the Absolute* is his more well-known text, Lacoste first lays out this vision in an analysis of temporality. In *Note sur le temps* (subtitled "an essay on the reasons for memory and hope"), he develops an account of human being before God as a challenge to being before death via a notion of the parousia. While human being toward death is the best account of human experience "in the world," we can envision an unsettling of this experience that might pose an alternative to anxiety before death with the hope of the eschaton. Lacoste thus tries to maintain the tension between not foreclosing human experience as finitude with a notion of eternity while also making a place for an alternative experience of hope beyond death. In a detailed and extensive analysis, he shows how certain moments or examples can serve to challenge and unsettle the more common experience.[44]

He distinguishes "kairos" from "chronos" and uses chronos to refer to our mundane experience of time, while he associates kairos with the theological or liturgical experience: "The kairological order breaks with the chronological order by allowing God's promises to resound here and now and permitting the human to respond to what is said to him."[45] This kairological time has to be thought as gift. The "logic of the eschaton" is in "no way inscribed in our facticity" and while we might "remember" aspects of the Gospel message in our daily lives, kairos has no continuity with chronos, but always interrupts it radically. To live "in Church" means to allow God to furnish the preconditions for memory and hope. Only here can the kairological subversion of time be encountered and in that sense the Church is without history: "the proximity of the kingdom constitutes the fundamental ecclesiological situation."[46] The Church is thus characterized by a pre-eschatological temporality. He concludes that "any liturgy takes place in the world and in the shadow of death. Nevertheless, it demonstrates the conditions under which the world, death, and history through certain gestures and certain silences cease to be . . . the sacrament allows for an *eschatological reduction* in which the definitive reality of the real appears."[47] Death is not the "final secret of time" because we have an eschatological vocation beyond the world.[48] He concludes: "*Imitatio (temporis) Christi* must be the final word of our temporality."[49]

In *Experience and the Absolute*, Lacoste also stresses the eschatological dimensions of liturgical time: "One exists liturgically from one's absolute future onward."[50] Indeed, sometimes he speaks of this as a non-time: the vigilant being-before-God is a "non-time," "that of a marginal or parenthetic existence."[51] History is bracketed and we exist in an absolute future. It is a time of "inchoation" in which the Absolute "disrupts" and unsettles us. The resulting restlessness is an experience of this anticipation of the parousia within the tension of its "not yet." Lacoste certainly does not claim that we live in the absolute of the eschaton now, quite the contrary. We exist in the continual tension between the "now" and the "not yet," the parousia is both radically separate from the present and has the possibility of displacing it at least momentarily and in fragmentary fashion. But being-before-God is framed entirely in terms of this eschatological notion of time; it is just that we cannot live liturgically all the time, that our being-before-God is always marked by disappointment, absence, and non-fulfillment. The tension between discordance and concordance—to use Ricoeur's language—is not within liturgy, but between "ordinary" life and "liturgical" life as utterly distinct from each other. It is telling that Lacoste's account of "liturgical" being is all about dispossession and disappropriation and kenotic emptying, never about feasting.[52]

As we have seen, Lacoste does not develop these ideas through any analysis of actual liturgical practices and insists that he is not speaking of "cult" or ritual, but about more fundamental structures of human existing. He is not providing a phenomenology of liturgical or even of more broadly religious experience, but a purely phenomenological analysis of human existing vis-à-vis the Absolute. Yet, as briefly suggested in the Introduction, it is not at all clear that these neat distinctions can be maintained or that such an abstract project is actually viable. Why should we presuppose that humans are ever faced with any Absolute, unless we look to the reality of religious experience that might suggest such a possibility? How can the notion of the eschaton, in particular, function phenomenologically without acknowledging its theological origin? Can "parousia" and other such theological (and decidedly Judeo-Christian) ideas simply be disconnected from their theological moorings and employed for a phenomenological analysis without a careful examination of how they structure "religious" being or existence in a particular tradition of practices? While a phenomenological analysis obviously cannot stop simply at descriptions of particular empirical practices, an analysis more rooted in the "lifeworld" of liturgy might ensure greater congruence between the phenomenological depiction and the actual manifestations of phenomena within liturgical experience. Let us push further the elements of liturgical temporality as highlighted by liturgical theology—the tension between memory and anticipation, the cyclical back-and-forth between fasting and feasting, and liturgy's emphasis on repetition—in light of the phenomenological discussions.

Between Memory and Anticipation

We have seen that many liturgical theologians claim that liturgy somehow brings past and future into the present. Although liturgy includes the hope of the parousia and memories of past events, both memory and anticipation occur in the present experience. They are not simply "recalled" into memory as a thought or even an image, but they are enacted; the memory becomes a present event within the liturgical "performance." Liturgy is mimetic by enacting the "having been" and the "will be" *within* the "now." Liturgy takes this experienced "present," the present of the liturgy, and fills it with meaning. *Our* present is seen as becoming the reality in which God is taken to be at work and encountered. In the liturgy and especially in our participation within it, time is experienced in soteriological fashion: each day gains meaning not just as "one more day" in the linear progression of salvation history, but rather as the very moment in which all of salvation becomes present. Soteriologically speaking, it is always "today," never yesterday or tomorrow. Each liturgical moment has meaning because it is always the "fullness of time." At the same time, each moment anticipates in this intensified fashion what all moments are supposed to become; the intense liturgical moment opens out onto and conveys the meaning of all moments. The liturgical present is at the same time the past and the future, our past and future, but only as we are part of our past and future, and as we are part of Israel's and the church's past and future.

This is exemplified by the fact that many liturgical texts, not just the eucharistic liturgy, but especially those that explore the theme of a specific feast or liturgical celebration, are written in the present tense (generally referred to as the "liturgical present").[53] Over and over again, the texts say "*Today*, the virgin gives birth to the transcendent one" (Kontakion for Nativity), "You have appeared *today* to the whole world" (Kontakion for Theophany), "*Today* is the prelude of our salvation" (Troparion for the Entry of the Theotokos into the Temple), "*Today* is the beginning of our salvation" (Troparion for Annunciation). Indeed, often this word "today" (or "this is the day") is set at the beginning of the poetic line (as if to make sure it is really heard) and repeated over and over again. Not only do the texts continually speak of "today," but even when they mention biblical characters and retell biblical stories, they frequently do so in the present tense rather than employing the past tense as one would expect for a historical description. What we might have thought happened long ago becomes our experience right now in the liturgical present.

Cuneo dismisses this as "permissive," "exotic," and "fantastic."[54] It somehow assumes that those "assembled engage in time travel."[55] He calls "incoherent" and "extravagant" the view that "the ordinary temporal divisions between past, present, and future no longer hold; liturgical reenactment somehow binds together all three temporal dimensions in one time frame."[56] This assumes, of course, that a linear, scientific account of temporality is the only valid and therefore "ordinary" one and that such an account can simply be assumed to have been the view of liturgical composers and all participants in liturgy even in the ancient world. Wolterstorff similarly argues that liturgical theologians are wrong both in their claims about how ancient peoples experienced ritual and in what such liturgy does today.[57] Both Wolterstorff and Cuneo understand temporality in a purely linear, objective, historical sense. "Today" would have to mean that the person saying so literally means that Jesus is ascending or is crucified on the present date in the calendar, that this specific historical event is occurring (again) in the present moment of celebration.[58] But obviously this is not what the liturgies claim.

Despite Heidegger's dismissive attitude about theological accounts of time, his analysis of temporality as ek-static in character is far more helpful than linear, scientific accounts for making sense of liturgical temporality. The liturgical present does not make claims about historical incidents reoccurring in some mysterious fashion within the celebration of the liturgy, but instead shows how the people participate in what affects them right now experientially. Time "concerns" us in liturgy: We have to "enter" into it, have to participate in it, cannot stand apart from it. The "past" is not a chronological "before" that happened "long ago," but it is an event experienced right now within our celebration of the liturgy. The "future" similarly is not "far away," expected to come only after a long wait, but it is experienced as breaking in now, as occurring in some form at this very moment within the liturgical celebration. In the experience of liturgy, past and future become present, but not as recreations or reenactments of *historical* events, but as *liturgical* events that are experienced "now," appropriated by our experience of the event in the liturgical moment. What is remembered is not the historical event of Jesus's crucifixion in year *x* or Mary's death in year *y*. Instead, it is the liturgical commemoration of

Christ's death or of the falling asleep of the Theotokos into which we enter as a present experience. We celebrate not a distant past as an objective moment in history that no longer affects us, but an event that comes to pass within the liturgical experience. We anticipate not a faraway future that will occur on some date on a future calendar, but a hope instantiated in the liturgical celebration right now. We are not magically transported back in time or mysteriously flying forward into the eschaton. Rather, in the experience of liturgy we stand ("ekstatically") in some way within liturgical memory and anticipation as our present experience. Instead of a linear experience that moves from past through the present to the future, time is experienced as the horizon within which we experience our liturgical being; it is the "how" of our "being" in its world. In the liturgical experience, the temporality of the liturgy serves as the horizon for our experience.[59]

In *Being and Time*, Heidegger makes the future primary and argues more broadly that the Western tradition has focused far too exclusively on the present and neglected the other two ekstases of time.[60] This is developed by Jacques Derrida and other subsequent thinkers into a critique of the "metaphysics of presence," namely philosophy's focus on presence as subsistence and permanence. Does the "liturgical present" succumb to such a "metaphysics of presence"?[61] It would do so if its focus on the present were a punctual now moment that proceeded in linear fashion from a past and synchronically moves on to the future. But this is precisely not a good description of how time functions in liturgy because the "present" of liturgy is actually the ek-statically experienced memory and anticipation, rather than the recreation of historical events. What has been and what will be become "present" in liturgy as "given" to us, but this is not a presence of "permanence" or "subsistence." Presence in liturgy is not the permanent locus of something fixedly present, but the shifting experience of the "then" within the "now" as "our now" assimilated to the pattern of the "then" as commemorated or anticipated. In that sense, the "present" or "now" is actually "subject" to past and future, although they become present within it, because past and future structure the present, fill it with "their" meaning, seek to "image" the present in terms of what was, what shall be, and yet is. Although the present is the primary locus of liturgical experience, past and future are in some way normative for it. The present is shaped by "having been as it reoccurs now" and "will be as it breaks in now" and yet past and future "are" only within our experience of them within the liturgical "today."

Similarly, liturgical time is neither simply "*vorhanden*" or available as an object, nor is it arranged in linear or chronological fashion, but the present happens *as* both memory and eschaton; it is not its own "time" but is meaningfully experienced only within the simultaneous experience of the other temporal ekstases as "now." Not only are they—to use Heidegger's language—equiprimordial in the liturgy, but they govern the very horizon within which liturgy makes any sense at all, its very *raison d'être*, its reason for being (or, more precisely, for doing). The liturgical present is only given meaningfully if it is precisely given *at the same time and within the same moment* as memory and anticipation. We can also note in preliminary fashion that in terms of its structure, liturgy here does not represent complete rupture with our "ordinary" experience of time, but actually significant continuity with it. The liturgical poets employ the "being-in-the-world" of their audiences by formulating dialogue that articulates what might be in the mind of the audience if confronted with a situation like that of the biblical story under consideration and placing them mimetically and ecstatically within it.

Yet does this liturgical temporality really map exactly onto the kind of experience Heidegger describes? It is not immediately obvious that it is *my* "no longer" that becomes "present" in liturgy or even solely *my* "not yet" that is anticipated or owned. Rather, anamnesis is memory of Christ or the saints; eschaton is anticipation of the "kingdom." These concern us intimately, but they are not solely about us and are not strictly speaking simply *our* past or future—and this "concern" is quite different from our usual "concerns" of life. Instead, this temporality of presence confronts us with another's experience that can become ours. The liturgical poets do not organize time solely around our present concerns. The recounting of stories is more theological and soteriological than it is a simple memory of either history or our personal experience. Indeed, liturgical poetry deliberately confuses our everyday experience of time. In liturgy, and especially in the way in which it handles time, personal identity becomes assimilated to a larger communal identity.[62] Louth surely is right to say that liturgical time "is not at all an individual experience of time, time has this shape through the liturgical celebration, regardless of how individuals relate to it. Individuals do not create it, they simply recognize it, take it into their experience."[63] To some extent, as in baptism, in liturgy we lose our own individuality and identity, our concern with ourselves, the organization of the entire world around "me." We are no longer the ones who open the world, but become dispossessed, swallowed up in the larger story, identified with its characters, part of the greater liturgical world. Our present reality is at the very least affected, possibly challenged and transformed by the liturgical reality that becomes present in our celebration of it. This possibility that liturgy displaces our focus on the self and invites us into *its* world must necessarily remain very preliminary and tentative at this point, but will be encountered again and given more substance in subsequent chapters.

From Fast to Feast

The tension of liturgical temporality is not only that between remembered past and anticipated future, but also the cyclical back-and-forth between fasting and feasting. This does not conflict with the temporality of the liturgical "today" just examined because in both fasting and feasting are characters and events remembered and appropriated for one's own experience. But the cycle of fasting and feasting also goes beyond mere memory and anticipation. It constitutes an experience of temporality that marks certain times as "more" than others, as qualitatively set apart from them. A feast is experienced more intensely than an "ordinary" day. The experience of time is heightened and intensified during the fasts and the feasts, and this intensification functions differently for different occasions.[64] Holy Week, for example, is an especially intense experience and this is particularly true in terms of its experience of time. Even in small parishes, one can spend hours and hours in church and going to all or even many of the services wreaks havoc on one's "normal" schedule—one enters into a different kind of temporality where regular time seems suspended. The services are long but it is not just that more time is spent in church than usually. The experience of time itself shifts; this time matters more than other times. Similarly, the first week of Lent is qualitatively different in its experience from the experience during "regular" time or even other fasting periods. The festal experience of the Paschal midnight service is heightened in various ways through temporal experience: the fact that it serves as a culmination of a week of long services, its own length (really several services packed into one: Nocturnes, Matins, Hours, and Liturgy), but also the fact that it takes place in the middle of the night, coupled with the anticipation of the feasting that will follow in many parishes into the wee hours of the morning with foods that have been prepared in the labor of many hours. The experience of the liturgical occasion is temporally weighted by the anticipation of the feast, the time-intensive preparation, and the memory of past feasting.

The cyclical pattern of fasting and feasting is also significant in another way. The liturgical "back and forth" means that the consciousness of the practicing Orthodox continually cycles between repentance or preparation and celebration or fulfillment. Both are temporal modes, one reflecting at least to some extent on the past and the other anticipating the future, albeit not quite in the way described in the former section. Here remembrance is not only about a biblical or historical event brought into the present celebration, but it is instead more particularly a remembrance of one's own shortcomings and failures. Again, these are not remembered in some scientific fashion as having taken place on such and such a date at such and such a time, but instead as aspects of *who I am now*, temporally shaped by my past actions. Contrition is a present experience regarding an ostensibly past but in some way still present experience. Our failures have marked us and continue to haunt us and to impact our relationships with the people we have wounded. To repent, to ask for forgiveness, to seek reconciliation is to acknowledge the present weight of the past, to renegotiate the link between past and present. It is not necessarily trying to "undo" what happened in the past but to deal with its current repercussions, with the ways in which the past is experienced now and still marked in its wounds. It attempts not an undoing but a healing, a release from the bonds of guilt and a restoration of relationships.

In quite a different way, feasting also addresses a fundamental human need. As we have already seen, feasting "thickens" time; time is experienced more intensely during the feast. Each moment of the feast matters more fully; we are more "present" to it than we are to the seemingly insignificant moments of our everyday lives. We set other things aside, we spend lots of time preparing for it, and during this preparatory time of cleaning, cooking, baking, and other activities, we are temporally already in the feast via anticipation. The feast thus works backward and forward into the rest of time. Lathrop claims that "a feast day gives organization to all time. The festival invites us all to see that the leisure and the intensity of enacted communal values, the activity and inactivity that fill the festival are why the other days exist; what a human being *is* is seen in the festival."[65] We will have to examine the claim about human "being" more fully, but it is certainly true that the feast in some way gives meaning to other days also. We prepare and work so that we can feast. We "give up" other time—sometimes even quite inordinate amounts of time—in order to "have the time" for celebration. The importance of the festal occasion is to some extent proportionally related to the amount of time and energy we are willing to expend in preparation. Feasts that we anticipate to occur only once—such as threshold moments of life celebrated in baptisms, weddings, funerals— or that occur only rarely (such as once a year) call for far greater commitments of time in preparation. Note also that we usually give this time quite willingly, the joy of the anticipated feast bleeds back into the preparation. Preparation for a feast, especially of those activities most directly linked to feasting such as the preparation of special foods, is not onerous but in some way part of the festal experience. In this respect it is also significant that most major feasts have what is referred to as the "forefeast" and "afterfeast." Feasts are not simply singular moments but are extended. Both fasting and feasting have duration; they are not points on a line. As Heidegger stresses about our experience of time, liturgical time is always distended, it involves extension or duration.[66] Indeed, the celebration of the "today" in liturgy can last several days, often eight—or even fifty in the case of the Pentecost season.

Perhaps most significantly, the liturgical back-and-forth between fast and feast points to the fact that both *together* are important and that the tension between them should not be collapsed. In fact, the rituals of most cultures similarly fluctuate between more somber or ascetic occasions and exuberant celebration. The human spirit (and body!) seems to need both and to require an alternation between them. One cannot remain at the height of celebration all year long. It is one of the fundamental mistakes of our consumer culture to pretend that we could be continually feasting.[67] This narcissistic indulgence not only eliminates fasting (though it is in a more destructive mode paralleled by the contemporary obsession with dieting), but also renders feasting meaningless. Feasts are meant to be rare, special, unusual, exorbitant; they interrupt our ordinary experience of time and heighten its meaning for the festive occasion. Even the weekly cycle acknowledges this: not every day can be a Sunday. Just as the Jewish tradition affirms that Sabbath practice ought to inform the entire week and yet we cannot manage to keep even one Sabbath perfectly,[68] so the liturgical height of Sunday or especially Pascha is to inform all of life while we realize that we cannot sustain it even once a week or once a year. In this respect, ritual experience across cultures and traditions seems to reflect a truth about human existence, about its fragility and finitude, about our inability to sustain harmony and fulfillment for any length of time. Here liturgy clearly at least to some extent mimetically takes up our real experience in the world. The liturgical present takes seriously our real struggles with the mess and chaos of our lives and our desire to make sense of them and give meaning to our existence. The back-and-forth arrangement of fast and feast constantly cycles between an acknowledgment that on the one hand we fall short and require repentance and on the other hand we desire the celebration of restoration and harmony.

Ricoeur refers to this experience of life in terms of the tension between concordance and discordance.[69] We seek to make sense of our lives, to give harmony and concordance to our existence. Yet we are continually confronted with the vicissitudes of life that undo our neat solutions and throw us into confusion and disharmony. Narratives and myths function as ways for people to grapple with this incoherence and to give a coherent structure or a meaning to the chaos of their own lives and that of the world around them. Narrative seeks to make sense, to re-establish concordance in the midst of discordance. Liturgy similarly recognizes the discordant and chaotic elements of our experience and magnifies them poetically. It thus does not erase human finitude or break with the chaos of the "world," but acknowledges it vividly. While penitential texts emphasize the experience of discordance, festal liturgies stress the desire for an overall cosmic harmony. For example, the liturgy for Dormition suggests that Mary's being taken up to heaven sanctifies all the elements and reestablishes harmony in the cosmos. Similarly, Christ's ascension and transfiguration are said to heal the ancient divisions of the cosmos, to bring earth and heaven together, to unite what was previously separated. We will return to the spatial aspect of this in the next chapter, but we should note here the way in which this is a particular kind of temporality, one that cycles between the acknowledgment of discordance and the desire to establish concordance. The progression is not from past via the present to the future, but a back and forth between a disordered, fragmented period (cf., Great Lent) and an ordered, harmonious temporality (cf., the Pentecost season).

Repetition and (Re)appropriation

Besides the two temporal movements of back-and-forth between fasting and feasting and the tension between memory and anticipation, more broadly speaking the liturgical cycles (daily, weekly, annual) lead to an experience of temporality as repetition. This aspect of repetition—even beyond the repetition of fasts and feasts—is crucial for the liturgical experience of time. The same prayers are read, the same texts chanted, the same hymns sung in the morning or evening of every day, on the same day of every week, or on the feast as it is celebrated every year. The same melodies and arrangements are used over and over again in various ways. The eight liturgical tones are repeated on a cycle that restarts after each Pascha, while certain tones are always associated with certain occasions. Furthermore, the feasts refer to each other, are patterned on each other. The feasts of Nativity and of Theophany liturgically imitate the feast of Pascha in terms of texts and organization on several levels. The cyclical nature of liturgical time has repetition naturally built into it.

Liturgical temporality, then, constitutes neither a radical rupture with this world and its temporality nor a completely smooth continuity.[70] Liturgy neither perfectly mirrors nor breaks entirely with "ordinary" time. Repetition is a kind of continuity but it is one that is interrupted and fragmented; it requires effort and deliberation. Repetition does not happen automatically, but is an active reappropriation of a previous instance. No repetition is ever entirely the same. Each time the horizon of the feast and the horizon of daily life have to meet anew. Although we encounter Great Lent again each year, we encounter it each time differently. Each time anew we have to make an effort at contrition: Each Lent the particularities of our concrete lives are different from how we lived and who we were even just a year ago. And both fasts and feasts certainly have elements of rupture with daily life. The rules for fasting, for example, alter not only one's eating habits but how one shops, cooks, interacts with others, on multiple levels. A kind of rupture is even explicitly expected: We are to change our life, turn around, abandon certain destructive practices and learn new habits. This is not a matter of simply continuing daily life in a new mode.

Repetition is a crucial element in liturgy. Liturgy lives and breathes by repetition (despite the continual threat of rite becoming dead or suffocating rote). The cyclical nature of liturgy enforces repetition, but there are many repetitive elements even within each specific liturgical occasion (most prominently the frequent repetition of the line "Lord, have mercy"). Individual phrases are repeated within each liturgy, prayers are repeated each day, the eucharistic liturgy is repeated weekly (or sometimes even more frequently), liturgical seasons and feasts are repeated each year.[71] If the "goal" of the Christian life is to become like Christ, Mary, or the saints, this is only slowly learned over time and needs to be reinforced continually. Krueger contends that "Byzantine religious experts and professionals understood that repetition formed interior religious dispositions. . . . Ritual repetition inculcated patterns of self-accusation and self-formation, as participants became the subjects of liturgy."[72] Identification with the models presented in liturgy is reinforced by repetition and continual practice. Each year, even each week, we again require times of repentance where we focus especially on reorienting our lives. The imitation of Christ and the saints must occur over and over again, and always be corrected by renewed experience of the same. Liturgy provides the continual practice to grow into this kind of life.

Aristotle speaks of the relationship between virtuous action and an excellent person in precisely this cyclical fashion: Only virtuous actions enable us to become virtuous people, but only virtuous people truly act virtuously.[73] That seems a vicious circle, until we realize that virtue is a matter of habit, of learning and practicing continually, of growing into a particular life through deliberate (and deliberated) repetition. This is, of course, a fundamental insight about the human condition: We learn nothing without repetition. Any acquiring of skill requires practice. Habits are shaped by doing things over and over again. Meaning only penetrates deeply when it is repeated over and over again. Liturgy, then, as the ancients already acknowledged, serves as the practice ground, as "medicine for the soul" and training for the body.[74] Don Saliers says that "certain affections and virtues are formed and expressed in the modalities of communal prayer and ritual action. These modalities of prayer enter into the formation of the self in community."[75] Liturgy helps us acquire salutary soteriological habits through their continual practice.

One cannot rush "salvation," it must permeate and shape all of life and this occurs only gradually. It takes time. Maybe this is one of the reasons for the length of Orthodox services. Many people complain that the services are so long and repeat so much, but there is a real if unarticulated recognition here that we are shaped by what we devote our time to and if all this time is wrapped up in consumerism and social media, then that is what will shape us and determine the meaning of our lives.[76] Liturgy can only transform us if we actually put our bodies and minds within it, spend time with it, are present to it. It is in this way that liturgy can form new habits, shape a new kind of life, and create identity over time. This does not happen automatically. If the contemporary horizon, where we find ourselves today within our lives, is to enter into relation with the liturgical horizon or even to be transformed by it, then its meaning cannot merely be engaged passively but must be appropriated in some fashion.[77]

Such appropriation need not always be completely conscious and deliberate. In certain ways, liturgy can probably have an impact on us without our being conscious of it the entire time. Habits are formed also at a subconscious level and even comprehension can often occur slowly over time without full awareness at each moment. Certainly meaning can be formed and can influence us in a very subtle and fairly unconscious fashion. Children, in particular, are shaped in their thinking and imagination through simply being present in liturgy, even if they are not entirely attentive or able to comprehend completely what is going on. They are formed significantly in unconscious ways by the worlds of meaning in which they are immersed. Indeed, part of the power of symbolism and poetry (especially when set to music) is precisely that its meaning is richer than can be fully comprehended, grasped, or put into words. Yet this more passive shaping and informing of our imagination is not sufficient. Liturgy has to be appropriated—that is, made our own. At some point participation has to become more conscious and deliberate. Catechesis and ascesis are required for full appropriation.[78] One has to enter the "world" and make its meaning one's own or, maybe more correctly, become part of its meaning. The repetitive nature of liturgy provides us with continually new opportunities for appropriation or application. Indeed, Ricoeur actually argues that such appropriation can function as a form of dispossession where I am confronted with new ways of being, which enable me to know myself more fully precisely in engaging with new possibilities that challenge my assumptions about the world.[79] Appropriation, then, allows us to make the meaning of liturgy our own, not in the sense of "possession" but in the sense of applying ourselves to it wholly and entering into it, allowing it to mold and transform our lives.

This has both personal and communal dimensions, although the two are not entirely separate. Identity is always shaped and appropriated in the context of association with (or even rejection of) other people. One chooses to belong to a community or not, usually from within that or another community. Faith is often much more about choosing to walk with others—or walking out on them when their world of meaning no longer seems convincing and the ties to its members no longer feel binding (*religere* means to bind or tie together).[80] Indeed, participation in religion is often far more about the relationships one establishes with a community or groups of people than mere assent to certain doctrinal statements, even in communities where such dogmatic adhesion is touted as central.[81] Thus, while faith must be at least on some level deliberate and maybe even deliberated for appropriation, such deliberation need not be purely intellectual or theoretical. At the same time, the meaning of liturgical actions must be communally and personally appropriated in order to function as more than mere imitation or rote practice.[82] Here, Heidegger's language about authenticity can be used positively: Practice must become "authentic" in the sense of conscious and deliberate appropriation rather than an "inauthentic" unreflective immersion in and going along with what the "crowd" says. While the language of authenticity and grasping of one's life is too individualistic for what happens in liturgy and smacks too much of self-sufficient autonomy, meaning always has to be reappropriated on some level in order to mean genuinely. And liturgy continually and obsessively encourages us to do so via its prayers—both personal and public—and its cycles of repetition. Each Lent is a new call to repentance, each Pascha a new invitation to celebration and gratitude.

Through repetition liturgical practice shapes an identity that is more contrite, more open to others, more generous, more hospitable. It sets before us constantly the images of the saints as models of who we are to become. We are directed toward them as models worthy of imitation. Here the pervasive paradoxical tension of liturgy between penitence and celebration reaches its height: Hermeneutically, we are the "worst of sinners" called to become saints. This tension is important and should never be collapsed. Although we are called to move from one to the other, to cease being "sinners" and to become "saints," it is crucial that liturgy never promises that we have stopped the one or reached the other. Here the cyclical nature of liturgical temporality is again significant: we must go through Lent each year anew and will never be finished with it. The identity shaped by liturgy is always one living *within* the tension of "sinner-saint." The tension can never be collapsed into pure celebration that would dispense with penitence or erase our finitude.

Repetition, then, is central to the liturgical experience of temporality. This is crucial because so often faith is presented as primarily hope in an afterlife or as an assent to certain statements about linear historicity (for example, that Christ lived, died, and was raised at a particular point in human history). Neither of these reflect the reality of liturgy, which is lived in its cyclical, repetitive nature as what concerns us now and celebrates the events (such as those of Christ's life) as mattering now and always anew. Liturgical experience as experience is neither about historical events in the deep past nor life after death in some far away future, but it is about liturgical events as they are experienced now and as they are real for us here. At the same time these are not singular, unpredictable (saturated?) events, but ones for which we must prepare, which we must always appropriate anew, for which one celebration is not sufficient. They are a repeated reality of our lives, we must enter them and leave them again, we cannot simply remain basking in them and they do not happen without conscious effort and diligent preparation.

Obviously, repetition can become rote or tedious; practices can become meaningless through endless repetition. Yet, it is precisely the repetition that gives the occasion meaning. The feasts are only such happy occasions because we anticipate them each year, because we have already experienced their celebration previously, because we have created habits of expectation by prior experiences of the feast. Repetition enables a deep familiarity that goes far beyond head knowledge or memorization to knowing something on a much more profound affective level. When we have repeated the hymns endless times, we have not just memorized the words or the tunes in some abstract fashion that makes it possible to recite them, but they have entered our subconscious being and affect us on deeply visceral levels. This includes the recognition that habits are only shaped by practice and repetition.[83] Repetition creates "habits of the heart"; it alters our being in the world permanently. Repeated practice becomes "rote" for the very same reason that it enters our existential being: It becomes a "natural" way of being in the world that has become absorbed and assimilated into our forms of existing.

And there is a further important phenomenological element to repetition. The repetition does not begin with us. We celebrate feasts that have been celebrated for centuries. We prepare foods that have been prepared by many before us and this is, in fact, what makes them so cherished. The cycles of fasting and feasting are meaningful precisely because we did not invent them, because they do not begin with us, because they transcend us while allowing us to participate in them. Liturgy precedes us, we are thrown into it, and we always come to it *in medias res*. Liturgy goes on before us and after us and without us. This obviously does not mean that we need not do anything; as we have seen, liturgy requires effort and appropriation. Yet such effort and appropriation are possible because others have done so before us and do so now with us. Our effort is meaningful and "succeeds" only as a participation in the cycle of repetitions. Although traditions surely change over time, they are experienced as stable or constant, as having always been done this way.

There is thus a way in which repetition institutes a time immemorial. Liturgy is not progressive or linear. In the "moment" (or *Augenblick*) of liturgy, eternity breaks in, in some manner what has "always" been true is experienced as here and now.[84] Only in this sense is Heidegger right that "theologically" eternity matters to Christian temporality. But it does so not because a confidence in the afterlife displaces a real experience of time or an authentic confrontation with one's death. Rather, it describes something about the qualitative experience of time: The moment is weighted with eternal significance. Each moment matters profoundly, not as one in sequences of nows, but as the moment that encapsulates all of time.[85] The heightened moment of the feast, then, in some way infects all of time, bleeds into the ordinary, and gives it significance.

Liturgical temporality, then, is characterized by several tensions. It is experienced in the present moment that is meaningfully shaped by memory and anticipation as occurring in the now-time of liturgy. This moment is always distended; it is not a mere fragment, but meaningfully connected through its place in the cycle of repetitions. Liturgy shapes our present experience so as to be weighted with a larger significance, magnified, but also colored by the given of liturgy: It is not simply my personal experience that becomes significant, but it is the meaning of the liturgical occasion as it opens unto us now and invites us into its events. This experience cycles continually between fasting and feasting, experiences of repentance and fulfillment. Here also, our daily experiences of failure and reconciliation are both taken up in and actively enabled by the liturgical movements, acknowledging both the discordance and fragmentation of our lives and our hope for greater concordance and harmony. Finally, liturgical temporality functions via repetition, albeit in continually new ways. Liturgy is not simply rupture with our ordinary lives but in some way structures and intensifies "ordinary" experience. The repetition of liturgy serves to habituate us to its movements and opens us up for a more deliberate entry into its temporality. We have already used spatial language here abundantly: invitation into, entry, and movement. Let us now turn more deliberately to the space in which liturgy takes place.

2

SPATIALITY

In the early sixth century, Procopius describes Justinian's recently rebuilt church, Hagia Sophia:

So the church has been made a spectacle of great beauty, stupendous to those who see it and altogether incredible to those who hear of it. . . . Its breadth and length have been so fittingly proportioned that it may without impropriety be described as being both very long and extremely broad. And it boasts of ineffable beauty, for it subtly combines its mass with the harmony of its proportions, having neither any excess nor any deficiency. . . . You might say that the [interior] space is not illuminated by the sun from the outside, but that the radiance is generated within, so great an abundance of light bathes this shrine all round. . . . Rising above this circle is an enormous spherical dome which makes the building exceptionally beautiful. It seems not to be founded on solid masonry, but to be suspended from heaven by that golden chain and so cover the space. All of these elements, marvellously fitted together in mid-air, suspended from one another and reposing only on the parts adjacent to them, produce a unified and most remarkable harmony in the work, and yet do not allow the spectator to rest their gaze upon any of them for a length of time, but each detail readily draws and attracts the eye to itself. Thus the vision constantly shifts round, and the beholders are quite unable to select any particular element which they might admire more than all the others.[1]

Liturgy is not just an organization of time, but it takes place in space—sometimes in a magnificently beautiful space, as depicted by Procopius, sometimes in much humbler environments. While this spatial situatedness may be an obvious and trite point, it is not always taken sufficiently seriously. There is no liturgy without the temporal and spatial dimensions. Liturgy does not take place in the abstract or in our heads; it is not simply beautiful thoughts or a timeless and placeless contemplation of the divine by a disembodied soul. Liturgy is performed rite, it involves bodies moving in—fairly organized and highly decorated—space, as well as handling objects that have a place. The "sacred" space is not only the backdrop against which liturgical experience occurs, but it is itself an important element of it. What does it mean for a space to be designated as "sacred"? The very performance of liturgy requires specific and explicit considerations of space: What sort of place must be built to accommodate it and how will such architecture be most conducive to what is supposed to happen within it? How are such places to be decorated or adorned; what images or architectural features will prepare the body, especially sight and touch, for worship and allow for its exercise? How are bodies expected to move within this space and how are its implements and other objects found within it to be handled most appropriately, that is, in accordance with their liturgical use? Where are choirs for chanting the liturgy to be placed and how must the space resonate acoustically for them to be heard? To what extent does the rest of the congregation participate in their singing and how is this encouraged or discouraged by the spatial arrangements?

It is clear already in these questions that the question of spatiality in liturgy is closely connected to that of corporeality. But it is also not completely separate from the question of temporality. In some ways, space also negotiates time; the liturgical calendar, its cyclical nature, and the "now" time of liturgy have an impact on considerations concerning the arrangement of space. Yet these are not merely "physical" or "material" questions that interest the architect, the artist, or the archaeologist; they are also deeply phenomenological questions. How do we experience the space of liturgy? How does its place affect our experience of other liturgical aspects? How does space "mean" for us? What role does it play in the "liturgical life" and hence in religious experience? To speak of the "world" of liturgy is already a spatial metaphor: What do we mean when we say that liturgy "opens a world" or "invites us into" such a world?[2] Where is this "world" and how is it related to the place of and the space within liturgy? Can we speak of a liturgical "being-in-the-world" or is the world of liturgy not related to the world "outside" liturgy?

Liturgical Theology and Ecclesial Space

The question of liturgical space is inextricably linked to the topic of Christian architecture.[3] At first Christian churches were modeled on the basilica form—that is, the public meeting house of the ancient Roman world.[4] A large nave served the congregation; often different areas were designated for different groups of people.[5] In the center was a bema, a slightly raised platform, from which the bishops or presbyters spoke to the congregation. The sanctuary area housed the altar on which the Eucharist would be offered and then distributed to the people who initially entered this area for the reception of the gifts and eventually only came to its edge. Although there was already a distinction between narthex, nave, and sanctuary in the early churches, the elaborate iconostasis developed much later. Even when architectural style shifted in Constantinople to the domed form,[6] there was no "wall" separating sanctuary from nave, although the two spaces become increasingly distinguished theologically, as can be seen in the liturgical analyses of Dionysius, Maximus, and Germanos.[7]

Especially under Constantine and Justinian, the building of churches as public gifts and monuments to their largess increased exponentially.[8] Byzantine emperors, empresses, other members of the royal family, and diverse wealthy citizens built and decorated churches and chapels. In the eyes of contemporaries, these are usually distinguished by their beauty, magnificence, imposing size, and lavish decoration (especially in Eusebius's descriptions of Constantine's building program and Procopius's descriptions of the churches built under Justinian).[9] Building a church to commemorate a martyr or supporting the decoration of a new chapel is often cited as evidence of the piety of an important person with means, functioning just like the ancient "liturgies"—gifts and donations on behalf of the state, including supporting its sacral functions. *Ekphrasis*, the laudatory description of a decorated space so as to evoke an experience of the space in the minds of the audience, became an immensely popular form of speech and writing.[10] In these descriptions, beauty, magnificence, and "sheen" (albeit not necessarily color) play an important role. The play of light on glittering implements or gold mosaic functioned differently at different times of day or night, in daylight or candle light. Thus, the experience of space was and is closely linked to visual, auditory, and other sensory aspects. It is consequently always also a corporeal experience of the body's movement and placement in space, as well as an experience of the senses, especially sight, hearing (in terms of acoustics), and touch. We will return to these aspects in that context in Chapters 3 and 4.

Maybe even more importantly, liturgical architecture from its very start implied an orientation and this orientation is meaningful in terms of its direction.[11] Churches are built to face east, liturgical actions are oriented toward the altar area, meaningful "regions" or areas of space within the church are carefully distinguished (especially narthex, nave, and sanctuary), movements are directed in deliberate orientation toward the sanctuary.[12] One moves naturally from narthex to nave and is oriented toward the altar or sanctuary area. The movements of liturgy circle around or move toward the sanctuary and are centered on it in some fashion. Ritual movements are not arbitrary or subjective, but often scripted by the rite. They instantiate a "reality" but not a reality in the scientific geometrical sense, not as something that can be measured with a ruler or measuring tape.[13] What signifies as meaningful spatially in liturgy does not correspond to an "objective" or "scientific" notion of space in terms of geometrical arrangement, although that certainly does not make it lack spatiality or embodiment.

Such movements did not always stay inside the church. In fact, processions or "stational" liturgy (liturgy moving from place to place, taking place at multiple "stations") was immensely popular in the ancient world.[14] In the early Jerusalem liturgy different services were held at different places, namely those most closely associated with whatever feast was being celebrated. Often it involved moving from place to place or church to church within the course of a service or several services strung together (especially true for Holy Thursday and Holy Friday). Both forms of stational liturgy were recreated in other places, the former more dominantly in Rome (alternating between churches for whole services, especially during Lent where liturgies were held at different locations throughout the city each week), the latter more popular in Constantinople (starting a service in one church and then moving to another or even a third in the course of the same service), although both versions can be found in the practices of several urban centers in later centuries. Baldovin argues that the stational form of so much of early liturgy was an attempt to "take over" the social and public space for the new faith. Worship "in the streets" tried to claim public space for Christianity. This social endowing of public spaces with religious significance applied not simply to architecture but to the ways in which space is traversed: "more than the buildings, it was the liturgy that made this 'conquest' both visible and viable by covering the city with liturgical action that had the bishop as its main participant. . . . Christianity, therefore represented the public religious life of the city by means of its cult. It made the *civitas* not only civilization, but also holy civilization, a civilization defended as much by icons and relics and processions as it was by walls and military and political power. Thus, the city as holy civilization was a concept that was expressed above all liturgically."[15] This use of space, then, conveys the "public" nature of liturgy, the ways in which it spills over into the world.

At the same time, stational liturgy constitutes an attempt to turn even "public" places into meaningful liturgical space in some way. Not only do the processions signal this, but it is also telling that portrayals of paradise tend to look like an enlarged Constantinople.[16] Both the regular processions that were part of the normal liturgical calendar (for example, the Hodegetria icon was carried each Tuesday to a different church in Constantinople[17]) and the more extraordinary experience of pilgrimage point to the way in which the "sacred" or "holy" is experienced in the spatial here and now. Baldovin claims that "this out-of-doors aspect of Christian worship in its stational form best exhibits Christianity's relation to late antique and early medieval urban life. It reveals that the city itself was sacred space and that its walls enclosed not only a geographical area but also an idea."[18] In a later text, he says that the "whole city becomes church."[19] Vicky Manolopoulo calls liturgical processions a "mobile form of prayer" and contends that they were "the form of the prayer of the city in the City."[20] While we will have to think more deeply about what this means today, it is clear that in the patristic and Byzantine experience—as indeed in most religions before the Enlightenment—religious experience is not confined to a private place separated from social and public life.[21] There are no clear boundary lines between personal, religious, social, political, economic, environmental, aesthetic, and historical elements of existence, but they are experienced as all interconnected and part of a larger whole. Religion is not a purely private affair to be relegated to the home as a form of personal "spirituality." Rather, although liturgy certainly occurs more intensely and more deliberately within a church or temple, it is not limited to such designated space, but includes and uses "public" space.

That is not to say that there is no distinction between them at all. The Byzantines did recognize the difference between carrying the icon of the Theotokos along the walls of the city in wartime for fear of invasion and venerating it during peacetime at a festival within a chapel. (Indeed, if there were no recognition of the difference, there would have been no perceived need to carry the icon along the walls with intercessions for protection from the enemy.) But these thoroughly public prayers are also liturgy; they do not cease being liturgical if they are offered in a public space. The many services and hymns written in commemoration of earthquakes constitute another striking example of such a public dimension of liturgy.[22] Just as an earthquake destroyed the first dome of Hagia Sophia and thus clearly impacted its "spatial" liturgical reality, so prayers were regularly offered for protection from future quakes and therefore seen as impacting natural physical phenomena. All this suggests that the line between "sacred" and "secular" is permeable and can shift. It is not an invisible or non-existent line—a difference between the Paschal service in church and its celebration later in the streets is clearly recognized—but it is not an absolute line, not a demarcation of total rupture between two incompatible realms or utter discontinuity between them. Thus, although liturgical space certainly is marked and experienced as "different" in some sense, it is not seen as utterly discontinuous with ordinary space or as a complete denial of it. Liturgical scholars often speak of the experience of liturgy in spatial terms as that of crossing a threshold or as a liminal space that is somehow at the "edge" of ordinary experience or pushes it beyond itself.[23] Such liminality frequently takes on cosmic proportions.

This cosmic dimension is especially vivid in the patristic mystagogies, which analyze the eucharistic liturgy and its significance. It is expressed most fully by Maximus the Confessor, although many others (such as Germanos of Constantinople, Symeon of Thessalonike, and Nicholas Cabasilas) reiterate it and seem to take it for granted, even when they stress other aspects more strongly. Maximus claims explicitly that nave and sanctuary—that is to say, the place of the congregation and the altar area respectively—"are" (or "represent" or "parallel"—translations differ in how they render this and thus already interpret Maximus's assertions about their relationship) several other spaces and relations: The nave corresponds to the realms of the created, the visible, the earth, the body, and vital faculties, while the sanctuary corresponds to the realms of the uncreated, the invisible, the heavens, the soul, and the intellectual faculties. We thus proceed from largest to smallest, but in each case the nave corresponds to one and the sanctuary to the other of a pair that can be distinguished but is also essentially related. Obviously not all of these levels refer to actual places (the smallest two are about the human being, yet conceived as a "microcosm," a miniature "world," and hence pictured in spatial terms) and not all of them are physical or geographical (the "invisible" obviously is not, although it is still often thought of as a "realm"), yet spatial language and especially comments about movement, place, or order and about parts and wholes pervade Maximus's account.[24] For him, the task of liturgy is to a large extent that of overcoming distinctions between different realms of reality and of unifying them into a harmonious whole. Language of "taxis" (position or placement) is prominent in his account. These claims about liturgy have significant spatial dimensions: spatiality for him functions on several levels and space is experienced as participating in several realms of multiple layers. Many of the patristic mystagogies assert such connections between cosmos and liturgy.[25] This "cosmic" interpretation of liturgy is now often simply taken for granted by contemporary liturgical scholars.

The relationship between arrangement of space and conceptions about it is reciprocal. Byzantine architecture to some extent tries to encapsulate this theology; it does not simply grow out of observations about liturgical places.[26] Rather, the particular vision of the cosmos had concrete impact on how churches were built physically.[27] The architecture employed for the building of churches reflected these assumptions about the cosmos and to some extent sought to represent the liturgical space as an image or archetype of the larger cosmos and its organization.[28] Whether this cosmos was imagined in an Aristotelian sense as circular spheres surrounding the stable earth at its center or—as became more prominent in later centuries—as modeled on the Jewish temple with the sky hovering as a tabernacle above a flat earth, in both cases the church was patterned on and assumed to represent the topography of the universe. Although nature imagery is not prevalent in Orthodox churches but, in fact, seems to have been explicitly banned early on due to the fear of "paganism," churches were always seen to participate in some way in the larger cosmos.[29] The ecclesial space tries to bring together "heaven" and "earth" visually through the combination of square and round architectural features, the arrangement of the imagery of saints and angels, the use of marble and glimmer of gold and their reflection by light, and other features. The icon program attempts to lead the eye from this physical earth to the invisible heavens, made visible in some measure through the interior architectural aspects and the iconography.[30] Although the cosmos and its elements (earth, heaven, rivers, plants, and so on) are deliberately no longer personified as was the case in much previous art, they are refigured in terms of the locale for liturgy. While they are not venerated, they are spatially significant. The exclusion of nature imagery from Byzantine churches does not mean that liturgy was experienced as a purely spiritual endeavor, quite the opposite.[31]

The liturgical texts, as they are still celebrated today, frequently speak of a joint celebration or even unification of heaven and earth on particular liturgical occasions. The liturgy insists on a real participation of the liturgical actions in these realms of heaven and earth—and of the participation of heaven and earth in the liturgical actions. Liturgical actions (and the theological "events" they celebrate) are at least claimed to have a real effect on the (physical) world.[32] For example, the liturgical texts for the feast of the Annunciation announce such unification on several levels: "Lo, our restoration is now made manifest to us: God is ineffably united to men. At the words of the Archangel error is laid low; for the Virgin receives joy, and the things of the earth have become heaven. The world is loosened from the ancient curse. Let the creation rejoice exceedingly."[33] The divine is united to the human, the heavenly to the earthly, the invisible to the visible. These are "glad tidings of joy" because "things below are joined to things above." Christ is taken to gather "together all the creation."[34] The feast of the Nativity creates harmony, both in the larger creation and, more narrowly, in human social and political arrangements.[35] "Heaven and earth are united today," a unification that concerns both heaven and earth and divine with human; it also always goes in both directions: descending (of Christ into the virgin, "bowing down" the heavens) and ascending (of the human via Christ into heaven, taking up the earth into it).[36] The texts for Ascension speak repeatedly of Christ's body ascending from "earth" to "heaven" and therefore bringing together earthly and heavenly, corporeal and incorporeal realms, simultaneously "renewing" the world. Therefore, "the earth celebrates and dances for joy, and heaven rejoices today on the Ascension of the Maker of creation, who by his volition clearly united that which was separated."[37] The kontakion also explicitly affirms that Christ's ascension "unites things on earth with the heavens."[38]

Even today, liturgical scholars often maintain such claims about the eschatological unification of heaven and earth within the liturgy. Joseph Ratzinger speaks of the altar as "the place where heaven is opened up. It does not close off the church, but opens it up—and leads it into the eternal liturgy."[39] Schmit argues that all this is purely symbolic: "It is not real experience that is presented in worship, but ideas about human experience or symbols of human experience. Thus, worship is a complex of symbols that reflects the breadth of human experience and exhibits a semblance of its range."[40] Limouris, conversely, takes it quite literally, arguing that church "is the experience—here and now in this age, in time and in space—of the kingdom of God, not of this world, the new heaven and the new earth of the new humankind in the new Jerusalem as foretold by the prophets, fulfilled in the Messiah and his Spirit, and beheld in the mystic vision of the apocalypse as the very life of the world to come."[41] Schmemann also consistently stresses this "cosmic" nature of liturgy:

> The liturgy of the Church is cosmic and eschatological because the Church is cosmic and eschatological; but the Church would not have been cosmic and eschatological had she not been given, as the very source and constitution of her life and faith, the *experience* of the new creation, the experience and *vision* of the Kingdom which is to come. And this is precisely the *leitourgia* of the Church's cult, the function which makes it the source and indeed the very *possibility* of theology.[42]

Some liturgical theologians even draw more explicit implications from this "cosmic" dimension of liturgy, such as environmental ones.[43] What do they mean by those claims and how do these connections impact how liturgical space is experienced? Are such claims about the liturgical dimension of the cosmos or the cosmic dimension of the liturgical space purely metaphorical or do they have implications for the physicality of the liturgical space? What is the relation between "metaphorical" space and "physical" place? How is such space experienced?

Phenomenology and Place

Although time is a much more prominent theme in *Being and Time*, Heidegger does briefly describe our experience of space as quite different from the "objectivity" of space assumed by science. We do not first of all measure space in abstract terms, but in terms of the relation of meaningful things in space to our bodies as "near" or "far." Something "far" away in terms of objective measurement can actually be much nearer to us than something that is, scientifically speaking, much closer. Thus, we touch the ground with the soles of our feet as we walk along and yet the friend we see coming toward us several blocks away is much "closer" to us than the street or the asphalt our feet touch.[44] I can bring a certain place "near" in memory or imagination, can even feel myself "there." I can obviously do so only because I have either been there and have had an experience of it that I now recall or have had sufficiently similar experiences that allow me to imagine it. Thus, such "nearness" does not mean some idealist or Gnostic abandonment of physicality, but rather a description of how space and place are actually experienced as we live within them as "spatial" creatures. In precisely these ways, space is meaningfully "near" or "far" in liturgy also: The action in the sanctuary may be experienced as much closer than the ground under my feet or the chair behind me or even the person next to me. Similarly, the processions of last year's Pascha may be much "closer" in experience than the previous Sunday if it has been imaginatively brought near in memory or anticipation. The liturgical space is not experienced as a purely geometrical arrangement of floor, walls, and ceiling; rather, it is experienced as meaningful space where certain aspects of the place weigh more heavily and are experienced more intensely than others.

Heidegger stresses that Dasein is not simply "in" space as an object could be inserted into a container. Although he speaks of "being-in-the-world" as one of the "existentials" of Dasein (one of the fundamental and primordial structures of human lived experience), this "being-in" is not that of an object inside another but more a "being-with" or an inhabiting. It is less a location than a way of "being there" (the literal meaning of *da sein*), a manner of dwelling. Our everyday involvement with the world is one of concern, of handling its objects, of knowing intuitively where they are placed without having to designate this space explicitly in conscious thought. We live within a whole "arrangement" of the world and of space that is meaningful in our ways of engaging it (cf. his famous analysis of the hammer in §15). The "spatiality" of this space emerges only when something is *not* in its place when I need it and I have to search for it (§16). This is when space (or the missing object) emerges into attention more explicitly. But even in that case, this is not at all a scientific or "objective" experience of space: As I tear up my apartment furiously looking for my keys,

I am intimately (and "affectively") involved with its space, but it is the absence of a thing, a missing place, the stuff that is "in the way" that hold my attention and which I experience, rather than the abstract physical dimensions of that space. In many parishes, the procession of the gifts during the Cherubic Hymn is done in silence during liturgies of the pre-sanctified gifts in Lent. This "absence" (in this case of sound but in a fundamentally spatial manner of processing) in many ways speaks more loudly than if words were spoken. Other "absences" and "lacks" that distinguish this liturgy from the regular one similarly catch our attention in ways they would not otherwise.

Even when one crosses a certain space in a very deliberate manner—a runner intimately familiar with the course to be traversed or a hiker mapping out the best route up the slope—it is a complex experience of space that involves the goal to be reached as much as the distance to be traveled: Particular features grab the attention more than others (an uneven surface around the first bend, a steep climb around a tight place between two rocks), and the crossed space clearly "means" quite differently in all these experiences. Space, then, is not a homogenous experience; not all of space is experienced similarly. One might say that space has "bumps" in it that catch us more than other aspects of space. Such spatial "bumps" in liturgy might be the small and great entrances, in which space is traversed deliberately, the royal doors that focus liminal movement in a heightened sense, or the space of the altar that is approached and treated quite differently than the rest of the sanctuary. All these spaces become places of a more intense and more focused experience of space.

Heidegger also notes that the world is "prior" in some sense to our awareness of it and always already serves as the condition for our being (§12). Indeed, space is always already "in" the world. We are not "souls" later inserted into "bodies" or "minds" encountering "space," but our very being is "spatial" and corporeal. Heidegger draws a distinction between *Umwelt*, the world that surrounds us, and *Weltlichkeit*, our manner of being in the world. He also distinguishes between the way in which we experience ourselves in the world and the way we experience things in the world (what he calls "inner-worldly"; we encounter them as within the world). Humans "have" a world in a manner objects—or even animals—do not, partly because this is a meaningful world and partly because it is made meaningful via our activity within and arrangement of it. Heidegger also highlights the importance of orientation: the way we orient ourselves and our activities toward the sun and its light (§22). This is obviously an important point for liturgy, inasmuch as its space is often deliberately oriented and, indeed, is oriented east, as Heidegger suggests here. Light matters for human beings and even more profoundly for human religious experience.[45] He also points to the fashion in which we become "familiar" with the world, especially with particular regions of it—they form a meaningful whole that orients our being within the world.

In a later essay called "Building, Dwelling, Thinking," Heidegger examines the relationship between building and dwelling, which he suggests have the same etymological root, and argues that our existence requires a spatial belonging, a kind of rootedness that is oriented via earth and sky.[46] Building is always already a particular sort of dwelling upon the earth: "We do not dwell because we have built, but we build and have built because we dwell, that is, because we are dwellers."[47] Dwelling, insists Heidegger, is a kind of safeguarding, a place of peace and freedom, where we are sheltered and "belong" within a fourfold matrix of earth and sky, mortals and deities.[48] Our essential task in dwelling on the earth is one of preserving and nurturing, which is also an activity of "gathering" the "fourfold" together.

Lacoste, who is probably the phenomenological thinker to have examined the question of spatiality in religious experience most fully and who employs Heidegger extensively, rejects this analysis of space almost entirely for religious being: "Neither the world, such as *Sein und Zeit* thinks it, nor the play of earth and world, nor the 'infinite relation' of earth and sky, offer to Dasein, and subsequently to mortals, the theoretical conditions which would enable them to come face-to-face to God—to the Lord of Being, to an Absolute who is someone, and who promises a relation with him. This is, with all due respect to him, reason enough to take leave of the philosopher."[49] Lacoste makes the radical claim that our "being-before-God" transgresses the topological and suspends our relation to "world" and "earth" in their Heideggerian connotations. "Liturgy" happens in a "nonplace" (and ultimately is a "non-experience" because it is not experience of being-toward-death in Heidegger's sense). The impetus for this firm rejection of Heidegger's notion of the Fourfold is informed by Lévinas's distinction between the "sacred" and the "holy" and the conviction shared by many that Heidegger's later work advocates for a "pagan" "sacrality of the earth" against a Christian effort of desacralization.[50]

For Lacoste, we do not "dwell" in liturgy, liturgy does not take place "in the world" or "on the earth," and it escapes or sets aside the Heideggerian struggle between world and earth. Liturgy's eschatological dimension comes to unsettle and displace our relation to world and earth in the Heideggerian sense because it is liminal in its very essence, although that does not mean that liturgy is not topological or has no spatiality.[51] For Lacoste, what he calls liturgy always occurs in a liminal or extraordinary space that ruptures and suspends our usual relations with earth and world.[52] Liturgical experience prevents us "from dwelling peaceably on the earth" and insists "on the transitory nature of every dwelling place"; thus, "no immanent logic of place is implied in liturgical experience."[53] Consequently, liturgy treats place with indifference and suspends any attachments to earth or home by "overdetermining" the relation between earth and world. Church is "the place of a fragile anticipation." Liturgical architecture "thwarts" the human desire to dwell.[54] Does liturgical space really have to be thought in radical distinction from the earth and the world, as Lacoste seems to claim? Does expectation of the "parousia" or the "eschaton" simply set aside our "ordinary" experience of space? Is liturgical spatiality a radical undoing of the spatiality of the world? Maybe starting from the "lifeworld" of concretely embodied liturgy (rather than from theological presuppositions as Lacoste often seems to do) will help in unfolding the phenomenological structures of liturgical spatiality as it is experienced.

Intentional Space and Orientation

Entering liturgical space, at least at first glance, is not experienced as total rupture with other forms of spatiality. Although the liturgical space in a church building is experienced as "different" from "ordinary" places and we step across a "threshold" to enter it, it is not experienced as a total rupture with other space. We still find ourselves on a ground, within a building, surrounded by walls, sheltered by a ceiling, and so forth. We can traverse this space, can sit or stand or kneel in it; it is organized in unusual but recognizable fashion with various implements that take up space. It is often filled with people. Yet such space is obviously different from a home or a public space such as a work place, government building, or educational institution. The space of the church can be distinguished as a particular and recognizable place, decorated in particular ways appropriate to its employment, containing familiar items specific to their use within an ecclesial setting (familiar in the sense that they are found in most similar places such as other churches or chapels). At the same time, although the space might be very familiar, it is often traversed differently than other familiar spaces, more closely resembling our traversing of ceremonial spaces or spaces that do not belong to us.

We do not "dwell" in church in the way in which we dwell in a home. In fact, the celebration of Mary's dwelling in the temple as a child, commemorated in the feast of her Entry into the Temple in November, clearly treats her living in the temple as unique and not as something to be imitated by all. At the same time, Heidegger's use of a well-known bridge as an example for dwelling implies that we can dwell also in "public" places. In this sense, the building of churches does imply a form of dwelling. To some extent—to be spelled out further—ecclesial space exists within the tension of familiar and strange, home and alien.[55] We cannot remain there permanently and yet we continually return.

Like liturgical temporality, so liturgical spatiality precedes us. Space is experienced as "there" "before" us (in both temporal and spatial senses) and we "enter" it. Of course, in some sense all space precedes us, not just liturgical space. We are always thrown into a world that exists prior to us. But liturgical space is prior in a special way: Liturgical space is experienced as prepared. This is not, first of all, a world we "create" (or even "open") as Dasein does, but a world that has been created and shaped before us in a very deliberate fashion. It also opens toward us, but not in an exclusionary fashion: It is thus opened to everyone. We find ourselves in a liturgical space not of our own making. Even the architect who builds a new church is not truly designing this space from scratch, but always participates in a much older tradition. The space of liturgy is thus not a world we appropriate or "grasp" in Heidegger's sense, but it is instead part of the "facticity" of the liturgical world; it is the context within which we experience our liturgical life in all its corporeal, sensory, and affective reality. The space provides the ground for our liturgical experience. Liturgy could not be experienced without spatiality. Like temporality, it is part of the horizon of the experience, maybe in some sense its most fundamental horizon, the literal "basis" or foundation of liturgical experience. We stand (or kneel or prostrate) on it when we are in liturgy. Being in liturgy thus always has important spatial dimensions.

Yet it is not only the empty space that precedes us. We always find ourselves there in an occupied space, surrounded by others who were there before us. This prior "gathering" of "others" is the case even if we are the first ones to arrive for a particular service. Ecclesial space is experienced as populated rather than empty, as participating in a tradition that has come before us. In Orthodox churches this is heavily reinforced by the icons and by the practice of greeting them via veneration upon entry into the church: The saints portrayed in the icons are always already there, they precede us, welcome us into this space, and accompany us in worship. Liturgical space is consequently experienced as given, as prior to us in some sense, and as a space of welcome. This does not mean, however, that the liturgical space becomes "home" or that we come to possess it in some fashion. Its open welcome remains that of another. If we welcome others into its space— friends, neighbors, strangers, visitors—we do not do so as its owners or as the hosts but as fellow guests. There are aspects of the space that remain alien, such as the altar area, set apart by the iconostasis, often veiled by a curtain, and not fully visible to the people. Liturgical space cannot be owned or possessed. Some of it remains "mysterious" and hidden.

This presence of others before us also implies that liturgical space is "weighty" space, loaded with memories. These are not just individual memories; they are the collective memories of centuries of arrangement of spaces and the meaningfulness of placement and things. Even someone not used to worshipping in churches will sense the accumulated memory of a place when stepping into a medieval cathedral, even when the space no longer functions as a place of worship (as in Hagia Sophia). The accumulated tradition of building churches, decorating their interiors, arranging their furnishings, placing their items creates a place of memory that precedes us and into which we enter. They are not directly our own memories but we experience them as weighty nonetheless and our more personal memories become interwoven with them and are "located" within the space of communal historical memory. Janet Donohoe in her important work on place and memory argues that our memories are "never truly our own" and always "transferred across generations and written on the world."[56] Yet while the memory generated by a liturgical space shares certain characteristics with the memories of public space, it is also different. The liturgical place is "weighty" not because it is old or because important events once occurred there (although some elements of this are probably at

work in martyria or ancient monasteries), but because the "events" celebrated are in some form "present" anew "now" in line with its temporal
dimension, as analyzed in the previous chapter. While we participate in the
memory of previous generations or in the saints depicted in the icons,
these are not particular memories of specific instances, but rather a participation in the memory of repetition, of the continual making present of
the liturgical events.

Yet space does not just precede us temporally, inasmuch as it was always
already there before we entered it, it also precedes us in other ways by orienting us and confronting us. At least to some extent, the space determines
where and how we stand, what movements are possible to us, how the
space impresses and affects us. There are places we do not go without per-
mission, such as the altar area. Our postures are influenced by the spatial
arrangements: One cannot sit where there are no chairs and one bows
before icons that are positioned in a predetermined space. The fact that
space is organized also means that it is deliberate space. Someone has to do
the organizing, the planning, the arranging. This arrangement is not arbitrary; it does not depend on personal whim but on a whole tradition of
liturgical spatial arrangement. Although all of these customs developed
over time, they now reflect longstanding traditions about arrangement of
the altar area, orientation of the whole building, the iconostasis itself and
the placement of icons on it, and so forth.

The space is also visually organized. The icon program, which in the
Eastern tradition follows an established pattern, organizes our visual field
in a particular way, with icons of Christ in several important places, icons
of John the Baptist and the Theotokos placed prominently next to or on
the royal doors (the main entrance to the sanctuary), icons of the saints
surrounding us, icons of the apostles and of angels in higher regions, the
icon of the Pantocrator in the dome or on the ceiling. The various gradations of holiness imagined (and experienced) as growing increasingly more
intense as one approaches the altar area similarly contribute toward the
sense of direction or orientation. What happens on the altar, even when
covered by a curtain or only obscurely visible, can be "closer" to us than the
ground under our feet or the wall behind us. The icon of the Pantocrator
looming from far above can be nearer, when our gaze rests on it, than that
of an icon hung on the wall next to us. An ordering or harmonizing of space
that goes beyond the building is indicated here. Liturgical space, then, is
intuited as meaningful, but this "meaning" becomes possible because it is

"intentional" space, because it has been prepared by the "intentionality" directed toward it and organized in concrete ways that allow for an intuitive experience to occur.

Furthermore, liturgical space is for movement. It is not static. This is true not only of the activities of censing and blessing by priests or deacons, but movement characterizes the experience of all participants in liturgy. One does not simply stand in the space of liturgy, but one exercises a variety of motions and gestures on and within it. (Again, the question of space is thus linked to that of body—of our bodies and of those of others.) Here what we have just said about movement, memory, and orientation finds a new significance. The "holy" places, in particular, are experienced as sites of memory, overlaid by new buildings and new practices. This memory is not mere mimesis whether as pure recall or as elaborate theater. Rather, the places themselves are thought to be significant. The memories are somehow alive in them. The places are meaningful because they are experienced as loaded, as saturated with memory. It is possible for the visitor to participate in some way in the accumulated and communal memory of the place.

We need to be careful here, however, with the language of "saturation," because it is not the kind of saturation Marion advocates that comes entirely without cause or anticipation and for which one cannot prepare in any form. The level of "saturation" or even "excess" in the experience of place (especially for pilgrimage) requires extensive preparation and at times laborious effort. That does not mean that the experience can be manufactured, that if one prepares "just so," one will have a profound "spiritual" experience. At the same time, no experience will come to us without preparation and without the spatial horizon of the place. The work it takes to perform the liturgical services, the effort and cost involved in erecting and maintaining the buildings, the preparation of spaces and the choirs within them, the dedication required for rising early or staying awake through long services, all these are intentional efforts preparing for intuitive experience, even if they do not manufacture it single-handedly.

This is thus not a disembodied or purely "spiritual" experience of space. To experience the "holiness" of an ecclesial site means one has to be there, has to stand in the place, feel its presence under one's feet. In the case of processions or pilgrimages, it also says something about the relation between explicitly liturgical spaces like churches and less explicitly liturgical spaces such as city roads or mountains. The sacred is believed to be able to "bleed" over into the regular or ordinary space and to transform it in some fashion. The "more" of liturgical space (manufactured by humans and thus in a continuum with other inhabited spaces) implies that a "more" can be possible in other experiences of space. The deliberate ordering or directing of liturgical space, its welcome to those who enter it, somehow implies that other spaces could be so ordered (or maybe differently ordered) and could "mean" by being focused or directed in some way. They might not signify in the same fashion and their orientation may well be quite different, but liturgical spatiality at least points to this possibility.

Hospitality

Liturgical space has to be entered. There is a threshold across which one must step both physically and metaphorically. Baptism functions as a similar "threshold experience" of entry. Several rites are performed in the narthex as preparation for entering the nave proper, such as the catechumenate leading up to baptism or the betrothal ceremony leading up to a wedding. The iconostasis separates and connects the nave from and to the sanctuary, something experienced even by people who never enter the sanctuary. These are liminal spaces where our experiences of space shift from a less intense to a more intense one. There are thus degrees of intensity of liturgical space.[57] Such degrees of "sanctity" have a long history in religion; most cultic spaces feature such degrees of increasing and decreasing holiness in terms of nearness or distance from a particularly holy center.[58] Yet this is not Lacoste's notion of liminality. It is not about a radical break or rupture, but rather about degrees or radiating circles of more or lesser intensity.[59]

In Orthodox liturgy, this increasing sense of holiness is conveyed especially by the iconostasis and the veiling and unveiling of the altar area that occurs through the closing and opening of the royal doors and their curtains. Although this clearly functions as a liminal space, it is not an absolute boundary, but is constantly traversed in various ways. The fact that curtains are opened and closed at particular times within the services, that all doors in the iconostasis are left open for the entire week after Pascha, that the iconostasis is covered in icons representing Christ and the saints, that bread and oil are carried in and out—all these serve to connect nave and sanctuary, not only to separate them. This is made especially vivid through the activity of censing: Although it begins in the sanctuary, it always includes the congregation and the rest of the ecclesial space. Censing and sprinkling with water are not limited to the most holy of places, but often extend to other spaces such as homes.

This activity of censing or blessing space constitutes a further important dimension of liturgical spatiality. At the beginning of liturgy and often at various points throughout a particular service, the priest or deacon cense the sanctuary and the nave, the icons and the people gathered in this place. At the feast of Theophany—and sometimes at other points such as the dedication of a new sanctuary or altar—the space is blessed with holy water (that has itself first been blessed). Such water is also used for the blessing of icons, vestments, or other liturgical objects. The activity is thoroughly spatial; it involves walking around the perimeter of the church, requires people to move out of the way, involves their bodies in bowing and turning, and so forth. The swinging of the censor marks space—and takes up room. In many places, some of the blessings of Theophany even take place outside by flowing water, including a retrieval of the cross from the water after the blessing. Here natural places, such as rivers, are made part of the liturgical space. In these cases, the space of liturgy extends out beyond the church and treats the earth as spatially relevant for liturgy— or, maybe more correctly, liturgy as relevant for it. Liturgy accordingly spills out into the "world"; it does not remain in the church, chapel, or temple. This brings us back to the claim that the space of liturgy is not merely architectural but somehow "cosmic," that liturgy unifies celestial and earthly realms.

Such a claim obviously makes little sense on "objective," scientific, or purely geometrical terms. Heaven has no physical properties; it has no measurable length or width. There is no visible boundary line, which would separate earth from heaven, the visible from the invisible "realms." The claim also cannot be substantiated phenomenologically if "heaven" were understood as a transcendent place (whether "real" or "mythical"), somewhere "beyond" our realm of vision. But the liturgical claim is quite different: It is a claim about the "immanence" of "heaven," about its experience here and now, united to and expressed through the experience of liturgical spatiality. When the Cherubic Hymn at the entry of the eucharistic gifts tells us that we mystically represent the "cherubim," it is not making a geographical claim about our entry into a netherworld but an experiential claim: This is what is experienced as "near" and as "now" as we "lay aside all cares of this life." There is a deliberate redirection of intentionality and orientation to an experienced space that transforms this place into something fuller and more meaningful. Liturgy here does not become a "non-place," but a "more-place" or a place where we experience a space opened to us but not focused on us.

This specific, particular sanctuary now comes to function as the dwelling of heaven here on earth. The notion of "sacred" space only makes sense if it is really this space here and now that becomes sacred and not some "other" place far away to which we have no access. The "sacrality" of the space emerges in the treatment and handling of it, not just its orientation, but who enters it, how, when, and for what purpose. It also matters that this space is not always equally "sacred"—it functions differently on the height of the synaxis during Pascha night than it does when the janitor is vacuuming it on a Friday morning. That is not to deny its "physical" reality but to notice that the meaning of the space emerges in terms of its experience, in terms of the actions that are performed within it and how these actions are perceived. Liturgical space is not a neutral or objective space, but it is "meaningful space"; it is both more and less than ordinary space. It invites us and transforms us, binds us to a community, gives "personal" meaning within the whole. It is space in *this* world; we cannot imagine another world that would not be spatial or corporeal.[60] Liturgy functions not as a suspension of either world or earth, but instead as a particular "arrangement" or "experience" of the world, which is possible because liturgy "opens a world" through orientation and directionality. Liturgy is not a non-place, but presents us with an intentional world. We can choose to enter this world (Lacoste surely is right that it is not forced upon us) and by doing so it also directs us in a particular way. There are gradations of continuity between "world" "outside" and "inside," not absolute rupture. Just as the time of liturgy does not break entirely with broader human temporality, but this human temporality is brought into the liturgical time, so the liturgical space has both continuity with the "world" and orders it in a particular fashion.

What appears or manifests spatially in this aspect of the liturgical experience is an experience of spatiality that is fully "here" and also "more" than here. It is essential to stress that we remain "here" on earth, in this space, and do not magically fly off into some other, purely spiritual, realm. Any experience of "heaven" drawing near in liturgy, is an experience that is fully immanent, fully spatial and corporeal. It does not deny or erase the spatiality of our being in this particular liturgical "world," but in fact instantiates it physically with its architecture and iconography. If the language of "heaven" or even of "cosmic liturgy" means anything, it has to mean, at the very least, a fully "incarnate" heaven and a liturgy that actually takes place in a physical cosmos. At the same time, the liturgical experience of space shows this space as "heavier" with meaning or more "deliberate" or "oriented" in its arrangement. It is a space that situates our experience in new ways, points it beyond itself. It opens up beyond itself without ceasing to be itself. This "more" involves corporeality and affectivity (much of its "weightier meaning" happens through movement, gesture, mood, music, and so on) and thus will necessarily remain a bit preliminary at this stage and have to be "embodied" more fully in the next chapters. But we can at least say that the idea of liturgy "opening" a world to us and inviting us to "enter" into this world is not false. Something is opened up *in* our experience and *as* our experience, not separate from it or somewhere far away. We do not step across a magic threshold (or go through a magic picture or wardrobe) in order to find ourselves in some other world. The world of liturgy is *this* world, *this* space, *this* place, but it is also opens up this place and shows it to be more than purely physical or geometrical. There is a sense in which liturgical experience introduces not another "dimension" somewhere far away, but broadens or widens or intensifies our experience of this space as more than itself. It also gives a focus to it, reveals or manifests it in a particular way.

Liturgical space is opened for us and by us in a particular fashion. Heidegger speaks of Dasein's relation with the world as "Erschlossenheit," which can be translated as "openness" or, more awkwardly, as "disclosedness." Yet openness has a passive connotation, while *Erschlossenheit* is an eminently active noun and is used by Heidegger in an active sense.[61] In *Being and Time*, it designates the grasping of one's existence, the activity of opening up something that has been closed (*geschlossen* means locked or closed) or of opening out something that has been hemmed in. Dasein's "disclosedness" unfolds the world for my authentic living within it, including my use of its tools for everyday comportment. Indeed, Lacoste counters this eminently active sense of Heidegger's Dasein by arguing that liturgy renders us passive, that being-before-God is characterized by an essential passivity. Yet while liturgy certainly does not allow for the same grasping attitude as Dasein displays it in its *Erschlossenheit* and rather calls us to "lay aside all cares of this life," this does not render the person in liturgy passive.[62] Entering into the liturgical world requires initiative and some sort of appropriation, albeit not in a "grasping" sense. It is more a deliberate participation than an appropriating as one's possession. Liturgy presents a world that invites us into it, rather than a world we must forcefully disclose. But we must enter it and participate in it; the world does not just overwhelm us or come over us without our willing participation. Contra Lacoste, liturgy opens us out and invites us to practice such opening in order to participate in it; it does not simply impose passivity upon us. We experience liturgy in its spatial dimensions as disclosing a deliberate and intentional world for us or maybe as opening our world differently and hence allowing for a different kind of dwelling, but not as a denial or undoing of world and earth.

The space of liturgy is then essentially a space of hospitality, in the sense that it is prepared and oriented by others and by the accumulated memory of its practices and previous participants, welcoming us to engage in its actions and enter its world. It does not ask us to leave the world behind but to bring our experience of the world with us and have it be opened out beyond its narrow confines, to be confronted with a wider and deeper dimension. The liturgical space and the world into which it invites us is a world with depth and breadth, a space for feasting and celebration where we are welcomed and fed. At other times it is a space that invites us to confrontation, contrition, confession, but it does not force them upon us. Even in the Lenten services, we are still *invited* (rather than forced) to confession and the liturgical space serves as a hospitable space for contrition regarding our failures and shortcomings. Liturgy does not deny our earthly finitude but provides a welcome to it; it deepens and widens our human experience such that it is defined not solely by finitude or frailty but able to open beyond its narrow focus on ourselves. We will see this tension between celebration and contrition over and over again, but it is crucial that both are welcome, both are acknowledged—liturgical hospitality always includes both. It allows us to be who we are—fragile, finite, spatial, corporeal creatures—and renders our existence meaningful without denying or erasing its finitude and fragility. (Much more will have to be said about this in subsequent chapters.)

It is then *this* space that becomes "heaven" for us, that is read as being part of the community of the "saints" or even the "angels"—who are imaged on the walls of this specific place.[63] Liturgical spatiality manifests as a more intense, fuller space, a place where our experience of space is "thickened." In this respect, it is interesting that the Kievan ambassadors in their famous description of the liturgy at Hagia Sophia did not claim to have "ascended" to heaven, but said that they "did not know" whether they were "on heaven or on earth." Their experience—or at least the description of that experience as it has gone down in history—confused (in a positive sense) the boundary lines between the two. One merged into the other. Earth is experienced as "heaven" in some fashion. And they affirm that "truly there God dwells among men"; thus, this richer or fuller or more "beautiful" experience of space—conveyed by and through its affectivity— is interpreted as God's presence in the real physical space where they found themselves rather than a removal to some other place. Liturgy undeniably happens in space and cannot do otherwise. There is no way to dispense with the "earthly" spatial dimension in order to "ascend" into heaven. Our bodies never leave this place, where our feet are rooted. Indeed, if liturgy welcomes "us," this "us" concerns bodies. Liturgy is always fully and intensely corporeal, which at the same times means spatial, because bodies are experienced within space and to some extent even as space.[64] Instead of dispensing with space or denying its earthiness and worldliness, liturgical spatiality instead orients it. The spatiality of liturgy allows us to experience it as directed and of ourselves as welcomed into its space. It has been difficult already to try to speak of the way in which liturgical spatial-ity affects us or how we "enter" into it without speaking at the same time of corporeality. The two are intimately connected. We will therefore now turn to this question of the body.

3

CORPOREALITY

Jean-Marie Gueullette describes an experience at the Lavra Petcherska in Kiev in the early 1990s:

> The faithful present in the liturgy were made up of two rather different groups: old ladies and young people. It was very moving to note how the old ladies, lost in their devotion, made the gestures in use in orthodoxy—metanoias, signs of the cross—without paying any attention to what was going on around them. Yet each of them was in fact followed by a line of young people who modeled their behavior on that of the ancestress. The young people discovered the practice of liturgy, made only just accessible through the fall of the Soviet Union. No one gave them any instruction, but the old ladies taught them without knowing, by the gestures they had always practiced despite the persecutions. Their gestures were those of the tradition, but they were also their own, they lived them with their entire bodies, while the gestures of the young seemed still maladroit, not very natural, because they tried to imitate them with sixty years of difference. I was overwhelmed by this scene of the silent transmission of a tradition via corporeal attitudes.[1]

While Gueullette is particularly interested in the way gestures express the beauty of liturgical spirituality, this account of the young people imitating the older women vividly illustrates the corporeal nature of liturgy.

Liturgy is inscribed upon and instantiated by bodies—by the way in which we stand, bow, kneel, prostrate, or move within the liturgical space.

Indeed, Orthodox liturgy is impossible without bodies. It is first of all a bodily exercise and includes many corporeal movements (some exercised only by priests and others serving in the altar, some by everyone): the putting on and shedding of various vestments through the service, the carrying of liturgical books including the Gospel, the swinging of the censor and the work involved in lighting it and keeping it lit, various processions or circumambulations both within the sanctuary and within the space of the nave, the lighting of candles, the venerating of icons, and so forth. Many liturgical movements are slow and deliberate, exercised with attention and intention. Liturgy is operated by bodies in movement, often in a sort of dance of call and response, where the congregation responds bodily to the corporeal movements of the clergy. During the processions, which were an important part of Orthodox liturgy for centuries and are still practiced in a more truncated form, the bodily movement is extended spatially beyond the church. Walking becomes worship. Each time anew, the body must enter into the liturgical space, cross the threshold between narthex and nave, approach the sanctuary for the reception of communion.

Not only do bodies appear in liturgy or "embody" the liturgy, but liturgy also expresses an explicit concern with bodies, especially in cases of illness or danger. This is visible in the oft-recited litanies included in almost any service: "For seasonable weather, for abundance of the fruits of the earth, and for peaceful times, let us pray to the Lord. / For travelers by land, by sea, and by air; for the sick and the suffering; for captives and their salvation, let us pray to the Lord. / For our deliverance from all affliction, wrath, danger, and necessity, let us pray to the Lord." Or "Remember, O Lord, the city in which we dwell, every city and country; those who in faith dwell in them. Remember, O Lord, travelers by land, by sea, and by air; the sick and the suffering; captives, and their salvation. Remember, O Lord, those who bring offerings and do good in Thy holy churches; those who remember the poor; and upon us all send forth Thy mercies." There are also extensive prayers for various occasions involving our corporeal wellbeing, which are prayed whenever there is need of them (cf. the liturgical "Book of Needs"). Often the prayers are for compassion and healing: "And as Thou didst not cast out the prostitute, the sinful woman who came to touch Thee, so have compassion on me a sinner who comes to touch Thee."[2] The liturgical prayers clearly display a concern with our corporeal frailty and finitude, including the dangers to which our bodies are exposed. (Presumably, people were far more vividly aware of such dangers in previous centuries, before we started hiding suffering bodies in hospitals or nursing homes.) And it is worth stressing that we are not praying only for our own protection or healing, but always also for that of others. Bodies play an extensive and multifaceted role in liturgical texts and actions.

The Body in Liturgical Theology

Liturgical theology has not ignored this important dimension of liturgical experience.[3] Nathan Mitchell reminds us that the body is "our primary mode of connecting with self, world, others, and God" and thus crucial for liturgical experience.[4] He focuses especially on the corporeal dimension of the Eucharist, which he interprets in terms of justice, saying repeatedly: "Bread is always about bodies, and bodies are always about justice."[5] Margaret Scott also stresses the connection between Eucharist and embodiment: "The Eucharist is the 'sacrament of body.' We participate in the eucharistic celebration as *embodied* people."[6] The connection between sacraments and corporeality is made frequently and may be the most obvious and most common instance of theological reflection on the role of the body in liturgy.

Probably the most extensive discussion of the body in relation to the sacraments is that of Louis-Marie Chauvet. The body is the primary field of expression and the fundamental setting for the sacraments. From this we learn that "the truest things in our faith occur in no other way than through the concreteness of the 'body.'"[7] Chauvet argues that the personal body is the site of convergence of social, traditional, and cosmic bodies, which all participate in the materiality of the sacrament. Consequently, "the sacramentality of the faith requires a consent to corporeality, a consent so complete that it tries to *think about God according to corporeality*."[8] He works this out later in the book under the assumption that "the body is the stage that gives liturgy its 'place.'"[9] The body functions for him as a kind of language where liturgy becomes word.[10]

Yet the consideration of the body's role in liturgy is not limited to reflections on the Eucharist. Pfattreicher points out concrete ways in which liturgical participation is inscribed on the body: "The liturgy requires the participation of the body in worship: standing, sitting, kneeling; seeing color and movement; smelling the aromas of incense and candle wax and wine; hearing words and songs and melodies; touching and tasting consecrated bread and wine." He also sees ethical implications of this: "Such participation of the body in worship must inevitably lead to concern for the plight of the needy who suffer physically and mentally as well as spiritually."[11] Anderson stresses that such bodily actions are necessary for formation: "Throughout this discussion I have been attempting to explore how faith 'gets into our bodies,' even how the liturgy 'performs' us. When we deny or ignore the ritual character of Christian worship, we make it difficult to attend to the ways in which what do in worship acts upon us."[12] Liturgy can have an impact on our lives because we are bodily creatures who then "embody" the liturgy in our actions. Indeed, Mitchell argues that "the most obvious aspect of ritual is *action*, and the most obvious aspect of action is *the body's movement through space and time*. Liturgy is embodied action. We belong to the liturgy by belonging to our bodies (in this world and the next)." He concludes: "The body is thus an inescapable 'site' of liturgical celebration, more primary and more essential than churches, sanctuaries, books, and furniture. 'Body' is the liturgy's native language, its first speech."[13]

This idea that corporeal movements can function as speech is not uncommon. Hughes concretely speaks of the *gestures* of liturgy as a kind of language: "The reality, then, is one thing, by no means to be discounted, but the *gesture* is another, also deserving attention: the liturgical forms do seek, do purport, to bring people before the Face of God, and to give them language wherewith to express their adoration, their regrets, their utmost hopes and deepest fears." Such gestures are significant in their impact: "Just occasionally for whole congregations, more regularly for particular members thereof, hearts and minds actually follow the gesture: there is an unrestrained turn towards the unbounded otherness which Christians and religious people generally name as God." He calls this the "vocative dimension" of worship.[14] Rashkover sees *postures* functioning in such a linguistic way: "Liturgical postures will be discovered both within and supplementary to scriptural texts as the lived practices that perform and interpret the Word in time."[15] Saliers states quite strongly: "In some respects our bodily movements, gestures, and dispositions may be the most deeply theological aspects of communal worship. For the human body is itself a primary symbol of God's glory . . . The bodily signs carry theological convictions at a deeper cultural level than do rationally expressed 'beliefs.'"[16] Corporeal positions, movements, actions, and gestures somehow communicate the meaning of worship.

What does it mean for the body—in its actions, postures, or gestures—to function as a kind of language? How is liturgy "embodied" and why do bodies matter in liturgy? How might a phenomenological discussion of the body illuminate or push further these theological claims?

Body and Flesh in Phenomenology

The question of the body is one of the most important and most difficult questions in phenomenology. Already Husserl distinguished between body as body in space (*Körper*) and body as lived or as "my" body (*Leib*). While I experience all other bodies as separate from me, as things I can touch and feel, I experience my own body not only as something that can touch, but also as something that *can be* touched, including by itself (the "touched touching"): I feel myself feeling. I experience all other people (and everything in the world) as *Körper*; I have no access to their *Leib*, no idea what it "feels" like to them to touch or be touched, except maybe through analogy with my own experience.[17] The two terms were translated into French at first as *corps* (for *Körper*) and *corps propre, corps organique,* or *corps vécu* (for *Leib*), but later *Leib* became translated as *chair* (flesh), which has become the standard translation in French.[18] English has a similar difficulty of rendering the German *Leib* for which there is no French or English equivalent.[19] Husserl scholars tend to translate *Leib* as "lived body" while those influenced by French phenomenology usually speak of "flesh." What complicates matters even further is the notion of the incarnation, which is formed from the Latin word *carne* for flesh (*sarx* in Greek) and for which German uses *Fleischwerdung, Verleiblichung* (occasionally even *Menschwerdung*) or *Inkarnation*, while both French and English generally say "incarnation," whether speaking of Christ's incarnation or of our own embodiment or "enfleshment" in a more phenomenological sense (for example, in the way in which it is used by Merleau-Ponty who is clearly aware of the use of the term in theology but appropriates it for a non-theological use to describe the interlacing of our flesh with that of the world).[20]

Heidegger, Merleau-Ponty, and Henry appropriate Husserl's insights to some extent and also criticize or modify them. In *Being and Time*, Heidegger specifically sets the question of the body aside and speaks only of temporality, although his analysis of the *Stimmungen* (moods) and *Befindlichkeit* (disposition or affectivity) of Dasein are certainly not irrelevant to a discussion of the "flesh" as it appears in the French thinkers and raises questions of affectivity.[21] Yet in the *Zollikon Seminars* he returns more explicitly to the question of corporeality and mentions both the famous discussion about the touched touching and the earlier Aristotelian question of the relation between vision and touch, questioning the model of seeing as the paradigm for understanding all the other senses, especially the sense of touch. He stresses that corporeality (*Leiblichkeit*) is always spatial and also always personal, always mine. This body is not an object in space (with volume or weight), but my way of inhabiting space (*leiben*). Heidegger also provides a brief and illuminating analysis of the gesture (*Gebärde*) as something other than "expression" (*Ausdruck*). Rather, it refers to "comportment," to my way of being "ecstatically" toward and together with others (*mitmenschliche Bezogenheit*). Language is not mere linguistic expression, but is corporeal and physical in hearing and speaking (for example, we talk about being "all ear"). Is the gesture a corporeal or "fleshly" manifestation of our being? How is it related to our *Mitsein*, our being-with-others? Heidegger raises but does not answer these questions here.[22]

Merleau-Ponty explicitly thinks body and world together. We are enfleshed not just through and in our bodies, but also in our intimate involvement with the world, which itself has flesh. While for most other thinkers only humans can have flesh (usually they do not even grant flesh in this sense to animals), Merleau-Ponty also speaks of a flesh of the world and sees it as closely connected to nature. The *Phenomenology of Perception* does not employ the language of flesh as fully as his later work does, but speaks in similar ways of the body (Section I). Merleau-Ponty shows how body cannot be understood in the traditional Cartesian or more recent scientific terms as extended thing or as something we "have." Rather, "the body is our general means of having a world" and therefore "I am not before my body, I am in my body, or rather I am my body."[23] In this text, Merleau-Ponty reads sensory experience entirely in terms of our corporeality. He focuses primarily on the ways in which our senses can go wrong or mislead us, especially in cases of illness, where there is a "disconnect" between world and unifying experience of the body. Yet, he also shows that I experience myself in some sense "in" the things or interlinked with them. This is qualified by the experience of time: I can "project" myself into a

thing in the world in anticipation or memory without having it percep-
tively present to me. Full sensory synthesis only occurs through the temporal experience. In *The Visible and the Invisible* (on which he was working
before his untimely death and which was published posthumously),
Merleau-Ponty adopts the language of flesh much more fully in order to
depict this interlacing with the world.

In contrast, Henry radically separates body and flesh. While the body is
what manifests in the world (and hence separates the phenomenon from
its phenomenality), the flesh is our interior and invisible life as it self-
manifests in the auto-affection of pathos as joy and suffering. It is the seat
of our affectivity and emotions, of joy and of suffering. It both generates
and experiences them; it is self-affective. Auto-affection—the interior
experience of pathos—is life itself. For Henry, the body is something external, an object in the world. We live our flesh, not our bodies. Incarnation
means to be generated into and as flesh not to become embodied in the
world. We are not related *to* our flesh, but we "are" our flesh, live *as* flesh;
it is utterly immanent and in that sense absolute.[24] Marion adopts this
notion of the flesh in his phenomenology of givenness as the third kind of
saturated phenomenon, which is saturated in regard to relation. That is to
say, the flesh is so utterly intimate and immediate that it undoes any category of relation to something external or separate and is "absolute" in
that sense.[25] He does return to an exploration of the flesh in *The Erotic
Phenomenon*, where he envisions the possibility of a "crossing" of two
"flesh," where I might give the other his or her flesh by exposing myself to
its impact on me.[26] He continues to maintain that I have no access to the
flesh of the other, but I can help the other experience his or her flesh.
Ultimately, the insufficiency of this experience and access has to be replaced
by a more verbal affirmation (the oath) and the coming of the third (the
child or God).[27]

Falque argues that this distinction between body and flesh is too strong
and that there can be no flesh without body.[28] In his work as a whole he
not only tries to overcome the dichotomy between body and flesh he sees
operative in problematic ways in the other thinkers, but also seeks to
retrieve a sense of an "organic" body that would take more seriously its
"chaos" of impulses and drives (he calls this our "animality"). He speaks
of the body as laid out or stretched/spread out (even "splayed out," as on
a bed) in illness, suffering, or crucifixion (*corps épandu*), in contrast with
the Cartesian sense of the body as extended thing (*corps étendu*) or the

Husserlian notion of the lived body (*corps vécu*). This body, as we observe it in sleep or on a hospital bed, bears the markers of its flesh and its organicity; it is not merely an object.[29]

At first glance, then, it seems that the phenomenological tradition does not agree on how to think body and/or flesh. To highlight just the starkest disagreements: For Henry and Marion the flesh is entirely interior, immanent, and invisible and has little interaction or connection with the world (or even the body), while for Husserl, Merleau-Ponty and Falque, flesh and body are not only fully interlaced with each other but also with the world and nature, which (at least for Merleau-Ponty) can in some way be said to have flesh and be affected in a mutual relation between my flesh and the flesh of the world. For Heidegger, corporeality seems distinguished both from temporality and from affectivity but linked with spatiality (although he does not work out these claims fully), while for Husserl and Merleau-Ponty they are all closely connected. For some (Henry and Marion), flesh is only about affect or emotion; for others (Merleau-Ponty and Falque) it is much more fully "corporeal." For some, we have no access to the flesh of the other at all (Husserl and Marion); it is a purely personal and completely intimate experience. For others, we can access the flesh of the other in caress, erotic encounter, or even in speech (Lévinas) or are even one with it in some fashion (Henry).

Yet what all phenomenological accounts, despite their diversity and even disagreement, share in common is, on the one hand, a rethinking of corporeality beyond Cartesian or scientific parameters as an object in space and, on the other hand, a recovery of our lived experience of the body.[30] This is much closer both to how the liturgical texts actually treat the body and to how corporeality functions in liturgy. Maybe the single most important obstacle in the recent theological controversies over the supposed dualism between soul and body in the tradition and the desire to retrieve "the body" (and with it affectivity, sexuality, and other bodily dimensions) as valuable, has been the assumption of Cartesian divisions between soul and body, the equation of body with extended object, and the dualistic, hierarchical thinking that results from both.[31] Employing a more phenomenological approach to speak of the body in liturgy—and maybe ultimately in theology more generally—seems far more productive in that respect.

The concrete disagreements about body and flesh do not necessarily imply that the phenomenological insights are not useful for the discussion of liturgy, but it does mean that we need to proceed carefully and develop any notion of liturgical corporeality in conversation with them, rather than simply adopting one model wholesale. For example, for now leaving aside Henry, who focuses primarily on affectivity rather than corporeality, we can say that, phenomenologically speaking, body is the way in which we experience space via movement, posture, and gesture. Space is meaningful inasmuch as it is inhabited or lived corporeally. Liturgical spatiality is similarly experienced via corporeality, but it structures that corporeality and its affectivity in a particular manner.

It is thus also important to stress again that the question of the body and that of the flesh are closely connected to that of spatiality (the body is always found in space or lives space in a particular way) and also to that of affectivity, emotion, and the senses (which are experienced by and manifested in and through the flesh). The world and spatiality are experienced through the body and the body opens the world to us in some fashion. Senses, emotions, even drives and impulses, are experienced in the body as flesh, although maybe not all of affectivity is reducible to flesh entirely. In either case, the discussions of spatiality, corporeality, and affectivity are connected and cannot be thought entirely separately from each other. The division of these topics into several chapters is thus somewhat artificial, but each also merits its own particular attention. For the purposes of the discussion of liturgy, this chapter will treat the clearly bodily aspects of movement and posture, while the next two chapters will consider the more "affective" aspects of sensory and emotive experience, respectively. This roughly corresponds to the distinction between "body" and "flesh" in the phenomenological literature (although, as we have just seen, not entirely). The distinction will here be employed provisionally, always keeping in mind their necessary connection and relationship.

Movement, Posture, Gesture

Liturgy cannot be experienced without bodies. Liturgy happens in a space that is entered corporeally and is manifested in sensory ways that are apprehended by and through the body. Liturgy is not only absorbed through the senses of the body—seeing, hearing, tasting, smelling, touching—but it is also expressed via the body in entering the space, positing oneself within it, participating in movements, responding via gestures, taking on specific postures, and so forth. Regular activities, such as lighting candles, singing the music, reciting the creed, or receiving the Eucharist, and less frequent ones, such as waving palms, processing around the church, or prostrating before the tomb, are all corporeal actions that not only require a body for their exercise, but indeed are meaningful only through their corporeality. Most of the time, we do not even notice this, as our movements, actions, gestures, and postures have become automatic.

Indeed, often bodily liturgical actions become habitual; many people cross themselves almost reflexively at certain points in the service or certain mentions of the Trinity or the Theotokos. It is important not to ignore or dismiss these "habitual" gestures. Liturgy is incorporated through such bodily movement, through the tracing of the cross on the body, through the inclining of the head, through bending, bowing, and kneeling. Our bodies are not objects in the liturgical space, but they are the way in which we experience liturgy and participate in it. The movements of liturgical prayer are inscribed on the body through such motions and posture. And these movements, postures, and gestures are oriented or directed; they are not senseless or purposeless.[32] We move toward the sanctuary, orient our bodies in its direction. Not only is the spatial arrangement directed or oriented, as we have seen in the previous chapter, so is that of our bodies in tandem with it. Our bodies themselves become spatial in some sense, inasmuch as the liturgical movements are imprinted and traced upon them corporeally. On the most basic level we can say, then, that the body is a vehicle or means for the experience of liturgy, not in a utilitarian sense, but as its mode of reception, as the place of its experience, as the mode of living this experience. And this experience is lived in our physical, material bodies, requiring bones and sinews for movement and gesture, not just in a spiritualized body or a disembodied mind. There is no liturgical experience apart from our real, physical, corporeal participation in it.

This is visible also in the fact that liturgical corporeality requires effort: We grow tired from standing, sore from kneeling or prostrating, bored from familiarity or inattentiveness. Liturgy is fully embodied with all the corporeal aspects like fatigue and boredom that this necessarily involves. It does not erase the normal functioning of our bodies; it does not alter our experience of their weight or their density, even if there might be moments of elation that "take us out of ourselves" in some fashion. Indeed, often the body in liturgy is experienced as distraction: To keep the body alert and focused requires attention and a repeated recalling it to itself. There is a sense, then, in which liturgy "trains" our bodies to move within it; one becomes accustomed to its length and its demands on our corporeality. Standing for a two hour-vigil or liturgy (in the past often much longer) takes real physical effort, and yet the body also habituates itself to it and becomes used to its rhythm.

And of course our bodies are never alone in liturgy; we are surrounded by other bodies who trace the same movements. The bodies of others can be experienced as both support and obstacle in the liturgical life. The presence of others can help or sustain our own bodily practice, as in the observation Gueullette depicts in the Kiev monastery with which the chapter opened. We learn from each other and in some way enter into liturgical movement and gesture together. While some gestures may well be personal expressions, they find their meaning only within the larger corporeal meaningfulness of liturgical gesture per se. If bodily gesture did not "mean" in liturgy, it could not be appropriated or expressed personally. And many liturgical actions and movements are simply impossible without a plurality of bodies. How would one practice the rite of forgiveness that begins Great Lent if we were not present together, asking for each other's forgiveness? And how would the service mean or signify differently—infinitely less—if we did not bow to each other and did not embrace? Forgiveness—both its request and its gift—is expressed in utterly corporeal fashion in this liturgical rite. Although words are said, it is the corporeal expression of forgiveness in bodily gestures and movement—including the way in which space becomes traversed in a giant circle around the nave in many parishes—that instantiates this liturgical rite and constitutes its phenomenological experience.

Similarly, the experience and even mood of a festal service is quite different when there are many people present celebrating together. The processions still held during high festal services, where bodies traverse the space around the church, holding candles and often singing or chanting, add a further corporeal and communal dimension to the feast. Walking with each other, waiting for each other, seeing one another's faces illuminated by the candle light are important parts of the festal experience, especially during Holy Week. And the number of embodied voices in the choir certainly matters to the liturgical experience. Yet the bodies of others can also be experienced as obstacle or distraction. Being pressed into a tight space with other bodies can make us physically uncomfortable. We rub shoulders with others with whom we might not usually associate.[33] An experience of the body in liturgy is always already an experience of others, even a communal or corporate experience. (We will return to this plural experience of liturgy more explicitly in a later chapter.)

Liturgy clearly is not primarily a mental exercise. Although it does not ignore or bypass the mind, it appeals to it through the senses (color and sound, rhythm and harmony, scent and taste). Its worship is intensely corporeal, including obviously how it is received in its sensory impact, to which we will turn more fully in the next chapter. Yet it should be noted here already that this receiving by the senses, just as the bodily experience, is not passive; it always involves movement and participation. Such participation occurs primarily through gestures: We kiss the icons, we bow when we are censed or when exhorted to prayer, we cross ourselves and fold our hands across our chest to receive communion, we bend low, we prostrate on the ground. The seeing, hearing, smelling, tasting, touching of liturgy is received bodily, not just in the sensory experience itself, but in the corporeal response to it. Corporeality, sensoriality, and affectivity move in tandem. Liturgy is an "incarnational" experience inasmuch as it is fully embodied and its experience received through and appropriated by the body.

The liturgical experience, then, employs the body as the site of worship, as the "where" and "how" of liturgical experience. The liturgical movements and gestures constitute our corporeal worship, the work of our bodily liturgy. If we are in some way "transformed" by the liturgical experience, this is always experienced as a transformation of bodies, of the human being as a whole. Liturgy does speak of redemption, but such "redemption" does not move us from corporeality to incorporeality or leave the body behind in favor of the soul. It is not a denial of the body, but happens within and as the body. There is never a moment in the liturgical experience, even at the heights of elation, when we can dispense with the body. Whatever happens to us in liturgy, or however we live liturgy, happens *within* and is lived *via* our corporeality and affectivity. Can we go beyond this "fact" of liturgical corporeality as the mode of liturgical experience and say something about its content or meaning? How do the movements and gestures of liturgy signify?

Veneration, Humbling, and Healing

We have already pointed to the orientation of movement toward the altar, to the postures of bowing, bending, or prostrating, to the gestures of crossing, kissing, and receiving. In the discussion of temporality, we saw that liturgy operates in a tension of two modes: fasting and feasting, repentance and celebration. The consideration of spatiality showed how this dual tension is ordered and directed via the liturgical space and our movement within it. The corporeality of liturgy gives further content to this and in some sense brings the two "sides" of this dual movement of liturgy together: The liturgical postures are primarily postures that express what one might call veneration and a kind of humbling, often both at the same time and related to each other, inasmuch as our veneration of what is perceived as holy and beyond ourselves induces and shapes the call for humility.[34] By bowing, kneeling, or prostrating, we express our awe or veneration and at the same time humble ourselves, lower ourselves, even "expose" our bodies in some way.[35] We take on postures we would not usually assume, postures that render our body vulnerable and exposed in a manner that implies that we offer it in some way to another and are not in complete or autonomous possession of ourselves.

The humbling posture of the body or bodily exposure of the self designates its openness and vulnerability. It is not a denial of the body, maybe not even a transformation of the body per se, but rather a transformation of its posture of self-sufficiency and self-absorption into one of humility and vulnerability. And these are obviously as much attitudes of the mind as of the body, so in some sense one might speak more appropriately not of a transformation of the body alone, but of a transformation also of the mind or soul or heart through the postures of the body. Liturgy seeks to transform who we are as a whole by training the body—and through it the mind, emotions, and affects—to be attentive to something other or beyond itself, to be "stretched out" before "God," to be "bent into" a shape that allows it to be receptive to the call addressed to it in liturgy.[36] The postures of veneration—bending, kissing, prostrating—are postures in which the body experiences itself directed and oriented toward another corporeally. The liturgical experience frames this orientation and endows it with meaning. The vulnerability of our bodies is in some measure exposed, its capacity for being wounded or violated is acknowledged in this exposure, and fear of such hurtful touch, which causes us to protect our bodies in our daily interactions in the world and to expose them in this manner only rarely, is linked with, maybe even taken up into awe or veneration.

The liturgies make clear that such humble exposure is partly due to the desire for healing. One exposes one's body in liturgy in some way as one exposes oneself to the touch of the physician. The liturgical texts and actions pray repeatedly, almost obsessively, for the healing of body and soul. Often this is linked to the Eucharist. Especially the prayers associated with communion, before, within, and after the eucharistic service itself, speak of it consistently in terms of such healing. The prayers to be read before communion reiterate this in almost every prayer. To cite just two representative examples: "Be pleased to allow me to receive Thy most pure Body and Thy most precious Blood for the healing of my soul and body, and the purification of my evil thoughts," and "Therefore, I pray Thee, O Master, for Thou alone art holy, sanctify my soul and body, my mind and heart, my muscles and bones. Renew me entirely, implant Thy fear in my fleshly members and let Thy sanctification never be removed from me." Here "muscles and bones" are to be sanctified, the "fleshly members" are directed toward God, soul and body are both healed. Similarly, the final line of the communion prayer during the liturgy prays that these mysteries may operate "the healing of soul and body." This is just as true of the prayers read after communion in which Christ (as "Creator" of the body) is asked to enter into the members and veins of the body, to give solidity to knees, to illuminate the senses, to purify and to adorn.

This language of healing is very prevalent in the liturgical texts and sin is often spoken of in terms of illness, especially in practices of penitence. The Lenten services are suffused with prayers for healing of soul and body. For example, two of the stichera during Forgiveness Vespers say: "Heal the wounds of my heart, inflicted on me through my many sins, O Saviour and Physician of our souls and bodies for Thou does always grant forgiveness of transgressions unto those that ask. Give me tears of repentance and remission of my debts, O Lord, and have mercy on me. Finding me naked, stripped of virtues, the enemy wounded me with the arrow of sin; but, O God, Physician of our souls and bodies, heal the wounds of my soul and have mercy on me."[37] The reference to the parable of the Good Samaritan, who cares for the wounded man by the roadside, is very frequent during Lent.[38] The Great Canon also goes back to it: "I am the man who fell among thieves, even my own thoughts; they have covered all my body with wounds, and I lie beaten and bruised. But come to me, O Christ my Saviour, and heal me."[39] God is consistently identified as the "Samaritan" who heals me as the one attacked by the robbers.

Indeed, the entire canon is full of descriptions of illness and prayer for healing. For example: "I have defiled my body, I have stained my spirit, and I am all covered with wounds: but as physician, O Christ, heal both body and spirit for me through repentance. Wash, purify and cleanse me, O my Saviour, and make me whiter than snow."[40] In these liturgical texts, illness and sin are often identified with each other, although sometimes the situation is painted in terms of deliberate transgression (and hence sin is identified as an illness of soul incurred by one's own fault) and sometimes described as the result of being made sick through the attacks of the evil one (hence illness is incurred as contagion and not as deliberate transgression). The lines between these two are fluid and they are often held together. For example in the following statement from the Great Canon, injury is both attributed to the "enemy" and to one's own deliberate choice: "I am wounded and smitten: see the enemy's arrows which have pierced my soul and body. See the wounds, the open sores and the injuries, I cry to Thee; see the blows inflicted by my freely-chosen passions."[41]

One should note, however, that although liturgy frequently establishes a link between sin and illness inasmuch as it treats sin as a kind of illness, it refuses the identification of illness as *punishment* for sin. The direct association of bodily disfigurement or illness with sin is consistently rejected, especially that of sin as a *cause* for personal illness (although larger natural disasters are often attributed to communal sin, especially social injustice).[42] Yet the reverse connection is made very frequently: Sin is a kind of illness and our sinful souls are disfigured as if they were sick with leprosy. For example, one of the prayers read in preparation for communion says: "And as Thou didst not disdain to enter and to eat with sinners in the house of Simon the leper, so now be pleased to enter into the house of my soul, humble and leprous and sinful." There are many more examples of this sort and the language is pervasive during the Lenten liturgies. While illness of body is never read as punishment for sin, illness of soul (that is, the vices) often are the direct consequences of sinful choices. At the same time, the complexity of finitude that can hurt or maim even without deliberate choice is acknowledged, as is the fact that failure is complex and not always caused directly by single-minded intention. This is clearly not an erasure or denial of our finitude or the fragility of our bodies. Even in the association between sin and illness, finitude or fragility as such are not equated with failure, but there is a kind of acknowledgment that failure can be inscribed on or manifested in the body and that it is a possible dimension of our finitude. Liturgy here enables an admission of our finitude in an environment that invites such vulnerable exposure and acknowledges its danger and need for protection and healing.

This may be partly why the rites of baptism involve such a radical stripping, an exposure of nakedness, an anointing of it (clearly indicating that such nakedness is not rejected or censured), and the "putting on" of new "garments." The body is not erased in the symbolic death of baptism, but cleansed and renewed, more truly itself. We do not baptize souls: We baptize bodies, sometimes very small screaming and slippery bodies who are fully there in all their incarnate reality, recently emerged from the womb, with all the messy physical processes that implies. Indeed, the patristic and liturgical texts often speak of the baptismal font as another womb (as they also do of the tomb). We are reborn in baptism, just as vulnerable in our exposure there as we were on the day of our physical birth. The rites of baptism leave the candidates for baptism with very little to do; almost everything is done to or for them. Even the verbal responses are replies to questions, not independent statements (and for an infant even those are made on his or her behalf by the godparents). Bodies in liturgy are as much, if not more, acted *upon* rather than acting themselves.[43] Even our movements are often a giving way (for the censor) or a reception (of communion). The gestures of liturgy—especially what we do with our hands and heads in crossing ourselves or bowing—reinforce this bodily posture of exposure and attention.

Exposure

Lacoste actually employs similar language of "exposition" to juxtapose our being-before-God to the disclosedness (*Erschlossenheit*) of being-in-the-world. While the relation to God is not necessary and "exposition" does not constitute an existential right, it does refer to the possibility that there might be a horizon within which we open ourselves toward the Absolute.[44] Lacoste thinks of this as "radically distinct from our opening onto the world" and as "an excess" or "surplus" of experience entirely grounded in "divine givenness."[45] It is an order that completely subverts Dasein's openness to the world and has nothing at all to do with being-in-the-world or with our facticity, but instead refers to our freedom to affirm the existence of an Absolute and the desire to exist in this presence. To be exposed to the Absolute means to exist no longer in the world and to become indifferent to opening the world. Instead, "the logic of exposition is thus first that of approval given to a presence and to its exorbitant demands."[46] Prayer constitutes a subversion of our relation with place and opens an existence at the limit or border of the world, living on the threshold of the eschaton: "Liturgy acts as the negation and the adoption of a position: it denies that the logic of inherence unveils all that we are and it affirms our desire to exist before God."[47] Lacoste also acknowledges that we rarely manage to live on this fragile threshold and often fall back into ordinary ways of being in the world. As he observes laconically: we do not pray continually.

Lacoste thus sees the body of being-in-the-world in opposition to the body within liturgy or prayer. Our liturgical experience of body (especially boredom and fatigue) turns upside down and breaks with our corporeal experience of Dasein. While Lacoste acknowledges that "place cannot be thought independently of the body," our being-before-God occurs in a "non-place" where our corporeality is eschatologically subverted.[48] The "dance" of liturgy invalidates the corporeality of being and of manifestation and puts all "worldly" spatiality into parentheses. It implies that we can "symbolically absent ourselves from the world and the earth" toward the ultimate.[49] Although Lacoste affirms that the tension between our earthly corporeality and spatiality in the world and the eschatological suspension of this in a non-place and non-experience always remains, it is clear that he expects them to be severed in the parousia, in which our "liturgical being" will be lived fully and not only temporarily.[50]

Lacoste is obviously right to note that the liturgical posture is not always maintained nor can be assumed without any intentional exposure to the other. Liturgy provides the space for its potential expression, but that does not happen in every liturgy; we can simply go "through the motions" without attentiveness to or acknowledgment of what they might mean. Yet the possibility for such exposure and humbling is there. And, contra Lacoste, this exposure happens within our bodily being in the world, within the liturgical space. Liturgy is first of all experienced in the here and now, not on the threshold of the eschaton. While the liturgical texts make theological claims about the "coming of the kingdom," the phenomenological experience of liturgy is one of bodies bent toward the altar or toward each other, not to some invisible non-place. If the "kingdom" or the "eschaton" arrives in liturgy, it does so here and now, in our experience in this place. We do not leave the world behind in prayer—at least not in any way that would be phenomenologically discernable. While we may desire to encounter the Absolute and may well come into liturgy with the hope of such encounter, to assume that encounter with the Absolute constitutes a radical break with the world is a theological interpretation, but no longer a phenomenological description of actual liturgical experience or of the overall structures it displays.

Yet, that does not mean that the liturgical postures and gestures constitute no challenge at all to our everyday manner of being in the world. As we have seen, Heidegger argues that authentic being in the world means to grasp one's possibilities, that disclosedness or openness to the world is Dasein's decisive or "resolute" assumption of its own destiny. The philosophical model of the most authentic life is almost always that of the self-examined, self-sufficient subject, in charge of its own life and thought. The posture of liturgy challenges this definition of the self in terms of autonomy and self-sufficiency. Contra Heidegger, such exposure of the body to the other may well be a more authentic way of being (rather than merely a fleeing of the self for the crowd) because it reveals us more fully to the other than a more protective stance does. In our more defensive postures, we hide and dissimulate the self even when this hiding occurs as a blustering inflation of the self. The protection, even "covering up" of the body (in its flight into appearances), is an important need in our society and probably essential for our survival in its competitive and often hostile environment, but it hides us from each other and from ourselves. Everyday being, then, as Heidegger himself indicates, is to some extent inauthentic being, a hiding or fleeing from more authentic modes of being. But such a more authentic mode may not ultimately be about a resolute grasp of one's own being (as *Eigentlichkeit* in *Entschlossenheit*), but instead an exposure and offering of one's self to the other—whether divine or human. The liturgical opening up or exposure of the body is a corporeal unfolding of the self, maybe even a kind of manifestation or disclosure.

Such exposure obviously should not be confused with self-display or self-exhibition. Exposing oneself must be phenomenologically distinguished from exhibiting oneself, which is also a kind of exposure, but for quite different purposes and in a very different posture. In that case, exposure is less a stance of vulnerability and openness than one of self-assertion and even self-exhibition. It draws attention to the self, folds the other in on the self, instead of unfolding the self beyond itself. Marion's analysis of idol and icon might be helpful here, albeit in a somewhat different fashion than he employs it. In his early work (*Idol and Distance* and *God Without Being*),

Marion speaks of both "idol" and "icon" as ways of seeing, as types of gazes, whether in regard to a physical object or a concept.[51] In the case of the idol the gaze is dazzled by the phenomenon, completely absorbed in it, adores it, but this very adoration, inasmuch as it captures the gaze entirely, is actually a mirroring of the self. It is idolatrous because it is at the measure (and under the control) of the self and imposes the measure of the gaze on the phenomenon. In the case of "iconic" seeing, the gaze becomes exposed to the icon and experiences another gaze weighing upon it. Here the self finds itself envisioned or envisaged by the other, by another gaze aimed toward it. For Marion, exposure is really at work only in the second case and is entirely "positive": It is an erotic gaze where I become devoted to the other (human or divine) who envisions me, ready to receive the other who bears upon me. This is the appropriate stance before the divine because it allows God to be manifested without constriction. While the "idol" is also a true vision of the divine for Marion, it is at our measure and on our conditions, which permits only what we can see or adore to be manifested. It does not go beyond us, does not allow for manifestation of the invisible, but merely mirrors what we have seen and what our gaze can bear.

But an exposure that is self-exhibiting also offers itself to the gaze of the other; indeed, its very goal is to focus the other's gaze upon me, to become an object of admiration or adoration for the other. One might say, using Heidegger's terminology, that this is an "inauthentic" mode of exposure, but one that reveals aspects of "genuine" exposure in its more "privative" (everyday?) sense. Both exhibition and exposure are forms of corporeality; both are ways of directing the gaze. In the former, the gaze is focused on me, on my body and on what is conveyed through my corporeality (which can include my mannerisms, my gestures, my affects, even my thoughts about appearances, and other aspects); in the latter, the gaze is directed away from me; my exposure serves to focus on the other rather than on the self. The former is "idolatrous" precisely because it seeks to turn the body of the self into the object of contemplation or adoration for the gaze of the other.[52] (Indeed, contra Marion's analysis, it might actually constitute a kind of refusal to serve as mirror for the other's gaze but instead wants to absorb that gaze for itself.) The latter is "iconic" inasmuch as it opens the self for receptivity of the other, exposes itself in all its finitude and fragility, not to attract the gaze of the other but to allow the other to touch me (without being able to control whether such touch will be healing or harmful, gentle or violent). We probably always hover uneasily between these two in the liturgical experience. Part of its temporality is precisely its distended and cyclical nature, which recognizes that no movement of liturgy, no feeling, action, or experience of the self is ever "complete" or reaches its telos entirely, but that they must be practiced over time and often fail.[53] Kenotic exposure does not happen in every liturgical experience, nor is it easy to come by (this is why we need repetition and practice). The liturgy invites to such exposure—it neither imposes it nor makes it magically happen overnight or on its own without our agreement or participation in enacting it.

This is not to say that bodies in liturgy become merely passive. Exposure does not constitute passivity, but a kind of disclosure that involves genuine effort. Standing, kneeling, prostrating, and so forth may be postures of vulnerability and exposure, but they have to be enacted, they have to be performed, they even require initiative. To say that liturgy acts on the body and that its corporeal postures expose the body and challenge our posture of self-sufficiency is not to say that our bodies no longer move and that we no longer have any sort of initiative, that liturgy merely happens to us or the Absolute overwhelms us (as seems the case to some extent in both Lacoste and Marion). Liturgy is hard work. Not only does the very term "liturgy" mean work, but this is also very evident in its practice. Especially the penitential practices of Lent are continually referred to in terms of the great effort they require.[54] The liturgical texts acknowledge at many points that liturgical practice involves heavy labor, dedication, tremendous effort. It is not at all passive. And it is certainly not easy. But this labor of exposure is done for and toward something. It is directed or oriented—as is our gaze and body during liturgy. The vulnerability involved in the exposure of our finitude is not simply for its own sake, but for the sake of opening the body into a receptive stance: a body that can see and hear and smell and taste and touch what is given, a body open beyond its focus on the self.

One might say, then, that in liturgy our preoccupation with "exhibiting" our bodies (but not the bodies themselves!) is set aside and reformed. Liturgy inscribes humility on the body: The body is no longer proudly upright and self-sufficient, but bent before the other and before "God," both for healing of the self and care for the other. Touching is no longer about grasping, but about offering. The body becomes a sacred offering, stretched out before the other. Liturgy is hence not a denial or erasure (or overcoming or suspension) of finitude, as Lacoste would suggest. Nor is it simply an affirmation or embrace of finitude, as Falque implies. Rather, it asks us in our very corporeality to make of our finitude an offering and to do so together, while acknowledging our fragility. In liturgy, bodies are not individual, extended objects in space, but they are dynamically related participants of a common liturgical experience that at least for some moments knits those bodies into one: one voice raised in song, one cup shared in common, one body broken for each other. Bodies are shaped and bent in liturgy, become open and vulnerable to the other, in some sense emptied of themselves and their autonomous subjectivity in order to share in a larger whole, become part of a body they create together. The frailty of corporeal bodies is not somehow "transfigured" liturgically into "glorious" bodies or pure souls communing with each other in some splendid "spiritual" fashion.[55] Rather, finite and fragile bodies become gifts or conduits and recipients of "grace" and "hospitality"; they are opened up beyond themselves but neither suspended nor erased. It might even enable a kind of permeability of bodies in this offering toward and for the other, as the connection of this language of bodily illness and healing within the Eucharist seems to indicate. In liturgy, our finite and fragile bodies are enabled to shed some measure of self-protection and self-enclosure in order to open ourselves to the welcome extended by the liturgy and to practice such welcome toward one another.

4

SENSORIALITY

Paul the Silentiary depicts the play of light on the marble in the ambo of Hagia Sophia:

The whole of it is adorned with skilful workmanship and glistens with the many hues of the natural stone. Its surface is covered, as it were, with eddying whirlpools, in places resembling an infinity of circles, while in others they stray from under the circles into winding curves. In parts is seen a rosy bloom mingled with pallor, or the fair brightness of human fingernails; in other places the brilliance turns to a soft white like the color of boxwood or the lovely semblance of bees-wax which men wash in clear mountain streams and lay out to dry under the sun's rays: it turns silver-white, yet not completely altering its color, it shows traces of gold. So, too, does ivory, tinged by the passage of long years, turn its silvery color to quince-yellow. In places it has a dark sheen, yet marvellous Nature did not allow this livid color to spread, but has mixed cunning patterns into the stone, and a changeful silvery light flashes over it.[1]

He goes on to compare various aspects of the architecture to the petals of white lilies, the rolling waves of the ocean, and to flowering meadows.

Orthodox liturgy is rich in sensory impressions.[2] Even the dismissive description often used of high liturgy—that it contains too much "smells and bells"—indicates its highly sensory nature. And indeed there is much to see, to hear, to smell, to taste, and to touch in liturgy. Sometimes the

101

senses are positively overwhelmed with the sensory stimuli presented. Special occasions, like the major feasts, seem to compete for sensory overload with even more visual decoration, more complicated chanting, more tasty food, more elaborate censing, more items to touch or venerate. Yet, most actions of liturgy, even the more "mundane" ones like the customary veneration of icons upon first entering a church, require sensory engagement. At the same time, this sensorial dimension of liturgy involves its spatiality and the many objects that appear in its spaces. We see icons on the walls and stands, we hear the choir's music echoing in the acoustical space, we taste the bread and the wine, smell the incense as it is carried around the perimeter of the church, and touch a variety of things. The analysis here will thus concern not only the activity of sensing, but what is sensed: the things of liturgy.

Probably the most obvious sensory experience in liturgy is that of sight.[3] Orthodox liturgical space is richly decorated. We see the space of the church, its architectural elements, their decoration, and especially the icons. We also observe candles, various liturgical implements, the actions and gestures of the priest or altar servers or those of other people around us. Thus, the spatiality and movement of liturgy is a crucial part of its sensory experience, especially in terms of sight but also involving the other senses. Another important aspect of this is color and glitter. Today, the liturgical colors of vestments and altar covers are linked to certain liturgical occasions—red for feasts of the cross or Christ, blue for the Theotokos, green for the Spirit, white for Pascha, purple for Lent, black for Holy Week, gold for many other occasions.[4] These colors "signify"; they are not merely intuitively visible to the eye, but convey sense. Intentionality is fully engaged here, not only in the deliberate association of certain colors with certain occasions, but also inasmuch as colors now create expectations and one intentionally anticipates certain kinds of meaning because of the signification conveyed by the colors.

In this regard it is interesting that the Byzantines apparently did not focus on color as much as on sheen or glitter, as several contemporary art historians have shown.[5] Thus, the kind and intensity of light was more important to the visual experience than the display of color, which for us today (at least in the West) tends to be primary.[6] This is particularly evident in the popular rhetorical form of *ekphrasis*, which—as in the example from the description of Hagia Sophia quoted at the start of the chapter—depicted the beauty of a space often primarily in terms of its dazzling effect on the viewer rather than providing detail about color and other aspects that might interest us today.[7] What is significant about this emphasis on brilliance, sheen, or glimmer is that it requires darkness and shadow. The glimmer or sheen of the glass in mosaic flickers in the light and the image is seen differently in different light conditions.[8] This is especially true when gold is involved because it is far more striking in semi-darkness and illuminated by candles rather than under the exposure of full light, when it simply becomes another color. Thus, icons in the apse or otherwise far away from the viewer are seen quite differently depending on the lighting conditions, whether the church is fully illuminated by daylight or whether it is in the semi-obscurity of a candlelight vigil.[9] (The introduction of electric lights obviously destroys much of this impression and it is usually not captured by modern photography.[10])

Scholars argue that the use of glass pieces and especially of gold in Byzantine mosaic conveys some of those very elements of ambiguity and hiddenness deliberately.[11] This dimension of hiddenness or concealing is an important part of the liturgical experience of sight. Its tension is always present in some form or other. In fact, much of the visual experience of liturgy is actually marked more strongly by what we do not see or what we only see partially in glimpses through the doors into the altar area. There is always a revealing and concealing going on, maybe more strongly in the later tradition after the development of the iconostasis or the ritual drawing and withdrawing of a curtain before the altar area. But the elements of mystery, of revealing and concealing are already highlighted in the fourth century by Cyril of Jerusalem and others. And even the most basic, most plain, most fully visible liturgy still has to cope with the mystery of the Eucharist, in which visible elements are taken to convey something essentially invisible and inaccessible to sensory perception.

Hearing is just as central an aspect of the liturgical experience as seeing. We hear the chants, hymns, and texts of the liturgy as they are read and sung. Often we participate in or respond to them. Liturgy is frequently dialogic in nature.[12] In fact, many of the early liturgical hymns were composed as dialogues, often sung by antiphonal choirs, responding to each other, thus even the performance itself was dialogical. Both Ephrem the Syrian (fourth century) and Romanos the Melodist (early sixth century), probably the two greatest eastern liturgical poets, employ dialogue extensively in their hymns.[13] Many such dialogues remain in the liturgical texts today in somewhat shorter form (especially in the canons for Matins or the verses for two central parts of the Vespers service, "Lord, I call" and the Aposticha).[14] The element of music or sound in liturgy has also recently received the increased attention of art historians, Byzantinists, and liturgical scholars.[15] Byzantine churches were designed for optimal acoustic effect, albeit not necessarily for optimal "comprehension." The impact of the music seems to have been more important than being able to distinguish or decipher each word, maybe paralleling the emphasis on sheen or glitter over that of distinguishing color.

The role of the sense of smell in liturgical and broader Eastern religious experience has been examined by Susan Ashbrook Harvey's important study on the "olfactory" imagination.[16] What does it mean to "scent salvation"? She highlights the many ways in which sanctity was associated with good smell or fragrance, especially in regard to the cult of martyrs. A particularly saintly person upon their death is often thought to give off a perfumed fragrance rather than a putrid or rotting smell. Such good smell is regarded as evidence of their sanctity.[17] She shows how this is carried over into liturgy: "Liturgy was the context in which every Christian act, practice, or perception was to be understood. Olfactory imagery was most often the marker that signified this orientation. . . . Olfactory imagery, then, functioned in late antique Christianity to integrate ascetic practice into the liturgical life of the church . . . Olfactory rhetoric held together asceticism, liturgy, and biblical exegesis, joining the practices of the individual into the ritual world of the ecclesial community."[18] She points out the frequent imagery of preparing a house with sweet-smelling fragrances as a simile for preparing one's body as dwelling for the divine.[19]

We also taste in liturgy. Schmemann opens his popular *For the Life of the World* by talking about the importance of food as an entry into liturgy. He cites Feuerbach's famous dictum that we are what we eat (*der Mensch ist, was er isst*). Within liturgy this is primarily confined to bread, wine, and water, but not only within the Eucharist. Blessed bread is eaten on many other occasions (for example, the litiya breads or *artoklasia*). Memorial services for the dead (*panikhida*) are generally followed by a meal or by the sharing of *koliva* (a sweetened boiled wheat mixture). Yet, probably the most explicitly sensory experience is that of participating in the Eucharist. Indeed, liturgical scholars often point to Cyril of Jerusalem's exhortation to the newly illumined catechumens to touch the eucharistic elements to their lips and nostrils, as if anointing the doors of the senses eucharistically.[20] How are the things of liturgy related to the sensory impressions they make? What is the phenomenological nature of so-called "liturgical elements"? Is the eucharistic "body" a "body" as things are bodies in the world?

Liturgical Theology and the Senses

Liturgical theology often insists on the importance of the sensory dimension of liturgy, although it does not necessarily expend a lot of time analyzing this dimension. Irwin argues that the arts "shape in very forceful ways, how the enacted liturgy is experienced, appreciated, and appropriated." This includes "architecture, painting, sculpture, music, choreography." And it extends to all the senses: "What participants see: lights and colors, harmony of the space; what they hear: voice, song, playing instruments; what they smell: incense, perfumed oils; what they taste: bread and wine; what they touch: offering the sign of peace, kissing the gospel book, exchanging a wedding ring and what movements they are engaged in: stational Masses, processions on Palm Sunday, Candlemas and Rogation days are all part of the experience of worship and require our methodological attention."[21] Saliers also suggests that "the visual theology of the stained glass, the iconography, the wall frescoes, or the statuary, is part of the prayed theology of the assembly" and insists that "the aural character of liturgy is powerfully formative of our embodied theology."[22] This also points to the role of the things—like candles, oil, bread, and wine—that are sensed in liturgy, whether through sight or scent, taste or touch. Flanagan points out the importance of touch: "Because Christian belief depends on dealing with the unseen, man cannot apprehend deeper spiritual meanings without some form of social embodiment of those meanings . . . one wishes to view liturgies as handling sensible signs that make known a hidden reality."[23]

Indeed, the "sensory" character of liturgy is most often explored in the context of reflection on the sacraments. Boff argues that everything ordinary or everyday can become a sacrament.[24] Therefore, "the structure of human life as such is sacramental. The more human beings relate to the things of this world and other human beings, the more the fan of symbolic and sacramental signification opens out for them."[25] Janowiak states emphatically: "Sacraments are not things. They are, first and foremost, events that express and celebrate God's saving acts in Jesus. . . . The liturgy employs elemental things like words and gestures, water, food and drink, and uses them in faithful memory to announce a new reality and to lead us into a future filled with hope."[26] Hughes does not deny that there are things in liturgy, but points to the way in which liturgy changes them: "But liturgy does not *leave* these things as we encounter them in their ordinariness. In many and various ways we subject them to what have been called 'ritualizing strategies': the ministerial party does not exactly *walk*, it processes; baptism is a form of *washing* but unlike any other lustration the candidate will undergo; the Eucharist is a *meal*, but one in which the bread is broken and given with a prayer and wine is consumed from a handsome cup; and so on, at pretty well every point."[27] Liturgy takes the ordinary and makes it extraordinary.

In fact, liturgical theologians often move quite quickly from the use of certain things in liturgy to their symbolic significance.[28] For example, Irwin argues: "The very use of candles is significant. These are commodities whose purpose is to shed light and, by their nature to be totally consumed in the act of being burnt. The purpose of the candle is to be burned, consumed. It is a complete oblation. Sacrificial overtones of complete self-offering are thus operative because of the nature of the candle as symbol."[29] Saliers also insists that "ritual symbols are never merely things" because "'things' like light, water, oil, or bread are already, for the Christian tradition, embedded in a history of shared social life. Such objects are not themselves 'symbolic' by virtue of using them to express our experience. Rather, only by being vulnerable to and learning to participate in the shared life toward which these symbols point is 'experience of the symbol' possible."[30] Chauvet puts it even more strongly: "All bread is essentially this symbol, even if it is only in the symbolic act of religious oblation that its essence as bread unfolds itself."[31] Lathrop similarly says that "the holy things of Christians are not static, but come to their meaning in action, as they are used."[32] He tends to talk about the way in which liturgical things function in quite exorbitant fashion: "Before the liturgy even begins, as the food is brought and set out on an offertory table or credence or prothesis, a Christian may rightly behold the loaf and think, 'Here is all human life,' or see the wine, thinking, 'Here is the universe itself.'"[33] Yet how does seeing the wine lead us to recognize the entire universe in it?

In fact, this connection between eucharistic elements and the larger creation is made fairly frequently. Chauvet insists that "bread cannot become Eucharist under just any conditions," namely not when it is the product of injustice and poverty: "To offer God this bread kneaded from the death of the poor is a sacrilege. . . . To pretend to eat the body of Christ unto life, when in fact this bread, taken from the mouths of the poor, is the bearer of death, is to condemn oneself." Consequently, "the theological economy of the sacramental cult is inseparable from the social economy of labor."[34] Senn contends that: "a reverent disposal of the elements which have been the bearers of Christ's sacramental body and blood can be a model for the reverential treatment of any of earth's creatures which have been the gracious bearers of life through a 'true use.'"[35] Lathrop similarly argues: "The meal held here tends toward being a model of sustainable consumption in which everyone is welcome to eat with thankfulness, no one hoarding, no one hungry, no one excluded, just enough made available. More: tasting enables seeing. Participants come to see that 'the Lord is good.' If this is so, perhaps they see more. Perhaps they see a new order in the cosmos itself."[36] Varghese goes even further: "The Church, as the priestly community, blesses the matter as well as the vegetation and asks God to make them a source of blessing and communion with God. In Christ, the Church asks God to integrate the whole creation with his saving plan and to restore them to their prelapsarian condition."[37] Such arguments are even more frequent in treatments that seek to show the sacramental or liturgical dimension as relevant for an ecological theology.[38] The lifting up of the bread and cup is frequently taken to have profound implications for all of creation.[39] Yet it is not at all clear why and how the handling of such items in worship necessarily has any effect on other objects or things outside of liturgy. More thinking is necessary here. Maybe a phenomenological analysis can point to a possible path.

Phenomenology and the Senses

Chrétien often stresses sensory elements in his discussions of language, which he sees characterized by an essentially dialogic character, as well as by a fragility and corporeality we often do not sufficiently acknowledge. In his *The Ark of Speech* he engages liturgical language in terms of the call of hospitality that shelters the world and gives voice to it. The "ark" of the title refers to Adam's naming of the animals, to Noah's ark that sheltered the animals from the flood, the arc of the rainbow of promise, and the arc of a bridge that forms a connection and makes a path for meeting across separation. The human voice is designed to shelter and safeguard all of creation, but is also addressed and protected by it in turn. Chrétien stresses the importance of hearing as something that precedes speaking, as a form of hospitality to the other. He explores prayer as a "wounded word," one that is not merely interior and silent but has to be vocalized and embodied. Yet silence is always a precondition for speech. Chrétien also discusses chant as a response to the beauty of the world. We sing the world, we give it voice in our liturgical prayer, but we can only do so because it has first sung us, because it gives us a voice. Thus, the praise of worship becomes an "ark/arc of speech" inasmuch as it welcomes the world in its offering of praise while simultaneously allowing itself to be spoken by it.

Chrétien returns to the phenomenon of praise in several contexts.[40] He always stresses its fragility and finitude, its situation of response and creatureliness. Our obligation to hospitality and to sheltering the beauty of the world is already a response to a prior address. And for Chrétien this must always be a cosmic liturgy, a praise that is offered together with all of creation and even in response to creation: "The world sings the human before the human can sing the world and in order for him to be able to do so."[41] Chrétien specifically responds to those who argue that the human has a unique task to give voice to the rest of creation—something often claimed by contemporary Orthodox theologians—by interpreting this praise as already a response to the song of creation of which we are but a small part. In liturgical praise we give voice to the "polyphony of the world" but on the one hand this is a "wounded" praise, marked by finitude and fragility, even by darkness and suffering, and on the other hand the song always precedes us, we can chant only because we are already chanted, because the world already bears us up in its own song.[42] Liturgical language is a gift offered to us—to our brokenness, fragility, and fragmentation—as much as it is our praise. We offer ourselves to each other and to the world as we respond to the call already offered to us. Chrétien argues that we can listen only because the call always already precedes us.[43] Although he stresses auditory aspects the most strongly, they are always linked to and expressive of the vulnerability of the body.

Marion argues more broadly that we experience sensory givens in two fundamentally distinct ways, either as "poor" phenomena (in the mode of "objects") or as "saturated" phenomena (in the mode of "givens").[44] In his essay "The Banality of Saturation" he gives an example for each of the five senses: We see the colors red, yellow, and green in approaching a traffic light or in contemplating Rothko's painting #212, we hear a voice over the loudspeaker at a train station or lose ourselves in the sound of a diva singing an aria at the opera, we smell gas or the fragrance of a perfume, we taste a poison or a fine wine, we stumble over various objects in a darkened room trying to find the light switch or we caress a beloved's body.[45] In the former cases, we experience objects, constitute them entirely in terms of concepts, understand them fully, and are really only interested in the information they provide. In the latter cases, we experience saturated phenomena, which we cannot constitute, cannot fully comprehend, cannot control; they come to us in surprising ways and without our initiative. Marion hence contends that cultural, aesthetic, or religious phenomena must be understood as such saturated phenomena and that interpreting them as objects minimizes and misunderstands their rich and excessive nature. Phenomena of revelation are especially overwhelming and saturated: bread and wine are not mere objects, but fully given, even abandoned, phenomena, which we experience as gifts.

Marion suggests that this identifies them as "saturated phenomena" in a particularly intense way, indeed so intense that it might be more appropriate to call them phenomena that are *raturé* (erased) rather than *saturé* (saturated), because they are abandoned so fully and in such abundance that nothing remains, nothing withdraws or is held back in this gift. Marion contends that Eucharist therefore emerges as the highest and fullest instance of phenomenality, as the most fully given gift, and can become a paradigm for all other gifts, and indeed for all other phenomena.[46] Yet, although this analysis provides a phenomenological sense of the language of offering and brokenness in the eucharistic liturgy, it seems to disregard the corporeal language of bread and wine, body and blood. Marion's eucharistic gifts are not manifested corporeally because they are so invisible, intense, absolute, and overwhelming that pure adoration can be the only response.[47] It surely says something about how the gift is given, but not much about how it is given as "body" offered "on behalf of all and for all." It also makes no attempt to grapple with the phenomenological manifestation of the larger eucharistic experience: the proskomedia, the anaphora, the procession with the gifts during the Cherubic hymn, the entry, the consecration, the lifting of the chalice, the saying of the creed and the Lord's Prayer, the reception of the elements, and their incorporation into our bodies (or their respective equivalents in other Christian traditions).

Falque pays much more attention to these corporeal elements and indeed follows the text of the (Roman Catholic) liturgical rite of consecration in his analysis, referring also to other aspects such as the reserving of the gifts and their use as "viaticum" for the sick.[48] The height of the eucharistic experience for Falque is the fact of incorporation: of the bread into our bodies and of our bodies into Christ. He applies his notion of the "spread body," briefly examined in the previous chapter, to the eucharistic "body," which becomes incorporated into our bodies, as we become incorporated into its "mystical" body. Yet Falque's analysis is heavily theological and makes any number of claims that cannot possibly be sustained phenomenologically.[49] He draws implications about sexual difference and a particular view of marriage from his analysis, some of which seem rather tenuously connected to the phenomenological experience of incorporation. Falque is surely right that Eucharist matters for bodies in all their materiality and that it cannot and should not be interpreted in a disembodied sense that invalidates the fundamental claims of incarnation (in both the theological and the phenomenological sense). But should we really abandon the phenomenological approach quite so quickly for a theological interpretation? Can we say a bit more about how "this is my body broken for you" is manifested phenomenologically? These claims about the Eucharist will be taken up in the final section of the chapter after returning to the questions of the senses in liturgy more generally.

Call and Response

Perhaps the most striking liturgical "commentary" on the senses is the rite of chrismation or anointing, whether in the context of a reception into the church or in the context of a healing service. Such anointing involves tracing a cross on each of the "entry points" or "doors" of the senses (both "outer" and "inner" ones): forehead, eyelids, nostrils, lips, ear lobes, hands (occasionally even chest/heart and feet). It thus conveys a touch (sanctifying? blessing? healing?) of all the places on the body that communicate or feel the world, including emotions (of the heart) and thoughts (brain/forehead). It is significant that this rite is traced with the liquid and fragrant oil on the body and not simply thought in abstract terms. It is not just a prayer for healing consisting of mere words or thoughts, but a direct and thoroughly sensory touch of the body. As both physical and even emotional pain are felt in the body not in some abstract realm separate from it, so healing must touch the body. At the same time, this touch is also highly symbolic and ritualized inasmuch as the same places are touched for every person, although their pain and need for healing might be quite different, and obviously the "external" body is touched while the pain might be lodged more deeply in the flesh and not directly visible on its anointed skin. It is also important that one *is* anointed and does not anoint oneself: One is touched by another. It is a touch of my senses by another. Healing or blessing is "mediated" by other people.[50] This brief liturgical example of sensory anointing highlights the close connection between corporeality and the senses. The body, as seen and touched by others, is taken as the person in his or her ability to feel and experience. Visible "parts" of the body, such as eyes, ears, or mouth, are read as "entry points" to the invisible experience of seeing, hearing, or tasting. The two are intimately connected.

The first—maybe obvious but still important—phenomenological point to make about liturgy thus is that anything that is "experienced" in liturgy is mediated through the senses. We experience liturgy as we see, hear, smell, taste, and touch. Liturgy is fully incarnate, corporeal, and sensory experience. Whatever experience liturgy conveys—even if it is taken to be an experience of "transcendence" or the "mystical"—such experience comes only as incarnate through or in affectivity and corporeality. The importance of the senses in liturgy also makes abundantly clear that there can be no flesh without bodies, at least liturgically speaking. Our corporeality is the "locus" of our experience of being affected. And this corporeality is spatial and temporal. All of the dimensions of experience discussed so far (and the ones still to be discussed) are connected and cannot function without each other. Liturgical experience is fully incarnated experience, enfleshed in the sensory experience of bodies, which themselves are experienced spatially and temporally. Liturgy is not a denial of our bodies, senses, or emotions, but works precisely through them and cannot do without them. It is through our affects and senses that we are "attuned" to liturgy and enabled to "hear" or "taste" it.

Let us begin with the auditory sense. Liturgy is busy: There is very little room for silence or contemplation within the liturgical experience itself.[51] Even the most solemn Holy Week services are full of chants and readings. In fact, for centuries Scripture was heard primarily if not exclusively within liturgy (and it was primarily *heard* rather than read in personal study) and for many people that may well continue to be the case today. Homilies are heard. We are often exhorted to listen. Almost all readings of Scripture, especially those of the Gospel, are preceded with the injunction: "Let us attend!" It is also immensely significant that almost the entire liturgy is sung or chanted, usually including the reading of Scripture (as chanted). All words and texts of liturgy have a rhythm and a texture. Music enters memory in far stronger ways than words without rhythm do, especially if movement is added to the combination of words and rhythm.[52] Poetry and musical lines are remembered longer and more vividly than simple prose. It is thus significant that liturgy is always sung or at least chanted.[53]

Music is not only about hearing but also about creating mood, even about crafting an experience of space. We experience liturgical music at least as much for the emotions and memories it evokes than for the "meaning" it conveys. Or, maybe more correctly, its meaning is conveyed also through mood, emotion, memory, and imagination, not simply through rational comprehension of signifying words.[54] Music signifies, and it does so in auditory fashion, but quite differently from the way in which we gain meaning from reading a text. Julia Kristeva distinguishes between a "semiotic" and "symbolic" function of language.[55] The semiotic refers to the visceral functions of language like rhythm and beat or even to the glossolalia of small children before they are able to speak in a recognizable language. Such speech is still (or already) verbal articulation and does convey meaning. Symbolic language, by contrast, signifies primarily if not exclusively through words and phrases. Music, especially the rhythm of plagal tones as they are employed in Byzantine music, is much closer to the semiotic than to the symbolic (in Kristeva's sense), although that does not mean that it has no symbolic dimensions. Meaning is evoked not only by what is said but by the *how* of its saying, by its rhythm, meter, and mood.[56]

At the same time, we not only hear in liturgy, we also expect to be heard.[57] An important part of every vesper service, including of a vesperal liturgy, is the hymn (based on Psalm 140/141[58]) "Lord, I call upon you, hear me." Similar references to calling and desiring to be heard abound throughout the liturgy. They are often taken from the psalms, which frequently express these desires. But beyond such verbal affirmations of hearing, the very presupposition of liturgy is that of being heard. There would be no point to all our singing, chanting, and praying, if it were not intended to be heard by someone. The petitionary nature of much prayer, even the prayers that do not ask for something but simply offer praise, all work with the presupposition that such prayers will be heard, that they are offered to someone who will listen to us. We come to liturgy not only and maybe not even primarily to hear, but to be heard. Orthodox liturgy has a profoundly dialogical structure, both in a general and in a more particular sense. Liturgy is hence not only about hearing things—bells, chants, homilies, litanies—but about being heard. Within liturgy we praise God, confess our sins, or call out for help. Almost all liturgical texts and many liturgical actions are directed and intended toward the divine. The abundant "God"-reference of liturgical language—both voiced and embodied—means that liturgy operates as a call upon and response to another. Yet beside this larger sense in which all of liturgy functions as dialogue, there are also very specific dialogic aspects within liturgy, such as the litanies, which occur at many places within any liturgical service. Each request addressed to God is followed by a response from the people that reinforces the request (usually through the line "Lord, have mercy" or on other occasions by saying "Grant this, O Lord"). Thus the larger implied dialogue with the divine is enhanced through a further dialogue between the one chanting the liturgical requests (often a priest or deacon, sometimes a reader) and the congregation as a whole.[59]

Liturgy not only portrays dialogue in its texts, it also initiates such dialogue via petitions for intercession, frequently directed at Mary as the Theotokos, but also often to the saints. One especially striking example is the repeated request on the Sunday of the expulsion from Paradise, in which the meadows, trees, and flowers of paradise are asked to offer prayer on our behalf.[60] This is again true not only of the liturgical texts, but also of actions performed in liturgy, especially the veneration of icons, where the saints portrayed are implored to pray on our behalf. Our experience of hearing in liturgy is thus doubled by our experience of calling and wishing to be heard. The very experience of hearing is enveloped within the calling and the call within the hearing. I can only call because I am hearing, only hear as I am calling. In some way, the call occurs in the very hearing itself, it is what we say that expresses what we hear and what we hear that expresses that we call. As Chrétien notes: "We can only beckon to ourselves what has already turned itself toward us, already manifested itself to us—what calls upon us to call: the full daylight of language is thus already well advanced before the dawn of any call." Therefore, "whenever we start to answer the call, we have already answered; when we embrace it as a call, it has already embraced us."[61] This is particularly true for those who are singing or chanting, which in principle ought to be everyone, even if in practice it is often relegated to a choir.[62] In the voice of the song the experience of hearing itself is made manifest. We sing and hear at the same time.

Liturgical language is dialogic also in another sense. Maybe one of the most important distinctions between liturgical prayer and individual prayer is that liturgical language is far more scripted. In the Orthodox tradition liturgy is almost entirely performed from a complicated network of prior texts (each service tends to require multiple books). Most Orthodox liturgical language, then, is essentially citation. Thus participants in liturgy listen to and participate in a language that *precedes* them. In praying liturgically, we make others' prayers our own. This is especially striking in something like the Great Canon, which operates in some sense a quadruple citation: the congregation prays as the priests chant St. Andrew's recitation of the biblical stories. Much of this long canon is written in the first person singular, deliberately identifying one's own prayer and conduct with the foibles and choices of the biblical characters. We thus allow others to "voice" us. We participate in the prayer of these characters, in the prayer of St. Andrew, and in the prayer of those who speak with us and on our behalf. And we do it each year, so in some way we are also citing ourselves each year anew. Language of praise is also almost invariably citation from the psalms or occasionally from earlier liturgical hymns. In all these our language participates in prior songs which we make our own as we chant them.

A similar dialogic back-and-forth also characterizes the visual experience of liturgy. In liturgy we not only see, but also *are seen*. This point has most frequently been made about icons, which are not merely seen but are experienced as seeing us. Marion argues that in gazing at an icon I experience another gaze weighing upon mine; I experience myself as being seen; I sense a gaze or aim directed at me and weighing upon me.[63] This is visually manifested by the inverse perspective employed by icons, which create the experience of our being envisioned by them instead of the Western perspective of objective contemplation by the viewer, introduced by the Renaissance. It is also exacerbated by the perpetuity of the icons in the liturgical space, which in most Orthodox churches cover all the surrounding walls and are prominently displayed on the iconostasis: their gaze meets us from everywhere. And for much of Orthodox history, these images of saints were conceived as being closely connected to the bodily reality of the depicted saint and to participate in it in some form.[64] We thus experience ourselves as seen from all sides by those who have gone before us and yet are imagined to worship with us. We do not simply observe or take in the liturgical space, but we experience our experience of seeing as wrapped into an experience of exposure to a gaze. The two are not two separate movements: First one sees, then one is seen. Rather, in liturgy the experience of being seen is part of the experience of seeing.

Here we can deepen the analysis of corporeal exposure provided in the previous chapter. The visual experience of liturgy, phenomenologically speaking, is not only that of seeing but also that of being seen, of becoming exposed or disclosed in our finite condition, of becoming vulnerable by admitting our frailties and failures, not only in words but in our visible bodily postures. Indeed, the liturgical texts often exhort precisely to this by portraying their participants as showing themselves fully and without pretense with all their foibles. This is obviously not solely a visual experience but also true of the other sensory and even emotive dimensions of liturgy. The sensory experience of liturgy is characterized by a liturgical back-and-forth. It is a doubled experience, in which we sense our own experience as always wrapped up with feeling ourselves also as experienced and exposed, in which we cannot see without being seen, cannot hear without being heard, cannot smell without becoming scent, cannot taste without becoming food, cannot touch without exposing ourselves to touch.

Although this dual aspect is maybe less immediately evident for the senses of smell or taste, there is a way in which it is true even there. Liturgy not only provides scents and fragrances to the sense of smell—burning candles, incense, scented oils, and so forth—but it functions to turn those who come into it into fragrant dwellings themselves. This is especially true of the burning of incense, probably the most obvious experience of smell in liturgical spaces. The censor is not merely something we passively smell. Rather, it represents in some way our prayer ascending to heaven as smoke rises. The liturgy also frequently speaks of good fragrance or smell of the saints or of prayers as being offered as scent.[65] What we "smell," liturgically speaking, are our own prayers mingled with those of all the others surrounding us, as they are offered up. It is certainly right that the way liturgy handles smell, informs and shapes the "sensory imagination" of those who participate in it.[66] But it does so not only passively; we are not simply overwhelmed by its very fragrances, but are encouraged ourselves to become the locus of such "holy" scent.

Just as the liturgy speaks of all of its participants becoming a fragrance, so it often exhorts us to become food. In ingesting the Eucharist, in some way we become "body of Christ." As the bread is offered to us, we are encouraged to offer ourselves similarly. Yet, we should not immediately move to the symbolic or metaphorical here. We do not first of all or primarily eat "meaning," but we taste the flavor of "physical" bread and wine. Whatever meaning emerges is conveyed in and through this tasting. It matters that the eucharistic elements become incorporated into our body, that we chew them and savor them. It is also worth pointing out that the senses are often all operative together: food is blessed after being displayed visually, by being censed, by having words spoken over it, by being sprinkled with water, and ultimately by being touched and consumed.

We have already spoken of touch in the previous chapter. We touch many of the elements of liturgical space: kissing icons and the cross, touching ourselves by tracing the cross on our bodies or by folding our hands over our chests in the reception of communion, sensing the elements on our lips and in our mouth, even the floor in kneeling and prostrating. In these experiences of touch we not only feel ourselves touching, in Husserl's sense, but we are also explicitly "touched" in liturgy in other ways—and not only in metaphorical but in quite corporeal ways. Practices of anointing, of eucharistic participation, of embracing each other, all involve not only giving touch but receiving it. This brings the dual tension we have discovered in the visual and auditory elements of liturgical experience—and to some, albeit lesser, extent also the olfactory and ingestive elements—to a head. Husserl's account of the touched touching, of the experience of *Leib* (rather than merely *Körper*) is in liturgy extended beyond touch to the other senses. We not only feel ourselves as we touch, but we also experience ourselves being seen by seeing, experience ourselves being heard in our hearing, become scent and food in our smelling and tasting. Phenomenologically speaking, within liturgy there is a constant tension or back-and-forth between an offering and a receiving dimension, between what is given to us and what we give, where one is always implicated in the other. What does this mean phenomenologically?

We spoke in the previous chapter of liturgical corporeality in terms of exposure of the body or as a disclosure of the self beyond itself. Here we can see more fully how this openness is effected: It is through the "doors" of the senses that we are accessed and open up; we see ourselves seen, hear ourselves heard, sense ourselves being touched. The sensory experience is always characterized by a call and a response structure, but the call is heard in the response and the response only manifested in the call. We do not only go from one to the other, alternately, but one is experienced *within* the other. We experience ourselves being seen within our experience of seeing, we come with an expectation to be heard within our hearing of prayerful music, we are told to become fragrant within our smelling of the liturgical scents, we experience tasting the Eucharist as an injunction to become food for others. These are not necessarily immediately "activities" in the fully corporeal sense—although they can certainly become such—but are experienced as part of liturgical sensoriality itself; the call-response structure is part of the sensory experience. Like liturgical corporeality, liturgical sensoriality hence establishes the possibility of an opening to something beyond ourselves, but it also gives a particular quality to that opening. It is a mode of "sensing" that is not closed in on itself, that does not merely draw the sensory experience into the self, but opens the self toward others who call upon me and touch me. Hearing is directed and oriented as calling upon others to engage in a dialogue. Chrétien concludes about the back-and-forth of call and response: "Our task is not to give an answer that would in some sense erase the initial provocation by corresponding to it, but to offer ourselves up as such in response, without assigning in advance any limit to the gift."[67] Taste, scent, touch, sight similarly do not simply come to us and end there, but come to us to open us up for response or even, as we have seen previously, for offering of self in some way (as food or scent).

Excess

Is such sensory experience always overwhelming, coming to us without preparation or precedent, a saturated experience that bedazzles and blinds us? Are sensory experiences in liturgy always so excessive and overwhelming that we cannot predict or control them, and that they come to us entirely out of their own initiative without our being able to prepare for them or anticipate them? Or, to use another term Marion frequently employs, do they come as anamorphosis, requiring us to "stand" in a certain place in order to "see" properly?[68] It is certainly true, as we have seen in the analysis of time and space, that liturgy is there "before" us and thus in some sense happens "without" us, not without our participation but beyond our individual control. Liturgy is a "given"—which is not to say that it does not change over time or is unalterable in some eternal fashion. But liturgy is indeed experienced as a tradition we did not make or choose (at least not its performance in *this* particular way) and that requires our participation in its own peculiar ways, not on our terms. In that sense "anamorphosis," standing in a specific place and becoming involved in the movements of liturgy as directed by the liturgy itself, does depict how liturgy impacts on consciousness. Furthermore, it is also true that a richly sensory experience of a particular liturgical occasion can be overwhelming and affect us in profound ways. Yet, is our seeing, hearing, smelling, tasting, or feeling always an excessive and overwhelming experience that comes without preparation, without cause, without fore-"seeing"?[69]

While these experiences are certainly marked by a kind of excess—our "ordinary" experience is not usually filled with such an abundance of flickering candles and heavy incense—this excess is not experienced as occurring without any preparation or intentionality. As has already been pointed out in other chapters, liturgy requires extensive preparation not only for those who "perform" it but even for those who participate in it. What expectations we bring to liturgy matters to its experience. It is not simply an utterly overwhelming and bedazzling event for which no preparation is possible or necessary. Indeed, it may often be experienced as more excessive, precisely when it has been preceded by more careful preparation or if it is intended in a particular way. We are not intuitively overwhelmed to such a degree that no intentionality can be at work. We also first of all experience these impressions as an excess of themselves, not necessarily as obvious pointers to something beyond it. We can be dazzled by the glittering of icons or overwhelmed by the smell of incense—maybe more intensely so at a festal liturgy than on a more "ordinary" occasion—but the bedazzlement comes from the sensory experience itself, not obviously from a "phenomenon of revelation." Certainly the experience can be interpreted in that way, maybe even "heard" or "read" in that way, but that is an activity of interpretation, not the immediate phenomenological experience.

Furthermore, liturgical experience is hardly *always* excessive and overwhelming. One can become easily habituated even to the most glittering decoration and most theatrical liturgical drama.[70] Such habituation or even mundanity is as much part of the liturgical experience. Indeed, much liturgy can be accomplished far more effectively, if those engaged in it know what they are doing from longstanding habit and familiarity, if they "breathe" the liturgy, rather than stumble through it. In contrast to Marion, Lacoste speaks of liturgical experience primarily in terms of boredom, fatigue, absence, and disappointment, because we find ourselves in the "in-between" or "clear-obscure" of the anticipation of the eschaton. For Lacoste, liturgy offers the promise "of a new mode of living, where things appear to us in their most secret truth."[71] Liturgy is an essential "restless-ness" because it is "man's ultimate act and the highest demonstration of his being possible for him,"[72] which, however, is not yet accessible, but only promised by liturgy. The truth is thus always veiled and the Absolute not fully manifested. He concludes: "Liturgy does not annul the a priori laws governing existence. But it does prove that transcendental forms of experi-ence do not constitute the entirety of our capacity for existence, and that the humanity of man does not let itself be determined exclusively by what comes to experience always, everywhere, and to everyone. The manifest God provides a future for man."[73] Yet, despite Lacoste's hesitancy, emphasis on nonexperience or nonmanifestation, and deferral to eschaton or parou-sia, too much seems assumed here. To claim that liturgy ultimately undoes "ordinary" experience and is radically discontinuous with it seems a theo-logical move rather than something that can be read "off" phenomenolog-ically from the experience. While boredom and fatigue are obviously often part of the liturgical experience and may indeed challenge some of our expectations about how the divine is supposed to be revealed in liturgy, these experiences are not themselves therefore indicative of God's "absent presence," nor do they indicate the coming of the parousia in any phenom-enologically discernable fashion.

The divine is thus not immediately or obviously present to sight, hear-ing, taste, smell, or touch, even as paradoxically absent in mystery. To see "God" in the eucharistic elements, to hear the divine in the words of the hymns or the homilies, to smell and taste "God's" goodness, to feel the divine touch, all require not only mediation through the "mundane" sen-sory experience, but also an activity of interpretation. This is not to say that such interpretation is purely arbitrary or merely subjective or con-demned to relativism. It is simply to affirm that there is no unmediated phenomenological experience of "revelation." And it is also to continue to bracket theological presuppositions about correspondence between "imma-nent" experience and "transcendent" assumptions, between what conscious-ness actually experiences and what it might assume about an existence "out there." At the same time, this also makes the important point that *if* this hermeneutic move is made and *if* "God" is said to be revealed in liturgy or religious experience more broadly, such experience is always mediated through the senses and the body. While it might go too far phenomenologically to identify what is manifested in the sensory experience of liturgy with God, the experience of being called to reception, welcome, and hospitality surely can be marked and described phenomenologically.

Things

We have already seen that Marion distinguishes saturated phenomena from phenomena that appear as objects and that he applies this especially to the eucharistic elements. Lacoste also argues that the language of the object is not appropriate for liturgy, but rather than identifying them as saturated phenomena he claims that we must always speak of the "things" of liturgy.[74] Again departing from Heidegger's analysis, Lacoste asserts that these things are neither simply "present" (*vorhanden*) nor are they "useful" (*zuhanden*); indeed, they are quite useless. He contends that in liturgy (in the large sense in which he employs the term as referring to any "being-before-God") there are neither subjects nor objects. The things of liturgy are "nonobjects in a pure state."[75] Before the Absolute, things are given to us and symbolize "beyond the world." They are not confined to the horizon of the world. Lacoste consequently suggests that "bread, wine, chalice, candles, icons" are primarily (maybe exclusively) signs or symbols and should be treated as such. In liturgy the body does not seek to possess or even to use; "things" are always more than themselves.[76] Our body's relation with these things is not one of grasping or holding, but a posture of reception. Indeed, he speaks of a liturgical reduction that "opens up a space in the world where appropriation loses its importance."[77] Although the discussion here is of voluntary poverty rather than of liturgy per se, he claims that such chosen poverty is a "pure example" of liturgy rather than derivative of it.[78]

This analysis, however, seems to conflate a much more varied and multiform experience of "things" in liturgy, if such an analysis becomes grounded in the corporeal and fully material experience of actual liturgical ("cultic") experience rather than a "symbolic" abstraction of any being before the Absolute. Not all "things" or implements of liturgy appear in the same way. For at least some of them, a tool analysis in terms of their use in a meaningful world in which we are engaged for particular purposes actually does seem quite illuminating of their "being" as it appears to us in liturgy.[79] The censor and the implements used for it, the knife for cutting the bread, the bowls in which the pieces are placed, altar cloths and so forth appear at least on some level as *zuhanden*, as part of a meaningful world in which things have their specific uses, although maybe not solely so. The fact that chalices and patens (and censors) were made from precious materials and quickly became decorated artistically, often with heavy symbolism,[80] indicates that they already signified toward something beyond their use as tools, but it did not erase the "tool-experience"—they were not venerated for themselves or contemplated as artistic objects, but actively employed within liturgical action. And even decorated objects remain fully material things.

Yet while Lacoste's suggestion about "holy things" may apply to some of the other things used in liturgy (although even there his emphasis on their "symbolic" nature seems rather too strong and disregards their materiality, which a phenomenological analysis does not erase), it is not an adequate phenomenological description of the eucharistic bread and wine. They are not treated or experienced merely as things, but our bodily posture toward and with them seems to imply more (at least in the Orthodox tradition; maybe other meanings would emerge for other Christian traditions). Phenomenologically speaking, the bread and wine of the Eucharist are experienced neither as things nor as objects—albeit certainly as "material" rather than purely symbolic or spiritual—but in some form as a "body" offered and received as gift.[81] The language of gift is obviously loaded phenomenologically, as it has heavily preoccupied phenomenological thinkers for decades, and not all of this discussion can be reviewed here. But maybe we can draw on at least some of it in order to reveal the phenomenological "nature" of the eucharistic gifts and their corporeal sense or implication more fully.[82]

What does it mean to speak of the eucharistic elements as gifts, as the liturgy indeed does—and does in terms of language of manifestation and revelation?[83] What ought to be clear up front is that phenomenology makes no metaphysical or ontological claims about what the eucharistic body "is"; language of substance and accidents or of a correspondence between the material of the bread to the sacrificed body of Christ cannot be sustained phenomenologically and are not really experienced, even when they are "believed." All such inquiries about correspondence and verification of substances must be bracketed phenomenologically. That does not imply, however, that there can be no reflection at all on the manifestation or appearance of these elements within the liturgical experience. It is the "metaphysical" or "scientific" parameters that are set aside in order for the experience of what is manifested to appear more fully and more clearly. How are these "gifts" manifested in the experience of the liturgy?

The first thing one might say is that the Eucharist is manifested corporeally, by our movements, actions, gestures, and bodily responses to it. Indeed, the entire eucharistic liturgy is spatial, corporeal, and sensory: we are told to "lift up our hearts" and we "lift" our eyes to the elevated gifts, we walk up to the sanctuary, we fold our arms over our chests, we open our mouths to receive them. It is a fully sensory, fully corporeal, and often "affective" experience of "really" experienced food and drink fully given. The chalice has weight and sheen, the liquid has color and flavor, the bread has texture and volume. While these certainly can be "measured" that entirely misses our very real experiences of them as physical elements. Their "spiritual" significance is not something added artificially "on top" of the scientifically measured features, but is inextricable from their very physicality. They mean in and through their physical experience; it is the very action of consuming *this* bread, drinking *this* wine, in *this* space and at *this* time that has significance and meaning as Eucharist, not something separable from these. Again, the "modern" distinctions between "objective" and "subjective" make no sense here: It is not that bread and wine "objectively" turn into body and blood of Christ by changing into a different "substance" that could be measured in scientific terms, nor is this "merely" a "subjective" experience of my mind or emotions, which "interpret" the bread and wine "as" something other. Rather, the experience is both of the "real" or "effective" (in Marion's sense), which is at the same time the concrete and particular within this specific experience, not some abstract observation of what is "out there." Eucharist signifies meaningfully within a liturgical world where incarnation (as embodiment) "happens." This also means that a discussion of Eucharist—or of sacramentality more broadly—should never be separated from its liturgical moorings. Eucharist only means within (or as an extension of) liturgy as communal, corporate, and corporeal experience.

The elements of the Eucharist are thus also first of all physical and material items. The bread is handled and placed, cut and held up, distributed and eaten. Many people respond bodily to certain words or proclamations in the eucharistic liturgy through bowing, prostrating, or crossing themselves. Although the corporeal responses highlight certain moments as especially important, the experience of Eucharist is distended—it does not occur just in a single moment or instant. The most significant "movement" of bodies occurs in the communal participation in the distribution of the eucharistic gifts. We touch and bend our bodies when we receive communion, and as we taste, swallow, and digest, the gifts are incorporated into our bodies. Indeed, the rules of preparation for communion that enjoin fasting from midnight until the reception of communion indicate that somehow our bodies must be prepared to incorporate this other "body" into it. The language about it speaks of it both in terms of food and in terms of fire (cf. the prayers connected to communion in which consuming Eucharist is linked to a fear of being consumed). The attitudes of veneration toward the bread, at certain moments within the liturgical process (such as the entry or the *epiklēsis*) and during the liturgy as a whole, indicate that these elements mean or signify in a way that is neither how we treat objects (as *vorhanden*) nor how we use tools (as *zuhanden*), but closer to how we handle something very precious or highly valuable (and yet not entirely, because we do not usually eat precious things and they tend to be more singular, while Eucharist is constantly repeated).

The most striking and probably most important part of the experience of the Eucharist is that it is eaten, that it is taken into our bodies. There would not be much point to the celebration of the Eucharist, to the consecration of the gifts, if they were not consumed (and, indeed, in the Orthodox tradition anything left in the cup does have to be consumed; it is not "reserved" for a future purpose).[84] And the attitude toward the bread, the care not to allow crumbs to fall on the floor or not to permit anything from the cup to be spilled, indicates the need for its consumption as the right "purpose" of the gifts. Although there are certainly Orthodox communities—and have been for centuries—where not many people approach the chalice for communion, this existential "fact" does not deny that everything about the eucharistic liturgy implies that the primary goal for the gifts is not veneration or adoration but consumption. The body that is consumed enters our bodies, becomes mingled with our body. The only way in which the "body of Christ" remains phenomenologically accessible after its consumption is in *our* bodies and as indistinguishable from them, fully consumed into them.

The prayers before, during, and after communion draw explicit connections between consuming the body of Christ and its effects on the human body that has eaten it. This is also true within the eucharistic liturgy itself, where Christ's "body broken for us" and offered "on behalf of all and for all" is liturgically linked to the request for the healing and safety of bodies: "Do Thou Thyself, O Master, distribute these Gifts here offered, unto all of us for good, according to the individual need of each, sail with those who sail, travel with those who travel by land and by air; heal the sick, O Thou Who art the physician of our souls and bodies." The eucharistic elements are offered as gifts for our bodies in travel, sickness, and other needs. Yet, in becoming assimilated to our bodies, one might suggest that liturgically our bodies begin to function in what may well be called a "eucharistic" fashion. Our bodies in some way come to embody the hospitality and orientation of the liturgical space and time, which is inscribed upon them through the movements, postures, and gestures of our bodies within them and marked by them. It exposes our bodies to each other and especially to the suffering other, while also expressing our own very real need and desire for healing. And such healing maybe begins precisely in letting go of our need to hide ourselves, protect ourselves, or secure our own benefits, by getting us out of our intense self-preoccupation and instead opening us up to concern for the other. The vulnerable postures of the body that we practice in liturgy enable and teach humbler conditions of the "soul," in which we do not stand upright in self-righteous pride but bent before and with the other in care and compassion.

5

AFFECTIVITY

The late-fourth-century preacher Proclus of Constantinople says in a homily on the nativity of Christ:

Beautiful is the lyre of the psalms,
inspired by God is the cither of the Spirit,
pleasant and terrifying is the song of prophecy.
Psalmody is always beneficial,
for through its melody it puts suffering to sleep.
For what the sickle is to thorns,
such also is a psalm to pain.
For while a psalm is sung,
it cuts away feelings of despondency,
it roots out pains,
it erases sorrows,
it lulls wailings to sleep,
it deals with cares,
it soothes those in pain,
it causes sinners to repent,
it awakens unto piety,
it causes people to inhabit deserts,
it chastens those in cities,
it establishes monasteries,
it encourages virginity,
it teaches gentleness,

it proclaims love as commandment,
it calls love for the poor happy.[1]

The feast eases sorrows or removes despondency; it inspires to love, repentance, and gentleness. He also suggests that feasting

causes you to forget pain.
It puts cares to sleep,
it cultivates joy,
it causes rejoicing,
it is a time for prayer,
a harvest for the poor,
an adornment for churches,
a time of rejoicing for cities,
shipwreck to enmity,
dawn of friendship,
heaven on earth.

Clearly, Proclus thought of liturgy as having a powerful effect on our emotions and affect.[2] Can liturgy still inspire such strong emotions and shape our dispositions in such fundamental ways? Are moods and emotions even an appropriate topic for liturgy?

Some liturgical texts can give the impression that emotions or feelings are a bad thing, to be suppressed or eradicated. Especially when speaking of the ascetic saints, the liturgical texts display some of the ambivalence about the body or the passions that asceticism often features.[3] The troparia for several saints speak of their triumph over the body or the passions and applaud their focus on the soul or on pure contemplation (*theoria*). For example, it is claimed of St. Theodore during the first week of Lent: "Thou hast slain the passions and shaken off the desires of the flesh, O victorious martyr."[4] John Climacus is lauded as having "burnt up the thorns of the passions" or having "quenched all the passions" with his ascetic struggles.[5] Similarly, Mary of Egypt is said to have "tamed the savagery of the passions" through her ascetic way of life and "broken the rebelliousness of the flesh."[6] Besides the liturgies for the commemorations of ascetic saints, much of the liturgy of Lent as a whole speaks of a domination or mastery over the passions. Especially the Great Canon of St. Andrew of Crete is full of language about the passions, which are usually portrayed negatively in the canon. It prays repeatedly "that I may escape the darkening of the passions" (here identified as seeking for pleasure) or asks God to "deliver us from degrading passions."[7] At times steadfastness in "suffering" (*pathei*) is almost indistinguishable from steadfastness against the "passions" (*pathei*). This is particularly true when speaking of Christ who "suffers his passion, delivering me from passions" (three uses of the same word in Greek).[8]

Yet at the same time there is plenty of emotion and even "pathos" (maybe in a different sense) in the liturgical experience. Both the liturgy itself, as well as patristic homilists, point to this dimension, especially in the experiences of contrition—often expressed by tears—and that of joy.[9] Penitential practices are frequently accompanied by a call to sorrow or even a desire for tears. For example, the Great Canon begins: "Where shall I begin to lament the deeds of my wretched life?" and continues with frequent references to tears or lamentation, including the request to "wash me clean in the waters of my tears."[10] Often these are made by pointing to examples in the biblical texts: "Like the robber I cry, 'Remember me!' Like Peter I weep bitterly, 'Release me, O Savior!' I croak like the publican; I weep like the harlot. Accept my lamentation as once the Canaanite woman . . . repenting with fear and crying with love." Indeed, often the liturgy explicitly asks: "Grant me tears of repentance!" and "Through Thy compassion grant me tears of compunction" (repeated during the Canon and at other times in the liturgies in various forms multiple times). Or it is affirmed: "No tears, no repentance have I, no compunction. But as God, O Savior, grant me these." In fact, tears are often conceived as the medicine or balm for the illness of sin, because tears are a sign of repentance and hence of healing, as in the Great Canon: "Heal, O Savior, the corruption of my debased soul, O only Physician. Apply the compress to me, and the oil and wine—works of repentance, compunction and tears."[11] The expression of emotion therefore can serve as a way to make "real" the experience of a particular occasion, to appropriate it for oneself on a more personal level, and to become the vehicle for the effect of liturgy on us, even a specifically hoped for "effect" like healing. Similarly, festal celebrations are often said to be marked by joy and joy is described as the appropriate and expected response, as in the quote from Proclus above. Here liturgy is clearly assumed both to evoke feelings and to soothe them. Liturgy and psalmody (the language of most of liturgy) is seen to be "beneficial" in the ways in which it deals with emotions.[12]

The use of ascetic examples within the liturgy, such as Mary of Egypt, John Climacus, Gregory Palamas, and the many other saints commemorated on different occasions, is particularly interesting in this respect, as they serve as a mimetic device for our own behavior and the liturgical texts explicitly treat them as such.[13] Already Aristotle argued that pathos can function productively in mimetic appropriation. Ricoeur's description of the world opened by narrative in three-fold mimesis draws on Aristotle and functions in similar ways. Yet, Ricoeur does not stress the element of pathos as strongly as Aristotle does. For Aristotle, the mimetic function of theater enables us to deal with our passions of "fear" and "pity" through the catharsis we experience in our identification with the characters in a tragedy.[14] At the same time, such cathartic identification not only eases the passions and allows us to grapple with them, but it teaches us how to live better lives and how to transform our character. Mimetic performance thus always has a strong ethical element for Aristotle; it teaches us *phronesis* (practical wisdom) through our emulation of its admirable characters and our identification with them through the plot. Liturgy may well be said to present similar admirable characters who we can emulate for the acquiring of wisdom.

As we have already seen, mimesis is a frequent theme in liturgical theology. Anderson mentions "the expression and catharsis of feelings" as one of the functions of ritual.[15] Such mimesis is rarely put in terms of affect, however, and there is not much sustained reflection on the concrete emotions involved in worship. In fact, although Guardini acknowledges that emotion in liturgy is "instructive" and "elaborate," he argues: "The liturgy as a whole is not favorable to exuberance of feeling. Emotion glows in its depths, but it smolders merely, like the fiery heart of the volcano, whose summit stands out clear and serene against the quiet sky. The liturgy *is* emotion, but it is emotion under the strictest control."[16] Saliers similarly stresses that emotion in liturgy is important, but should not be disorderly: "Our emotions and deep affections are necessarily involved because a living symbol brings together the other and the self in a crucible of ordered ambiguity in our experience. The ambiguity is not confusion or disorder; rather, it is richness or experienced meaning that holds opposites in tension: dying to self and yet alive to God, renunciation yet fullness of being, remaining in this world yet citizens of another, and so on."[17] Thus, although the presence of emotion is acknowledged, there seems to be some hesitation over its expression that has to be controlled or ordered.

Others mention emotions, especially joy, more favorably. For example, Morrill says: "Assembling to hear the word requires a genuine submission to the Gospel, real faith trusting in God amid the full range of our human strengths and weaknesses, joys and sorrows, virtues and sins."[18] Wainwright comments on the Eucharist as involving joy.[19] Senn points to the joy associated with feasting: "In a genuine festival, people show a lack of restraint, a joyful abandon, that they would not display in their everyday lives."[20] Andrew Mellas goes further in his analysis of the affect evoked by the Great Canon to argue that such emotions have liturgical significance: "Emotions were not simply constructed within a social and cultural milieu, but within a liturgical event. Emotions became imbued with a theological dimension—which presented a mystical unity of the human race—and were dramatized as participating in the grace of the Incarnation and a communion of saints."[21] Ritual creates "an affective and mystical space" where emotions and their "somatic markers" are shaped such that they enable an "encounter with the divine."[22]

Sometimes awe and reverence are mentioned as a result of liturgical participation: "The union of love between Christ and the church remains pure gift; it yields a humble awe and reverence and joy within the Body's gathering, not a self-focused attention on worthiness, communal or individual."[23] Flanagan, however, bemoans the fact that "certain terms have vanished from the liturgical vocabulary" and points to reverence as a prime example. He thinks that its elements of "deference and restraint" are "at odds with contemporary liberal theological assumptions giving power to the marginal." In contrast: "Reverence conveys a sense of awe, of being before something greater than the self. It acts as a defence against the risk of self-glorification in the liturgical act by imposing a sense of humility on the actor."[24] It is not clear, however, that Flanagan (or others) think of awe or reverence as emotion or as connected to affect in any explicit sense.

There is somewhat more extensive discussion of how liturgy shapes our dispositions. Janowiak speaks of identity as an "interior disposition" that is also "bodily in expression."[25] As noted already, Saliers draws explicitly ethical implications from the formation of affect and virtue in liturgy: "The relations between liturgy and ethics are most adequately formulated by specifying how certain affections and virtues are formed and expressed in the modalities of communal prayer and ritual action. These modalities of prayer enter into the formation of the self in community."[26] Mitchell similarly argues: "Liturgy leads us to the brink of chaos in order to tutor our desire, to reverse its triumphalism and megalomania."[27] Hughes also stresses the liminal nature of the liturgical event. Those responsible for worship must be aware "that the work in which they are engaged is a 'boundary' or liminal' (threshold) event; that it takes place at a kind of virtual 'edge' of what we can manage conceptually and emotionally."[28]

Chauvet says even more explicitly than Mitchell that liturgy cultivates desire: "It is desiring human beings as such who bare themselves to the divinity. It is the very drama of their ex-sistence that they present to God." This presenting oneself to God results in a moral conversion of desire: "At least, Christian prayer orients believers in this direction, a pedagogy aimed at conversion of desire passing little by little from the simple asking of needed objects . . . to the request for God as such." He continues: "Liturgical rituality is thus the symbolic expression of the human in its total corporality and as a being of desire. By revealing in full view of the divine Other the whole human being as a body of nature and culture, of history and desire, it 'acts out' before the Other the existential anguish of this singular entity which, always in quest of the lost object that would satisfy its desire, still can experience only the non-satisfaction of what it aspires to and which thus learns to see there, painfully, a longing for the other (named 'God' by religions) that expresses itself in its needs."[29] Yet, the transformation liturgy is taken to effect in our dispositions and desires is not necessarily explicitly linked to affect in the theological literature. Maybe phenomenology can add a dimension here that has not yet been examined in much detail.

Affectivity, Attunement, and Emotions of the Heart

Although the emphasis on emotion and affect is strongest in the French phenomenologists, their interpretations often draw on Heidegger's account of affectivity in *Being and Time*.[30] For Heidegger, affectivity (*Befindlichkeit*) is a fundamental ontological structure of human existence, equiprimordial with understanding and discourse (*Rede*).[31] It is expressed ontically by *Stimmungen*, translated as "moods" or "tonalities." The latter translation tries to capture the connotation of the German that connects it with music, with the idea of being "attuned" to something. (Such musical attunement is obviously particularly apt for liturgical "tonalities.") The German *Befindlichkeit* refers to how one "is" or "feels oneself" and etymologically evokes something like how (or the state in which) one "finds" oneself.[32] Heidegger argues that we are always in the world already in particular dispositions, attuned to our facticity in particular ways. We find ourselves "thrown" into the world and opened onto it via the "how" of our being there. Moods

(*Stimmungen*) come over us, they are not always consciously or deliberately created; we experience them as both ours and on some level imposed on us. Furthermore, *Befindlichkeit* points to the ways in which the world and its environment always already concern us. It hence designates our deep involvement with and in the world. *Befindlichkeit* is an ontological structure for Heidegger, inasmuch as it is a foundational way of being in the world that characterizes our existence as such, rather than a particular mood experienced at some instance or in some circumstance or other. (One might say that *Befindlichkeit* communicates the truth "that" we are always in a "how" but not the specific "this" of this how.)

In *Being and Time*, Heidegger discusses fear (*Furcht*, not *Angst*) as one of the modes of *Befindlichkeit* (§30). It shows a particular being as threatened and fearful. Fear and its various modifications are one of the ways in which we can find (or experience) ourselves within the world; they are existential possibilities of Dasein's essential attunement to the world. Later he will call *Angst* (fear in the sense of anxiety or dread) a *Grundbefindlichkeit*, more fundamental or foundational than fear (§40). Anxiety confronts us with ourselves at the deepest existential level because it is not a fear of some specific danger but rather a dread concerning our very being itself and shows how we are essentially oriented toward death. It deeply unsettles us, reveals to us the ways in which we are not at home in the world, and thereby opens us to our existential possibilities and enables us to grasp them. *Befindlichkeit* is grounded in throwness (*Geworfenheit*) and thus for Heidegger connected to our having-been (*Gewesenheit*), that is, the temporal ecstasis of the experienced past (§68b).

Lacoste suggests that there might be several dimensions of affectivity (which, in line with the French translations of *Sein und Zeit*, he uses to render *Befindlichkeit*) in the liturgical experience, but identifies joy and peace, as well as boredom and fatigue in a different sense, as the most dominant.[33] The line between affectivity as "emotion" (or even specific emotions or moods such as joy) and affectivity as the underlying existential dispositionality of *Befindlichkeit* is not always clear here. He returns to the topic of affectivity also in other places, in one case suggesting that liturgy might allow for a kind of co-affectivity or coaffection (*Mitbefindlichkeit*). In fact, liturgy always assumes reconciliation and communion in Lacoste's view.[34] Yet, he also contends that liturgy transcends our senses or affects. The "secret of the liturgy" does not reside in some "shared sensibility" but rather in the participation in a "drama."[35] Because liturgy is primarily about transcending or transgressing being-in-the-world for Lacoste, he thinks that any sensibility in liturgy always suffers from ambiguity. He admits that there are liturgical "emotions": "To be at peace with the Other, to rejoice that he is there, and (if need be) to share his suffering with him: there is no lack of affective tonalities that would witness a 'with' lived as communion."[36] But he thinks of the sensibility of liturgy as speaking mostly of "a destiny that goes beyond the world. . . . And when the 'with' takes, liturgically, the shape of being-at-peace or of shared joy and the like, we then have a presentiment of a use of the ego, of affection, and so forth that lives in advance of an eschatological destiny and signifies here and now an order of experience that is no longer that of the world, an order of manifestation that exceeds all being-in-the-world."[37] Being together in liturgy really has no "particular experiential content" and the sensibility of which we have a "presentiment" in liturgy "transgresses the everyday rules of appearing."[38] True *Mitbefindlichkeit* hence is deferred to the eschatological future.[39] In a more recent essay on "sacramental intuition" he argues that liturgy (here designating real sacramental practice and not only being-before-God in a general sense) has its own "inalienable *Befindlichkeit*," although he does not tell us in what this might consist or analyze it any further.[40]

Although Steinbock draws primarily on Husserl's rather than on Heidegger's analysis, his investigation into the essential structures of what he calls "moral emotions" or emotions "of the heart" parallels Heidegger's claim about the structural nature of *Befindlichkeit*.[41] The phenomenological analysis can uncover the fundamental nature of these "emotions" of the heart, such as pride, shame, guilt, repentance, hope, despair, trust, love, and humility, under three categories (emotions of self-givenness, of possibility, and of otherness). In pride, shame, and guilt I am given to myself in a particular way. He also notes that shame and guilt are rooted in pride. Repentance, hope, and despair open new possibilities to the self and prod us to transformation. Trust, love, and humility directly engage us with others and thus open an interpersonal dimension. Steinbock is particularly interested in the cognitive structures of these emotions and argues that they have their own kinds of evidence. (He explicitly excludes moods like boredom or anxiety and distinguishes moral emotions from affects.[42])

Repentance is of particular interest here for our purposes. Steinbock claims that "shame and guilt acquire their deeper significance not simply as independent experiences unto themselves, but elicit the overall movement of repentance."[43] He argues that repentance liberates us "from fixed meanings of ourselves and our past deed as one could accomplish such a deed" and thus enables us to reconceive ourselves and engage in new interpersonal relations. It leads to a "revolution of the heart" and must be accompanied by repentant praxis, including a divestment of self and "non-attachment to self."[44] Steinbock admits that some of the moral emotions he has described might function differently in other cultural or religious traditions (for example, Buddhist rather than Abrahamic), but that the phenomenological analysis is also not simply arbitrary, but clarifies "the *essential structures* of these experiences" and points to the essential features of the actions that express them in our living in the world.[45] Steinbock also stresses—in a way Heidegger does not—the intersubjective dimension of these moral emotions. They operate in "the irreducible interpersonal dimension of experience" and the "moral tenor" of such an emotion is "weighed according to how it opens up or closes down the interpersonal nexus."[46] Loving and humility especially are fundamental experiences for him and are able to counter pride. He points to the relationship of humility with religious experience, but notes that it should not be limited to religion.[47]

Pathos and Emotions

There are many different kinds of emotions at work in liturgy and some of them are mentioned explicitly by the liturgical texts. For example, the homilies or the liturgy for Holy Friday frequently refer to fear, those for Holy Saturday to awe, those for Pascha to abundant joy, and so forth. Often the "mood" appropriate for a particular occasion is conveyed by the music.[48] Certain tones or "modes" were thought more fitting for "sad" occasions, while others are considered to be celebratory.[49] Music can "make or break" a liturgy. Music—obviously not just liturgical music—has the possibility of "transporting" us out of ourselves in some way, it not only "sets" a mood, but has the potential for deeply affecting our emotions.[50] Thus the emotional imagination is shaped by the music that is heard and experienced in a particular service. In this respect it is also significant that we have to make and become the music, as the music in an Orthodox liturgy is produced entirely by human voices, whether in Greek plainchant, Carpathorussian unison, or high Russian harmony.

It is therefore not true that liturgy bans all forms of pathos or condemns emotions in blanket fashion as distracting or even evil. Certain emotions and their physical expression seem not only appropriate for liturgy, but are explicitly enjoined upon us by the liturgical texts. Tears of repentance and grief over sin are consistently applauded or even set up as an example. Joy is endorsed as a perfectly appropriate expression of celebration. On Pascha we are even invited to "feast sumptuously" although admittedly several homilists through the centuries also warn against excessive feasting leading to drunkenness and other inappropriate behaviors.[51] This tension between sorrow and joy—often combined in the same experience as in the solemn joy of the first week of Lent—embodies the tension of liturgical temporality between fasting and feasting, conveys its experience through and in our affectivity. The liturgical emotions thus inscribe the directedness and orientation of liturgy not just upon the body, but within the very experience of the flesh, not only in its sensory but also in its affective dimensions.

In either case, such emotions are different from the "passions," which we are consistently counseled to flee or to work at subduing. In the liturgical texts, such passions are almost always associated with destructive, indulgent, and selfish desires. False pathos refers to emotion and desires that govern and overwhelm us in ways that lead us to focus only on ourselves and to do so in the most damaging ways possible. Such self-indulgence is injurious to the body and the "soul" (to employ the liturgical language) because it refuses to be taught, trained, or healed by succumbing to excessive and harmful desires. These passions will lead to further illness of soul, just as indulging in too much and the wrong kind of food leads to illness of body. Instead, the pedagogy or medicine of liturgical affectivity serves to train and discipline the body and soul in the right way, to teach it appropriate pathos that will lead to contrition, repentance, change, and holiness of life.

At the same time, liturgy does not simply reject such more destructive pathos out of hand in simplistic fashion. Rather, it helps us to express and redirect our emotion in healthier ways and to train our pathos in a new manner. The sadness and joy counseled and expressed within liturgy are not simply "other" emotions than these debilitating passions, but they are emotions that will help train our affective faculties to cope with emotions in healthy ways and habituate ourselves to feeling and expressing them consistently. This is presumably one of the reasons why the call for tears of repentance is so often repeated. If we felt such emotion automatically and easily, we would not need to be told this so frequently. Even the rhetorical excess of the statements that affirm that "I have sinned more than anyone" or that "there is no worse sinner than I am," serves to reinforce the same message: it is not about a literal measurement of my sins as exceeding those of others, but about an emphatic statement that moves us to identification with, incorporation of, and personal expression of the sentiment. We are to feel ourselves contrite and the excessive language tries to ensure we do so (and also points to the fact that it is not automatic, that very often we do not manage this). Part of this training also comes from the fact that these emotions are experienced in community, something we will examine more fully in the next chapter. And this is true not only of the sorrow that leads to contrition, but also of the joy and exuberance related to feasting: It is difficult—albeit obviously not impossible—not to feel joy when everyone around us is rejoicing and when we have associated this particular occasion with festal joy for many years.

Thus, the affect evoked during liturgy clearly is supposed to act on the participants and to open and even transform them. This is also obvious in the practices of fasting. The patristic (and contemporary) homilists frequently remind their audiences that fasting is not primarily about abstaining from food, but about training the emotions.[52] Even the liturgy itself reinforces this: "Let us observe a fast acceptable and pleasing to the Lord. True fasting is to put away all evil, to control the tongue, to forbear from anger, to abstain from lust, slander, falsehood and perjury. If we renounce these things, then is our fasting true and acceptable to God."[53] Furthermore, the affective emotions of sorrow and awe are conveyed (maybe to some extent even induced) by the liturgical bodily postures of humility and veneration. The structure and orientation of the time and space of liturgy similarly provides a framework for such affects. By training our bodies through gestures and postures to move in certain ways we are more open to experiencing the kind of affectivity liturgy tries to produce in us.

Liturgy hence does not train us to eliminate emotions, but to evoke a different kind of affectivity. Sorrow is indeed a kind of pathos; it is a "suffering" that is supposed to induce a particular predisposition (or mood or attunement), namely that of contrition (coupled with or resulting in humility). This is particularly striking when our "bad" passions are contrasted and connected to Christ's Passion on our behalf, for example when the Great Canon speaks of "routing the passions of the night," so that I may see the "glorious Passion of Christ." Liturgy, then, emerges as a way to guide or direct pathos, to deal with the passions appropriately. Indeed, one might say that the state of *apatheia* (passionlessness), often advocated by the ascetic tradition, does not mean that one will no longer display any sort of emotion. It is not apathy or indifference. A more phenomenological reading of the passions permits us to interpret *apatheia* as focused dedication or single-minded attention, hence as a kind of openness or even receptivity, not a closure. The passions of pride and self-indulgence close us in on ourselves and shut us off from hearing the call addressed to us in liturgy. Liturgy consequently requires continual effort of turning away from distracting thoughts and focusing on the movements of the liturgical prayer.

And these movements are often corporeal ones: Affect is guided by our bodily postures, encouraged by physical gestures, ordered through the orientation given to our movements. The awe or reverence of worship is enabled and reinforced through bodily postures and gestures of humility, such as bowing and veneration. Such affect is also supported through the sensory experience of the smell of incense and the visual experience of beauty or abundance. The affect of sadness and contrition over wrongdoing is enabled and encouraged through bodily postures and gestures that express guilt or admission of failure, such as prostration. They receive sensory support through the lighting of candles, the ephemeral quality of their flickering light. The interpersonal dispositions of hospitality or peace are expressed and formed physically through embrace and the sharing in the same food and drink or other such gestures that involve concrete touch. The emotions of joy or exuberance are reinforced, shaped, and made possible through celebratory music, festive foods, lavish decoration, and similar elements. Affect is always instantiated in sensory and corporeal ways and made possible through them.

One might also suggest that the emotions liturgy portrays and evokes are in some ways the most primordial ones, but maybe also the ones most difficult to express. The sadness of sorrow is linked to deeper "moral" emotions (to use Steinbock's language) of pride, shame, guilt, and even anxiety or dread (in Heidegger's sense). In this respect it is telling that the liturgy for the Orthodox funeral service confronts the physical reality of death starkly rather than immediately consoling us with a hope for heaven or an afterlife. The troparia sung at the end of the funeral service are quite graphic about the dead person having been "cut down like grass," now being "covered with earth," and soon to be "consumed by worms in darkness." The organs of the body are now "idle" and "the beauty of the face has turned to dust and death has withered up the flower of youth." There is prayer for "rest" but no promise of resurrection (at least in this context).[54]

Instead of mollifying our fear of and grief over death (our own or that of a loved one) or immediately folding it into a vision of eternity, liturgy provides a language for acknowledging these emotions, confronting them honestly, and to some extent enables us to cope with them precisely by expressing them and by doing so in a ritual fashion surrounded by a consoling community who grieves with us.[55]

Moods and Dispositions

Expressing particular emotions creates and evokes certain moods and forms corresponding dispositions. As we have already seen, various aspects and occasions of the liturgical year convey different moods, often not just one mood but a complex set of moods that are in creative tension with each other, such as the combination of "joy" and "somberness" in the services of Great Lent. Moods thus work together in complicated ways. Cuneo points this out in his analysis of liturgical immersion by commenting on the way in which content and presentation can be "colored" in diametrically opposite ways: "For example, in the rite of the burial of Jesus, the content of the narrative calls for something like sorrow. Its musical presentation, by contrast, calls for that difficult-to-describe emotional reaction characteristic of being in the presence of something of great beauty. When combined, the reenactment calls for something like that state of sorrow in which we are moved by beauty" in such a way that these disparate elements "are fused in one's experience."[56] The question of how "beauty" functions to create mood is an especially complicated one. Many people experience Orthodox liturgy as beautiful, but it is hard to tell whether this is a structural or a purely empirical aspect of the experience, as it depends to a large extent on musical preferences and subjective responses to visual and other stimuli. One might at least say that whatever beauty is experienced through the performance of the services contributes to a mood of awe and reverence because these are explicitly evoked any number of times.[57] And it is certainly clear that the careful preparation, deliberate actions, lavish decoration, elaborate musical settings, and the various other aspects of the experience all contribute to these solemn moods, whether the solemnity is "negative" (sorrow) or "positive" (joy or beauty) or a combination thereof.

Furthermore, although this mood is "sensed" by the participant in liturgy, it is sensed as created by the liturgical occasion and its elements (including the music and the lighting). It is therefore not simply about the personal mood (frustration, anger, expectation, elation, or others) with which one might come into liturgy, but also about the mood that is conveyed within it and that one can choose to enter or try to bar from affecting oneself. We can give ourselves up to the mood of the liturgy, immerse ourselves in it, respond to it, or we can keep our distance, guard ourselves, and dwell on our own private thoughts and feelings. Both (and any mix of them) always remain possibilities of "attunement." Beyond specific moods, one can say more fundamentally that the experience of liturgy is never "neutral," but always characterized by an essential "atmosphere" that is sensed on multiple levels, even if the specifics of the atmosphere shift and its "sensing" is different for different participants and for different occasions. It is thus crucial to remind ourselves that the phenomenological analysis is not about the empirical emotion a particular person feels on a certain liturgical occasion, but rather about the very structure of affectivity that liturgy displays.

It might be worth distinguishing here between particular emotions (or even broader moods) and underlying dispositions or attitudes. We have already briefly pointed to the emotions of sadness, guilt, shame, sorrow, and others, all associated in some form with the attitude of contrition. One might say, in fact, that contrition is the underlying, deeper affectivity that some of these emotions express, maybe in a manner parallel to how angst or dread underlies fear in Heidegger's analysis. Feelings of guilt, shame, inadequacy, or failure, which all haunt us, are expressed in the fundamental mood of contrition. Similarly, one might say that joy and other celebratory emotions are linked to the "mood" or attunement of "awe." The moral posture of contrition, and the commitment to metanoia (turning around) to which it leads, is a deeper phenomenological experience than the specific emotions of shame or guilt and this posture is to some extent made possible by such feelings. The experience of realizing that one has hurt or harmed someone in a specific situation is qualitatively different from the deeper existential experience of inadequacy or failure that can result from it.

Something similar might be said of a momentary feeling of pity for someone and a deeper disposition of compassion. Liturgy teaches not just "apathy" (in the qualified sense discussed above), but also "empathy." The descriptions of Adam and Eve, the "publican" and the Pharisee, Zacchaeus and the prodigal son, as well as the many other "characters" of liturgical narratives not only invite us to imitation, but maybe above all teach us compassion. In entering into the narrative liturgical world opened by the hymnography, we are moved to identify empathically with their grief, their fear, their anxiety, their frustrations, but also their hope, their joy, their gratitude. The rhetorical magnification of the emotion of the biblical characters within the liturgical setting enables us to sense their distress and joy and to be moved by their plight.[58] Such narrative identification not only helps us to express our own versions of such emotions or to articulate them more fully, but it also teaches us to empathize with the characters and thereby with others experiencing such pathos in their lives. We will come back to this imitative function in a moment, but can at least say so far that liturgy also seeks to teach us the important (and active) disposition of compassion with others, the pathos that goes out to others.

This is also evident by the fact that the liturgy constantly refers to God as the lover of humanity,[59] as the one who is merciful and compassionate toward us. We plead for God's mercy more than for anything else in liturgy; the phrase "Lord, have mercy" is reiterated more than any other request. God is frequently referred to as compassionate or the divine compassion invoked or requested (as in some of the passages cited in the opening of the chapter). The gestures and actions of liturgy—our bowing, kneeling, prostrating, and offering of candles and bread—similarly signify our imploring for mercy. The attitude of contrition that permeates so much of the liturgical experience itself also functions as a call for compassion. Yet we have also noted—and will explore in more detail in the next chapter—that such attitudes and postures are not singular or individual, but that we engage in them together. We do not just call for mercy for ourselves, but always for all of us. We express the shared recognition that we all stand in need of mercy. Liturgy thus structurally fosters compassion—not just requested but exercised—by evoking it in community, by recognizing our own failures in conjunction with those who have gone before us and those prostrating besides us. We are exhorted to forgive and embrace each other, by both the words and the actions of liturgy. We are to be compassionate as our "heavenly Father is compassionate" (Luke 6:36). It may not be incidental that the Beatitudes are sung as the third antiphon at every eucharistic liturgy, which bless the meek, the pure in heart, the merciful, and those who are suffering.

While the particular emotions of boredom or joy or sadness or even guilt characterize the specific experience of liturgy at a concrete moment,

the "moods" (or "attunements") of contrition, awe, and compassion designate the fundamental phenomenological liturgical attitude of openness to
each other. This attitude or disposition is concretely expressed in corporeal
postures (as examined in the previous two chapters) and characterized by
specific emotions (as examined in this chapter), but can also be described
as a more fundamental or more primordial shared experience. There is no
access to these dispositions without the concrete corporeal and affective
dimensions, but they are not simply reducible to them. We might say,
then, that liturgy is more fundamentally about contrition than it is about
inducing guilt, more fundamentally about cultivating an attitude of awe or
gratitude than it is about a specific feeling of admiration or even rejoicing,
more fundamentally about compassion than about moments of pity, but
these more fundamental dispositions form the basis for and enable the
particular emotions or moods.

In liturgy, we are consequently invited to expose our deepest insecuri-
ties, to admit that we are flawed and that we often fail, to recognize the
ways in which our inadvertent and deliberate failures have hurt and
wounded others. We are given words and examples for expressing such
emotions and for grappling with the harm we have inflicted on others.
Liturgy allows us to bring our pain and despair, as well as our faults and
failures, to articulate them honestly and to grapple with the consequences
of our actions. It gives us the language for expressing the most fundamental fears of our existence—our fears of failure, insufficiency, inadequacy,
and abandonment. Liturgy recognizes the ways in which despair can consume us. Yet it also recognizes the ways in which even small mistakes can
cause damage to others in ways that make us guilty or ashamed even when
we did not intend to cause such harm. And it certainly points to the more
explicit and deliberate ways in which we intentionally hurt others. It thus
acknowledges the slippery line between deliberate fault and inadvertent
failure linked to human finitude. (In fact, these are constantly conflated in
the liturgical texts, as we have seen in some of the citations from the Lenten
liturgies.)

But liturgy also directs us to the other, opens us out to each other,
teaches us to ask for and accept forgiveness, models compassion with others.
The fact that we say the words together, prostrate together, expose ourselves together—and that we do so modeled on centuries of examples—
enables us to see our despair and failure as no purely private affair but as
part of the larger human condition. Liturgy acknowledges (or helps us to

acknowledge) that while our failures can feel extraordinary and over-whelming, they are in many ways very ordinary—and yet able to do much harm. It does not trivialize our failures but sets them in the context of a deeper existential condition shared with others, with even the greatest of saints. Liturgical affectivity appropriates and instantiates the exposure of the body via a disclosure of our deepest selves in our emotions and gestures of contrition and compassion.

At the same time, this makes clear that body and affectivity (or flesh) are not separate, but always work together. Emotions, affects, and even dis-positions are always experienced across and via the body and expressed through and by it. These elements are always already intimately connected, separated only in thought or description, not in experience. Not just sen-sory impressions but emotions are clearly felt in and through the body not just some incorporeal flesh. And the dispositions of contrition, awe, grati-tude, or compassion are felt and cultivated through all the corporeal and affective aspects we have explored: the senses, emotions, postures, gestures, movements, and so forth. The vulnerability exemplified by liturgy is marked in the body and the flesh together, expressed via the exposure or disclosure of our supplicating bodies just as much as via the affective dis-positions of shame or admission of failure. The frequent reference to tears in the liturgical texts illustrates this as well: Tears are an emotive and affec-tive expression par excellence and yet a visible, corporeal phenomenon produced by our bodies.

There is then a twofold dimension to liturgical affectivity: On the one hand, it acknowledges our finitude and frailty and gives them room for expression in the various demonstrations of guilt, sorrow, and even despair. On the other hand, it allows for a redirecting and even transforming of dis-abling and destructive emotions and directs them toward a deeper under-lying affect of contrition, desire for forgiveness, and determination to change. It cultivates new dispositions: compassion for others, mutual for-giveness, gratitude, generosity, and peace with one another. The structures of liturgy not only express the desire for forgiveness by an admission of our own faults, but also enable us to forgive each other in the gestures that bend us toward each other, encourage us to bow low before one another and to embrace. By fostering such mutual forgiveness, liturgy ultimately works toward healing and peace with one another.

The disposition of peace is fostered by various gestures and actions in liturgy. Although in contemporary practice the people no longer exchange a literal kiss of peace during the anaphora, the deacons and priests still do, and the liturgy certainly evokes it structurally (and hence at least symbolically).[60] And kissing and embracing are often practiced in various other ways, during the rite of forgiveness, but also greeting each other after Pascha and on other occasions. We are told to glorify God "with one mouth and one heart" and we pray to "complete the remaining time of our life in peace."[61] Peace is also structurally instantiated by the liturgy in the sharing of the same cup and bread. We are called upon to offer the gifts "in peace" and exhorted to draw near to partake "in faith and in love."[62] All these are affective dispositions that position us toward and together with others. Yet peace and forgiveness are probably impossible without the cultivation of compassion. It is only when we are directed toward the other with mercy, kindness, and generosity that we are open to mutual forgiveness and to living together in peace and harmony. Although these affects are dispositions for which the litanies constantly pray, they are made real in our experience through dispositions of compassion cultivated by the structures of liturgy.

Models

As we have seen at several points, the liturgical texts often use medical imagery for sin and failure, which is pictured as a kind of illness or sickness that requires healing. While this runs the danger of interpreting physical illness as a sign of sin—although this is explicitly refused and such identification condemned by many writers and by the liturgical texts themselves—it does highlight something about our experience of both: The breakdown of the body feels like a kind of failure or betrayal in a way that is analogous to how we experience the breakdown of the "soul." And such analogy goes in both directions: On the one hand, we sometimes experience our physical illness as a sort of failure (not having lived a "healthier" life) even when that is objectively speaking not at all true;[63] on the other hand, we often experience our inadequacies and failures as a kind of illness or even as something beyond our power. Here the ascetic use of "pathos" (as both suffering and "passions"), as it is expressed in the liturgical texts, contains a deep phenomenological insight about the way in which both suffering and tendencies to give in to temptation or even to act in ways that are identifiably "evil" are often experienced as something that comes to us from without, something that overpowers us and renders us "passive," as something stronger than us that takes over and acts in our place, although that does not absolve us of responsibility for our actions.[64] The "mastery" of the "passions" in this sense is actually at least to some extent a way of reasserting control over oneself, of not allowing oneself to be governed by impulses or powers, of becoming one's own. Attributing such influences to the "devil" or to "demons," as ascetic and liturgical texts often do, externalizes them more fully and presents them hermeneutically as a foreign power, which one can resist and with which one can struggle. Yet liturgy always portrays such struggle in communion with others. It is not an isolated struggle that we must undertake on our own, but it is one that the liturgical characters have already undergone and in which all the people around us are similarly engaged.

Not all of the models we encounter in liturgy are about inducing recognition of sin and penitence. The professed goal of liturgy is also to shape us into the image of Christ via the examples of the saints.[65] This is evident in the way churches were laid out and decorated after the period of iconoclasm, it is visible in the iconographic tradition, and it is also obvious in hagiographical texts that were often employed liturgically.[66] One of the primary goals of commemorating saints within the liturgy and of hagiography more broadly, which especially in monastic settings is often read in conjunction with liturgy—and was clearly highly consumed in previous centuries, judging by the number of manuscripts that have survived—is presenting a saint as model for imitation.[67] That is precisely one of the main reasons why such stories are often highly inflated and use standard rhetorical tropes, rather than emphasizing the individuality, uniqueness, or particular historicity of the character. They are presented as patterns and models, not necessarily as unique individuals. The readers are not really all that interested in their peculiar histories, but rather in how their search for the divine might be imitated. The texts are read not for entertainment or for historical accuracy but as a guideline for our own lives.[68] Even when the liturgical texts do not explicitly exhort us to such imitation, the cumulative visual and auditory effect of the constant presence of the images and stories of the saints prods the liturgical consciousness to experience them as models.

In this hearing of the liturgically modeled acknowledgments of failure and penitence or the petition for assistance in the midst of suffering, we see our own needs and struggles mirrored and know we are not alone. Grief, pain, and failure can be immensely isolating experiences that shut us off from others who we suspect cannot share our pain and have no idea what it "feels like" to us or before whom we are ashamed and who we do not wish to know of our inadequacies. To see such feelings and needs expressed in liturgy assures us that we are not alone in our struggles.[69] And to express them together provides a formal, ritual way of binding us together in our pain and finitude. When we are in despair or suffering, we already feel that our pain is unique and cannot be shared. In that context, we are far more interested in knowing that others have faced and undergone similar struggles than to persist in our uniqueness or seek for originality. When I feel that I really am "the worst of sinners," it is encouraging to realize that Symeon the New Theologian or Basil the Great felt the same and wrote these words we now (all!) say. Although every illness and struggle, in its physical and emotional dimensions, is a particularly personal and intimate experience, it helps to know that others have confronted similar struggles of their own. John Chrysostom, pointing to the biblical story of the poor Lazarus says: "We, for our part, even if we suffer a multitude of troubles, can at least gain sufficient comfort and enjoy consolation from looking at him. Finding companions in our sufferings either in fact or in story brings a great consolation to those in anguish." Indeed, not to have such examples "is enough to darken one's soul."[70] The "singular" experience of the self, highlighted so strongly by the ascetic literature, is here enfolded in the plural struggle portrayed in liturgy.

Liturgy allows for the transferal of this ascetic struggle into a communal and ritual context. No longer does one struggle alone in the desert (albeit under the guidance of a spiritual mentor; even the ascetics rarely undertook such struggle entirely alone), but we can now express it in the terms of all those finite and frail creatures who have preceded us and who have undergone similar struggles. Liturgy allows for daily, weekly, and annual structured and formal expression of such finitude and inadequacy. It does not deny our finitude, does not seek to erase it, does not equate it with failure, even when it draws connections between the two. It provides the communal space for acknowledging our finitude, facing it, coping with it as who we are and how we live, rather than denying or ignoring it (thus hindering us from the kind of hubris that causes us to think we are invincible or better than others and that can be so deeply destructive of our lives and those of others). Liturgy allows for acknowledging our failure, facing its debilitating impact on our lives and relationships, coping with it rather than denying or ignoring it. And it also provides the space for the "in-between" experiences of inadequacy—those that do not designate explicit failures or faults but can still cause harm to others unintentionally through misunderstanding or circumstances beyond our control. Finally, liturgy reminds us of all this when we forget it or try to ignore or repress it. It confronts us with ourselves in sometimes brutal honesty. We can obviously close our ears to it or refuse to heed its call, but the structures for hearing it are there. The importance of experiencing this in the context of community has already been mentioned repeatedly, so let us turn to that dimension of the liturgical experience more fully.

6

COMMUNITY

At the end of the service that begins Great Lent, Forgiveness Vespers, every person bows before every other, saying "Forgive me, a sinner." Each responds "God forgives and I forgive" and both embrace. In most parishes, the line of people bowing and hugging creates a large circle all around the nave of the church. In some places, people even do full prostrations before each other, rather than just bowing low. The penitential effort of Great Lent begins with this communal act of forgiveness. As isolated as our sins and failures can often make us feel, at least during Lent we engage together in acts of confession, postures of contrition, and prayers for transformation. Most Orthodox churches have far more services during Lent than during any other time of the year: the Great Canon during the first and fifth week, the liturgies of the presanctified gifts on Wednesdays and Fridays, various Akathist services and liturgies for the departed, all culminating in the intense services of Holy Week and finally Pascha night.

Liturgy cannot be done on one's own. The very term means work of the *people*.[1] Liturgy is plural and is experienced in its communal nature. Liturgy's goal ostensibly is to make its participants part of a body, to bring them together into a whole that is larger than a mere compilation of individuals. We have already encountered what one might call the "plural" dimension of liturgy on a variety of levels. The temporality and spatiality of liturgy imply that others have gone before us. We experience

146

the space of liturgy as inhabited by others before us, as preceding us, as shaped by those who were there before. We also come into the space of liturgy surrounded by others. Especially for the person baptized as an infant there is no conscious "before" they are part of the community; they always already belong to the people who gather liturgically. But adult converts are maybe even more conscious of entering into a community, joining something larger than themselves, a tradition of generations of people who have worshipped and practiced in this way. Similarly, the temporal circularity of liturgy, its repetitiveness, is always plural. Fasts and feasts are entered into and celebrated together. Not just the rite of forgiveness on the eve of Great Lent, but the waving of palms on Palm Sunday, the processions during Holy Week, the prostrations before the tomb, the celebration of Pascha and its sumptuous feasting—all these experiences would be far less, quite different, maybe entirely impossible, without other people.

The bodies of liturgy are plural. We engage in the movements, the postures, the gestures together. While there are certainly individual adaptations of bowing and crossing, a lot of this happens in unison and its effects even on our personal bodies are experienced as the weight of a tradition of such corporeal engagement. It would feel utterly strange to cross oneself if no one else ever did so. All the corporeal movements of liturgy are shared and communal movements. Even baptism, although undertaken individually, is always done with the support of godparents or a sponsor and participates in a tradition of all those others baptized before and after me. Although the creed is formulated in the first person singular ("I believe"), it is recited together (again, even at baptism together with the sponsor or for an infant by the godparents together on behalf of the child) and we say words that have been formulated by others before us. Our affects are shaped by the larger moods of liturgy and by the communal experience of them. The examples we meet in the liturgical texts move us to compassion with others. Not only do we happen to be several people experiencing a particular liturgical occasion in the same spot, but the plurality is part of the very experience. Liturgy is accordingly always a plural experience; indeed, priests are prohibited from celebrating a liturgy without people present.[2] How does the fact of its plurality, of the ways in which we encounter others within it, how we are as persons in liturgical community, emerge in and shape the experience?

Liturgical Theology and Community

Liturgical theology has often stressed the communal dimension of worship. Irwin speaks especially of Lent as "a communal experience."[3] Baldovin points to the fact that in the early Christian world, especially in Byzantium, participation in liturgy was tantamount to being part of the society: "Worship was not a specialized activity as much as it was an expression of membership in society itself. At the same time, church services were not exclusively religious but also upheld the structure of society. Processions were organized and relics and icons were paraded along the ramparts when a city was under attack. To distinguish too sharply between the civil and the religious in such a situation would be a mistake."[4] He stresses that especially the stational worship of processions spread out over the entire city "was essentially public in nature" and concludes: "To participate in civilization and to be a Christian were now one and the same thing."[5] He thinks that even today worship ought to "have political and economic consequences if those same Christians are to offer credible and authentic witness in the contemporary world."[6]

Saliers similarly points out that "the distinction between individualistic devotional prayer and the Church's common prayer was foreign to the early Church."[7] In another context, he also stresses the communal dimension of the early church: "Prayer, for the early church, was never isolated. ... A dichotomy between individualistic devotional prayer and the church's common prayer is foreign to the Spirit in Christ's body. A dichotomy between individualistic devotional prayer and the church's common prayer is foreign to the spirit of the early church."[8] Like Baldovin, he also thinks that this has implications for today: "Finally, intercessory forms of prayer force us to recognize that religious faith must be lived in the world of power, conflicting passions, and in moral ambiguity. In our social circumstances prayer as praise must be linked with prayer as love of neighbor."[9] He interprets this primarily in terms of solidarity: "Our lives and our liturgies are incomplete until we learn solidarity with others who suffer, and allow others to touch our suffering. Only in this way can we cease being alienated from our own experience of the pathos of the world. ... There is no authentic liturgy without such a radical identification and no true service of others without praying with Christ for them."[10] Lathrop also speaks of the communal dimension in terms of hospitality, juxtaposing personal and communal with each other: "Hospitality should be paired with reverence, the personal with the communal, respect for the individual with respect for the center of the meeting."[11] Personal and communal must be held together.

Varghese stresses the communal dimension for the West Syrian liturgy and the need for active participation: "*Ordo* is an ordering of a vision; it expresses the mind of the community. It orders and orients the community, by assigning each member his/her role and function in the celebration. In the Syrian Orthodox liturgy, there is no place for passive participation. Each member 'con-celebrates' with a prayer, hymn, gesture or movement. *Ordo* implies the presence and participation of the people. Thus the meaning of the *ordo* is inseparable from that of the Church."[12] Mitchell contends that this is true not only of Christian liturgy, but more broadly of any ritual action: "In a nutshell, what is at stake in ritual behavior—as it develops in individuals and is ritually enacted by groups—is nothing less than the survival of the social order."[13] He insists that "meanings are socially constructed" and "flow from *communal* discoveries based on a shared humanity."[14] Anderson, as previously cited, thinks that communal enactment shapes the worldview of the church: "liturgical sacramental practice, while an expression of the faith of a community, is a practice that norms and constitutes that community as a particular community of faith. It exercises claims upon us as a religious people. While our practice is a means by which the community of faith *enacts* a theological grammar and narrative, it is also the means by which the community *appropriates* that grammar and narrative."[15] Liturgy formulates a worldview that the church then enacts in its practices.

Janowiak links the communal dimension to God: "A community at worship is in harmony and rhythm with the very life and being of the triune God."[16] He argues that "the liturgy enacts the sign and reality of the community's conscious, public act of *identity-making in the Spirit*, because God's desire and Jesus' bodying forth of that Love transforms those who gather in its power and grace."[17] And he ultimately connects this to the Eucharist: "All these dynamic actions and actors are interconnected, revelatory of a presence whose various modes exhibit a rhythm and a harmony of the Spirit hymning the life of God in us. Standing together in the community of God, singing and moving to the rhythm of the triune life: this is the shape of a worship whose participants are willing to be taken, blessed, broken, and shared for the life of the whole world."[18] Not only is liturgy a communal experience, but it is undertaken on behalf of the whole world.

Kuruvilla also grounds the communal nature of church in the Eucharist, which he takes to anticipate the eschaton: "This is not a private act of an individual believer; it is an act of the local community of believers in communion with the church catholic in space and time. It is also an act of communion with the rest of creation and the heavenly court." He considers it significant that "the Eucharist is offered not on an 'altar' but on the 'thronos' of God. The church is gathered before the throne of God in eschatological anticipation, recalling the past and giving thanks for the past, present and future."[19] Wainwright similarly thinks of community in liturgy in an eschatological sense: "Every local congregation has in varying measures the possibility to anticipate that community across time and space which characterizes the inhabitants of the city of God in the final kingdom. The church is both a cultural and a transcultural community."[20] Thus, the present communal dimension somehow instantiates the coming heavenly unity.

Often explicitly ethical implications are drawn from this emphasis on the communal dimension of liturgy. Anderson says: "The contemporary challenge of liturgical catechesis is to understand the liturgical life of Christian communities as patterns of formation into particular forms of a moral way of life." He thinks that liturgy "is the primary place in which the community participates in its 'work of salvation' as the work of the Christian life on behalf of the world."[21] Anderson and Morrill claim that "the Christian pattern teaches one, shapes one, to have an attitude of awesome wonder and deep recognition of suffering and death. When the community prays (in life as well as in worship), continually lifting to God those who suffer, the world in its actuality is held, openly and honestly, before God."[22] Morrill puts it even more strongly in a different context: "We verify—make true in our lives—our faith in the God revealed in word and sacrament only through ethically embracing the attractive and the revolting, the beautiful and the broken, the calming and the upsetting, the clear and the confusing in our own unsettled world and ever-changing lives."[23] Lathrop warns, however: "The liturgy, then, engages us in a quest for justice in the human community but does not propose to us a concrete program."[24]

At the same time, several liturgical scholars raise questions about how the communal dimension can still function today. Baldovin points out that we no longer share common symbols that would make liturgy possible and hence approach it in individualized fashion.[25] He also argues "that the liturgy cannot do everything" and suggests that "it is unrealistic to imagine that an hour or so a week, and often less than that, of involvement in the liturgical assembly is going to be able to attune people to the value system and way of life to which the Gospel invites all Christians." Therefore, "the liturgy, supremely important as it is in the life of the Christian community, can only be the ritual highpoint of Christian life set in the context of rich communal activity."[26] He thinks that most people come to liturgy with "overblown expectations": "To expect liturgy to create a community that does not otherwise exist in any way, shape, or form is to confuse symbolic or ritual activity with daily life. These are inseparably interrelated but they are not interchangeable."[27] We must work at creating community; it does not happen magically just by virtue of being within liturgy.

Hughes frequently challenges what he sees as many liturgical theologians' facile assumptions in regard to liturgy's implications for contemporary culture. Pickstock also criticizes liturgical reform for a "sinister conservatism" that "failed to challenge those structures of the modern secular world which are wholly inimical to liturgical purpose" and "perpetuate a separation of everyday life from liturgical enactment."[28] Hemming similarly laments the rationalistic outlook of much liturgical reform that treats the human as individualized subject.[29] Guardini, conversely, despite a chapter on the importance of fellowship warns: "Their fellowship consists in community of intention, thought and language, in the direction of eyes and heart to the one aim; it consists in their identical belief, the identical sacrifice which they offer, the Divine Food which nourishes them alike; in the one God and Lord Who unites them mystically in Himself. *But individuals in their quality of distinct corporeal entities do not among themselves intrude upon each other's inner life.*"[30] Working out exactly how liturgy creates community or how its communal dimensions function seems fraught with difficulties.

Phenomenology and the Experience of the Other

French phenomenology has been especially preoccupied with the experience of other people. This issue is raised and discussed already by Husserl and Heidegger, albeit in quite different ways. Most philosophy, including phenomenology, proceeds from the question of the ego or the self to that of the other, although some phenomenologists have tried to correct this by pointing out that we are first with others before developing a sense of personal uniqueness or identity. Husserl confronts the question explicitly in his *Cartesian Meditations*, where he posits the question of the other as that of an "alter ego": Can we constitute the other not as an object of our experience but as a subject, as a constituting consciousness of his or her own? He suggests we do so through analogy and empathy. The other acts as I do and responds to phenomena in the world in ways that resemble my own; therefore I can assume a parallel between us and deduce that the other must also be a consciousness experiencing the world. But this remains a hypothetical parallel and is always based on my own experience of phenomenality. I do not truly have access to the other, certainly not to his or her consciousness—although there is also always an assumption that what I analyze in phenomenology is not simply my personal consciousness but consciousness as such and so it already assumes the experience of others to some extent, at least latently.

The analysis of body and flesh strengthens this point of inaccessibility: While I perceive and experience the other's body, I do not have access to the other's flesh. I do not know what things "feel like" to the other. Max Scheler, Edith Stein, and others try to explore this question further with an analysis of empathy, the idea of "in-feeling," being able to access the other's feelings via analogy with my own.[31] Heidegger condemns this attempt in the strongest terms.[32] We do not need to establish some sort of artificial relation with others via empathy, but always already find ourselves in a plural world: Dasein is a being "with others." Our experience of self and of our "ownness" only comes within our experience of a public and communal world shaped in interaction with other people. Yet for Heidegger, this dimension, although primordial (fundamental to being-in-the-world), can quickly become, or more correctly, always already is, "inauthentic": We lose ourselves within the "crowd," do as "they" say, act as "one" does.[33] The others become determinate for me as they form the background to my own flight from myself, to my inability to confront my angst, and to my refusal to embrace my possibilities. Heidegger's analysis of death demonstrates this in particular: I can always only live toward my own death and die my own death. I cannot die for the other, because even if I sacrifice my life on someone's behalf, the other still must die his or her own death; it has just been delayed.[34] The prospect of my death and my angst over my finitude structures my possibilities and the way in which I project myself toward them. The dread (*Angst*) of death is thus the most individuating experience possible, because it is the most fundamentally concerned with my own possibility of existence.

Merleau-Ponty insists even more strongly than Heidegger that we experience ourselves first of all in a communal and relational world, not as isolated individuals who need to encounter an "other" or constitute the other as "subject" rather than "object." The question of the subjectivity of the other, he suggests, is a purely philosophical dilemma, which ignores how we actually experience the world, where we have no doubt about the fact that others exist and experience the world roughly as we do.[35] We must return to the intuition of the child who experiences the world as fully interlaced and relational and does not think of the self as an individuated consciousness standing over and against the world as separate from it and from other "selves." Yet he acknowledges that even our shared experiences of communal or public activities, although they clearly presume that the world is experienced always already as plural, contain an element of self consciousness and of "personal" experience that cannot be shared.[36] I experience my participation in a collaborative project as *my* contribution, experience my elation at a concert or sports event as *my* joy or enthusiasm, even though they are only possible in the shared event and depend to a large extent on the presence of others. Merleau-Ponty thus agrees that one can have no genuine experience of the other's affectivity, although he also reiterates that the phenomenological I by necessity already assumes a shared plurality and does not refer to my empirical experience. In that respect Merleau-Ponty's claims reflect what we have seen about liturgy: The plural dimension both precedes us and shapes our experience or consciousness of the personal.

Husserl himself also tried to articulate a phenomenological account of community in his later writings. He seems to envision such a community as an association of consciousness, as plural minds thinking together, while also encapsulating something about the "transcendent" ego of the phenomenological reduction that is not a specific empirical philosopher thinking inside a solitary head, but the phenomenological I "as such," referring to *any* consciousness instead of a particular one. And we certainly do speak of the "mind" of a people, of a culture, or even of an age (and many Orthodox frequently refer to "the mind of the fathers" as if this were one cohesive, identifiable, and singular "spirit"). And yet such a mind has to be embodied in some way.[37] The "mind" of a culture, if it is anything at all, is not just an abstract ephemeral idea, but is embodied in paintings, in music, in social and political structures, in ways of interacting with each other. Even cultural "mentality" is embodied, which is precisely why it can become so quickly offensive to others who embody a different mentality: It is about how we touch each other, how we eat with each other, how we speak to one another in the gestures we use. So if there can be a phenomenological community of "consciousnesses"—and Husserl seems to think there can be—it must also be corporeal in some fashion.[38]

Michel Henry explicitly links such an account of community to the flesh.[39] While it is our body that distinguishes us from others and individuate us, our flesh—our true self—constitutes our living experience of Life itself, in which we all equally participate. In his later work, Henry uses explicitly "Christian" language to articulate this, claims that it is a primary insight of Christianity, and occasionally appeals to patristic thinkers, such as Irenaeus and Tertullian, to illustrate it. Henry argues that we all share the life of flesh as "auto-affection," which in his final works he identifies with the life of God. It is only because we are eternally and continually generated in the divine life that we are alive and have the capacity for experience. But this capacity is not an autonomous "I can" (I cannot give myself life), but *pathos*—what I undergo, what is given to me, what affects me in my flesh and as my flesh. Henry thinks of all "livings" as united in a community of Life/flesh in which all share the same life, which generates all of them as their source, continually nourishes them, and is expressed in them. Although he speaks of this as utterly immanent "flesh," not as body in the external world, he draws on the notion of the "mystical body" to stress the oneness of this community. For Henry, we share in each other's life because we all share the same life, the life of God, communicated to us through the "Arch-Son," Christ. He maintains that this is not a simple merging into one, but that a measure of individuality is still possible within this community of flesh. I am both self and wholly part of the other, of all others. I become a self only via my participation in the pathos of life in which we all share and which we all express.

In contrast to Henry, where personal experience becomes collapsed entirely into the communal (or, more precisely, into the divine), Lévinas provides a radical account of alterity that seeks to refuse any reduction of the other to the self. Although Lévinas's philosophy is often described primarily as an ethics (he himself claimed that "ethics is first philosophy," although he does not mean anything like traditional doctrines of morality), more fundamentally it is an attempt to articulate a genuine notion of alterity in phenomenology. The impetus is there already in his earliest work and becomes exacerbated through the experience of totalitarianism in the Shoah and the Second World War. His first major work, *Totality and Infinity*, begins with the question of war and the threat of totalitarianism, while the second major work, *Otherwise than Being*, describes encountering the other as fission and as becoming hostage to the other.[40]

Lévinas is probably the thinker to challenge Heidegger's focus on the self and its embrace of finitude as my ownmost possibility the most strongly in favor of a focus on the other. There is nothing benign or pretty about Lévinas's notion of alterity, even in its well-known terminology of the "face."[41] For Lévinas, one cannot get away from the other, the other constantly confronts me, interrupts me, disturbs and haunts me, will not leave me alone.[42] This encounter with the other is a primordial and individuating experience, but in a quite different sense as in Heidegger: Although it structures our very experience of the self, it does so as interrupted and confronted by the other. I "am" only as I am called to response and responsibility, only as I face up to the vulnerability of the naked exposure of the other, even when, especially when, I'd rather avert my face, ignore the call, extinguish its inexorable claim on me.

Lévinas is insistent that alterity cannot be assimilated, that any attempt to reduce the other to the same, to a version of myself, is not only a kind of violence that turns the other into an object but ultimately also is impossible because utter alterity always escapes my grasp. Complete otherness cannot become a phenomenon, cannot be experienced as alterity. It can, however, enter consciousness through the call, through the anonymous "rustling" of strange absence in the darkness of night (as explored in *Time and the Other*) or through the trace that is left by the one who has always already passed and cannot be held or grasped (in the later texts). Such "relation" with the other can never be reciprocal, but is always asymmetrical, requires substitution rather than empathy or an abstract equality. Substitution does not mean that I "stand in" for the other or replace the other—already Heidegger had condemned this by articulating care for the other (*Fürsorge)* instead as a being "ahead of" the other that makes a place for the other—but that the other's death matters more than mine, that it is the very impossibility of possibility, the closing of the horizon not only of *my* experience and existence (as in Heidegger), but of any experience.

Marion's phenomenology, which is deeply influenced by Lévinas's work, is explicitly posited as an attempt to overcome the split between the empirical ego and the phenomenological subject evident in Husserl and to some extent also in Heidegger and Merleau-Ponty.[43] He does so in a two-fold fashion, on the one hand by elaborating a notion of the self as completely devoted and given over to the saturated phenomenon, as recipient of an abundant givenness that comes entirely from elsewhere and cannot be expected, predicted, or controlled (hence divesting the self of any lingering remainders of Cartesian subjectivity), and on the other hand by developing a phenomenology of erotic experience in which I completely devote myself to the other and discover myself loved by the other, especially and primordially by the divine other. Marion assumes both Henry's notion of the flesh, which is always intimately mine and cannot be shared (although he does not adopt Henry's notion that we are all part of the life of God and thus of each other's flesh), and Lévinas's account of the other, which he develops into his notion of the (phenomenological) icon, where the invisible gaze always proceeds from the other and is encountered only as it weighs upon mine invisibly. Marion strongly contends that only a notion of love can individuate the other (and the self), can speak of the other adequately as *this* other and not just any other.[44]

In his study of Augustine's *Confessions*, entitled *In the Self's Place*, and in several articles, he rearticulates this notion of the self as addressed by and open to the divine. I am "a question to myself" and find myself in a "non-place," having to receive myself from another: "If I am neither in myself as a self identical to itself nor outside myself as departing from self, but indeed without a place, I can at the very least conclude from this that the question of my place cannot find a response through myself, who does not have a place. . . . This place without me, before me, but only thus *for* me, who remains essentially outside and foreign to it, God alone is found there."[45] And he concludes: "The ego does not even accede to itself *for* an other (Levinas) or *as* an other (Ricoeur); rather, it becomes itself only by an other—in other words by a gift."[46] And because "I cannot myself give to myself" I must receive myself from God.[47] Marion does think of the *Confessions* as a kind of liturgical text that structures confession as prayer before God and before the community. The self is again discovered as one who risks everything in loving abandon and thereby finds itself always already loved: "For I am what I love, since I put in this place all that I am, what I love offers me in return the self's place." The self comes to know itself only within an incomprehensible and infinite love.[48]

Marion's account of eucharistic experience also develops such experience as an entirely kenotic self-giving of the divine as gift, calling forth a similar devotion in the worshipping recipient. Despite Marion's attempt in the final part of *Being Given* and in the *Erotic Phenomenon* to overcome a notion of the self as a strong Cartesian subject and to replace it instead with a sense of being devoted or given over to the other, the focus is still almost exclusively on the singular self, even if it is conceived as a receptive self rather than a dominating or controlling one. At best, there are two individuated selves, wrapped in erotic embrace or devoted in silent adoration, but no account of a plural or communal experience. Lacoste's "being-before-the-Absolute" is similarly always singular, even if it can encounter others in the context of liturgy. He even explicitly says, "Being *coram Deo* is always phenomenologically first mine. Only in second place is it ours," although he then does go on to speak of a kind of plural being.[49] In all of these accounts—whether "secular" or "religious"—we begin with the individual and move from there to an experience of the other, even if—as with Lévinas and Marion—the experience of the (also singular) other becomes constitutive of the self.

The question of alterity, then, has been central in phenomenology from its very beginning and is particularly strong in the French context. It is usually raised in a very specific fashion, however, regardless of whether the focus is solely philosophical or includes theological or religious considerations. The assumption is almost always that one begins with the individual, the self, the cogitating subject and must constitute "the other" from this starting point. Heidegger and Merleau-Ponty challenge this very briefly, but both go on to focus again on the self as the appropriate perspective for phenomenology. In the more explicitly theological appropriations, such as in Marion or Falque, the important question is always that of *haecceitas* or individuation.[50] Even Lévinas's strong philosophy of alterity can in some sense be read as a philosophy of a dislocation of the subject and hence of the self as constituted by the other. Even the earliest phenomenologists, like Husserl, Scheler, and Stein, tried to access the other through analogy with the self in terms of empathy. When something like plurality or community is envisioned (in Husserl, in Henry, to some extent in Heidegger, or in the question of eros in Marion or Eucharist in Falque[51]), this always occurs on the basis of and from the starting point of the self or the individual.[52] Ultimately, for contemporary phenomenology I am always myself first before I can participate in community.[53] Does such phenomenology fit the communal experience of liturgy?

Liturgical Community

As we have already seen repeatedly, liturgy assumes a communal experience. The liturgical texts are, for the most part, in the plural (the creed is an exception, although, as noted, in liturgy it is still recited together). We say "our Father," pray for God to have mercy on "us"; the prayers of the litanies are for the "world," for the health and well-being of people who govern, are sick, are traveling, and so forth. The words of liturgy are always addressed to the whole community—unfortunately often dissimulated in English because the second person is identical in singular and plural and can thus be heard as "singular" even when it is plural. They always address all of us together, including those who are not present. This plural flavor of the language of liturgy is significant and points to the experience of liturgy as always communal. Indeed, we experience ourselves in liturgy as part of a larger community, even when not all of those people are physically present. The community extends beyond the specific bodies in this space, to people represented by the icons on the wall, to those who have shaped these traditions and worshipped in this way before us. Ritual always assumes a certain kind of antiquity; it is experienced as having been done by many people in this way, maybe from time immemorial.[54]

The only time we speak in the singular within liturgy is in penitence and confession of sins, although even there one's personal voice is identified with that of many others who have gone before, as in the Great Canon. Baptism welcomes us into the community and we remain in it until the moment of death, unless we absent ourselves from it by deliberate choice. Even in death it is hoped that the person who has died is now "gathered with all the saints" or may "enter into the court of the righteous" or find him- or herself "where the just repose."[55] Although these (penitence, baptism, death) are three instances of apparently singular experience, even there the actual experience is plural: We sing the Great Canon or recite the prayer of St. Ephrem together, we bow and prostrate together, we confess our sins before one another—in the early centuries quite publicly, but even today before at least one witness (usually the priest, who also confesses to another). In baptism, we join the community and are held by others as we do so. In death, we leave this community, accompanied by its prayers, to join another community (at least that is how it is liturgically portrayed, obviously the experience of the dead, if there is such experience, is not something open to phenomenological examination). It is significant that even these intensely personal experiences—birth, death, confession of sins—happen within community and accompanied by others. In many ways these are our most vulnerable moments and so it matters that we do not go through them alone.

In this respect, what has been said about affectivity in the last chapter needs to be reiterated. If liturgy gives us a language for expressing our deepest pains and sorrows, our most abject failures, our most haunting fears about ourselves and our actions, it does so by giving us the language of others, of a community who says those same words and hence by extension shares a similar experience. Liturgy does not leave us alone with our failures and fears. If it gives us a manner to cope with them, this is always a plural and shared manner—and one that also leads us to consider the frailties and failures of others compassionately. The prayers invite us and enable us to recognize ourselves as sinners, express our deepest despair, and yet they do so for *each* one of us, everyone says these prayers and expresses this despair and hopes for healing.

At the same time, penitence also has a further plural dimension inasmuch as the failures and faults we confess have harmed others. Our sins never concern just ourselves but always impact the community. Lying, stealing, murder, adultery, but even basic unkindness, arrogance, selfishness, disrespect, small slights—all are acts against other people that harm them in major or minor ways. By confessing them, we take the first steps toward reconciliation and restoration of community and relationships. Here it is immensely significant that the liturgical event that begins Great Lent is the rite of forgiveness (described in the opening of this chapter) in which we bow or even prostrate before all members of the community and ask for their forgiveness. Confession must on some level be a communal affair, precisely because the actions and dispositions that require confession harm the community, because they are destructive of peace and harmonious relationships.

The plural dimension is also significant for celebration. We cannot feast in the singular. Feasts require the participation of several or even many people. What would it mean to feast on one's own, as an isolated individual? Celebration, especially exuberant celebration and sumptuous feasting, calls for community. It requires music and hence the plurality of voices. It induces a mood of expectancy colored with memory, created only when others have gone before us and when we have such shared memories with them. It requires abundant food, which must be prepared by many and especially consumed by many. (A solitary and lonely festal meal is one of the saddest things imaginable. Even the strictest ascetics joined the community for the paschal celebration. Most did so every Sunday.) The joy of the feast is heightened by the number of people present. The awe of the occasion is proportionate to the hushed expectation of a crowd of people. When a church crammed full of people suddenly goes entirely silent and dark before the first paschal candle is lit, it is an entirely different experience from an empty space in which lights have been extinguished as a matter of course. Even the shared silence of a community is a significant plural experience. And in all the instances and aspects of liturgy just mentioned the plural precedes any singular experience or serves as its condition. None of these experiences is first singular and then plural, but they are always already communal.

Invitation and Individuality

The plural experience of liturgy thus creates a space for the gathering of community. As we have seen in the chapter on spatiality, liturgy is essentially and structurally welcoming. Although particular liturgical communities may not practice a hospitable atmosphere and very ethnic parishes for instance can seem quite inhospitable to a first-time visitor, the structures of liturgy are structures of hospitality.[56] Liturgy is designed to welcome us, to invite us in, to call us to participation. (When individuals or specific communities do not practice this, it is their failure, not the failure of liturgy per se.) Almost everything about the space of liturgy speaks of welcome: It is designed for crowds, invites us to come and see and hear and taste and smell. The corporeal postures of liturgy—from the embrace of forgiveness, to the exposure of prostration, to the sharing of the cup—are structurally postures of hospitality, of openness to the other. The sensory duality of liturgy that invites us to being seen in our seeing, being heard in our hearing, being touched in our touching, and so forth, is an invitation to participation. The tunes of liturgy, their rhythm and frequent repetition, enter us, whether we are singing them out loud or not. They are present in our consciousness and memory and their reoccurrence each year contributes to the hospitality of the occasion: They invite us into the event by their very familiarity.

Again, that is not to say that liturgy always "works" or that any of this occurs automatically. One can feel intensely lonely in a crowd or utterly depressed at a boisterous celebration and the fact that one's personal experience contradicts the prevalent mood around us can exacerbate the pain of such experiences of isolation. But here one's personal experience contradicts the structures of liturgy; it is painful precisely because one is unable to participate in the plural experience and sense it for how it gives itself. Furthermore, liturgy is not easy; preachers and homilists across the centuries often remind their congregations to practice hospitality more deliberately and to work harder at instantiating welcoming community. Here the various affective and corporeal dimensions of liturgy serve to reinforce and embody its plural dimensions of hospitality and community.

Phenomenologically speaking, these experiences are quite different from independent subjects encountering "the other" (apart from the final, disjunctive instance of loneliness just mentioned). The liturgical experience described and presupposed by liturgy is not that of individuals coming into it and participating in it, but it is always already a communal and plural experience. The festal experience is not that of lots of distinct individuals "dipping into" something separate from them, but the festal experience is precisely constituted by its plurality; it is plural from the start. Liturgically speaking, we are first of all "being-with" (or maybe even better "being-within"), not individual selves reaching out to other individual selves. Although today we probably often enter liturgy as individuals because our culture predisposes us to do so, the liturgical experience itself is structured in plural and shared fashion and does not consider or treat us as individuals. The other dimensions of liturgical experience we have already examined support this further. The temporality and spatiality of liturgy requires plurality and structures community. The liturgical postures and gestures of the body serve to expose or disclose it within the communal context. The affectivity of liturgy leads us to contrition and repentance that are directed toward others: to cultivate compassion, to forge forgiveness, to pursue peace. In all these ways, the actions and structures of liturgy presuppose and sustain a plural experience.

Besides this most basic point that liturgy is always addressed to the plural "you" and formulates a plural "we" or "us," the very notion of liturgy includes the "laos," the people. And indeed this point is made by the patristic homilists over and over again: We are inseparably connected to each other and so if a part of the body suffers all of it does; we have an obligation to each other and to all others, especially the poor and suffering. This is the highest Lenten obligation, far more important than personal mortification. Not to care for the poor is to abandon Christ. Liturgy imposes such a responsibility for the other on us in a variety of ways: in the biblical texts that are read, in the liturgical texts, in the patristic homilies and liturgical chants. Although we bear a responsibility for ourselves, expressed in the constant call to and practice of penitence, such responsibility is always expressed as also a responsibility for the other, especially compassion, care, and concern for the other's suffering. The "sanctity" of the "saint," in particular, is understood to have benefit for all others.[57] Our ascetic struggles are never just our own, but a struggle within, together with, and on behalf of the community. The experience of others matters for our experience, their salvation matters for ours, indeed, they are inextricably linked. We are not "saved" alone, but redemption is a plural experience.[58] The plural dimension of liturgy is both "before" me—I always enter into liturgical experience only as it has already been constituted by the community and as a participant in that community—and "after" me, because liturgy calls me to service of the other and for intercession on behalf of others. Liturgy is both intensely personal and communal, but even the personal is experienced within the communal, as an appropriation of its plural dimension *for me* as part of the community. Indeed, the texts of the liturgy and the homilies delivered during liturgy exhort the church to become one body.

Imitation and Identification

At times, the liturgical texts treat us in even more "unifying" fashion, deliberately erasing distinctions between persons or collapsing the distance between ancient and contemporary. This is particularly evident in the way in which the figure of Adam is used, who can indiscriminately (sometimes within a line or two) refer to a first human person, to Christ as the "real" or preeminent human being who takes on all of humanity, to each person praying within the liturgy, or to all of us together as humanity. The pronouns often shift fluidly between first person singular and plural, sometimes the second person singular and plural, and finally the third person

singular: Adam is "he" and "I" and "us" and "you" (in both senses of "you").
While this is much clearer in the texts, it is also to some extent marked in
the experience of liturgy where we pray the texts together in unison as a
body, most of the time without distinction of persons. The Eucharist at
least symbolizes such unification by breaking one bread for all those present who all partake from the same cup. And at the height of a festal celebration we may well experience ourselves as swept up into a shared
experience that is so exuberant that one does not experience it as *my* experience but as *ours*. Yet even the more mundane gestures and postures of the
body, when they are performed together, in unison, can provide an experience of absorption in shared experience that makes my particular experience not only inseparable from but in fact impossible without the
experience of the community as a whole. In music especially we become
experientially one as the harmony of our voices merges together and produces something new.[59] The ritualized music of liturgy, which is remembered and hence always anticipated, is experienced like a dance where one's
body and consciousness becomes absorbed in the communal experience
rather than standing outside of it.

Furthermore, liturgy is not experienced as primarily focused on us or
exercised for us. Although prayers are indeed offered on our behalf—especially in the litanies—liturgy is not exclusively, or even primarily, about
our personal needs, but structured as an event not manufactured by us. It
is given to us and we enter it, but it is not dependent on us and it continues
without us. Its space and time precede us, its movements are on some level
imposed on us, its gestures sweep us up in participation but are not
invented by us, its postures are exercised by us in imitation of others, and
even its moods and affect are in some sense always already "there": open to
us but not focused on us, dependent on us, or determined by us. Liturgy
is experienced as a "phenomenon" in the literal sense, as what appears or
reveals itself to us, as an event we may enter and in which we may participate but which we do not produce. In its very structure, it is not a "subjective" experience inasmuch as its structures and its world are experienced as
spread out before us rather than created by us.

The plural dimension of liturgy thus functions to divert the focus on
ourselves: to lay aside our personal cares, to become part of the larger whole,
and to receive what is offered to us. Even failure can become an intimately
personal obsession that wholly wraps us up in ourselves in unhealthy ways.
The ritual structures of liturgy, especially in their focus on imitation and

examples, serve to make us one of many, to absorb our peculiarity and self-absorption into the larger "I" or "we" of liturgy so as to free us from ourselves and open us up to each other. This is not an anonymous "they" that absorbs us into the crowd where we flee our obligation to authenticity (as in Heidegger). Instead, it is an explicitly named and imaged "crowd" of witnesses, which redefines "authenticity" in a quite different manner than the phenomenological accounts of ipseity. Death to self is liturgically imaged, especially in baptism, as "rising with Christ" or even as "becoming Christ." Imitation is not a replacement of selfhood with alterity, not a simple substitution of the "other" (even the divine other) for the I. Identifying with Adam, Abraham, Moses, and David, or Sarah, Rebekah, Tamar, and Rahab, shapes the audiences' soteriological self-understanding and encourages them to pattern their lives on these examples.[60] They matter to us today because in some ways *we are and are to become* Adam and David and Tamar and Sarah. Each of us is the publican and the Pharisee and the harlot and the recalcitrant prophet.

Yet each of us is also the blind man who was healed, the sinful woman who becomes the apostle to her people, the prostitute turned glorious example of sanctity.[61] In identifying with these liturgical "characters," we are not erased in our own selfhood, but become more truly ourselves. The distinction between the manifold "models" for imitation and our own experience in liturgy is never erased. If we are "absorbed" into them in any way, we also "absorb" them into ourselves, make their experience in some small measure our own, claim them for ourselves precisely by identifying with them. It may actually be the plurality of the experience that guards against total identification with a singular character. There are simply too many of them and too many of us for total absorption or complete identification. The diversity of characters as models and the diversity and plurality of those appropriating their examples matters in the process. To say that "I am Adam" tells me something about myself, reveals some part of myself to me, opens new possibilities for me, but it also does so for the person next to me who is chanting these words at the same time. It allows us to participate in something larger than ourselves, to expand the narrow and constricting boundaries of our self-absorbed egos, to divest us of our isolating subjectivity. The loss of self in liturgy is maybe a little like the loss of self in the absorption of an all-consuming task or in the creative act, which takes us "out of ourselves" but not at all in the sense of erasure or annihilation of self. Indeed, the goal of imitation is always ultimately participation,

participation not only in the particular liturgical moment or occasion but participation in what it seeks to accomplish. To stand on the outside (or edge) of liturgy "looking in" as a mere spectator, is to refuse such participation. In its essence, liturgy should not just be observed or contemplated, it has to be practiced and appropriated.[62]

We are thus not simply wholly submerged within the shared or communal experience. Merleau-Ponty and others are surely right that the experience of our consciousness can also be distinguished in some measure as our own in a way that is different from the affectivity and thoughts and experiences of another consciousness. I live in my own skin and my own flesh, not in that of the other. While there is much we can indeed assume about and surmise of the other based on shared experience, there are also aspects of alterity that remain irreducibly "other" and must necessarily (and ethically) remain so. These are real aspects of our lived experience of alterity that we deny at our detriment by trying to reduce them to only one version of otherness, but also by making them exclusively dependent on a prior notion of subjectivity.[63] We are in liturgy with others, before and after others, beside others, and for others. It is neither simply a matter of standing "face to face" before the other nor solely being "for" the other. Liturgy opens the possibility for all of these; it is not limited to only one of them. Although liturgy is always, first of all, a plural and communal experience, this experience unfolds in manifold ways: There is no reason it has to decide phenomenologically between accounts of the other as only "being-with," only being "alongside," or only being "face-to-face." There are elements of all of them in human experience and in liturgical experience. The other is always already before me and we thus are within relationship and community and publicness. Yet that does not mean that there can be no experience of the self at all.

This is particularly true of the experience of contrition or confession. The confession of sin is always made in the first person singular, albeit in conversation with the examples. Liturgy never accuses of sin, but enables penitence. It confronts me with myself inasmuch as I recognize myself in its examples of sin and penitence, not by imposing a specific accusatory vision of myself. Thus, the "identity" of myself as someone who has failed is not imposed upon me by liturgy, but liturgy opens the space in which I can recognize my faults, to which I can bring my failure, and through which I can exit from its isolating loneliness by (re-)entering into a community or fellowship that allows for forgiveness and transformation. At the same time, the plural dimension of liturgical identity, not just in identification with the examples of others, but in the fact that this individual recognition or confession occurs within the context of community, even before and toward each other, means that the plural identity provides the horizon and context of the personal one and indeed enables it in some fashion. We "each" come into liturgy folded into the "all of us" as we gather, pray, move, gesture, fast, and feast together. This holds the dimensions of "individuality" and "plurality" together: We are "each" only as we are part of "all," but participating in "all" allows us also to experience ourselves as "each," not an isolating "each," but a particular "each."

The experience of "self" or "person" that emerges in liturgy phenomenologically is consequently neither that of an autonomous individual subject nor an entirely passive singular self overwhelmed by the abundant (and hence presumably incommunicable) divine givenness. Instead, it is a fully corporeal, embodied self whose affects and emotions include both "active" and "passive" dimensions. Liturgical selves experiences themselves first within the context of community, in a prepared and oriented space and time, which precedes them and provides horizons of experience that enable intentionality. Through the postures and gestures modeled for us by and within the whole community we are enabled to open up toward others and to expose ourselves in vulnerability, albeit always together with others, not separate from or simply in front of them. In such self-disclosure, the person in liturgy experiences the self as seeing and seen, calling and hearing, touching and being touched, oriented toward others but also welcomed in hospitality together with them. Maybe above all, we are opened beyond ourselves and find ourselves directed away from obsessive preoccupation with our own self. We are constantly confronted with our own failings, yet in such a way as to enable contrition and change rather than despair. It may not be coincidental that liturgy exhorts to "lay aside all cares of this life" while simultaneously constantly prodding us to self-examination and exposure of our faults and frailties. In liturgy, our finite and fragile selves are welcomed into the plural experience of the community.

7

INTENTIONALITY

Phenomenology operates at the interplay between manifestation and intentionality. Now that it has been examined how liturgical experience is manifested in its temporality and spatiality, as well as in its corporeal, sensorial, affective, and communal dimensions, can anything be concluded about its overall intentionality? How are we directed to what is revealed to us within liturgy? What sort of intentionality is at work in it? Can liturgy be said to shape intentionality and, if so, how does it do so? What is ultimately "revealed" or "manifested" within liturgical experience?

The troparion for the feast of Theophany (the "phainesthai"—appearance or manifestation—of "theos"—God) affirms that on this day of the celebration of Christ's baptism "the worship of the Trinity was made manifest" and that it "revealed" Christ as the Father's "beloved son" who "appeared" in the world. Similarly, the troparion for the feast of the Annunciation speaks of it as "the manifestation of the mystery that was from eternity." The transfiguration "shows" the disciples Christ's "glory." There are many similar claims made within liturgical texts about the revelation or manifestation of the divine. This question is also explicitly raised in the controversy over icons and thus becomes liturgically explicit in the liturgies for the Sunday of Orthodoxy (on the first Sunday of Great Lent), which celebrates the affirmation of icons as appropriate vehicles for divine manifestation. What is "revealed" or manifested in liturgy, at least according to the liturgical texts, is Christ's glory or even the mystery of the Trinity.

Liturgy is taken to be worship of God, encounter with the divine, manifestation of the kingdom of God.

At the same time, it is striking that all these revelations and manifestations remain mysterious and veiled in various ways. Even if we are said to encounter them "today" within the liturgy in some form, they are mediated to us via stories and images. In fact, the claims about revelation and manifestation are often highly qualified even within the liturgy itself. Both the troparion and the kontakion for Transfiguration, for example, affirm that the disciples only beheld Christ's glory "as far as they could bear it," acknowledging that it might not be possible to confront the divine fully or endure all of God's manifestation directly. The controversy over icons ended up concluding that it was acceptable to portray images of the saints and of Christ, because they were human and incarnate beings who could be painted in material media, but that any veneration of them is directed beyond the visible and material to the invisible and immaterial. Our veneration is never of the wood or paint directly, but ascends to the "prototype" portrayed in the icon. Furthermore, a careful distinction was made between veneration (*proskynēsis*) and worship (*latreia*); while images of saints or Christ are venerated, only God is worshipped (the liturgical texts for the occasion emphasize this: "we depict the likeness of Thine outward form, venerating it with an honour that is relative" or "we shall glory in the ikon of the Word made flesh, which we venerate but worship not as an idol"[1]). God "as such" cannot be portrayed in material form and liturgy does not give us direct access to the inner life of God.

What would it mean, then, to speak of the divine phenomenologically? Can "God" be investigated phenomenologically? Can a particular experience be identified securely as proceeding from the divine or being an experience of God? Can intentionality be directed at "God" and is that what "liturgical intentionality" does? Can "God's intentionality"—whatever that would mean—be said to be directed at us during liturgy?

Liturgical Theology and God's Role in Liturgy

Not surprisingly, liturgy's relation to the divine is a frequent topic in liturgical theology. Irwin insists that "what we celebrate in the liturgy is the fullest experience we can have of the triune God through Christ's paschal mystery here and now before the coming of God's kingdom."[2] For Morrill, everything in liturgy is meant to enable us to encounter God: "All of these—

people, architectural fixtures, movable objects, sounds, silence, and actions—both relate in their ways to beliefs in the Christian tradition and relate within a particular liturgy to one another so as to create in that ritual enactment a concrete encounter with God in Christ."[3] Dalmais emphasizes that liturgy manifests and enables redemption: "The liturgy is, above all else, a work, and indeed *the* work *par excellence*: the one that manifests and brings to fulfillment God's saving action among and through human beings."[4] Liturgy, then, at least theologically speaking, is about manifesting God's work and enabling us to participate in it, such that we are redeemed. Anderson summarizes William Easum as saying: "The only normative criterion to be applied to worship is whether it fosters an experience of God. There are no other normative claims to be made by worship."[5]

Taft qualifies this by insisting that liturgy "is not how we seek to contact God" but instead "it is a celebration of how God has touched us, has united us to himself and is ever present to us and dwelling in us." Relying on the interplay between anamnesis and eschaton, he argues: "It is not a reaching out for a distant reality but a joyful celebration of a salvation that is just as real and active in the ritual celebration as it was in the historical event. It is ritual perfected by divine realism, ritual in which the symbolic action is not a memorial of the past, but a participation in the eternally present salvific Pasch of Christ." Therefore, liturgy "publicly feasts the mystery of our salvation already accomplished in Christ, thanking and glorifying God for it so that it might be intensified in us and communicated to others for the building up of the Church, to the perpetual glory of God's Holy Name."[6] Guardini similarly says: "The primary and exclusive aim of the liturgy is not the expression of the individual's reverence and worship for God. It is not even concerned with the awakening, formation, and sanctification of the individual soul as such." Instead, "in the liturgy God is to be honored by the body of the faithful, and the latter is in its turn to derive sanctification from this act of worship."[7] God is at the center of liturgy; liturgy is worship of the divine who has come to us; liturgy can even ultimately be said to be initiated by God.

Hemming concurs with this. In his phenomenologically inspired theology of liturgy, he insists on the dimensions of revelation and manifestation. He argues that it is in conformity with Heidegger to say that "what we call divine revelation is God's approach *toward*" us and insists: "God's divine self-disclosure—his revealing of himself, his disclosing of himself so that he can be seen to be true—is *God's*, not *our*, initiative."[8] He contends that it is the work of liturgy "in which God reveals himself in the person of his Son through his Spirit to the believer who anticipates God's self-disclosure in faith and hope."[9] This happens most appropriately within the church: "The Church is the proper place of God's self-revelation to man, it is its home, and its completion."[10] In terms of the signification of liturgy, this means that it "opens the intellect to the activity—the self-disclosure—of God in his divine Son."[11] In fact, liturgy "*performs* its meaning, which means: makes its meaning available such that it *is* what it signifies."[12] That is to say, the liturgy "*measures us*, it is the divine means by which we are gathered into God."[13] Therefore, "the liturgy is the very making possible of this understanding. What is understood is at the same time what is effected: to understand is to be brought in to the divine *self*-understanding."[14] In short, liturgy reveals the divine and deifies us, but this is something that happens to us, not something we do or accomplish. Mitchell also thinks that liturgy somehow incorporates us into the divine life, but distinguishes this from understanding God: "Liturgy's goal isn't meaning but *meeting*. And meetings are always risky. Christian worship is not doctrine disguised in ritual shorthand but action that draws us into the dynamic, hospitable, yet perilous space of God's own life."[15] Liturgy thus for these thinkers somehow enables access to God's very life and self-understanding.

In contrast, in his philosophical reflections on liturgy, Wolterstorff also stresses the divine dimension, but sees it located more in our orientation toward God: "When we assemble to enact a liturgy, we turn around and orient ourselves toward God." Through this orientation and liturgical enactment, "we engage God directly and explicitly." He is unambivalent about this: "When we kneel, there is no creature before whom we are kneeling; we are kneeling before God. When we stand with hands upraised, there is no creature before whom we are standing with hands upraised; we are standing with hands upraised before God. When we sing hymns of praise, there is no creature whom we are praising; we are praising God." In fact, "being directly engaged with God is what liturgical enactments are *for*."[16] Although he thinks that worship of God is primarily adoration, it is also for "learning who God is and what God has done," "for the purpose of learning and acknowledging the excellence of who God is and what God has done."[17] He reiterates this later in the book: "A central thesis of my discussion in this volume is that Christian liturgical enactments are for worshipping God—not for placating God, not for appeasing God, not for 'centering oneself'—but also not for expressing worshipful feelings."[18]

While all these claims are about our orientation toward God, he does also consider God's orientation toward us in liturgy, primarily through the activity of speaking to us.[19]

Many liturgical scholars draw ethical implications from this divine self-revelation in liturgy. Liturgy is not only about meeting God, but even more fundamentally about being shaped into the sort of people God wants us to be, people who act justly in the world.[20] Saliers contends that "liturgy is doing God's will and work in the world while providing human beings with a time and a place for recalling who God is and who we are before God, and identifying the world to itself—what it is in God's eyes—the pathos of this terrifying and beautiful world."[21] Dalmais speaks of this even more explicitly in terms of an arrangement of the whole cosmos: Rite "owes its properly religious value to the fact that it emphasizes the importance of fidelity to traditional observances that have for their purpose to express in a symbolic way the very order of the universe as willed by God and to ensure its continuance."[22] Liturgy therefore has profoundly transformative power. It not only changes people, but it affects the whole world.[23]

This is claimed especially in regard to the sacraments. Morrill examines the ritual of the Eucharist "in order to understand how the faithful thereby receive the revelation of God in Christ so as to embody the Spirit-life of the crucified and risen Jesus in the world."[24] Sokolowski, who draws on Husserlian phenomenology for his reading of the Eucharist as a theology of disclosure, contends that "the Eucharist reminds us that we can and should see our own lives as the will of the Father."[25] God "is the ultimate agent in the sacrament."[26] Chauvet, who employs Heidegger heavily for his analysis of symbolism and sacramentality (including that of Scripture), argues that the sacrament functions as "a symbol of identity that unites believers as sons and daughters of God and brothers and sisters in Christ" and provides a liturgical justification for "their practice of justice and mercy."[27] The sacraments enable and shape a corporeality of faith in such a way as to work "upon the subjects in their relations with God and with one another."[28] Through the symbols of liturgy, the confession of faith in the otherness and graciousness of God takes place in practice and takes flesh in us."[29] Yet the fundamental aim of liturgy is "the communication of the gratuitous gift of God, entrance into the mystery of Christ's passover." It is a "grave error" to think that "the properly Christian quality of the celebration depends on its human qualities."[30] Hughes similarly warns that "to conceptualize God as at the 'edge' of our known world is to posit that God remains to us essentially, or largely, *un*familiar, that God is fundamentally *other* to us, is *not* coextensive with known reality." He criticizes those for whom "God is to be apprehended *in* ordinariness—albeit in its depth—not at the edge of ordinariness."[31]

Despite the fundamental agreement that liturgy is concerned with God, there is thus profound disagreement over whether it is fundamentally motivated by our intentionality directed toward God—in awe, reverence, worship, petition, or other such acts—or whether it is a self-revelation of the divine toward us. Furthermore, there is just as much disagreement over the thrust of liturgy: Is its primary goal to understand, meet, and worship God, or does liturgy have a transformative goal of shaping us into certain kinds of people, cultivating moral character, and working justice in the world?[32] Is liturgy about meaning and understanding or is it about action and transformation? Does it take up the ordinary reality of our lives—maybe in order to transform it—or is it utterly incommensurable with the rest of our lives? Several of these theologians employ phenomenology in their work: Sokolowski draws on Husserl, Chauvet and Hemming on Heidegger, Mitchell on Marion. Can these claims about God's activity and self-revelation in the liturgy be sustained phenomenologically? Can phenomenology help resolve the issue of what sort of effect liturgy is supposed to have on our lives? What would it even mean to detect God phenomenologically in our experience? What phenomenological access could we possibly have to the divine "self-understanding" or to God's intentionality? In short, can phenomenology investigate the divine?

Phenomenology and God

Husserl rejected the possibility of a phenomenology of religion precisely for this reason: God is always transcendent (or at least talking about God always assumes a notion of transcendence, while phenomenology is about the exploration of immanence, of consciousness) and thus must be radically excluded by the epochē, by the setting aside of "transcendent objects" out there and even an examination of their "existence."[33] Heidegger similarly argued in the strongest terms that theology does not concern the question of God, but rather the question of the believing human Dasein.[34] While there might be a phenomenology of "religious life," there cannot be a "phenomenology of God." In contrast, most of the recent French thinkers contend the opposite; one of Lacoste's books is even called *The Phenome-nality of God*.[35] Lévinas, Marion, and Lacoste all try to speak of God in ways that safeguard the divine transcendence or alterity while also provid-ing a phenomenological account of God as revealed or manifested in human experience. While none of them explicitly addresses the question of liturgy (Lacoste's account, as we have noted, is about more general being before the Absolute), they certainly do consider the experience of the trace of the divine (Lévinas), the possibility of a phenomenon of revelation (Marion), and the "non-experience" of our being-before-God (Lacoste).

What presents particular challenges in this context, is the strong insis-tence on divine alterity or transcendence in all three thinkers (what one might call a strongly apophatic leaning), which makes it difficult not only to figure out how to identify any experience as proceeding from the "wholly other" if it is indeed entirely "other," but also, conversely, to discern how to account phenomenologically for the difference between human and divine other. Lévinas especially speaks of both in terms of absolute alterity. Marion claims that not only is Lévinas unable to individuate the other, that is, to give an account of a particular other and not just any other, the other per se, he also is unable to distinguish between divine and human other.[36] Although the face (of the human other) stands in the trace (of the divine), there is no access to the divine as separate from the account of human alterity. Lévinas himself repeatedly stresses that there is no access to God directly, but that we are always instead turned to the (undesirable) human other. Falque goes so far as to claim that for Lévinas we are all the Messiah, all the face of God to each other (which Falque sees as a Jewish and not a Christian notion, because for Christianity there is only one Mes-siah, Christ).[37]

In Lévinas, "God," if such a notion makes any sense, always stands "behind" or has already passed "before" the human other. We never encoun-ter God directly, but always only the face that stands in the trace of the divine. And yet "God" functions as a way to hold open the utter alterity of the human, to prevent the collapse of the human other back into its absorption by the same. It is "God" who holds open the demand: "Thou shalt not kill!" continually anew, even when we have sought to silence the other through war or murder. Yet Lévinas strongly stresses the divine alter-ity: "God is not simply the 'first other,' the other par excellence, or the 'absolutely other,' but other than the other, other otherwise, other with an alterity prior to the alterity of the other, prior to the ethical bond with the other, and different from every neighbor, transcendent to the point of absence, to the point of a possible confusion with the stirring of the *il y a*."[38] Although here Lévinas insists on a distinction between divine and human alterity, at the same time the transcendence of the divine is so dissimulated and inaccessible that it cannot be distinguished phenomenologically from the traumatic anonymity of the faceless void of being.

In Marion, human and divine alterity are somewhat more carefully distinguished, although even there they often threaten to collapse into each other. The motivation of Marion's entire phenomenological project can be said to consist in making it possible again to think the divine philosophically as a phenomenon of revelation.[39] He has tried to work this out in a variety of ways, most fundamentally with the notion of the saturated phenomenon, which comes to us in utterly overwhelming and unpredictable ways, thus cannot be constituted and suspends our intentionality. The phenomenon of revelation manifests as the paradox of "the unforeseeable, the excess, the absolute," as a phenomenon entirely given to us and abandoned to our receptivity.[40] Marion frequently argues that the language of phenomenology can be employed for the givenness of revelation because to acknowledge it as revelation is always already to speak of its manifestation and self-showing or self-giving.[41] In his Gifford Lectures, published under the title *Givenness and Revelation*, he tries to develop an account of Trinitarian manifestation based on his phenomenology of givenness.

Yet there is an uncanny similarity between the phenomenon of revelation and the saturated phenomenon of the "other" as the face (the fourth kind of saturated phenomenon which suspends modality, modeled on Lévinas's account of the face), which both are said to bring together all aspects of the other saturated phenomena.[42] Although Marion talks about the phenomenon of revelation in *Being Given* as a doubled paradox, which raises the level of saturation to a second degree, in a way that seems considerably higher than and different from the other four types of saturated phenomena, in fact, this higher phenomenon often becomes collapsed back into the others. Most of the time Marion speaks of it simply as "a" saturated phenomenon—especially in his analyses of the gift, Eucharist, love, and so forth—a phenomenon that comes to us in bedazzling and blinding ways due to its unpredictable excess and super-abundant intuition. In terms of its phenomenological characteristics, it does not seem fundamentally different from his account of the erotic phenomenon, where God as first lover also ultimately appears behind the human lover and divine and human love are thought in entirely univocal fashion.[43] In his book on Augustine, God and the religious community are envisioned as two interlocutors of the *Confessions*: One confesses to God (one's sins) and to the others (to reorient them toward praise of God).[44]

Structurally speaking, at least on Marion's own terms, it is difficult to see how the saturated phenomenon of revelation (that is to say, a manifestation of the divine) can be identified as different from the saturated phenomenon of the loving gaze or the overwhelming event. They are all intense, all give too much, all cannot be borne, cannot be predicted or anticipated, escape all control or constitution, are not perceived against a horizon but simply received in their overwhelming impact. With such intense saturation, how can levels of saturation (or of negative certainty) be distinguished? Would that not mean to impose concepts on the phenomenon, to control or at least "parse" it in some inappropriate fashion? If the only appropriate response to the saturated phenomenon is always utter devotion, complete giving of self in receptivity, how can degrees of such givenness be determined that would allow for distinction between devotion to God and love of the human other? The fact that the Eucharist becomes the gift par excellence and this gift ends up determining all of phenomenality is itself telling. Indeed, in several accounts Marion has begun to develop the notion of the human as an image of the divine, almost as "impossible" or "absolute" as God in terms of phenomenality.[45] Phenomenologically speaking, an encounter with the divine and an encounter with the human cannot be distinguished if both are experienced as radically saturated phenomena and if a "measuring" of saturation is a priori forbidden, as Marion consistently asserts explicitly as a crucial aspect of his account.

This is exacerbated by Marion's insistence that there can be no intentionality at work in the encounter with the saturated phenomenon. It comes in such an excessive and bedazzling manner that it overwhelms us with intuitive excess that renders our intentionality inoperative. To receive "means nothing less than to accomplish givenness by transforming it into manifestation, by granting that what gives itself to show itself on its own basis."[46] The recipient becomes like a "filter or prism" making visible the given, a screen on which its impact crashes and hence becomes phenomenalized. While we can respond by receiving the phenomenon, such receptivity must consist in total abandonment to the phenomenon, becoming entirely given over to it, devoted to it, possibly even addicted to it (the term *adonné* that Marion employs to depict the "self after the subject" has all of these connotations): "Screen, prism, frame—*l'adonné* takes the impact of the pure, unseen given, holding back the momentum of it in order in this way to transform its longitudinal force into a slack, even, open surface. . . . . the extent of phenomenalization depends on the resistance of *l'adonné* to the brutal shock of the given. . . . The greater the resistance to the impact of the given . . . the more the phenomenological light shows *itself*."[47] Similarly, to allow the given of the sacrament to unfold itself from itself, to manifest it as a phenomenon, is at the same time to understand it as a gift given to us in abundance and in complete abandonment.[48] One cannot prepare for this phenomenon and one's identification of it is ultimately always arbitrary and anonymous.

This is of a piece with his insistence that there can be no human interpretation of the Eucharist, but that the only right "interpretation" is always provided directly by God.[49] To speak theologically—that is to say, to employ appropriate "logos" of the "theos"—we must employ a "eucharistic hermeneutics" in which we allow ourselves to "be said" by the divine.[50] Similarly, to "praise" is to move from an idolatrous description *of* the divine to an iconic way of letting ourselves be "baptized" into the name and receiving our name from it.[51] Yet in that case how can the experience of the divine itself be described if it is always immediately transmuted by its overwhelming effect? Must not all words fail us or dissolve in an infinite variety of non-sensical words that do not describe but simply mark its excess?[52] Has not saturation reached the breaking point of language here, reducing us to silence or meaningless chatter?[53] Can such a phenomenon still be identified as a phenomenon of revelation or of the divine?

Lacoste is critical of precisely such analyses of religious experience in terms of inchoate feeling or overwhelmed awe before the divine, although he associates them primarily with Otto and Schleiermacher. He seeks to distinguish a "mystical silence" from "sacred mutism" and argues that "liturgical" silence is open to speech and understanding, hence that even mystical texts are intelligible on some level.[54] In that respect, the word (*parole*) allows us to go beyond speech and is a much richer experience than that of language (*langage*), which we share even with machines. The "event" of speech or of the text coming to presence can be analyzed. Although we have no mastery of the text or the spiritual experience, we must not abandon the effort to make sense of the gift of presence or its superlative appearing within the liturgical event. The excessive speech of mystical prayer or liturgical experience disrupts ordinary speech and dislocates us. It promises an event that transcends the world and hence is always at the limit of existence.[55] "Liturgical" speech confronts the nihilism of the contemporary world and breaks its "closure." In that respect, it is a "utopic" speech that puts the world into parentheses, although it does not abolish it.[56] Prayer speaks before God but often in God's apparent absence and always in the face of the threat of boredom and acedia. Within liturgy we can experience the truth of the event of God's presence, yet we always do so only partially and in anticipation. In this respect, liturgical language is both eschatological and always functions as rupture of the world and history.[57]

Thus here also, albeit in a slightly different sense, identifying a phenomenon as an instance of revelation or directly connecting it to God becomes impossible. In contrast to Marion, it is not the overwhelming and excessive nature of the phenomenon that forbids it, but instead its elusive absence and parousical distance. For neither Lacoste nor Marion do we seem capable of truly coming into God's presence; God either appears in such an overwhelming fashion that we cannot bear this phenomenality or we are too bored, too inattentive, and too much wrapped up in this space and time to enter the eschaton proleptically. Lacoste himself constantly stresses that liturgy is non-experience because God's "presence" (or even absence) in liturgy cannot be confirmed, but is only expected eschatologically. Yet, as has been pointed out repeatedly, we have no phenomenological access to such eschatological expectation; it is a theological assumption that cannot be verified phenomenologically. Similarly, if a phenomenon of revelation is characterized primarily by its excessive and overwhelming character, by the "fact" that it has no discernable cause and that we cannot manufacture it ourselves (like Descartes's idea of the infinite), but if all saturated phenomena, including aesthetic, cultural, and erotic ones are characterized by such abundant, overwhelming, bedazzling excess, then no meaningful distinctions can be made between them and no such overwhelming phenomenon can ever be identified as a phenomenon of revelation. Some intentionality must be present to enable such identification. It becomes impossible to provide a fully phenomenological description of our encounter with the divine, because there is both too little and too much continuity with other kinds of experiences. It is precisely the divine absence or "wholly/holy otherness" that leads to a conflation of such a phenomenon with other kinds of phenomena. It cannot be identified sufficiently to emerge as its own phenomenon.

There are some other attempts to speak of religious experience in contemporary phenomenology. Falque focuses extensively on the human encounter with the divine, but he conceives of this more as being "with" God rather than "before" the Absolute.[58] Overall, there is far more emphasis on immanence, incarnation, continuity with the human condition, and God's presence with us in Falque's account. It is nevertheless telling that his *God, the Flesh and the Other* deals with God before either considering our experience of the flesh or our encounter with the human other.[59] Similarly, his trilogy on the Paschal Triduum is predominately preoccupied with Christ, despite his supposed starting-point of "the human as such" (*l'homme tout court*). As we have seen, he also often argues for a close parallel between erotic and eucharistic experience, where marriage becomes patterned on eucharistic incorporation. Although Falque insists that we must start with the (agnostic) human condition as we encounter it in the world today, he moves far more smoothly back and forth between phenomenology and theology than the others, drawing on all kinds of theological presuppositions in his exploration of our experiences of birth, death, resurrection, and the flesh.

Kevin Hart also raises the question of whether God can be investigated phenomenologically explicitly in his recent *Kingdoms of God*. He argues that "in phenomenology, the evidence that counts is *Evidenz*, the making evident of something, and no rules are set in place to limit what makes itself evident."[60] This makes it possible to read Scripture as revealing God: "The phenomenality of sin consists in allowing death to come forward . . . and the phenomenality of God is registered in love impulsively coming forward, freely manifesting itself by way of overwhelming compassion." A biblical text "is open to a phenomenological reading" and "is itself an example of phenomenology" inasmuch as it reveals the Kingdom of God.[61] He repeatedly uses the terms "phenomenology of Christ" or "phenomenology of God," although he is clear that "we cannot figure God as a phenomenon." Instead, "once God has revealed himself this revelation may be made more fully manifest."[62] The phenomenological epochē can thus function as a kind of conversion that frees us from ourselves and makes us open to the kingdom and to the arrival of the phenomenon of God.[63]

Yet can we really speak phenomenologically of an incorporation into the very life of God or of a "phenomenology of Christ"? Are these not theological assumptions that cannot be verified phenomenologically? In a similar, albeit less fundamental, fashion, it seems deeply problematic if an encounter with the erotic body, the eucharistic body, and the suffering and dying body, are superimposed on each other, as Falque attempts to do repeatedly, or if the "fully human" in genuinely phenomenological existence turns out to be the resurrected human raised above animality and metamorphosed into Christic existence.[64] For Chrétien also there is continual slippage between human and divine or even the flesh of the world.[65] Even for Kearney it is often indistinguishable whether we are sharing a cup of cold water with "the least of these" or whether we are feeding the divine; often the one seems deliberately conflated into the other.[66] John D. Caputo, in a somewhat different fashion but with similar consequences, speaks of the "insistence" of God as the call of the other or as the desire of "I know not what," the love that disturbs me. God becomes simply another name for such love, such disturbance of the ordinary.[67]

Part of the problem in this precisely seems to be a fairly narrow focus on individual prayer or speech before God in the abstract rather than any concrete engagement with actual liturgical texts or occasions.[68] Many of these accounts are focused on individual being before God. For Marion, I am swept away by the overwhelming abundance of the bedazzling divine excess to which the only response possible is total abandonment, devotion, and adoration. For Lacoste, the confrontation with the divine ruptures my relation with the world, gives me hope beyond death, leads to an abnegation of my will, and presents me with the possibility of kenotic existence, albeit only in limited and anticipatory fashion. His examples of the individual before God are invariably ascetics or monastics, even when he acknowledges that they are inscribed in a tradition and receive certain prayer practices within a communal context. In either case, it is not coincidental that Lacoste sets aside concrete ritual in his account and instead investigates human being before the divine. It is really the individual encounter with God that is at stake for him, even when he admits that such an experience always ultimately eludes us. For Falque, the one partaking of the Eucharist becomes incorporated into the divine life, but it is not clear that this is a shared communal experience in any sense of that term or that the broader liturgical context is of relevance to it.

Can liturgy help with some of these confusions and slippages? Can we provide a phenomenological account of our experience of God within liturgy? Is it possible to identify liturgical language as "eschatological" or concerned with the "parousia" without looking at specific texts or concrete liturgical occasions, without engaging the actual "lifeworld" of liturgy hermeneutically? Can God's apparent absence or at least only partial presence in prayer be securely interpreted as pointing to some eschatological fulfillment without fuller examination of the nature of that absence or presence and the liturgical experiences within which it is experienced as such? Can we speak of this sort of experience as "saturated" without unfolding the particular ways in which it overwhelms our senses, speaks to our emotions, affects our bodies, reorients our location in place and time, or has other concrete effects on us? Must not any excessive or superlative nature of the religious experience emerge through the concrete ways in which religious practices are experienced? Can our concrete exploration of the actual phenomenological structures of Orthodox liturgy, as undertaken so far, provide some further substance here?

What Appears

One disclaimer is necessary up front. Even if we might be able to provide a philosophical account of our experience of revelation or of the divine, it would always be an account of *human* experience, never of *God's* experience. There is no way, at least phenomenologically, to access God's *own* experience, whatever that would even mean. This is true even in the claim that God becomes incarnate. We can perhaps make certain theological assumptions about Christ's consciousness, inasmuch as it is presumed to be a fully human consciousness, based on what we can say about human consciousness per se, but we do not have any access to an experience of the hypostatic union directly. Phenomenologically speaking, Christ's experience cannot be taken as a paradigm for all of human experience, because we have no experiential access to his experience, but only either to our own empirical experience or to broader structures of human experiencing as such. We can never assume or pass over to God's position phenomenologically, but always speak from within our human—albeit shared and communicable—experience. Yet, with that caveat, we can indeed describe how humans *claim* to encounter the divine within liturgy and how liturgy structures such encounter or even manifestation.

Liturgy certainly operates with the assumption that God is encountered there. The *texts* of liturgy all imply and even explicitly claim this. Liturgical language abounds with references to the divine. How could it not? The very presupposition of liturgy is that it is service of God, worship of the divine. While it is the "work of the people," theologically speaking, as evidenced by the discussion of liturgical theology in the first section of this chapter, it is conceived as work for and toward God and as encounter with God or revelation of the divine. The language of liturgy is language of praise of or petition to God, often drawing on the psalms in order to call upon the divine. At the same time, while the texts of liturgy address the divine, they do so in our words or in the words of the psalmists. In liturgy, we are directed toward the divine, rather than hearing God speak to us in any sort of straightforward fashion. These are therefore *hermeneutic* claims about what the texts and their language say, not necessarily phenomenological claims about what is experienced within liturgy.

To encounter icons, Eucharist, or liturgy more broadly as a revelation of the divine may thus require a hermeneutic predisposition or judgment to recognize them as such manifestation. We kiss the icon and intend for it to venerate the person portrayed. We bow our bodies and mean for this to express our devotion or penitence. We raise our hands and hope that our prayer is heard by God. We taste the bread and the wine and take them as the body and blood of Christ. Yet how do all these actually present themselves to us in experience? They appear within our experience of seeing and touching the icons, our experience of tasting the bread and the wine, our experience of hearing the words of Scripture, our experience of being oriented toward the sanctuary. Thus, any manifestation or revelation always occurs through and within the concrete experiences of liturgy, the way in which it orders time and space, the way in which it directs and orients our bodies, the way in which its various aspects are sensed, the way in which it affects our emotions and moods or shapes our dispositions, the way in which we share the experiences with others and our experience is wrapped up with theirs, and so forth.

Our experience in liturgy is thus shaped by the manifold aspects of the horizon of liturgical experience more broadly. God is never experienced apart from the temporal, spatial, corporeal, communal contexts of manifestation. God does not come in entirely unforeseeable, unpredictable, utterly overwhelming fashion, but whatever is experienced in liturgy is experienced in temporal, spatial, corporeal, sensorial, affective, and communal ways that have been prepared for us and precede us. We experience them as structures that invite us to penitence and celebration, as orienting us in our movements, postures, and gestures toward another before whom we humble ourselves in the hope of healing, as structures that encourage us to expose our bodies for such healing touch but also as directed to one another, as structures that enable hearing and being heard, seeing and being seen, touching and being touched, as structures that call for change of ourselves and compassion with others, as structures that are always shared and communal. If there is an experience of God—as the one to whom we are oriented, as the one who heals, as the one who requests our penitence, as the one who helps us to turn around, as the one who calls us to compassionate care for the other, as the one who gathers us in peace—it is only in and through these structures and experiences.[69]

One must thus be careful to distinguish the hermeneutic from the phenomenological dimensions here: While hermeneutics can examine what the liturgical texts say explicitly about the divine, this is always an interpretation, not a direct experience. Phenomenology instead (albeit not in opposition) examines how such expectation is marked in human experience, how it shapes the self, what it does to our bodies, minds, and emotions. Phenomenology makes no claim about whether "God" is "actually" encountered in liturgy in this way in the concrete experience of a specific person, rather it examines the liturgical structures as they are manifested and open to examination.[70] We can say that liturgy is structured such that it fosters an attitude of repentance, awe, and gratitude with an expectation that these are directed toward the divine, but phenomenology cannot (and should not try to) proceed further than that.[71]

At the same time, the fact that the liturgical texts speak so abundantly of God and that liturgy operates with the presupposition of being directed toward the divine does affect how we disclose ourselves in liturgy. It raises the "stakes" of liturgy to another bar: Our exposure is not just to each other but also before the invisible we hope and maybe also fear to encounter, our admission of contrition is not just before each other but also before someone we assume to know us intimately and accordingly may well induce greater honesty and transparency than would otherwise be the case. The presumption of the possible presence of the divine in liturgy adds a dimension of depth, seriousness, and profundity to the experience. Everything we do in liturgy—our postures, our gestures, our affects—have more weight if they are performed before "God" and not just before each other. Thus, while it is probably impossible to explore God's "presence" in liturgy in any direct way, at least phenomenologically, it is entirely possible to examine the ways in which the hope or expectation for such divine presence is experienced and shapes the affect and behavior of the participants.

That is to say, we can phenomenologically examine the ways in which liturgy shapes our intentionality.

Liturgical Intentionality

Even if God cannot be "constituted" as a phenomenon that appears within liturgy, liturgy requires that our intentionality be directed toward God. Liturgy proceeds not first of all *from* God, is not simply given *by* God (at least not in the way in which it is experienced), but is oriented *toward* God. As we have seen throughout, liturgy is directed or oriented. This direction or orientation is conceived by the texts—and may be experienced by those shaped by the world of those texts—as a direction toward the divine. We are enjoined to raise our hearts and minds—and certainly our voices and hands—toward God. The posture of the body is either stretched out or raised up before "God." The posture of liturgy is structurally conceived (though not necessarily always empirically experienced) as exposure to the divine. We come to liturgy as broken and frail human beings and spread this frailty before God, offer this brokenness to the divine for healing and transformation. "God" is thus first "envisioned" as the one before whom we stand, the one to whom we offer ourselves and our gifts, the one upon whom we call in praise and petition.[72] Liturgy prepares for encounter with the divine by placing us in the position of offering ourselves. This means that we must (quite literally and physically) come into liturgy, must enter into its space, must prepare ourselves, must be willing to disclose ourselves.

Simultaneously, there is an expectation that "God" is always already there, that the space into which we come is in some sense sacred, set aside for God, that it is where God dwells. The experience of liturgy is shaped by this expectation that we are entering "God's house" and that somehow what we do there is visible to God, is witnessed by the divine, is heard by God. We prepare for an encounter with the holy, because we assume that we find ourselves in a holy space and our intentionality is directed toward such manifestation.[73] It does not come out of nowhere without preparation or expectation, but is an intentional experience. The way in which we handle the "things" of liturgy and the manner in which we experience them also speak of this expectation. Ecclesial spaces and vestments are blessed and dedicated in elaborate fashion. Similarly, icons are blessed.[74]

The space and the people are censed at the beginning and sometimes multiple times during a service. All the actions we perform, all the items we handle, all the attitudes and postures we assume, are intended to prepare for encounter with the divine, sacred, or holy. This expectation can be "read off" our postures, interactions, movements, handling, and so forth; it becomes visible there.[75] What becomes manifest here, then is not first of all a person or event identifiable as "God," but instead a human posture of expectation, desire and preparation.

Yet the experience given to intuition within liturgy is neither entirely empty (Lacoste) nor exceedingly and overwhelmingly full (Marion). Rather, our experience within liturgy is filled hermeneutically by the texts and actions: the ways they speak of or point to God. For example, when we come to the Eucharist, the texts guide us to "confess" that this is "truly" the body and blood of Christ. The anaphora, i.e. the eucharistic prayer, of Saint Basil even prays that the bread and wine would be "revealed" or "shown" or "manifested" as the body and blood of Christ. These are thus phenomenological affirmations, not (or at least not primarily) ontological ones; they are descriptions of our intentionality. We are directed to this phenomenon of bread and wine as intending the body and blood of Christ, praying to experience its manifestation in this way. Similarly, when we praise or petition "God," we are turned toward the divine in our intentionality, even if this intentionality does not receive intuitive fulfillment every time (or ever). Phenomenology does not "prove" God's "presence" in liturgy—or God's existence in the world. Phenomenology describes the intentional structures liturgy provides for a possible encounter. We must be prepared for and by liturgy in order to experience how it gives itself. The continual repetition enables the formation of such liturgical intentionality.

Perhaps even a little more can be said about the intentional structures of our expectation. As we noted earlier, the single most repeated line in the Orthodox liturgy is "Lord, have mercy" (which constitutes the response of those gathered to almost anything that happens or is said) and the divine is over and over again referred to as the "merciful one" and the lover of humanity (*philanthropos*). We thus expect to encounter the "divine" first of all as an expression of mercy.[76] The pervasive language of illness and healing, pollution and cleansing makes a similar point. God is described and envisioned as the one who has mercy on us, who heals us, who cleanses our sins. Liturgy forms intentionality in such a way as to approach liturgy with

the expectation of encountering a merciful God. The intentionality with
which we engage in liturgy is shaped by this expectation. Thus, liturgy
manifests not only a generic expectation of an encounter with God, but
rather the more specific expectation of divine mercy and healing. We
expect to be touched and fed. The intentionality of liturgical consciousness
is an attitude of receptivity, a hope for healing, an expectation of being
nourished, in short, a hope for merciful and compassionate hospitality—a
welcoming of our finitude.

The way in which liturgy structures our intentionality is thus not only
about God, but also about us *before* God. We spread our finitude before
God, come with our failures and needs, joys and sorrows. We have seen
that liturgy on the one hand welcomes us into its space as we are and
enables us to express our frustrations and our despair with honesty and
transparency. Liturgy structurally provides a space in which such emotions
and fears can be articulated because it gives us the words and postures for
exposing them openly, authentically, but also "safely," inasmuch as it is
done communally and ritually. (No one checks what specific frailties mark
me or what particular sins I have committed when we together—but also
each personally—pray for healing or accuse ourselves as being "the worst
of sinners." Because petition for help and confession of sins is "expected"
by the structures of liturgy, it does not come as a total surprise and hence
is presumably less traumatizing to admit. All of us are "exposed" as "sinners" together.) On the other hand, it confronts us with ourselves, calls out
our failures, and helps us confess them and cope with their consequences.
For much of our daily lives, we can hide the various ways in which we have
failed or harmed others and seek to forget them, but liturgy continually
reminds us of this. Over and over again, it calls us to repentance in the
most insistent fashion. It thus both protects our vulnerability or finitude
and encourages us to deal with our failures, not equating the two yet
aware that they are often connected. It does not simply condemn our failures, but enables us to turn around by presenting us with models of
transformation.

Furthermore, liturgy not only provides a space for grappling with our
finitude—whether in terms of our own vulnerability to harm or in terms
of our awareness of causing harm to others—but also orients us away from
our obsessive self-preoccupation. Liturgy structurally directs us to the
other, teaches us postures of awe and reverence, cultivates attitudes of
compassion, and promotes living together in peace. Liturgy humbles and

encourages us, invites us to participate in something larger than ourselves, to become part of a shared community of those who are together oriented toward the divine in expectation and hope. Liturgy always goes beyond us and is structurally experienced as greater than us, as not just about ourselves. It is experienced as welcoming us into its space rather than something we manufacture on our own. Much of it is given to us, not so as to erase our intentionality or in defiance of it, but rather as orienting us and forming the intentionality with which we are to approach it.

In all these respects, Ricoeur's three-fold mimesis, as laid out in the Introduction, works well for liturgy. Liturgy is prefigured in life (especially in our experiences of finitude), it configures life (via the liturgical "world" of penitence and celebration), and it therefore enables a refiguration or transfiguration of our lives. Liturgy is not some alternative ultra-religious experience that has nothing to do with our human condition, but it is both a way of grappling with that condition in various ways and a possibility of transforming it, opening it out beyond our narrow and restrictive expectations, asking us to "lay aside" the preoccupying cares of our individual finitude in favor of a fuller—yet still fully human—life. Liturgy does not erase finitude, it does not sweep us up into heaven, it does not eliminate our senses and affects. Instead, it welcomes finitude, fills our senses and affects with the celebration of life lived more intentionally, directed toward the divine and human others within the shared, plural, liturgical experience.

The choice between liturgy being *either* our human labor *or* something purely given by God, then, is a false dichotomy. Liturgy is not *either* our worship of God as a merely human act *or* God's manifestation of which we are simply passive recipients. It is not a matter of *either* a human experience in continuity with our ordinary lives *or* a complete conversion of our lives exercised upon us by God in such a way as to deny or erase our finitude and leave us stunned in silent adoration of the wholly other. Liturgy is not simply a formation of the self or some sort of ethical exercise that might also be accomplished in myriad other ways, but it is also not a divine revelation dropped from heaven without context, history, development, or human involvement. Liturgy, at least phenomenologically speaking, structures the human experience of gathering together before another whose revelation we desire and directs its intentionality to be open to such manifestation in concrete corporeal, sensory, and affective ways. Whatever manifests in liturgy is revealed precisely *within* our shared worship not in opposition to it. We experience what liturgy reveals in and through our human entering into the liturgical world together temporally, spatially, corporeally, affectively—and all these require human structures of time, space, movement, gesture, and so forth. At the same time, this experience is one of being reoriented, transformed, called out, confronted, healed, touched, forgiven—as something that liturgy does to and for us. Our intentionality is directed toward an experience—or, rather, manifold and multiple experiences—that are experienced precisely as given and not as manufactured by ourselves. Within the liturgy, we find ourselves welcomed in all the dimensions of our human finitude.

CONCLUSION

This book has attempted to give a substantive account of liturgical practice in a particular religious tradition, that of Eastern Orthodox Christianity. The hope was that paying close attention to the "lifeworld" of a specific tradition would help us to ascertain its structures more easily without the kind of abstraction often practiced in the (philosophical) study of religion while also not remaining at a purely empirical level. The practices and structures of liturgy examined here, although particular, are obviously not foreign to other Christian traditions. Roman Catholicism shares many of these liturgical features (the liturgical calendar, the cycles of feasts, significant parallels in the arrangement of liturgical space, some of the postures, many of the gestures, and quite a few sensory and affective dimensions as well), as do at least some Protestant denominations (certain forms of Anglicanism/Episcopalianism or "high church," mainline Lutheranism). Beyond Christianity, many aspects of ritual are practiced in almost all religious traditions, even if the concrete ways in which they are practiced may differ and they may well signify differently in the context of a particular religious expression: Many religious traditions cycle between fasts and feasts, many engage in certain deliberate postures for prayer, many have patterns of communal meetings in specifically designated spaces, many light candles or share other sensory aspects of liturgy, almost all prepare special foods and consume them in ritual fashion. There is much potential here both for analyzing the specific practices of particular traditions and for discerning larger patterns of religious behavior and comparing them across traditions. In many ways, this investigation has intended to open the phenomenological investigation of liturgical and ritual practices with the hope that others will build on it and surely also correct aspects of this preliminary study.

How does this examination of liturgy respond to the three audiences identified in the Preface? What does it contribute to liturgical theology? Can we draw broader phenomenological implications from this particular study of Eastern Orthodox liturgy? And can we say something about what insights it has provided for the Eastern Orthodox tradition in a philosophical sense? Let me briefly address each question in closing.

Liturgical Theology and Phenomenology

One problem that has returned again and again in this study is the relationship between liturgy and culture, or liturgy and the rest of our lives, or liturgy and the "world" outside of liturgy. Anderson, for example, insists that we must "see the connection between the practices of prayer, belief, and ethical action. If liturgical sacramental practice is constitutive and normative for the nature and identity of Christian persons and communities, then it is oriented towards the life of such persons and communities in and with the world."[1] Part of the problem is that although pretty much all liturgical scholars are convinced that liturgy is not and should not be hermetically sealed off from the rest of the world and that what we do in liturgy does have and should have an impact on our lives, there is very little agreement about how this can or should take place. The various examinations of the relationship between liturgy and world fall roughly into three broad models, of which the first has several iterations.

First, there is the claim that liturgy constitutes a "token" or special part of our lives, where we practice more intensely what should shape our lives as a whole. To cite Anderson again: "Liturgy represented by baptismal and eucharistic practice, is directly related to belief and life in the world. The catechesis of the self practiced in liturgy and sacrament is a catechesis for Christian belief *and* action."[2] The implication is that while all our lives should be lived in saintly fashion, we concentrate on this especially on a particular day of the week or a particular season of the year. Such more deliberate focus presumably ensures that such transformation is more likely to occur because we pay special attention to it and lavish more effort upon it. This sense of liturgy as a token also recognizes that such intense effort cannot be sustained everywhere or all the time. If we cannot even do one liturgy "perfectly," how are we to live all our lives in such devoted fashion?

At the same time, beyond an acknowledgment that the intensity of liturgy might not be sustainable across all of our lives, it can also mean that the token is more something like "on behalf of" or that it is a sacrifice "for." This seems implied in Schmemann's contention that liturgy is "for the life of the world" and that what we do in liturgy matters outside of it, that the chalice is raised on behalf of "all and for all," even if not everything or all are present. To bless some things, such as water or oil, means in some way the sanctity of all. To set aside some bread, some space, some time is to affirm that all food, all space, all time are holy in some way. This helps understand some aspects of liturgy but is also unsatisfying in certain ways. It makes liturgy arbitrary, too special, too disconnected from what we are "really" all about for most of our lives, although it may present accurately the way in which we often experience liturgy, as a respite or a tithe of our time. It also often remains unclear how the partial "token" is exactly related to the rest of life. How does blessing a vat of water once a year on Theophany exactly affect all the water on the planet?[3] It certainly has no clearly discernable impact on our polluted waterways or the rising of the oceans. While such impact of blessing ceremonies or other liturgical activities is often claimed, it is left largely unexplained how such impact actually occurs or how it might be concretely detected.

Another mode of picturing this relationship of liturgy to the rest of life is to see it as the most authentic version of spirituality, practiced more intensely in liturgy than possible otherwise. Taft says that "liturgy is the salvific relationship between God and us, and that our liturgies, a privileged ground of this encounter, embody and express that relationship." After examining sixteen theses of what liturgy "does," he concludes that liturgy is "the most perfect expression and realization of the spirituality of the Church," namely "the common expression of the Mystical Body's personal relationship to God, which in turn is simply the relationship of the man Jesus to his Father, given as his Spirit, his gift to us" but warns that "unless we encounter this total Christ, head and members, not just Christ in himself, but also in others, in faith, hope, and charity, it will not do or mean what it's supposed to for us."[4] This is a somewhat narrower claim that sees liturgy primarily in relation to the rest of spirituality rather than to all life in the world.

A further way of picturing this idea of liturgy as a token or part of the larger lifeworld is the idea of degrees or gradations of holiness, especially in spatial terms. We already encountered this in the chapter on spatiality. In the Hebraic tradition, the entire land was considered holy, holier than the world surrounding it. Yet Judea was holier than the more outlying areas. And Jerusalem was thought holier than other cities. And the temple precinct is holier than the rest of Jerusalem. The temple itself is holier than the area surrounding it. And the innermost sanctuary is the "holy of holies," an even more intensely sacred place (maybe the interior of the ark of covenant functions as the highest locus of holiness). Similar gradations of increasing holiness are recreated by Byzantine architecture and assumed by the patristic mystagogies. Yet because nothing on earth is holy in comparison with God, these are all relative degrees and do not constitute a radical break between lesser and more holy spaces and times. At the same time there is always a tension between a site that is holy inasmuch as it conveys God's presence or mediates it in some fashion and the utter holiness and alterity of the divine that remains inexpressible and unmediated and in "comparison" (although there can be no comparison because there can be no measurement) with which all else pales.[5] Thus, the space, time, and actions of liturgy are maybe only slightly holier (or slightly less impure) than all other space, time, and action in comparison to God's utter alterity, which cannot truly be mediated. While such a model of gradations of increasing or decreasing liturgical intensity is useful inasmuch as it acknowledges that there are no radical breaks between one aspect of our lives and another and that to enter liturgy is not to live in utter schizophrenia, this does not really explain how the realms relate to each other or how liturgy might impact the rest of our lives concretely.

A second, almost diametrically opposed model, suggests that liturgy is not only the highest form of spirituality or of the Christian life, but that it is the only true reality and hence the only "real world." Here liturgy is not a (maybe slightly artificial) token (of the eschaton?) in contrast to the "real" world occupying most of the rest of our lives, but it is the only real experience in contrast to the inauthenticity and falsity of the world. Kavanagh and Fagerberg's shared claim that liturgy is "doing the world as it is supposed to be done" encapsulates this position. For example, Kavanagh contends: "*What* the liturgical assembly does is the world. *Where* the liturgical assembly does this is the public forum of the world's radical business, the *Thingplatz* of a restored and redeemed creation. *When* the liturgical assembly does this is the moment of the world's rebirth—the eighth day of creation, the first day of the last and newest age. Nothing less rides upon the act of the assembly, determines its style, lays bare its service and mission for the life of the world."[6] What this implies is that all of life ought to function in the way liturgy does and that we should actively work to transform it into such. This is a much more "aggressive" version of liturgy that sees liturgy and world as opposed to each other. Liturgy is the only "true" world, which must serve as corrective to the disorientation and fragmentation of the (false) world around us. Liturgy is not merely a token, which maybe can increasingly radiate outward to other aspects of our lives, but it is an alternative world, which must combat and maybe completely transform the (secular) world hostile to it. There is little to no continuity between these two "worlds." This position recognizes that "faith" cannot be limited to a small part of one's self, isn't just a pretty occupation for a Sunday morning, but that in some sense religion is always a "total vision," not a purely private affair. If liturgy is "public work" it has implications for all of reality and does not remain neatly delimited to a church. Yet such a totalizing vision runs the danger of becoming militant or insular, causing either a separation from the "world" into a small alternative subculture or an engagement with a hostile world only in terms of combat and annihilation. This easily lands us in a liturgical fundamentalism.[7]

A third, quite different, option is one advanced by the Jewish liturgical scholar Lawrence Hoffman in regard to what he identifies as the particular nature of Jewish blessings and some of the ceremonies that accompany them.[8] Instead of understanding "blessing" (in a "Christian" manner) as *conferring* sanctity, as making something sacred or holy through the rite, he argues that Jewish blessings instead function to *acknowledge* the sanctity of the world that is already there and instead of rendering it "holy" actually removes it from sanctity sufficiently to allow for our use of it. The "normal" state of things and the world then is "holy," set aside for God. We are able to engage with things and to use them, to live in the world without perishing, by acknowledging this sanctity and ritually "neutralizing" it enough that we can live with it. There may well be some elements of this also in Orthodox liturgy. There certainly is always a sense that the whole world is God's creation and therefore wholly good (and our use of it a gift) and the idea of using blessing ceremonies *in order to* sanctify actually seems fairly late.[9]

In a slightly different way, many theologians increasingly try to stress the holiness of the everyday and to help us see all things as sacred in some fashion. And some contemporary scholars have carried this much further by suggesting we abandon any distinctions between sacred and secular and simply speak of the whole world in liturgical terms.[10] While it is certainly wrong to deny the sacral dimension of the larger creation—and indeed it is often emphasized by aspects of the Orthodox tradition—does it make sense to abandon all distinctions between the sacramental dimension of the creation as a whole and the more structured sacramentality of ecclesial liturgy? Phenomenologically speaking, we certainly do experience a difference between standing in liturgy and being at a football game or preparing dinner or some other such activity. And while we can invent personal rituals, we experience them differently from rituals that precede us and into which we enter as part of a larger tradition. In fact, phenomenology insists that we can distinguish between our perception of experience within liturgy, our anticipation of it in imaginative expectation, and our memory of it in conscious recall. To erase all distinctions between liturgy and "world" is to disregard the very real way in which ritual is experienced as different, deliberate, special, and an experience of heightened intensity.

Can the phenomenological analysis we have attempted to provide in this study help illuminate some of these pressing questions about the relationship between deliberate liturgical rite and the rest of our lives as lived in less deliberate, less obviously liturgical fashion? It certainly will not be able to resolve the fundamental theological questions about the meaning and purpose of liturgy nor should it attempt to do so. Yet it can certainly say something about how we experience liturgy in relation to our everyday existence, based on the various aspects of phenomenological experience we have examined.

First, liturgy is experienced as organized and structured in a way that goes far beyond the order and structure of the rest of our lives. Liturgy is deliberate and highly scripted. In much of the rest of our lives, such intense scripting and organization would probably feel suffocating and constricting. Yet in liturgy, it enables an opening of the self and the formation of habits; the order and structure provide the familiarity and security that allows for disclosure; the repetitive insistence on it issues a continual invitation to contrition and change. The order and structure of liturgy is far more formal and far more deliberate than everyday life, yet that is precisely part of what heightens its experience into one of greater intensity and weight. The structured time and place of liturgy enables a kind of focus that we would not experience otherwise. At the same time, it frees us from other concerns, as we enter this space and time deliberately.

Second, this suggests that while liturgy might be a more saturated—even excessive and at times overwhelming—experience than other more transitory or mundane moments, it is more intense or excessive because it involves greater intentionality, not because it eliminates intentionality. Liturgy is more deliberate in its ordering, involves more memory and anticipation in its experience, and requires greater preparation. It thus provides a space and time deliberately and intentionally set aside for instantiating and practicing a certain way of being. At the same time, this requirement of focused intentionality does not give us control over it. Liturgy precedes us and is prepared for us, even as we must also prepare for it and appropriate it. Again, this exceeds the preparation and appropriation we experience in other events and situations of everyday life, but it is not completely discontinuous with them.

Third, the temporality and spatiality of liturgy allows us to experience it as a space of hospitality. Other public and even communal places and times are not necessarily so structured. Liturgy issues a welcome and invitation in its moods and gestures, its arrangement of space, its implements, even its plural dimension. Liturgy does not force itself upon us, does not expect particular displays of our bodies in terms of their appearance or adornment, but invites us to present ourselves as we are. This kind of unconditional hospitality, such offers of feeding and healing, are rarely encountered in our everyday lives and yet respond to a fundamental human need.

Fourth, we have seen that the postures, gestures, and affects of liturgy open us out beyond ourselves; they invite us to exposure and disclosure of ourselves. The deliberate liturgical space—prepared via temporal and spatial arrangements, habits of body and affect, particular language and concrete practices—gives us the opportunity to be more honest with ourselves; it challenges and confronts us in ways regular or ordinary times and spaces do not. Its corporeal and affective nature shapes us in particular ways that direct us toward such disclosure within the context and horizon of its communal nature. Liturgy, then, is a deliberate place and time where we can learn to be more truly ourselves in openness to the other in ways that are very difficult if not impossible to acquire in most of the rest of our lives in the society that surrounds us.

Fifth, liturgy challenges our conception of the self-sufficient ego by calling us to contrition for our actions, encouraging repentance before others, and inviting us to change our lives. Rarely are we prompted so clearly and so frequently to honest confrontation with our failures in other contexts. At the same time, liturgy provides the safe and structured space for expressing such emotions together with others and provides language for coping with their impact on us and on those around us. It thus enables us to grapple with our faults and frailties in a way that can both free us and allow us to change. In liturgy we can experience our finitude in all its varied dimensions—whether positive, neutral, or negative—and when it becomes destructive we can learn to orient it in healthier ways.

Sixth, liturgy sustains and promotes the formation of such healthier habits by its repetitive practices that are pursued far more intentionally than would be possible in a less structured place. Yet such habits fundamentally shape who we are and therefore do not apply only to liturgy. Attitudes of contrition, awe, gratitude, and compassion can become fundamental dispositions of the self that are practiced not only in liturgy but above all in our everyday interactions with others.

Finally, liturgy provides a communal experience that conceives of and treats the self primarily as part of the plurality of the liturgical community, past and present. In that respect, it challenges the individualism and autonomy of our culture and presents the model of a different way of being. This may be the dimension most discontinuous with our everyday experience, at least in Western cultures. This "clash" between liturgical and "secular" worldview goes beyond merely challenging our thinking of ourselves as autonomous individuals, but also applies to the ways in which we exhibit ourselves in social media or are encouraged to do so by advertising and consumerism. In liturgy, we are exhorted to care for things and to practice compassion for others, rather than to consume or exploit them. Here, liturgy trains us to act differently in the world: to live in gratitude rather than grasping greed, in awe rather than anxious acquiring, in compassion rather than compulsive competition.

Liturgical Practice and Phenomenology of Religion

Several aspects of this study of a particular tradition have bearing on the phenomenology of religious experience more broadly conceived. We have explored liturgy as what most fundamentally welcomes our finitude and at the same time challenges us to open up beyond ourselves. This is obviously not a particularly startling or novel claim.[11] Liturgical "being," to use Heideggerian language, is indeed a kind of opening or disclosedness (*Erschlossenheit*), but not as a call to grasp one's own being more authentically, but rather an opening onto something beyond its own self and beyond the preoccupation of care. To some extent, then, liturgy is not a confirmation of the self, but a kind of loss of the self, not as an erasure of the person but a shift of focus away from the self (and as itself becoming a site of manifestation for others in its opening toward them). This is not simply an ethical claim, that liturgy frees us from preoccupation with ourselves and opens us onto the other. It does not simply turn *Sorge* into *Fürsorge* or confront me with my absolute responsibility for the other. Liturgy neither simply says "me voici" (Lévinas) nor is it simply a reversal of the gaze (Marion). This basic insight of exposure or disclosure in liturgy has been phenomenologically unfolded into its various and manifold manifestations and thus shown to be far from simple. Liturgy's opening of the self (in some way always already thought as plural) beyond itself is a complex phenomenon that cannot be put simply in terms of liminality, saturation, rupture, or even transformation. Rather, it is organized and prepared in terms of time and space, manifests corporeally and affectively, and shapes a plural identity. What concrete implications for the philosophical study of religion does this have?

First of all, it shows that an in-depth philosophical study of the particular liturgical practices of a religious tradition is possible, that patterns of behavior and structures of practices can be discerned, that they are meaningful, and that they tell us something about religious behavior, at least in that tradition, but maybe also in a broader sense. It suggests that we have been right not to focus solely on doctrine, statements of belief, or personal faith, but that a religious tradition is expressed in its practices and that an examination of them constitutes a meaningful and productive philosophical engagement.

Second, this study has raised at least some questions about the phenomenology of religious experience as it is currently practiced by (mainly French) philosophers. Although their work has extensively influenced this study on multiple levels and often been employed in fruitful ways, it has also been shown to be limited in certain ways due to its explicitly Roman

Catholic confessional context. This is not to say that doing philosophy from a confessional perspective is always wrong or problematic. But it can lead to a certain narrow vision that disregards aspects of religious behavior in other traditions. One example of this is the exclusive focus on the Eucharist in the contemporary literature with almost total disregard of other aspects of liturgical practice. Concrete aspects of these philosophical approaches have also been challenged: contra Henry, the body matters and not only the flesh; contra Marion, the saturation or excess of experience in liturgy requires preparation and intentionality; contra Falque, the "fleshly body" of liturgy is quite different from the eroticized body or a body spread/splayed out in illness; contra Lacoste, liturgy is not nonexperience and not solely deferred to eschaton and parousia.

Third, and more positively, other aspects of religious practice have emerged that may well be not just particular to Eastern Orthodox liturgical practice, but characteristic of religion in much broader terms, albeit filtered and expressed differently in other traditions. That religion allows us to express our deepest needs, desires, fears, and failures, that it enables us to grapple honestly with our finitude, that it expands us beyond ourselves, that it invites us to exposure for healing or concern for the suffering other, that it confronts us with our faults and challenges us to change—all these are not just experienced in Eastern Orthodoxy. We have seen here one particular way in which they are structurally instantiated and practiced in a specific tradition, but this may enable us to discern such patterns and structures more easily also in other traditions. And the conversation between the particularities of a tradition, while not disregarding their differences, may enable us to gain insight into the human religious experience per se, may help explain why the human has been *homo religiosus* almost from the beginning and in almost all times and places of human history.

What, then, does all this mean for religious experience more broadly speaking? First, it has implications for how we speak of the "relation" between "ordinary being" and "liturgical being": Based on this more extensive analysis of the dimensions of liturgical life, we can say that liturgical "being" is neither complete rupture with the ordinary ("before" God), as Lacoste contends, nor a simple continuation or affirmation of the ordinary (God "with" us) as Falque argues. The movements of liturgy are far more complex than these black-or-white juxtapositions would indicate. Liturgy is neither the complete affirmation of our true self as always already in the self-affective life of God (Henry) nor is it always an utter bedazzlement of abundant saturation that compels us to offer ourselves in pure receptivity and devotion (Marion). There is surely some saturation and some rupture, but also some taking up of the ordinary and continuity with it. The kind of singular, absolute claims made by many phenomenologists disregard the complexity of life and the complexity of liturgy, which can rarely be grasped in such extreme either-or terms. Liturgy operates in the constant, dynamic tension between both mimetic and transformative dimensions.

The "meaning" or orientation of liturgical being or liturgical life, as opening the self beyond itself in a variety of ways and dimensions, may also point to an insight about religion more broadly speaking. It may well be true not just of "liturgical" being, but in a broader sense of religious being as such. In fact, such opening of the self may not even be limited to religion, although it takes on a particular form there, but also occur in other dimensions of the human condition, such as art or music or poetry (and obviously liturgy draws on all of these). Maybe one of the functions or goals of liturgy is precisely to prepare us to see and even practice such forms of disclosure in other places, in the world more generally (where it might be more fraught with danger or less visible). If this "beyond itself" of liturgy points to a dimension of the "sacred" or the "transcendent" or even "God," then maybe the deliberate engagement in liturgy can also begin to open us to the "holy" in all things, to dimensions of the "sacred" in the everyday, to traces of the "divine" in all of creation.[12]

Second, a similar methodological point can be made about the often extreme contrasts drawn between phenomenology "as such" and the study of religious phenomena. It is just too simple to contend either that phenomenology can function "only" as illustration for religious phenomena (in some sort of entirely passive fashion) or that theology/the study of religious phenomena can "correct" phenomenology (as if it had some great authority over it). The dialogue between them can be enriching and productive in far more subtle ways. In some cases, applying a phenomenological analysis to a particular feature of liturgical experience "fits" perfectly, to describe it in phenomenological terms illuminates something about it we would not have been able to see otherwise, it enriches our understanding of it. In another case, the "fit" is only partial, the phenomenological description helps us get an "angle" at understanding or describing an aspect of liturgical experience, but we must modify the description for it to fit; we can see other phenomenological aspects at work in the liturgical experience for which the explanation we have tried to employ is not fully adequate. At times this partial fit is simply left at that—we use as much of it as we can and try to supply other aspects "on the go." At other times, the altered phenomenological description we must give of the experience can actually illuminate our phenomenological understanding and contribute something to it. That does not mean that here "religion" works as a "corrective" to "philosophy," but simply that the attentive depiction of particular phenomena has revealed aspects of phenomenality of which phenomenology was not yet aware or which it has so far disregarded. Finally, there are also cases where the examination of religious experience might actually correct phenomenological assumptions or descriptions and show some aspect of them to be untrue, not borne out by the evidence of experience. But that is hardly always the case or necessarily a desirable paradigm for interaction between the two. The dialogue thus can be enriching in both directions, but it remains a dialogue not a conflation.

A "phenomenology of liturgy," then, or more broadly a "phenomenology of religion" need not be all of phenomenology, indeed, should not try to be all of phenomenology. While phenomenology does and should have an interest in investigating "religious" phenomena, just as it examines historical, aesthetic, cultural, ethical, social, or political phenomena, because they are an important part of the human experience, this does not mean that this becomes all of phenomenology or that it transforms phenomenology in some fundamental fashion or serves as paradigm for it. An examination of religious experience surely can make a *contribution* to a wider investigation by illuminating some aspects of phenomena that are not purely religious; after all, our lives and our experience do not unfurl in watertight categories. Many religious phenomena also have aesthetic and broader cultural dimensions; many historical phenomena cannot be understood without their religious dimensions and contexts. Thus their phenomenological investigations also overlap and inform each other. But it goes too far to treat religious phenomena as the paradigm for all of human experience or to argue that an examination of religious phenomenality fundamentally shifts the broader study of phenomenology. This is not say, as Heidegger does, that theology is merely an ontic or "positive" or merely particular science like chemistry or architecture, while only phenomenology reaches the deeper and broader ontological structures of human existence per se. Religious expression—maybe especially engagement in ritual practices—do reach a primordial level of human experience (assuming levels must be distinguished in this way in the first place). Neither the exclusion of religious experience from phenomenology nor a theological subversion of phenomenology are desirable and both end up restricting phenomenology in unhelpful or distorting fashion that limits our phenomenological access to human experience.

Phenomenology and Eastern Orthodoxy

Have we gained any insights specific to the Eastern Orthodox tradition? One caveat before drawing any conclusions: This is not and does not want to be an "Orthodox philosophy of religion." This study is neither done as an exemplification of certain personal confessional commitments—being on the "inside" of liturgy might help one describe it more fully, but a very careful and generous, albeit personally non-committed observer, should also be able to do so—nor is it somehow trying to extrapolate a larger Orthodox "philosophy" (whatever that would even mean). It is a study of the particular contemporary lifeworld of Eastern Orthodox liturgy in order to perceive the phenomenological structures of liturgical practices as a form of religious experience. No more than that. So what may this particular phenomenological study of liturgical experience say to people who affiliate with the variety of Eastern Christian traditions?

First, it says that the rather facile appeal to experience in so much of twentieth-century Orthodox theology—often in deliberate distinction from what was perceived as Western sterile "scholasticism"—can be given more substance than it has been given so far (and without the derogatory implications about the Western tradition). Experience need not be a purely subjective, relative, empirical, intensely personal whim, but can be given philosophical substance by examining its broader structures rigorously and observing them closely. Orthodoxy can engage and use philosophy profitably. The substantive phenomenological account of Orthodox liturgical experience that has been attempted here hopefully shows that crucial aspects of the meaning and signification of Orthodox liturgical practice can be ascertained from a *philosophical* investigation.

And, second, it can do so from itself, from its own starting point. It need not adopt a foreign starting point or paradigm and then artificially adapt it to point out the differences of its own peculiar tradition. Although this study has obviously drawn from Western philosophical thinkers, such as Heidegger and a group of contemporary French Catholic phenomenologists, it has always begun from the particularities of the liturgical experience and tried to unfold it from itself, drawing on phenomenological insights only for the analysis, not as unexamined presuppositions or governing principles. And—as has just been elucidated—this has also led to challenging aspects of their work or pointing to lacunae they have failed to consider because of the particularities of their own traditions.

This also means, third, that Eastern Orthodoxy need not fear philosophy as some distorting, dangerous, or even heretical endeavor. While some Orthodox Christians might be disturbed by the fact that God has been mentioned so little in this study of their liturgy, when the liturgy itself is full of references about the divine, this does not mean that God is either excluded from religious experience or somehow explained away philosophically. Philosophy is a particular practice limited to the insights of its specific field of expertise; it does not rule over all of reality or encapsulate all forms of knowledge. When phenomenologists speak of "experience"— even if this means experience *of* the divine—they mean *human* experience (whether of God or not) and such human experience can be examined as such, without theologically extrapolating in regard to the existence or nature of God. Surely something can also be said about what is perceived as experience of the divine and how such experience might be distinct from other kinds of experiences. That has not been the focus here, but that does not mean that it is not possible.

Fourth, and more specifically in terms of the content of what has been explored here, Orthodox liturgical practice has been shown to be deeply involved in time and space, to be instantiated in bodies, senses, and affect, to shape identity in community. Orthodox liturgy is not simply some sort of highly spiritualized transport to heaven, but is meaningful for our lives here and now. Many books on Orthodox spirituality give the impression that Orthodoxy is a religion for male monks sequestered on Mount Athos, an angelic life not involving human bodies or "worldly" concerns. That is simply not true—or at least it shouldn't be true. Orthodox liturgy is fully temporal, spatial, corporeal, and affective. Using theologically inflected language, one might say that it is fully incarnate. To contend—as many do—that it is "cosmic liturgy" must also mean that it concerns *this* cosmos, not some other, heavenly, world, removed from this one. Liturgy matters to our lives as they are lived in their day-to-day existence on this earth in our flesh and bones, engaged with the real people around us, their (and our) affects and emotions in all their concrete, particular, finite, frail, and fully human reality.

NOTES

Preface

1. Pavel Florensky, *The Pillar and Ground of Truth*, trans. Boris Jakim (Princeton: Princeton University Press, 1997), 5.

2. Ibid., 9.

3. Vladimir Lossky, *The Mystical Theology of the Eastern Church* (Crestwood, N.Y.: St. Vladimir's Seminary Press, 2002 [originally 1957]), 7–11. This popular text has served as an introduction to Orthodoxy to countless people.

4. For example, the Orthodox liturgical theologian Alexander Schmemann says: "To take but one example, the liturgy of the Paschal *Triduum*—Holy Friday, Great and Holy Saturday and Sunday—reveals more about the 'doctrines' of Creation, Fall, Redemption, Death and Resurrection than all other *loci theologici* together; and, let me stress it, not merely in the texts, in the magnificent Byzantine hymnography, but precisely by the very 'experience'—ineffable yet illuminating—given during these days in their inner interdependence, in their nature; indeed as epiphany and revelation." In Thomas Fisch, ed., *Liturgy and Tradition* (Crestwood, N.Y.: St. Vladimir's Seminary Press, 1990), 63. For a detailed examination of the claims about experience as Orthodoxy's most essential marker, see my "The Category of Experience: Orthodox Theology and Contemporary Philosophy," *Journal of Eastern Christian Studies* 69, no. 1–2 (2017): 181–221.

5. Alexander Rentel, "Where is God in the Liturgy?" *St. Vladimir's Theological Quarterly* 59, no. 2 (2012): 213.

6. Gordon Lathrop, *Holy Things: A Liturgical Theology* (Minneapolis: Fortress Press, 1993), 33.

7. Paul A. Janowiak, *Standing Together in the Community of God: Liturgical Spirituality and the Presence of Christ* (Collegeville, Minn.: Liturgical Press, 2011), 180.

8. Robert F. Taft, *Beyond East and West: Problems in Liturgical Understanding* (Rome: Edizioni Orientalia Christiana, 1997), 295.

9. Graham Hughes, *Worship as Meaning: A Liturgical Theology for Late Modernity* (Cambridge: Cambridge University Press, 2003), 222.

10. Jean Grondin notes this in his *La philosophie de la religion* (Paris: PUF, 2009). See also my "Faith: Belief or Practice?" *Journal for Cultural and Religious Theory* 14, no. 2 (2015): 299–318. A couple analytical philosophers have also recently had this insight. Nicholas Wolterstorff bemoans the fact that philosophers of religion "have focused almost all their attention on just four topics: the nature of God, the epistemology of religious belief, the nature of religious experience, and the problem of evil. If someone who knew nothing about religion drew conclusions about the religious mode of life from this literature she would come to the view that, apart from the mystical experiences of a few people, the religious life consists of believing things about God. She would have no inkling of the fact that liturgies and rituals are prominent within the lives of most adherents of almost all religions, including the religion dominant in the West, namely, Christianity. Between the priorities of analytic philosophers of religion and the priorities of most religious adherents there is a striking discrepancy." *Acting Liturgically: Philosophical Reflections on Religious Practice* (Oxford: Oxford University Press, 2018), 1. Similarly, Terence Cuneo, who seeks to provide a philosophical treatment of Orthodox liturgy from an Anglo-American analytical perspective, claims that "the discussion in contemporary philosophy of religion is detached from the religious life" and that "the topic [of worship and religious experience] is simply not addressed" in philosophy. *Ritualized Faith: Essays on the Philosophy of Liturgy* (Oxford: Oxford University Press, 2016), 6, 5. Both of these authors entirely disregard the fact that many philosophers working in the phenomenological tradition have focused for several decades primarily, and in some cases almost exclusively, on precisely such an analysis of religious life and practice (even if it is not an analysis of liturgy per se). Although Wolterstorff, for example, interacts extensively with Nathan Mitchell's work, he never acknowledges or mentions Marion, although Mitchell relies on him heavily. Similarly, Cuneo discusses the role of narrative and mimesis extensively without any mention of Ricoeur's important work on this topic.

11. Indeed, almost all contemporary sociologists of religion now assume that practices are a much better indication and source for the examination of religion than affirmations of "faith" or doctrinal statements. See, for example, Martin Riesebrodt, *The Promise of Salvation: A Theory of Religion*, trans. Steven Rendall (Chicago: University of Chicago Press, 2010).

12. John Panteleimon Manoussakis is an important exception. He has engaged phenomenology extensively and employs a phenomenological perspective in much of his work. Cf. *God After Metaphysics: A Theological Aesthetics* (Bloomington: Indiana University Press, 2007); *The Ethics of Time: A Phenomenology and Hermeneutics of Change* (London: Bloomsbury, 2017). Neither of these texts attempts to be distinctly Eastern Orthodox (they make a much broader contribution to the discussion) and neither explicitly engages liturgy.

13. See my "Overwhelming Abundance and Every-Day Liturgical Practices: For a Less Excessive Phenomenology of Religious Experience," in *The Future of Continental Philosophy of Religion*, ed. Clayton Crockett, B. Keith Putt, and Jeffrey Robbins (Bloomington: Indiana University Press, 2014), 179–96; "L'expérience de la liturgie comme phénomène religieux commun: Emmanuel Falque et Jean-Luc Marion sur l'eucharistie," in *Une analytique du passage. Rencontres et confrontations avec Emmanuel Falque*, ed. Claude Brunier-Coulin (Paris: Éditions franciscaine, 2016): 135–53.

14. Paul Ricoeur, *Figuring the Sacred: Religion, Narrative, and Imagination*, trans. David Pellauer, ed. Mark I. Wallace (Minneapolis: Fortress Press, 1995), 35, 37; emphasis his.

15. Indeed, he is quite suspicious of a "phenomenology" of religious experience, especially when it is concerned with the "manifestation of the sacred," which he associates with non-Christian forms of religious experience, especially as they are highlighted by the anthropology of Mircea Eliade. In this respect it is interesting that Eliade was a practicing Orthodox—see David Tracy's reflection on Protestant, Catholic, and Orthodox approaches to religious experience in his "Paul Ricoeur: Hermeneutics and the Dialectic of Religious Forms," in *Hermeneutics and the Philosophy of Religion: The Legacy of Paul Ricoeur*, eds. Ingolf U. Dalferth and Marlene A. Block (Tübingen: Mohr Siebeck, 2015), 31.

16. Laurence Paul Hemming argues most emphatically for a normative centrality of liturgy in the Roman Catholic tradition. On the one hand, "to practise faith is to be a liturgical practitioner"; on the other, "liturgical theology means: theology *as such*, and *from whence* every other theological discipline must take its license, and *to which* every other theological discipline is subordinate." *Worship as a Revelation: The Past, Present and Future of Catholic Liturgy* (London: Burns & Oates, 2008), 44, 45; emphases his.

17. Aidan Kavanagh, *On Liturgical Theology* (Collegeville, Minn.: Liturgical Press, 1984), 49.

18. For example, John Meyendorff says: "In the final form it assumed in the ninth century—the later enrichments were only peripheral—the Byzantine hymnographical system is a poetic encyclopedia of patristic spirituality and theology. Its importance for our understanding of Byzantine religious thought cannot be exaggerated. Medieval Byzantium never attributed to schools, to intellectual

speculation, or even to the magisterium the importance which they acquired in the West, but the centuries-old hymnographical tradition will be referred to—for example by Gregory Palamas against Barlaam—as a certain criterion of orthodoxy and as an expression of Church tradition *par excellence.*" *Byzantine Theology: Historical Trends and Doctrinal Themes* (New York: Fordham University Press, 1983), 123. Theophan the Recluse claims that liturgy is the entire "theological science" and that it serves as a full book of Christian instruction. Hilarion Alfeyev, who cites this passage, argues that the liturgical texts have an even higher authority than the Fathers (a striking claim for a tradition that is obsessed with the fathers) and that liturgy is the primary school of prayer and theology in the East. Hilarion Alfeyev, "La liturgie orthodoxe comme école de théologie," in *Le feu sur la terre,* ed. Job Getcha and Michel Stavrou (Paris: Presses Saint-Serge, 2005), 82–84. On the relationship between liturgy and theology more generally, see Robert F. Taft, "Liturgy as Theology," *Worship* 56, no. 2 (1982): 113–17; Teresa Berger, "Liturgy—a forgotten subject-matter of theology?" *Studia Liturgica* 17 (1987): 10–18, and "Liturgy and Theology—An Ongoing Dialogue," *Studia Liturgica* 19 (1989): 14–16; Paul F. Bradshaw, "Liturgical Theology," *Studia Liturgica* 30, no. 1 (2000): 1–128; Burkhard Neunhauser, "Liturgiewissenschaft: Exakte Geschichtsforschung oder (und) Theologie der Liturgie," *Ecclesia Orans* 4 (1987): 7–102.

19. Paul F. Bradshaw, *The Search for the Origins of Christian Worship: Sources and Methods for the Study of Early Liturgy* (Oxford: Oxford University Press, 2002), and with Johnson E. Maxwell, *The Origins of Feasts, Fasts, and Seasons in Early Christianity* (Collegeville, Minn.: Liturgical Press, 2011).

20. Paul F. Bradshaw and Lawrence A. Hoffman, eds., *The Making of Jewish and Christian Worship: Two Liturgical Traditions* (Notre Dame, Ind.: Notre Dame University Press, 1991). See also Andrew B. McGowan, *Ancient Christian Worship: Early Church Practices in Social, Historical, and Theological Perspective* (Grand Rapids, Mich.: Baker Academic, 2014); Lutz Doering, *Schabbat: Sabbathalacha und -praxis im antiken Judentum und Urchristentum* (Tübingen: Mohr Siebeck, 1999); Eugene Fisher, ed., *The Jewish Roots of Christian Liturgy* (New York: Paulist Press, 1990); Elizabeth T. Groppe, "Holy Things from a Holy People: Judaism and the Christian Liturgy," *Worship* 81, no. 5 (2007): 386–408; Harvey H. Guthrie, *Theology as Thanksgiving: From Israel's Psalms to the Church's Eucharist* (New York: Seabury, 1981). For an illuminating examination of early Sabbath practices, see Heather McKay, *Sabbath and Synagogue: The Question of Sabbath Worship in Ancient Jerusalem* (Leiden: E. J. Brill, 1994).

21. Hemming, *Worship as a Revelation,* 78. He thinks that most contemporary liturgical theologians are confused about the meaning of this word and reverse the relation between visible and invisible in its meaning and use (he criticizes Catherine Pickstock's account in particular).

22. Kavanagh, *On Liturgical Theology*, 57.

23. Susan Holman, *The Hungry Are Dying: Beggars and Bishops in Roman Cappadocia* (Oxford: Oxford University Press, 2001); Marcel Hénaff, *The Price of Truth: Gift, Money, and Philosophy*, trans. Jean-Louis Morhange (Stanford: Stanford University Press, 2010).

24. On the development of Christian architecture, see Hans Buchwald, *Form, Style and Meaning in Byzantine Church Architecture* (Aldershot, UK: Ashgate, 1999); John Wilkinson, *From Synagogue to Church: The Traditional Design* (London: Routledge, 2002); Constantin Akentiev, ed., *Liturgy, Architecture, and Art in the Byzantine World* (St. Petersburg: Byzantinorossica, 1995).

25. On the importance of rhetoric in early Christianity, see George A. Kennedy, *Classical Rhetoric and Its Christian and Secular Tradition from Ancient to Modern Times* (London: University of North Carolina Press, 1980) and *Greek Rhetoric under Christian Emperors* (Princeton: Princeton University Press, 1983); Averil Cameron and Robert G. Howard, eds., *Doctrine and Debate in the East Christian World, 300–1500* (Farnham, UK: Ashgate, 2011); Christopher Hannick, "Exégèse, typologie et rhétorique dans l'hymnographie byzantine," *Dumbarton Oaks Papers* 53 (1999): 207–18. Concerning preaching more specifically, see David Dunn-Wilson, *A Mirror for the Church: Preaching in the First Five Centuries* (Grand Rapids, Mich.: Eerdmans, 2005); Ekkehard Mühlenberg and Johannes van Oort, eds., *Predigt in der Alten Kirche* (Kampen: Kok Pharos Publishing, 1994); Karl-Heinz Uthemann, "Die Kunst der Beredsamkeit in der Spätantike: Pagane Redner und christliche Prediger," *Neues Handbuch der Literaturwissenschaften* 4 (1996): 327–76.

26. John F. Baldovin, *The Urban Character of Christian Worship: The Origins, Development and Meaning of Stational Liturgy* (Rome: Pontificum Institutum Studiorum Orientalium, 1987); Vicky Manolopoulo, "Processing Emotion: Litanies in Byzantine Constantinople," in Claire Nesbitt and Mark Jackson, eds., *Experiencing Byzantium. Papers from the 44th Spring Symposium of Byzantine Studies, Newcastle and Durham, April 2011* (Aldershot, UK: Ashgate, 2013), 153–71. Pentcheva claims that "the Byzantines believed in the connection between processions and salvation." Bissera V. Pentcheva, *Icons and Power: The Mother of God in Byzantium* (University Park: Pennsylvania State University Press, 2006), 167.

27. See Geoffrey D. Dunn and Wendy Mayer, eds., *Christians Shaping Identity from the Roman Empire to Byzantium* (Leiden: Brill, 2015).

28. For a fascinating account of children in Byzantium, see Arietta Papaconstantinou and Alice-Mary Talbot, eds., *Becoming Byzantine: Children and Childhood in Byzantium* (Cambridge, Mass.: Harvard University Press, 2009).

29. Cf. Pentcheva who describes these traditions in detail in *Icons and Power*.

30. For example, William T. Cavanaugh, *The Myth of Religious Violence: Secular Ideology and the Roots of Modern Conflict* (Oxford: Oxford University Press,

2009). This historical shift has come to be reflected in analytical philosophy of religion in particular, which focuses almost exclusively on questions of faith or doctrine (and their rationality or coherence) and entirely ignores religious experience or practices. Cf. Cuneo, *Ritualized Faith*, 1–19.

31. Gregory of Nyssa, *Oratio de divinitate Filii et Spiritu Sanctu*, PG 46, col. 557b, cited in Kallistos Ware, *The Orthodox Church* (New York: Penguin, 1963).

32. As reported in the *Russian Primary Chronicle*, attributed to the 12th century monk Nestor (and cited in almost all introductions to Orthodoxy or Byzantium). This translation is taken from Taft (*Beyond East and West*, 144), who cites it in the context of stressing the centrality of liturgy to Eastern Christian self-understanding and identity.

Introduction

1. For example, in the Introduction to Nesbitt, *Experiencing Byzantium*, 8–9.

2. For an example of an empirical (sociological) examination of liturgical experience, see Martin Stringer, *On the Perception of Worship: The Ethnography of Worship in Four Christian Congregations in Manchester* (Birmingham, UK: Birmingham University Press, 1999).

3. Their disagreement lies more in the focus of the method—whether it examines the "objects" of consciousness in order to provide evidence for them or whether it opens the question of the meaning of Being as such. It is outside the scope of this analysis of liturgical experience to engage the controversies over specific interpretations of the work of the phenomenological thinkers employed. Consequently, I rely almost exclusively on primary sources and try to give a fairly straightforward reading. Although I have consulted much of the secondary material on the thinkers I mention (especially the French), none of those treatments deals with liturgical experience per se, and has thus not been discussed here in any detail. (I should also stress that I am not a Husserl or Heidegger scholar and this book is not intended to make some sort of contribution to secondary scholarship on these—or indeed other—phenomenological figures.)

4. Husserl's description of phenomenology went through several iterations with significant shifts in terminology. Some of the most important texts include: Edmund Husserl, *Ideas Pertaining to a Pure Phenomenology and to a Phenomenological Philosophy* (usually referred to as *Ideas I*), trans. F. Kersten (The Hague: Martinus Nijhoff Publishers, 1982); Husserl, *The Idea of Phenomenology*, trans. L. Hardy (Dordrecht: Kluwer Academic Publishers, 2010); Husserl, *Cartesian Meditations: An Introduction to Phenomenology*, trans. Dorion Cairns (The Hague: Martinus Nijhoff, 1960).

5. Martin Heidegger, *Sein und Zeit* (Tübingen: Max Niemeyer Verlag, 1993), §§1–4; *Being and Time*, trans. John Macquarrie and Edward Robinson (New York: Harper, 2008), 2–35.

6. See the preface to his *Phenomenology of Perception*, the thrust of which this entire paragraph summarizes. This preface as a whole is an eminently lucid account of phenomenology and its method. Maurice Merleau-Ponty, *Phenomenology of Perception*, trans. Donald A. Landes (London: Routledge, 2012), lxx–lxxxv. Phrase cited from page lxxxv.

7. For introductions to Jean-Yves Lacoste's work, see Joerij Schrijvers, *An Introduction to Jean-Yves Lacoste* (Farnham, UK: Ashgate, 2012), and Kenneth Jason Wardley, *Praying to a French God: The Theology of Jean-Yves Lacoste* (Farnham, UK: Ashgate, 2014).

8. Heidegger actually uses the expression "being-before-God" himself in his 1924 lecture to the theology faculty at the University of Marburg. "Der Begriff der Zeit," *Gesamtausgabe 64: Der Begriff der Zeit* (Frankfurt/M: Vittorio Klostermann, 2004), 46, 107.

9. Jean-Yves Lacoste, *Experience and the Absolute: Disputed Questions on the Humanity of Man*, trans. Mark Raftery-Skeban (New York: Fordham University Press, 2004), 2 (trans. lightly modified).

10. "Man says who he is most precisely when he accepts an existence in the image of a God who has taken humiliation upon himself—when he accepts a *kenotic* existence" (*Experience and the Absolute*, 194; emphasis his).

11. *Experience and the Absolute*, 193 (trans. lightly modified).

12. The main secondary sources on Marion include Robyn Horner, *Jean-Luc Marion: A* Theo-*logical Introduction* (Hants, UK: Ashgate, 2005); Tamsin Jones, *A Genealogy of Marion's Philosophy of Religion: Apparent Darkness* (Bloomington: Indiana University Press, 2011); Shane Mackinlay, *Interpreting Excess: Jean-Luc Marion, Saturated Phenomena, and Hermeneutics* (New York: Fordham University Press, 2010). For a basic introduction, see my *Marion and Theology* (London: T&T Clark, 2016).

13. Marion works this out most fully in *Reduction and Givenness: Investigations of Husserl, Heidegger, and Phenomenology*, trans. Thomas A. Carlson (Evanston, Ill.: Northwestern University Press, 1998), and *Being Given: Toward a Phenomenology of Givenness*, trans. Jeffrey L. Kosky (Stanford: Stanford University Press, 2002).

14. For the most thorough study of saturated phenomena, see his *In Excess: Studies of Saturated Phenomena*, trans. Robyn Horner and Vincent Carraud (New York: Fordham University Press, 2002).

15. For a theological interaction with Henry's work, see Joseph Rivera, *The Contemplative Self after Michel Henry: A Phenomenological Theology* (Notre Dame, Ind.: University of Notre Dame Press, 2015).

16. Michel Henry, *I Am the Truth: Toward a Philosophy of Christianity*, trans. Susan Emanuel (Stanford: Stanford University Press, 2003), and *Incarnation: A Philosophy of the Flesh*, trans. Karl Hefty (Evanston, Ill.: Northwestern University Press, 2015).

17. The texts translated into English include: *Under the Gaze of the Bible*, trans. John Marson Dunaway (New York: Fordham University Press, 2015); *The Ark of Speech*, trans. Andrew Brown (London: Routledge, 2004); *The Call and the Response*, trans. Anne A. Davenport (New York: Fordham University Press, 2004); *Hand to Hand: Listening to the Work of Art*, trans. Stephen E. Lewis (New York: Fordham University Press, 2003); *The Unforgettable and the Unhoped For*, trans. Jeffrey Bloechl (New York: Fordham University Press, 2002). He has published more than twenty other works that are not yet translated.

18. Emmanuel Falque, *Crossing the Rubicon*, trans. Reuben Shank (New York: Fordham University Press, 2016).

19. Emmanuel Falque, *The Guide to Gethsemane: Anxiety, Suffering, Death*, trans. Georges Hughes (New York: Fordham University Press, 2019); *The Metamorphosis of Finitude: An Essay on Birth and Resurrection*, trans. Georges Hughes (New York: Fordham University Press, 2012); *The Wedding Feast of the Lamb*, trans. Georges Hughes (New York: Fordham University Press, 2016).

20. Emmanuel Falque, *Le Combat amoureux. Disputes phénoménologiques et théologiques* (Paris: Hermann, 2014), 137–93.

21. See especially Chapter 7, *Le Combat amoureux*, 265–96.

22. For example, Heidegger claims that a philosopher does not believe: "Der Philosoph glaubt nicht," *GA 64*, 107; cf. *Sein und Zeit*, 48–49. For a detailed exploration into this issue, see Laurence Paul Hemming, *Heidegger's Atheism: The Refusal of a Theological Voice* (Notre Dame, Ind.: University of Notre Dame Press, 2002). Hemming does argue that Heidegger's atheism leaves open the possibility of Dasein's encounter with the divine in Christ (271–90). He also vigorously disagrees with Marion's critique of Heidegger on the question of God's "being" (249–69). See also Didier Franck, *Heidegger et le christianisme. L'explication silencieuse* (Paris: Presses Universitaires de France, 2004). Husserl addresses the question in §58 of *Ideas I* (among other places), where he argues: "an extra-worldly 'divine' being . . . would therefore be an *'absolute' in the sense totally different from that in which consciousness is* an absolute, just as it would be *something transcendent in a sense totally different* from that in which the world is something transcendent. Naturally, we extend the phenomenological reduction to include this 'absolute' and 'transcendent' being. It shall remain excluded from the new field of research which is to be provided, since this shall be a field of pure consciousness" (*Ideas I*, 134, emphases his). See also Angela Ales Bello, *The Divine in Husserl and other Explorations*, trans. Antonio Calcagno (Dordrecht: Springer, 2009) and her earlier *Husserl sul problema di Deo* (Rome: Studium, 1985).

23. Emmanuel Housset cites several of his letters that speak quite cruelly about all three projects. He also tries to provide a context for these remarks and then shows how the concept of God nevertheless plays a role in Husserl's work, or at least can be read from implications of Husserl's oeuvre. *Husserl et l'idée de Dieu* (Paris: Cerf, 2010).

24. Heidegger, "Phenomenology and Theology," in *The Religious*, ed. John D. Caputo (Oxford: Blackwell, 2003), 49–65.

25. Marion, *Being Given*, 367n90.

26. For example, Lacoste, *Experience and the Absolute*, 2; Falque, *Rubicon*, 104–6.

27. "The reader who has seen the term in the table of contents of this work must therefore be advised: what 'liturgy' designates in these pages is, in fact, as convention would have it, the logic that presides over the encounter between man and God writ large. I am not denying that this encounter is also attested to in worship, or that worship has an order and that this order is rule governed. But the limits of what I understand here by 'liturgy' exceed the limits of worship— though I concede unreservedly that anything to do with worship is not foreign to the domain of the 'liturgical'" (Lacoste, *Experience and the Absolute*, 2).

28. It is not incidental that when we finally get an examination of a more concrete experience it is always an analysis of the sacrament of the Eucharist (in a particular, post-Vatican II, French version).

29. Anthony Steinbock, *Phenomenology and Mysticism: The Verticality of Religious Experience* (Bloomington: Indiana University Press, 2007), and *Moral Emotions: Reclaiming the Evidence of the Heart* (Evanston, Ill.: Northwestern University Press, 2014).

30. In fact, Ricoeur points to this as a much broader problem for phenomenology, saying of Husserl: "Even the last works devoted to the *lifeworld* designate by this term a horizon of immediateness that is forever out of reach. The *Lebenswelt* is never actually given but always presupposed. It is phenomenology's paradise lost. It is in this sense that phenomenology has undermined its own guiding idea in the very attempt to realize it. It is this that gives to Husserl's work its tragic grandeur." *From Text to Action: Essays in Hermeneutics II*, trans. Kathleen Blamey and John B. Thompson (Evanston, Ill.: Northwestern University Press, 2007), 14. See also his more detailed earlier critique in *Freedom and Nature: The Voluntary and the Involuntary*, trans. Erazim V. Kohák (Evanston, Ill.: Northwestern University Press, 1966/2007).

31. A preliminary version has appeared as "Mimesis or Metamorphosis? Eastern Orthodox Liturgical Practice and its Philosophical Background," *Religions* 8, no. 5 (2017): 1–22.

32. Heidegger, *The Phenomenology of Religious Life*, trans. Matthias Fritsch and Jennifer Gosetti-Ferencei (Bloomington: Indiana University Press, 2004).

33. For the fullest example of this see his Gifford lectures, now published under the title *Givenness and Revelation*, trans. Stephen E. Lewis (Oxford: Oxford University Press, 2016).

34. Marion claims this in several places, especially in *Believing in Order to See* (New York: Fordham University Press, 2017), although so far he has not done much to work out exactly what this would look like for phenomena other than saturated ones. See Anthony Steinbock's critique of this in "The Poor Phenomenon: Marion and the Problem of Givenness," which, although written a while ago and hence only addressing Marion's earlier work, still seems valid. In Bruce Ellis Benson and Norman Wirzba, eds., *Words of Life: New Theological Turns in French Phenomenology* (New York: Fordham University Press, 2010), 120–31. Marion's introduction of the notion of "negative certainties" raises further questions of a similar nature: *Negative Certainties*, trans. Stephen E. Lewis (Chicago: University of Chicago Press, 2015). See my "Marion and Negative Certainty: Epistemological Dimensions of the Phenomenology of Givenness," *Philosophy Today* 56, no. 3 (2012): 363–70.

35. See his "Epiphanies of the Everyday: Toward a Micro-Eschatology" in *After God: Richard Kearney and the Religious Turn in Continental Philosophy*, ed. John Panteleimon Manoussakis (New York: Fordham University Press, 2006), 3–20; *Anatheism: Returning to God After God* (New York: Columbia University Press, 2010); with Jens Zimmermann, *Reimagining the Sacred: Richard Kearney Debates God* (New York: Columbia University Press, 2016).

36. This is why it is essential to stress that no conclusions should be drawn by the reader about the author's "personal" religious experience. Philosophically speaking, the personal (and subjective) experience of the one describing the phenomenological structures of experience per se is completely beside the point.

37. Heidegger increasingly insisted on a kind of "tautology" in phenomenology, which simply seeks to think the "same" rigorously again and again: "The most difficult thing is to say the same again and the ultimate difficulty is to say the same of the same." *Zollikoner Seminare*, ed. Medard Boss (Frankfurt/M: Vittorio Klostermann, 2006), 30 (trans. by Franz Mayr and Richard Askay as *Zollikon Seminars* [Evanston, Ill.: Northwestern University Press, 2001]). Indeed, Heidegger's continual desire to return to the ancients and allow us to hear their insights anew is not at all unlike the Orthodox desire to be faithful to the patristic heritage and to understand and convey the "mind" (*phronema*) of the fathers. See George Florovsky, *Bible, Church, Tradition: An Eastern Orthodox View*, vol. 1 of *Collected Works* (Belmont, Mass.: Nordland Publishing Company, 1974), 109. Phenomenology is thus not some dangerous new method that would deliberately or accidentally distort ancient insights. See also Hans-Georg Gadamer's analysis of the importance of tradition in *Truth and Method*, trans. Joel Weinsheimer and

Donald G. Marshall (London/New York: Continuum, 2004), Part II, Chapter 4, Section B (i).

38. Jean Greisch is an important exception and makes an explicit argument for hermeneutics as the most viable form of philosophy of religion. See his three-volume *Le Buisson ardent et les lumières de la raison. L'invention de la philosophie de la religion* (Paris: Cerf, 2002–2004), especially Part V (volume 3), which makes this argument in over 1,000 pages.

39. Michel Henry, *I Am the Truth*, 215–33; *Paroles du Christ* (Paris: Seuil, 2002). See my "Can We Hear the Voice of God: Michel Henry and the Words of Christ," in *Words of Life*, 147–57; "The Truth of Christianity? Michel Henry's *Words of Christ*," *Journal of Scriptural Reasoning* 13, no. 1 (2014). For a critique of the treatment of Scripture in particular in Henry, Marion, and Falque, see my "Phenomenology, Hermeneutics, and Scripture: Marion, Henry, and Falque on the Person of Christ," *Journal for Cultural and Religious Theory* 17, no. 2 (2018): 281–97.

40. Jean-Yves Lacoste, *Recherches sur la Parole* (Louvain-la-Neuve: Peeters, 2015), 3.

41. See especially *In Excess*, 104–27 and his *Reprise du donné* (Paris: Presses Universitaires de France, 2016), 58–97 (revised version of his Marquette lecture "Givenness and Revelation"). I criticize this in detail in my *Degrees of Givenness: On Saturation in Jean-Luc Marion* (Bloomington: Indiana University Press, 2014).

42. *In Excess*, 33, 123–27.

43. Ibid., 29.

44. As Merleau-Ponty claims it must: "Phenomenology involves describing, and not explaining or analyzing" (*Phenomenology of Perception*, lxxi).

45. See also Ricoeur's essay "Phenomenology and Hermeneutics," *From Text to Action*, 25–52.

46. Falque, *Crossing the Rubicon*, 29–75.

47. Richard Kearney and Brian Treanor, eds., *Carnal Hermeneutics* (New York: Fordham University Press, 2015).

48. The introduction to Nesbitt, *Experiencing Byzantium*, for example, explicitly states as its primary interest to re-constitute the experience of the past through its descriptions and to "interpret the various experiences of 'self' in Byzantium" (6). Similarly, Derek Krueger interprets ritual practice in Byzantium in order "to consider how Byzantine Christians came to view themselves through the liturgy." He acknowledges the difficulties of doing so without autobiographical sources addressing such questions and therefore focuses on normative rather than on descriptive dimensions: "liturgical texts, their modes of performance, and Byzantine reflections on the meaning and work of liturgy reveal a sophisticated, if largely unarticulated, indigenous Byzantine theory of how liturgy was

expected to work, especially to work in producing Christians." Derek Krueger, *Liturgical Subjects: Christian Ritual, Biblical Narrative, and the Formation of the Self in Byzantium* (Philadelphia: University of Pennsylvania Press, 2014), 3, 8. See also Robert Taft, *Through Their Own Eyes: Liturgy as the Byzantines Saw It* (Berkeley: InterOrthodox Press, 2006). John Baldovin warns about the danger of drawing contemporary implications from historical practices in his "The Uses of Liturgical History," *Worship* 82, no. 1 (2008): 2–18.

49. There might also be a way in which hermeneutics is more attentive to the singular and particular, even when it understands it within or by recourse to a larger context, while phenomenology examines the particular or even empirical primarily for extracting from it larger structures of meaning that would be true in broader fashion and apply not simply to one empirical instance alone. Yet, the very activity of interpretation also seeks such broader meaning, even when it is focused on a very particular and specific text.

50. Bridget Nichols, *Liturgical Hermeneutics: Interpreting Liturgical Rites in Performance* (Frankfurt/M: Peter Lang, 1996); Joyce Ann Zimmerman, *Liturgy as Language of Faith: A Liturgical Methodology in the Mode of Paul Ricoeur's Textual Hermeneutics* (New York: The University Press of America, 1988). See also her more recent brief introduction: *Liturgy and Hermeneutics* (Collegeville, Minn.: The Liturgical Press, 1999). Kieran Flanagan also uses Ricoeur somewhat more briefly in his *Sociology and Liturgy: Re-presentations of the Holy* (London: Macmillan, 1991), 274ff. More recently, Brian Butcher has explicitly employed Ricoeur for an analysis of Orthodox liturgy: *Liturgical Theology after Schmemann: An Orthodox Reading of Paul Ricoeur* (New York: Fordham University Press, 2018). See also my "Toward a Ricoeurian Hermeneutics of Liturgy," *Worship* 86, no. 6 (2012): 482–505. Engagements with hermeneutics more broadly include Margaret Mary Kelleher, "Hermeneutics in the Study of Liturgical Performance," *Worship* 67, no. 4 (1993): 292–318; Martin Stringer, "Text, Context and Performance: Hermeneutics and the Study of Worship," *Scottish Journal of Theology* 53 (2000): 365–79.

51. The literature on language and especially symbolism in liturgy is extensive. Examining it in detail is outside the scope of this study. For an exploration of (eucharistic) liturgy in conversation with phenomenological sources that focuses especially on the dimensions of sign and symbol, see Louis-Marie Chauvet, *Symbol and Sacrament: A Sacramental Reinterpretation of Christian Existence*, trans. Patrick Madigan and Madeleine Beaumont (Collegeville, Minn.: Liturgical Press, 1995).

52. *Figuring the Sacred*, 221–23; "Hermeneutic of the Idea of Revelation," in *Essays on Biblical Interpretation*, ed. Lewis S. Mudge (Philadelphia: Fortress Press, 1980), 9. In "Philosophy and Religious Language" he says: "Through fiction and poetry new possibilities of being-in-the-world are opened up within everyday

reality. . . . religious texts are kinds of poetic texts: they offer modes of redescrib-ing life, but in such a way that they are differentiated from other forms of poetic texts" (*Figuring the Sacred*, 43).

53. Gadamer, *Truth and Method*, 303–6, 326–36, 363–71.

54. Heidegger, *The Hermeneutics of Facticity*, trans. John van Buren (Bloom-ington: Indiana University Press, 1999). See also *Being and Time*, §31.

55. Ricoeur, *Time and Narrative*, trans. Kathleen McLaughlin and David Pel-lauer, 3 vols. (Chicago: University of Chicago Press, 1984–88), especially Vol. I, Chapter 3.

56. Ricoeur, "Philosophical Hermeneutics and Biblical Hermeneutics," in *From Text to Action*, 89–101.

57. Cf. Maximus Confessor, *Selected Writings*, trans. George C. Berthold (New York: Paulist Press, 1985); Germanus of Constantinople, *On the Divine Liturgy*, trans. Paul Meyendorff (Crestwood, N.Y.: St. Vladimir's Seminary Press, 1984); Symeon of Thessalonika, *The Liturgical Commentaries*, ed. and trans. Ste-ven Hawkes-Teeples (Toronto: Pontifical Institute of Mediaeval Studies, 2011); Nicholas Cabasilas, *A Commentary on the Divine Liturgy*, trans. J. M. Hussey and P. A. McNulty (London: SPCK Press, 1960).

58. Andrew Walker White, *Performing Orthodox Ritual in Byzantium* (Cam-bridge: Cambridge University Press, 2015). In his view, Orthodox liturgy is not influenced by the theater, as an emphasis on mimesis might suggest, but only by ancient rhetoric. Although he is probably right that liturgy was not conceived as a form of theater, his argument assumes that rhetoric had no mimetic functions, which is patently untrue.

59. For example, ibid., 41, 46.

60. Ibid., 52.

61. See especially, Chapters 4 and 5, *Ritualized Faith*, 66–105. Byron Anderson also speaks of ritual in terms of mimetic performance and distin-guishes between three modes of ritual practice: "(1) Ritual performance is a communicative event that discloses, or perhaps manifests, a particular complex of meanings and relationships. Ritual makes something—some meaning, some form of relationship—present to us. (2) Ritual performance is experienced in the present and as such has a 'pre-reflective' meaning. We do not know what or why we experience something; we are 'in' the experience. (3) Ritual perfor-mance offers the possibility for the transformation or construction of meanings, relationships, and ways of being. Because ritual performance is an experience of the present, even as it is connected to a history and future, it draws us into its own meaning now and, in doing so, requires that we set aside our conscious connections to that past and future." *Worship and Christian Identity: Practicing Ourselves* (Collegeville, Minn.: Liturgical Press, 2003), 93.

62. Wolterstorff disagrees with this account (see *Acting Liturgically*, 149).

63. Cuneo, *Ritualized Faith*, 87. Cuneo distinguishes between two theories of "liturgical reenactment," namely "anamnetic theory" and "dramatic representation theory" (76). The ancient term of mimesis obviously encapsulated both.

64. Krueger, *Liturgical Subjects*, 59.

65. Ibid., 65.

66. Ibid., 212.

67. Ibid., 7.

68. Luke Timothy Johnson, in his book on the body as site of revelation, treats liturgy similarly as a sort of highly structured mode of "play": "all of these mark the liturgy even more decisively as play of a distinct and elevated kind." Citing traditions of sitting and standing or exchanging the kiss of peace, he argues that "to the degree that Christian liturgy maintains these formal elements of play, it enables participants to experience a form of transcendence. Worshipers so internalize the patterns of liturgical play that they can move in spirit beyond their individual bodies and into the larger body of the community, in a form of 'going beyond' that does not eliminate but enhances the significance of the individual as part of a meaningful whole." *The Revelatory Body: Theology as Inductive Art* (Grand Rapids, Mich.: William B. Eerdmans Publishing Company, 2015), 99. He also argues that liturgy provides a kind of freedom: "Precisely because the 'rules of the game' are formal, established, and not open to negotiation, they liberate worshipers from self-consciousness and free them to enter joyously into the common action that unites them all in a body that is greater than they are, yet embraces each of them bodily" (ibid., 100). The entire discussion of liturgy in this book that claims to be a phenomenology and theology of the body is only two pages long.

69. Romano Guardini, *The Spirit of the Liturgy*, trans. Ada Lane (New York: Crossroad Publishing, 1998, originally 1930), 61–72; Johan Huizinga, *Homo Ludens: A Study of the Play-Element in Culture* (Kettering, Ohio: Angelico Press, 2016, originally 1938). Dalmais also claims that liturgy functions as play, inasmuch as "the gestures and words of the liturgy carry a meaning and an energy that becomes present and operative each time that the liturgical action is repeated." In Martimort, *Church at Prayer: An Introduction to the Liturgy* (Collegeville, Minn.: Liturgical Press, 1987), 235.

70. Gadamer, *Truth and Method*, 109. He does think that this kind of play is a "transformation into the true" (112). Later he speaks of the "true meaning of the religious image or play" for which its "performance" is essential (115).

71. *Truth and Method*, 102–10.

72. Lacoste, "Liturgy and Coaffection," in *The Experience of God: A Postmodern Response*, ed. Kevin Hart and Barbara Wall (New York: Fordham University Press, 2005), 99.

73. Ibid., 97–98.

74. Ricoeur, *Oneself as Another*, trans. Kathleen Blamey (Chicago: University of Chicago Press, 1992), Chapters 5 and 6 (113–68).

75. Ricoeur, "Life in Quest of Narrative," *On Paul Ricoeur: Narrative and Interpretation*, ed. David Wood (London: Routledge, 1992), 20–33.

76. Nichols suggests that there is significant continuity between liturgy and ordinary life, not just because we return to it, but also because liturgy draws on it: "Liturgy *can* address the practices of ordinary life, because such practices have provided its background and its symbolic tissue. By attending to the integrity and value of what it recalls each time it is celebrated, liturgy can give back to these practices a dignity that lifts them above the level of the quaint or the mundane. It can even preserve the sense of a sacred universe where even the most ordinary aspects of life are precious, central, and consecrated in the community's gathering of itself towards the inheritance of salvation" (*Liturgical Hermeneutics*, 274). Kevin Irwin goes even further: "Liturgy is anthropologically fitting in the sense that the *combination* of using words, symbols, gestures, and silence in a whole ritual action articulates the way human beings communicate." *Text and Context: Method in Liturgical Theology* (Collegeville, Minn.: Liturgical Press, 1994), 314.

77. Alexander Schmemann, *For the Life of the World: Sacraments and Orthodoxy* (Crestwood, N.Y.: St. Vladimir's Seminary Press, 1973). The original 1965 title was just *Sacraments and Orthodoxy*.

78. Ibid., 27.

79. Kavanagh, *On Liturgical Theology*, 100.

80. Lathrop, *Holy Things*, 212, emphasis added. Another Protestant liturgical scholar argues: "The worship of God is the purpose for which other things are done in and by the church. The mission of the church is to enlist worshipers who shall perform the true worship of the true God (*orthodoxia*). The purpose of proclaiming the word and celebrating baptism and the Lord's Supper is to form a community of priests who will offer a sacrifice of praise and prayer *for the life of the world*." Frank C. Senn, *The People's Work: A Social History of the Liturgy* (Minneapolis: Fortress Press, 2006), 55; emphasis added. He warns, however, in a different context: "As liturgical forms, content, and style of celebration are changed, we must ask probing questions of any liturgical material. What theology is being prayed? What experience of (what) God is being promoted? What in the story of Christ is being proclaimed? What understanding of the church is being generated? What attitude toward the creation is being cultivated? What relationship to the world is being strategized? What kind of worship is being made possible? What kind of hospitality is being extended? How are new Christians being made? What values are being instilled? What doctrines are being expressed? Cultural anthropologists have learned through case studies that a change of ritual forms can bring about a change of doctrine.

Such data need to be taken seriously lest the community of faith gain the whole world and lose its soul. As a ritual system, liturgy expresses nothing less than a worldview. A worldview is a complex system of interpretations of experiences and orderings of relationships that provides a cohesive way of understanding reality and operates within particular cultural boundaries." *New Creation: A Liturgical Worldview* (Minneapolis: Fortress Press, 1997), xi.

81. David Fagerberg, *Theologia Prima: What Is Liturgical Theology? A Study in Methodology* (Chicago: Hillenbrand, 1992), 190, emphasis added. Passakos claims this specifically of Orthodox liturgy: "Based on the above-mentioned principle, worship does not exist in order to meet our alleged religious 'duties' and 'needs'. Rather *worship embraces our whole life, the whole space and time, the whole universe.* This is the reason why the Orthodox church sanctifies with its worship every aspect of the personal and social life of its members: worship refers not only to the so-called 'transitional stages' of a human being's life (birth, marriage, death) but actually to every moment of the member's life. Moreover, it liturgically articulates space and time (the day, week, year) transforming them in this way as the framework within which the church awaits the coming of Christ, and prepares the whole universe for it. Consequently, the final aim of worship is the transformation of all in the direction of the kingdom of God." In Thomas F. Best and Dagmar Heller, eds., *Worship Today: Understanding, Practice, Ecumenical Implications* (Geneva: WCC Publications, 2004), 23.

82. Kavanagh, *On Liturgical Theology*, 161.

83. Robert Taft, *The Liturgy of the Hours in East and West: The Origins of the Divine Office and Its Meaning for Today* (Collegeville, Minn.: Liturgical Press, 1993), 343. See also his "What Does Liturgy Do? Toward a Soteriology of Liturgical Celebration: Some Theses," *Worship* 66, no. 3 (1992): 194–211 (a slightly revised version is included in Taft, *Beyond East and West*, 239–58).

84. Irwin, *Text and Context*, 346. Earlier he affirms, however, that "liturgy allows creation to be creation; it does not (and does not need to!) transform creation" (327).

85. Simon Chan, *Liturgical Theology: The Church as Worshiping Community* (Downers Grove, Ill.: InterVarsity, 2006), 84. Anderson asks it in slightly more detail: "The normative question asks: How do liturgical sacramental practices establish and maintain particular standards for the Christian life? The constitutive question asks: How do these practices function to organize or construct Christian identity both individually and communally?" (*Christian Identity*, 34). Wendy Mayer argues that "there is a reason why the shaping of Christian identity (in which performative ritual plays a part) is a topic that is currently exciting much attention." "The Changing Shape of Liturgy: From Earliest Christianity to the End of Late Antiquity," in *Liturgy's Imagined Past/s:*

Methodologies and Materials in the Writing of Liturgical History Today, ed. Teresa Berger and Brian D. Spinks (Collegeville, Minn.: Liturgical Press, 2016), 290.

86. Indeed, Hughes argues that there is a clash "between the meanings proposed in the liturgy and the meanings proposed by the world to which the worshipper returns" (*Worship as Meaning*, 42). He criticizes the liturgical theologians (like Schmemann and Kavanagh) for ignoring the reality of the contemporary world, while also indicting "liberal theologians" for the opposite (namely devaluing liturgy and focusing only on the "world"). Hughes hence thinks of the meaning and language of liturgy and ordinary life as being in essential conflict and it is his primary task in the book to articulate a way in which one might still make sense of the "meaning" of worship against the radical difference of the culture in which we live most of our lives. Yet if there is really such radical discontinuity between them, can one simply draw on language about "ordinary" experience in order to analyze specifically liturgical experience? Lathrop raises this question specifically about the language of sacrifice within liturgy: "Shall we be done with the language of sacrifice altogether? Shall we find other metaphors expressive of the inversion and transformation of our own religio-political culture? Or, shall we give the answer of critical classicism? That is, given the importance of this language in the tradition and the perdurance to our own day of the human interest in holy gift and holy violence as a compelling link with deity, we should maintain the language, even increase its use, but do so with a fierce insistence on breaking and converting its power. We should recover the sense of the sacrificial metaphor and use this metaphor in the manner of biblical rhetoric. Such is the answer of this book" (*Holy Things*, 155–56).

87. Rentel, "Where Is God in the Liturgy?," 223.

88. Ricoeur, *From Text to Action*, Part II (105–222).

89. This especially is an issue raised by many contemporary liturgical scholars, often in explicit critique of earlier work on liturgy. Irwin says, for example: "In trying to underscore the priority of the *lex orandi* in doing theology many of the authors reviewed here have tended to emphasize liturgical *texts*. The positive value of this emphasis is that it gives due weight to texts which have been crafted over centuries of Church life and prayer and which are essential to the ritual enactment of liturgy. The negative side, however, is the danger of using liturgical texts as 'proof texts' and of textual fundamentalism. Liturgy is far more than texts. Liturgy is an enacted communal symbolic event with a number of constitutive elements and means of communication, including, but not restricted to, texts. . . . The succeeding chapters are intended to shed light on an elusive task—how to develop liturgical theology based on the multifaceted *event* called liturgy" (*Text and Context*, 32). Baldovin also points this out: "Much of the current discussion of the relation between the rule of prayer and the rule of

belief (*lex orandi/lex credendi*) would, in my opinion, benefit from a fuller appreciation of the fact that the 'rule of prayer' consists not only in the texts that are prayed but also the manner in which they are prayed and the social and ecclesial setting in which they take place." John F. Baldovin, *Worship: City, Church, and Renewal* (Washington, DC: Pastoral Press, 1991), viii. Dalmais similarly stresses: "The liturgy is an *action*. Consequently, we cannot treat it as though it were a doctrine and be satisfied to make theological use of the texts alone. In fact, the texts are properly liturgical only to the extent that they have their place within the cultic whole of which they are but one component. The whole includes, in addition, the gestures and melodies that underscore and clarify the theological meaning of the texts. In making theological use of liturgical texts, then, we cannot argue from them as though they were the same in kind as other documents of the tradition. These texts are integral parts of an action, and it is this action, and not simply the texts in it, that must be the subject of study for theologians who wish to base an argument on the liturgy" (in Martimort, *Church at Prayer I*, 274). He concludes from this: "An exegesis of the liturgy that does not take into account its poetical character, the importance it gives to verbal correspondences, and its deliberate allusions to details of a rite or a situation, is likely to be misleading. Theologians must put themselves inside the categories proper to cultic and social accomplishment of the mystery of salvation if they are to derive from the liturgical data all the fruits these are capable of providing" (274). See also Richard McCall, *Do This: Liturgy as Performance* (Notre Dame, Ind.: University of Notre Dame Press, 2007).

90. Baldovin even goes so far as to speak of liturgy's use of the city in its processions and movement between different liturgical "stations" in terms of a language: "A city can be compared to a language. Monuments, public places, thoroughfares, the center, edge, and important outlying spots are the vocabulary of this language, while the social and cultural life of the city is the language's syntactical expression. If this is so, then the stational liturgy was one of the most elegant forms of the urban syntax, the use of urban language at its best" (Baldovin, *Urban Character*, 267).

91. I should say, however, that I have deliberately tried to avoid quoting too many texts and focused instead on describing the practices, partly to avoid the trap of much previous philosophical investigation that relies so heavily on texts and frequently ignores the lived experience. It is curious, for example, that Wolterstorff's treatment of liturgy is called *Acting Liturgically*, yet he relies almost exclusively on quotation from texts (rather than descriptions of actions) for his reflections. Many of his questions circle around what participants might mean when they *say* certain things in liturgy. The same is true of Catherine Pickstock's *After Writing* (although with more justification considering she is specifically responding to Derrida's distinctions between speech and writing). Her argument

relies almost exclusively on abundant (Latin) quotations from the medieval Roman rite. *After Writing: On the Liturgical Consummation of Philosophy* (Oxford: Blackwell, 1998).

92. Gadamer, *Truth and Method*, 291–99.

93. Maybe in this respect it can give a two-fold response to Florovsky's claim that "the very nature of the Church can be rather depicted and described rather than properly defined. And surely this can be done only from within the Church. Probably even this description will be convincing only for those of the Church. The Mystery is apprehended only by faith" (*Bible, Church, Tradition*, 58). A fully phenomenological depiction of liturgical experience may well on the one hand help "those of the Church" to appreciate and understand it more fully and on the other hand make it accessible in some sense, at least as a viable experience, to those outside it.

1. Temporality

1. Sergius Bulgakov, *The Orthodox Church*, trans. E. S. Cram (London: Centenary Press, 1935), 152–53, trans. lightly modified.

2. For example, the dating of Dormition on August 15th was connected to the dedication of a church in the holy land, not to any attempt to find or provide a historical date for Mary's death. For the development of the Marian feasts, see Chris Maunder, ed., *The Origins of the Cult of the Virgin Mary* (London: Burns & Oates, 2008); Leslie Brubaker and Mary B. Cunningham, eds., *The Cult of the Mother of God in Byzantium: Texts and Images* (Farnham, UK: Ashgate, 2011). For the development of the dormition traditions more specifically, see Stephen J. Shoemaker, *Ancient Traditions of the Virgin Mary's Dormition and Assumption* (Oxford: Oxford University Press, 2002).

3. Note Andrew Louth's analysis of the significance of this for understanding liturgical time in his "Space, Time and the Liturgy," in *Encounter Between Eastern Orthodoxy and Radical Orthodoxy: Transfiguring the World through the Word*, ed. A. Pabst and C. Schneider (Farnham, UK: Ashgate, 2009), 215–31. See also his "Experiencing the Liturgy in Byzantium," in *Experiencing Byzantium*, 79–88. For the historical background on the liturgical development, see Bradshaw and Maxwell, *Origins of Feasts*; Thomas Talley, *The Origins of the Liturgical Year* (Collegeville, Minn.: Liturgical Press, 1991 [1986]). For daily prayer, see Paul Bradshaw, *Daily Prayer in the Early Church* (New York: Oxford University Press, 1982); Gregory W. Woolfenden, *Daily Liturgical Prayer: Origins and Theology* (Aldershot, UK: Ashgate, 2004); Taft, *Liturgy of the Hours*. For the development of the Byzantine rite more broadly, see Taft, *The Byzantine Rite: A Short History* (Collegeville, Minn.: Liturgical Press, 1992); Thomas Pott, *Byzantine Liturgical Reform: A Study of Liturgical Change in the Byzantine Tradition*, trans. Paul Meyendorff (Crestwood, N.Y.: St. Vladimir's Seminary Press, 2010);

Job Getcha, *The Typikon Decoded: An Explanation of Byzantine Liturgical Practice*, trans. Paul Meyendorff (Yonkers, N.Y.: St. Vladimir's Seminary Press, 2012); Miguel Arranz, "Les grandes étapes de la liturgie byzantine: Palestine—Byzance—Russie. Essai d'aperçu historique," in *Liturgie de l'Église particulière, liturgie de l'Église universelle* (Rome: Edizioni Liturgiche, 1976); Daniel Galadza, *Liturgy and Byzantinization in Jerusalem* (Oxford: Oxford University Press, 2018). For a Western account, see Aimé G. Martimort, ed., *The Church at Prayer IV: The Liturgy and Time* (Collegeville, Minn.: The Liturgical Press, 1986).

4. "The Lord's Day is not 'one out of several' days of the week and does not belong to time, just as the Church is 'not of this world,' and cannot be a part of it. But at the same time the Lord's Day, the first and eighth day, does exist in time and is revealed in time, and this revelation is also the renewal of time, just as the existence of the Church in the world is its renewal and salvation." Alexander Schmemann, *Introduction to Liturgical Theology* (Crestwood, N.Y.: St. Vladimir's Seminary Press, 1986), 139.

5. For a more qualified treatment, see Bradshaw and Hoffman, *Jewish and Christian Worship*.

6. Although the late first-century text *Didache* polemically *opposes* these days to the supposedly Jewish practice of fasting on Mondays and Thursdays, it now seems more likely that the choice of days was actually *influenced* by Jewish practice, maybe by the Essenes who seem to have inspired many early Judeo-Christian traditions. See Gerard Rouwhorst, "Liturgical Time and Space in early Christianity in Light of their Jewish Background," in Alberdina Houtman, Marcel J. H. M. Poorthuis, and Joshua Schwartz, eds., *Sanctity of Time and Space in Tradition and Modernity* (Leiden: Brill, 1998), 265–84.

7. Louth remarks that "it is a 'vulgar error,' popular among some theologians, that cyclical time spells meaninglessness, in contrast with the purposeful nature of linear time" (in Nesbitt, *Experiencing Byzantium*, 82). The introduction to *Sanctity of Time and Space* points out: "Sacred time takes on characteristics of its own and should not be measured by quantitative standards. As an important element of human experience, sacred time is in that respect no less fundamental and 'real' than the more quantitative clock-time. Sacred time is a complex phenomenon: it can be linear and it can be cyclical and it can be traversed in different directions and through different dimensions" (1). Frank Gorman similarly claims: "the dichotomy often made between 'cyclical' views of time and 'linear' views of time is too simplistic to account for the *views* of time in the Priestly ritual material." *The Ideology of Ritual: Space, Time and Status in the Priestly Theology* (Sheffield, UK: Sheffield Academic Press, 1990), 227.

8. Irwin claims: "The determination of times for the celebration of the daily rhythm of the Liturgy of the Hours, the seasons of the Church year and some feast days is derived from the rhythm of the cosmos" (Irwin, *Text and Context*,

133). See also Maxwell Johnson, ed. *Between Memory and Hope: Readings on the Liturgical Year* (Collegeville, Minn.: Liturgical Press, 2000); Marianne H. Micks, *The Future Present: The Phenomenon of Christian Worship* (New York: The Seabury Press, 1970).

9. This is already the case for Melito of Sardis's early Paschal homily and continues in most early homilies for that feast. Cyril of Alexandria often depicts the abundance of spring in his Paschal letters. Maybe the most popular example is Gregory Nazianzen's homily on New Sunday (the Sunday after Pascha), which Maguire suggests became a trope for most subsequent descriptions (*ekphraseis*) of spring in the homiletic tradition. Henry Maguire, *Nectar and Illusion: Nature in Byzantine Art and Literature* (Oxford: Oxford University Press, 2012), 65. This obviously raises issues for celebration in the southern hemisphere where Pascha does not coincide with spring but with autumn. See Anscar J. Chupungco, *Cultural Adaptation of the Liturgy* (New York: Paulist Press, 1982) and *Liturgical Inculturation: Sacramentals, Religiosity, and Catechesis* (Collegeville, Minn.: Liturgical Press, 1992).

10. See Vassa Larin, "Feasting and Fasting According to the Byzantine Typikon," *Worship* 83, no. 2 (2009): 133–48.

11. The only feast that has no explicit link to the life of Christ or the Theotokos, though it has a theological link with Christ, is that of the Elevation of the Cross on September 14.

12. The fast that leads up to the fixed feast of St. Peter and Paul on June 29th begins a week after Pentecost and thus the length of the fast is variable; it can be as short as "minus three days" (if following the new, i.e. Gregorian, calendar) or even longer than the Great Fast (especially if following the "old," i.e. Julian, calendar), depending on when Easter falls in a given year.

13. Schmemann stresses this in his *Great Lent: Journey to Pascha* (Crestwood, N.Y.: St. Vladimir's Seminary Press, 1996, originally published 1969).

14. Hemming argues that "the passage of time is the means by which the liturgy of the heavenly Jerusalem unfolds into human life" and laments the loss of this dimension in the Western tradition (*Worship as a Revelation*, 125).

15. Anderson, *Christian Identity*, 195.

16. Irwin, *The Sacraments: Historical Foundations and Liturgical Theology* (New York: Paulist Press, 2016), 317.

17. Ibid., 253, 254.

18. He continues: "All these expressions must not be taken as poetic hyperboles in the Orthodox church hymnography. In fact, they reflect the existential experience of the church's worship and belief in the resurrection and the presence of the Spirit in its midst. The church becomes the risen, living body of Christ through its reception of the Spirit and the sacramental presence of Christ. In this way, then, the believer shares in the reality of Christ when he shares in the

spiritual reality of the church." Gennadios Limouris, ed., *Church, Kingdom, World: The Church as Mystery and Prophetic Sign* (Geneva: WCC, 1986), 24.

19. Philip H. Pfattreicher, *Liturgical Spirituality* (Valley Forge, Pa.: Trinity Press International, 1997), 115, 247.

20. For example, he claims: "The original understanding of the Feast Day, which we find in the early Christian experience of the Lord's Day or of the Passover, was rooted primarily in the awareness of the Church herself as a Feast Day, as the actualization of the 'eschaton' in this world. Hence its profound connection with real time, with the time of 'this world.' The early Christian theology of the 'eschaton' did not destroy, did not empty time, or abolish its significance, but transformed it into the 'time of the Church,' into the time of salvation. Within the Church time becomes a progressive movement toward the fullness of the Kingdom of Christ, toward His cosmic and historical triumph . . . it acquires the life of a new creation . . . an anticipation of the unending day of the Kingdom" (Schmemann, *Introduction to Liturgical Theology*, 137–38). This theme of eschatological entry into the kingdom within the liturgy pervades his work. Morrill criticizes this realized eschatology: "The statement betrays a significant problem in Schmemann's theology, especially in his concept of eschatological symbolism. . . . Schmemann's error lies in identifying the signs of the kingdom *only* in the liturgy, where they are glorious . . . [instead] the liturgy must enable Christians to perceive the poor and suffering as the special object of God's favor, as well as kenotic deeds of service as signs of the Christ . . . If one overidentifies the signs of the kingdom in the liturgy with the signs of the glorious victory of the Second Coming, then it becomes difficult to expect the participants in the liturgy to be able to perceive the Spirit of the kenotic Christ acting in the world." *Anamnesis as Dangerous Memory* (Collegeville, Minn.: Liturgical Press, 2000), 134. Instead, he stresses the ethical dimension far more strongly: "Thus, the eschatological nature of the liturgy carries an irreducible ethical and social imperative, our own call to know Christ by following him in words and deeds, participating in the reign of God that has come in him, the one who will come again." *Encountering Christ in the Eucharist: The Paschal Mystery in People, Word, and Sacrament* (New York: Paulist Press, 2012), 5. See also his "The Liturgical Is Political: A Narrative Theological Assessment of Alexander Schmemann's Work," *Questions Liturgiques/Studies in Liturgy* 98, nos. 1–2 (2017): 41–59.

21. "Like the Lord's Day in the week, so also Easter each year manifests and 'actualized' that eternal beginning which in the old world appears as an end, but which in the Church signifies an End that has been turned into a Beginning, thereby filling the End with joyous meaning. Easter is an eschatological feast in the most exact and deepest meaning of this word, because in it we 'recall' the resurrection of Christ as our own resurrection, eternal life as our own life, the fullness of the Kingdom as already possessed. As the beginning

and end of the Church year Easter links this eschatological fullness with real time in its yearly form. Life in the world becomes a 'correlative' of the eternal Easter of the New Aeon. Thus Easter reveals the essential nature of every Feast Day, and is in this sense the 'Feast of Feasts'" (Schmemann, *Introduction to Liturgical Theology*, 165).

22. Saliers, *Worship as Theology* (Nashville: Abingdon Press, 1994), 14. He also insists that "the eschatological reality of what God had accomplished in Christ pervades the whole temporal pattern. It is this celebrated pattern of time known as the Christian year that itself bears witness to the eschatological hope made present in the community's worship" (ibid., 55). Similarly, Chan says: "Worship is the time to heighten and renew the eschatological tension of the church's existence" (*Liturgical Theology*, 130).

23. Kavanagh, *On Liturgical Theology*, 142.

24. Irwin, *Text and Context*, 99.

25. Gerard Rouwhorst, "How Eschatological Was Early Christian Liturgy?" *Studia Patristica* XL (Leuven: Peeters, 2006), 93–108.

26. Robert Taft, "Historicisme: une conception à revoir," in *Temps et Liturgie. La Maison-Dieu* 147.3 (Paris: Cerf, 1981), 61–83. See also his "Historicism Revisited," in Taft, *Beyond East and West*, 31–49.

27. Khaled Anatolios also insists on this in his "Heaven and Earth in Byzantine Liturgy," *Antiphon* 5, no. 3 (2000): 1–10.

28. Pfattreicher, *Liturgical Spirituality*, 108.

29. "At each celebration, the participants find the same sacred time . . . Sacred time 'appears under the paradoxical aspect of a circular time, reversible and recoverable, a sort of eternal mythical present that is periodically reintegrated by means of rites.' In ritual, *then* and *now* become one, joined in a representation of that eternal present, which is an experience now of the time of heaven when all will exist in an eternal present, when time will be no more" (Pfattreicher, *Liturgical Spirituality*, 79).

30. Anderson also points out the importance of repetition as "writing in and on the body a form of memory through which we recognize in sight, sound, and affect God's way in the world and by which we are disposed to act in accordance with this way" (*Christian Identity*, 196).

31. Janowiak, *Standing Together*, 54.

32. Senn, *New Creation*, 21.

33. Lathrop, *Holy Things*, 36.

34. Edmund Husserl, *On the Phenomenology of the Consciousness of Internal Time (1893–1917)*, trans. John Barnett Brough (Dordrecht: Kluwer, 1991).

35. Merleau-Ponty, *Phenomenology of Perception*, 433.

36. Ibid., 438.

37. Ibid., 446–52.

38. Heidegger, *Sein und Zeit*, §5, 17. The most important analysis of time in *Being and Time* occurs in §65, although all of Section II is devoted to a discussion of temporality (*Zeitlichkeit*). See also his earlier (1924) discussion of time in *Gesamtausgabe 64* and the later *Zollikon Seminars*, 38–67. For an excellent succinct analysis of Heidegger on time, see Françoise Dastur, *Heidegger et la question du temps* (Paris: Presses Universitaires de France, 1990).

39. GA 64, 107. Several of the French philosophers respond to this particular claim. Falque, for example, argues in *The Guide to Gethsemane* that Christ has a genuine experience of anxiety or anguish over his death, as evident in the account of his agony in the garden of Gethsemane and that he approaches death as we do rather than with ready-made assumptions about eternity that would make his experience fundamentally different from the way in which we experience death.

40. This is worked out most fully in *Experience and the Absolute*, but also the case for most of his other works. See also his *Présence et parousie* (Paris: Ad Solem, 2006) and—especially in regard to time, although less so in regard to liturgy—his *Note sur le temps. Essai sur les raisons de la mémoire et de l'espérance* (Paris: Presses Universitaires de France, 1990).

41. *Présence et parousie*, 69 and 79; *Experience and the Absolute*, 65, see also §17, §39, and §40.

42. *Présence et parousie*, 72–83.

43. *Experience and the Absolute*, 66, 61.

44. He argues, for example, that the time of creation is the "(eschatological) recapitulation of our time" (*Note sur le temps*, 85).

45. Ibid., 188.

46. Ibid., 191.

47. Ibid., 201; emphasis his.

48. Ibid., 202.

49. Ibid., 214.

50. *Experience and the Absolute*, 72.

51. Ibid., 83.

52. He does, however, speak about joy as an important feature of being-before-God—for example, *Experience and the Absolute*, 193–94; *Note sur le temps*, 174–77. See also his discussion of peace in *L'intuition sacramentelle et autres essais* (Paris: Ad Solem, 2015), 147–75 and 109–12.

53. Varghese argues: "The offices of the day, whether Nativity, Epiphany, Good Friday or Easter, reiterate the expression 'today' or 'on this day.' This shows that the feast makes present the reality that is being celebrated. A feast manifests the reality and the implication of the economy of salvation in our life. It reminds us that its meaning and implication are not limited to the present life and that it

provides a 'glimpse' of the eternal life. 'Today' refers to the 'sacramentality' of the liturgical time. Time 'distorts' and makes eternal reality imperfect, multiple and successive. It makes the economy of salvation an event of the past and its fulfillment a 'remote' experience. Liturgical time transcends duration. In the presence of God, everything becomes present. In God, there is but one moment, in which everything is included." Baby Varghese, *West Syrian Liturgical Theology* (Aldershot, UK: Ashgate, 2004), 141.

54. Cuneo, *Ritualized Faith*, 68, 71.

55. Ibid., 72.

56. Ibid., 76, 72–73. Wolterstorff also repeatedly calls this "extraordinary" and even "fanciful."

57. Wolterstorff, *Acting Liturgically*, 188–208.

58. Ibid., 208.

59. This experience of the past is also inflected by memories of past celebrations of the feast. We commemorate Christ's death and resurrection via our memory of the celebrations of the previous years.

60. Yet although in *Being and Time* Heidegger makes the ekstasis of the future primary, in his later work his focus actually increasingly shifts to the present. In the *Zollikon Seminars*, for example, it is the present that becomes central. By analyzing what it means to "have" time, he describes the ways in which it is directed toward the "to come" (*gewärtig*) by dwelling or abiding with what is present (*gegenwärtig*) and by "keeping" or "owning" (*behalten*) what is no longer—all in a present (*anwesend*) experience (*ein dreifältiges Zeitigen des Aufenthalts*). This experienced "now" is hence not simply about "subsistence" or "permanence"; it is "*Verfügung*" not "*Vorhandenheit*."

61. See also Lacoste's essay on this in "L'intuition sacramentelle," which is subtitled "the Eucharist beyond any 'metaphysics of presence'" in *L'intuition sacramentelle*, 29–57.

62. Heidegger does acknowledge that time is "public" or shared (*Zollikon Seminars*, 62). But this is a slightly different point from what is going on in liturgy.

63. Andrew Louth in Nesbitt, *Experiencing Byzantium*, 83.

64. Gorman claims that ritual time must always be "understood in terms of qualitative tone or texture" (*Ideology of Ritual*, 227).

65. Lathrop, *Holy Things*, 111; emphasis his.

66. Heidegger, *Zollikon Seminars*, 78–80.

67. See Greg Kennedy's insightful analysis of this in *The Ontology of Trash* (Albany, N.Y.: SUNY Press, 2007), 11–22. Obviously, we can only continually "feast" in the West because of the exploitation of much of the rest of the world, hence condemned to continual non-voluntary fasting. See also Baldovin's

argument for a stronger distinction between celebration and commemoration in *Worship*, 37–38.

68. See Heschel's analysis of the Sabbath, although this is a fairly common conviction. Indeed, the affirmation that the Messiah will come if even one Sabbath is kept fully, echoes the same insight. Abraham Heschel, *The Sabbath: Its Meaning for Modern Man* (New York: Farrar, Strauss and Giroux, 1951).

69. Cf. "Life in Quest of Narrative."

70. Liturgy does present at least one liturgical event as a fairly radical rupture with our ordinary experience, namely baptism. The symbolism and the text of the baptismal liturgy speak of it as a threshold experience that begins something new, that inaugurates a new time. This new temporality actually begins with death. Liturgical temporality, then, is not primarily governed by anxiety over death, by concern over one's self, but begins with a death of the self. Even this "initial" event is part of a larger cyclical pattern. We join in the celebrations of other baptisms as in some way also a renewal of our own. Theophany celebrates and commemorates not only Christ's baptism but all baptisms and even a renewal of the cosmos each year. At the beginning of every Lent the liturgies exhort us to renew our baptismal vows. So although baptism is a one-time event and even an occasion of rupture, it is in some way continually repeated and actively part of the cycle of repetitions.

71. Baldovin points to the element of repetition in a more surprising context: "Earthquakes, barbarian invasions, sieges, fires, and other disaster all provided likely occasions for services of prayer if not panicked supplication. What is so remarkable about the worship system of medieval Constantinople is not that these events were times for immediate liturgical expression, but that their anniversaries were commemorated year after year for centuries" (*Worship*, 17).

72. Krueger, *Liturgical Subjects*, 221.

73. Aristotle, *Nicomachean Ethics*, Chapter II. Aristotle also frequently stresses the importance of following good examples in order to lead an ethical life (*Nicomachean Ethics*, chapter VI and *Poetics*). Pierre Hadot argues that most of ancient philosophy was conceived as teaching a "way of life" through the acquirement of certain practices. See his *Philosophy as a Way of Life: Spiritual Exercises from Socrates to Foucault* (Oxford: Blackwell, 2011), and *What Is Ancient Philosophy?* (Cambridge, Mass.: Harvard University Press, 2004).

74. "Athlete-imagery" is very common in patristic texts. For example, this is how Theodoret of Cyrrhus refers to the Syrian ascetics, especially Symeon the Stylite, already in the fourth century. Theodoret of Cyrrhus, *A History of the Monks of Syria* (Kalamazoo, Mich.: Cistercian Studies 88, 1985).

75. Saliers in E. Byron Anderson and Bruce T. Morrill, *Liturgy and the Moral Self: Humanity at Full Stretch Before God* (Collegeville, Minn.: Liturgical Press,

1998), 17. Baldovin similarly acknowledges: "The formative work of the liturgy is gradual and subtle; it inculcates Christian identity by the pattern of worship repeated ritually week after week" (*Worship*, 70).

76. Baldovin points out that "the whole way in which we celebrate the liturgical year needs reflection. In order to understand the justice implications of the Christian calendar, one also has to understand what it means and what it *has* meant to celebrate the year by means of a liturgical calendar." In a later chapter he warns: "For some reason many preachers tend not to realize that the liturgical life of Christians is cumulative in its impact. Everything does not happen all at once every Sunday. Rather, the liturgical experience is the gradual process of people being formed more deeply into what they already are—the Body of Christ" (*Worship*, 64, 230).

77. See Ricoeur, *Interpretation Theory* (Forth Worth: Texas Christian University, 1976), 43–44.

78. See Fagerberg's *On Liturgical Asceticism* (Washington: Catholic University of America Press, 2013).

79. *Interpretation Theory*, 94–95.

80. See Greisch, *Buisson ardent*, 14–16 and Grondin, *La philosophie de la religion*.

81. Anderson says: "Such an understanding of liturgical practice challenges the dominant Western ethos of worship as a private act done in a corporate setting. It suggests that liturgical sacramental practice, while an expression of the faith of a community, is a practice that norms and constitutes that community as a particular community of faith. It exercises claims upon us as a religious people. While our practice is a means by which the community of faith *enacts* a theological grammar and narrative, it is also the means by which the community *appropriates* that grammar and narrative" (*Christian Identity*, 192).

82. See Fagerberg, *What is Liturgical Theology?*, 198.

83. Anderson acknowledges: "Yes, repetition and ritual breed familiarity. But it is just this familiarity that is required for our ability to take the music into the depths of our being" (*Christian Identity*, 197).

84. Irwin also puts this in terms of eschatological anticipation, although he does not interpret the eschaton primarily in terms of rupture: "The genius of commemorating the liturgical year is that it enables us to experience salvation in time and according to time's seasons and to yearn for time's fulfillment in the endless day of eternal life" (*Text and Context*, 330).

85. Houtman says: "The fragmentary nature of sacredness of time—not the whole week is holy, but only one day—can be interpreted as a *pars pro toto*: the partial time set apart as a holy day, contains in itself the program for time as a whole" (*Sacrality of Time and Space*, 2). Andronikof describes the temporality of

Orthodox liturgy: "Liturgy unfurls in time, but at each moment figures eternity." Constantin Andronikof, "Le temps de la liturgie," in A. M. Triacca and A. Pistoia, eds., *Eschatologie et liturgie* (Rome: Edizioni Liturgiche, 1985), 21.

2. Spatiality

1. Procopius, *De aedificio*, I.i.23ff., in Cyril Mango, *The Art of the Byzantine Empire 312–1453* (Toronto: University of Toronto Press, 1986), 72–75.

2. For Ricoeur, texts do not "literally" open a spatial world, but the expression refers to the "world of the text" in an apparently purely metaphorical sense. (Gadamer also uses spatial language by speaking of the horizon. And although he does address architecture briefly in *Truth and Method*, he does not explicate any concrete physical aspects of the notion of horizon.) In his work on religion, Ricoeur focuses almost exclusively on texts, primarily the biblical texts, although he certainly also speaks of action and life in other contexts. He did very briefly twice explore the possibility of a parallel between his notion of three-fold mimesis and architecture. Yet although Ricoeur himself never explored any application of this to religious spaces (and probably would have recoiled from any consideration of sacred space, which he associates with the "paganism" examined by Eliade), liturgical scholars consistently speak of sacred space in terms of liminality and threshold and at times explicitly appeal to Ricoeur for doing so (for example, Nichols, cf. the Introduction). Even when no such explicit applications are made, the language of "world" or even "cosmos" is frequently employed. Surely this spatial imagery is telling and deserves further exploration.

3. For analyses of Byzantine architecture, see Thomas Mathews, *The Early Churches of Constantinople: Architecture and Liturgy* (University Park: Pennsylvania State University Press, 1971); Cyril A. Mango, *Byzantine Architecture* (New York: Abrams, 1976); Richard Krautheimer, *Early Christian and Byzantine Architecture* (Baltimore: Penguin, 1986); Allan Doig, *Liturgy and Architecture: From the Early Church to the Middle Ages* (Farnham, UK: Ashgate, 2008); J. M. Hussey and Andrew Louth, *The Orthodox Church in the Byzantine Empire* (Oxford: Oxford University Press, 2010); James and Susan White, *Church Architecture: Building and Renovating for Christian Worship* (Nashville: Abingdon Press, 1988). For a more specific analysis of the architecture and decoration of Hagia Sophia, see Rowland J. Mainstone, *Hagia Sophia: Architecture, Structure and Liturgy of Justinian's Great Church* (London: Thames and Hudson, 1997); Nadine Schibille, *Hagia Sophia and the Byzantine Aesthetic Experience* (Farnham, UK: Ashgate, 2014); Leslie Brubaker, *Talking about the Great Church: Ekphrasis and the Narration on Hagia Sophia* (Prague: Byzantinoslavika, 2011); Robert F. Taft, "The Liturgy of the Great Church: An Initial Synthesis of Structure and Interpretation on the Eve of Iconoclasm," *Dumbarton Oaks Papers* 34–35 (1980-81), 45–75; Walter D. Ray, *Tasting Heaven on Earth: Worship in Sixth-Century Constantinople*

(Grand Rapids, Mich.: Eerdmans, 2012). For the artistic decoration of churches, see Bissera V. Pentcheva, *The Sensual Icon: Space, Ritual and the Senses in Byzantium* (University Park: Pennsylvania State University Press, 2010); Oleg Tarasov, *Icon and Devotion: Sacred Spaces in Imperial Russia* (London: Reaktion Books, 2002); Thomas F. Mathews, *The Clash of Gods: A Reinterpretation of Early Christian Art* (Princeton: Princeton University Press, 1993), and Chapter 4 in his *Byzantium: From Antiquity to the Renaissance* (New York: Harry N. Abrams, Inc., 1998); Robert Ousterhout, "Holy Space: Architecture and the Liturgy," in *Heaven on Earth: Art and the Church in Byzantium*, ed. Linda Safran (University Park: Pennsylvania State University Press, 1988), 81–120. For the description of the interior of buildings, see Paul the Silentiary's *Ekphrasis* and Procopius, *Buildings*, trans. H. B. Dewing (Cambridge, Mass.: Harvard University Press, 1940) and the text by Brubaker on Hagia Sophia mentioned earlier.

4. It is interesting that there was no attempt to imitate either pagan temples or the Jerusalem temple. Clearly, by the time they started building churches, Christians did not want to be associated with either (and there is a constant rhetoric against "paganism" and Judaism in early Christian literature, much broader than architectural questions). This does not mean that Christians thought that previously sacred sites had become "secular," quite the opposite. Ze'ev Safrai contends that it is "quite likely that the location of Christian sacred sites was influenced by the fact that these spots were already considered to be holy" and that "as far as the concept of sanctity is concerned, church and synagogue went almost simultaneously through a very similar process of sacralization" ("The Institutionalization of the Cult of Saints in Christian Society," in Houtman, *Sanctity of Time and Space*, 203, 278). Sites associated with pagan sanctity were often deliberately avoided because of the fear that demonic powers operated in them. Paganism was not simply assumed as untrue, but as an alternate form of the sacred that could do active harm. In either case, the use of the basilica form also confirmed the idea of liturgy as "public work" and often poverty relief and other social aid was organized from and within the church building. Stringer claims that Christian architecture begins in the cult of the saints: "The bodies of the martyrs, however, were not polluting; they were the site of sacred power and the focus for worship. If the churches of the cities were to become the sacred places of the new discourses, then the sacred dead needed to be brought in to sanctify these spaces. It was no longer enough simply to have a worshipping congregation; something more concrete, a specific sacred 'place,' was needed, and this was provided by the relics of the martyrs and saints." Martin D. Stringer, *A Sociological History of Christian Worship* (Cambridge: Cambridge University Press, 2005), 88.

5. For early descriptions of how churches were to be built, their interior arranged, and what spaces designated for which groups, see *Constitutiones*

apostolorum II.57 and *Testamentum Domini* I.19. Excerpts from these and many other relevant texts are included in Mango, *Art of the Byzantine Empire*.

6. For an analysis of its theological significance, see Kathleen McVey, "The Domed Church as a Microcosm: Literary Roots of an Architectural Symbol," *Dumbarton Oaks Papers* 37 (1983): 19–21; Anscar J. Chupungco, *The Cosmic Elements of Christian Passover* (Rome: Editrice Anselmiana, 1977); Nicolas Ossorguine, "Éléments cosmique de la mystagogie liturgique," in *Mystagogie: Pensée liturgique d'aujourd'hui et liturgie ancienne,* ed. A. M. Triacca and A. Pistoia (Rome: Edizioni Liturgiche, 1993), 243–51.

7. Tamara Grdzelidze, "Liturgical Space in the Writings of Maximus the Confessor," *Studia Patristica* XXXVII (Leuven: Peeters, 2001), 499–504. See also Torstein Theodor Tollefsen, "The Mystery of Christ as a Key to the Cosmology of St. Maximus the Confessor," *Studia Patristica* XLII (Leuven: Peeters, 2006), 255–58; Alain Riou, *Le monde et l'eglise selon Saint Maxime le Confesseur* (Paris: Beauchesne, 1973).

8. This included extensive building in the holy land, especially Jerusalem, which had spatial significance in a different way, both in regard to the association of the geographical locations with events in Jesus's life and increasingly as a site for pilgrimage, which afforded a different experience of "sacred" space. The most famous account of this is that of a Gallacian nun, now usually named Egeria, who describes various churches and geographical locations and provides an extensive account of liturgical life in late fourth-century Jerusalem and its environs. See John Wilkinson, *Egeria's Travels* (Westminster, UK: Aris & Phillips, 1999). Pilgrimage to Palestine was not unusual at the time; we have another much briefer report from a pilgrim from Bordeaux who traveled there around 333, and there is extensive archaeological evidence of various kinds of mementos that were sold to pilgrims (a whole tourist trade seems to have developed around pilgrimage sites from very early on). Pilgrimage was also a popular practice before the Christian era, so its development within Christianity does not come without context or precedent. On this topic, see Andrew Louth, "Theological Reflections on Pilgrimage," *ΠΡΑΤΙΚΑ ΙΒ ΕΠΙΣΤΗΜΟΝΙΚΟΥ ΣΥΜΠΟΣΙΟΥ* (Thessaloniki: University Studio Press, 2001), 97–102; John Wilkinson, *Jerusalem Pilgrims before the Crusades* (Westminster, UK: Aris and Phillips, 2015); Brouria Bitton-Ashkeloni, *Encountering the Sacred: The Debate on Christian Pilgrimage in Late Antiquity* (Berkeley: University of California Press, 2005); Peter W. L. Walker, *Holy City, Holy Places? Christian Attitudes to Jerusalem and the Holy Land in the Fourth Century* (Oxford: Clarendon, 1990); Gary Vikan, *Early Byzantine Pilgrimage Art* (Washington: Dumbarton Oaks Byzantine Collection Publications, 2010); Edward David Hunt, *Holy Land Pilgrimage in the Later Roman Empire AD 312–460* (Oxford: Clarendon Press, 1982); Vincent and Edith Turner, *Image and Pilgrimage in Christian Culture* (Oxford: Basil Blackwell,

1978); Catia Galatariotou, "Travel and Perception in Byzantium," *Dumbarton Oaks Papers* 47 (1993): 222–41.

9. For a detailed examination, see Vasileios Marinis, *Architecture and Ritual in the Churches of Constantinople: Ninth to Fifteenth Centuries* (Cambridge: Cambridge University Press, 2014).

10. For one prominent example (besides Procopius and Paul the Silentiary), see Patriarch Photios's tenth homily, which describes a new chapel in the palace. Photios, *The Homilies of Photius Patriarch of Constantinople*, trans. Cyril Mango (Cambridge, Mass.: Harvard University Press, 1958).

11. Gorman claims: "The way a particular culture views and 'interprets' space and time is an important part of its world view and, hence, of its cosmology." Ritual "is a way of construing, actualizing, realizing, and bringing into being a world of meaning and ordered existence. Ritual is thus seen as a means of enacting one's theology" (*Ideology of Ritual*, 10, 232).

12. Already the early *Apostolic Constitutions* says: "First, let the church be elongated (inasmuch as it resembles a ship), turned to the east, and let it have the pastophoria on either side, towards the east." It goes on to give various other instructions regarding exterior and interior arrangement (*Constitutiones apostolorum* II.57.3 in Mango, *Art of the Byzantine Empire*, 24).

13. In this respect, the *ekphraseis*/descriptions of ecclesial buildings by Procopius and other early writers are telling: They highlight not specific architectural features per se, but describe their meaning. Their description is neither "objective" nor "subjective" in our use of those terms, they are not descriptions of physical or geometrical extension nor are they descriptions of personal "subjective" impressions, rather they are "meaningful" descriptions, one could even call them phenomenological descriptions, inasmuch as they highlight the significance of the space as *any* viewer should experience it (or would experience it by coming into the space with the right intentionality). For example, Choricius describes the church St. Sergius of Gaza: "When you enter, you will be staggered by the variety of the spectacle. Eager as you are to see everything at once, you will depart not having seen anything properly, since your gaze darts hither and thither in your attempt not to leave aught unobserved: for you will think that in leaving something out you will have missed the best" (*Laudatio Marciania* I.23, in Mango, *Art of the Byzantine Empire*, 61).

14. Baldovin's *Urban Character* is by far the most thorough exploration of stational liturgy.

15. Baldovin, *Urban Character*, 257.

16. See Jane Baun, *Tales from Another Byzantium: Celestial Journey and Local Community in Medieval Greek Apocrypha* (Cambridge: Cambridge University Press, 2007). The political arrangement in Byzantium was also supposed to instantiate the heavenly *topos* in some (albeit limited) form. Mango claims that

"the Byzantines imagined God and the Heavenly Kingdom as a vastly enlarged replica of the imperial court at Constantinople . . . their mutual resemblance was taken for granted." Social relations were to conform "to the harmony of the universe: life on earth . . . assumes some resemblance to life in Heaven." *Byzantium: The Empire of the New Rome* (New York: Charles Scribner's Sons, 1980), 151, 218.

17. Pentcheva, *Icons and Power*, 110. She also reports that there were processions to Blachernai every Friday evening.

18. Baldovin, *Urban Character*, 267.

19. Baldovin in Getcha and Stavrou, *Le feu sur la terre*, 94.

20. Vicky Manolopoulo, "Processing Emotion: Litanies in Byzantine Constantinople," in Nesbitt, *Experiencing Byzantium*, 153, 159.

21. Marinis also discusses the "nonliturgical" use of churches, referring to "devotion to sacred objects, to healings and miracles, to funerary rites, and to other functions." He argues that it "is difficult, and occasionally imprudent, to insist on completely separating" liturgical and nonlitugical acts, pointing to personal devotions in the context of a service as an example. He also points to other examples: "Nonliturgical activity is usually taken to refer exclusively to private devotions, but there is another, more elusive category of nonliturgical acts: the use of sacred space for such informal occurrences as resting, sleeping, eating, and drinking. These could be the result of circumstances—a weary traveler finds a church on his way and rests there—or more institutionalized, such as the *diaklysmos* or collation partaken by monastics in the narthex." In fact, "sometimes churches became part of celebrations that took place during popular festivals." For example, "there are tantalizing allusions to people wearing costumes even inside churches: the canonist Balsamon refers to priests who, on certain feast days, appear in the middle of the church dressed as soldiers with sword in hand, or as monks, or even as four-legged animals" (*Architecture and Ritual*, 100, 101, 111, 112).

22. André Lossky examines these in his "Commémoration liturgique des séismes et confession de la toute-puissance divine," in *Liturgie et cosmos*, ed. A. M. Triacca and A. Pistoia (Rome: Edizioni Liturgiche, 1998), 131–51.

23. Pfattreicher, for example, claims: "Sacred space, marked out and enclosed by a church building, is a declaration of the paradox of a timeless proclamation embedded in time, the Eternal born in mortal flesh at a specific moment and in a particular geographic area. It is a window of heaven and a door to eternity carrying our sight and spirit beyond the confines of this world and into the next as far as the human spirit can penetrate and understand. Temples are always liminal" (Pfattreicher, *Liturgical Spirituality*, 173). Similar comments are frequent in writing on liturgy and ritual, often relying on Eliade's analysis of sacred space.

24. See the detailed study by Pascal Mueller-Jourdan, *Typologie spatio-temporelle de l'Ecclesia byzantine. La Mystagogie de Maxime le Confesseur dans la culture philosophique de l'Antiquité tardive* (Leiden: Brill, 2005).

25. See Enrico Mazza, *Mystagogy: A Theology of Liturgy in the Patristic Age*, trans. Matthew J. O'Connell (New York: Pueblo, 1989).

26. Louth summarizes these in his "Experiencing the Liturgy in Byzantium." Stringer says: "Many different symbolisms were possible but the all-embracing sense was of a space designed to represent heaven on earth and to be the meeting place between earth and heaven. . . . This represents the hierarchy that is believed to exist as a fundamental part of the structure of the universe. As well as the space itself reflecting the meeting of earth and heaven, the liturgy, as performed within that space, was seen to make that meeting a reality. The singing of the liturgy in particular reflected this merging of heaven and earth" (*Sociological History*, 126, 127).

27. Marinis qualifies this: "The Divine Liturgy was both a cosmos and a history. The same was true for the building. In light of such mutually reinforcing understandings, the interchange of architecture and ritual in Constantinople cannot be distilled into a simple question of how function affects form. . . . The evidence, however, supports none of this. Rather, as long as a church building continued to be used, the dialectic between architecture and ritual endured. . . . For all the professed preoccupation of the Byzantines with taxis and the rigidity that this concept implies, both space and function show remarkable fluidity. . . . it is the story of an architecture and ritual continually in the process of becoming" (*Architecture and Ritual*, 117–18).

28. To cite again from Choricius's description of the church of St. Sergius at Gaza: "To gaze up at it [the roof of the church] you will require a neck accustomed to straining upward, so high is the roof above the ground, and with good reason, since it imitates the visible heaven" (*Laudatio Marciani* I.39 in Mango, *Art of the Byzantine Empire*, 63). Procopius describes the marble of Hagia Sophia as giving the impression of "a meadow in full bloom." *De aedificio* (in ibid., 76).

29. While early Christian churches seem to have featured extensive mosaic with "pagan" themes, depictions of nature, of rivers and sources of water, even of "pagan" gods, these were progressively removed. Increasingly, mosaics are no longer used for floors but instead for walls, no longer using flowers and vines, but portraying human figures (biblical or the saints). See Henry Maguire, *Nectar and Illusion* and his earlier *Earth and Ocean: The Terrestrial World in Early Byzantine Art* (University Park: Pennsylvania State University Press, 1987).

30. See, for example, Bissera V. Pentcheva, "Hagia Sophia and Multisensory Aesthetics," *GESTA* 50.2 (2011): 93–111.

31. Maguire points out that a significant transition in the depiction of nature imagery occurs during iconoclasm where all sides accuse each other of worshipping the material rather than the Creator and all scrupulously try to avoid giving any impression of doing so. Yet, a refusal to worship nature or the material was not tantamount to a rejection of it, as arguments on both sides clearly showed.

The most famous is probably John of Damascus's claim that we "venerate matter" because Christ "became matter" for our sake and henceforth matter "is filled with divine energy and grace." John of Damascus, *Three Treatises on the Divine Images*, trans. Andrew Louth (Crestwood, N.Y.: St. Vladimir's Seminary Press, 2003), I.16, 29–30.

32. Stringer claims: "The incarnation, including the crucifixion, the resurrection and the ascension, was seen as the point at which heaven and earth met most profoundly and in which the permanent links between the two were made. To recreate that moment in the liturgy, therefore, was the ultimate goal. The liturgy expressed this dramatically through its texts and also through a series of movements from the space behind the iconostasis to the nave and back again." He also argues that "the liturgy was seen to be an end in itself, a means for achieving the unity of heaven and earth, the action that enables people to touch heaven if only for a moment. The liturgy took on cosmic proportions. It was done because it had to be done, not because there was any specific benefit for those who took part." Thus, "the celebrating of the liturgy was a way, the primary way for most, of tuning in to the cycle of the world and the way in which the world was. It was a means of entering into the cosmic pattern of creation. For some, however, it was more than this. It was a way not just of enabling a meeting between heaven and earth, but of becoming one with heaven. It was a way of bringing the earthly into the heavenly realms, of making the mundane and the ordinary into something special, something cosmic" (*Sociological History*, 127, 128, 129, respectively). Presumably these are descriptions of the theological claims of certain historical texts rather than sociological claims per se.

33. Lity at Compline, Feast of the Annunciation of the Most Holy Theotokos, in *The Festal Menaion*, trans. Kallistos Ware and Mother Mary (South Canaan, Pa.: St. Tikhon's Seminary Press, 1998), 445.

34. Ibid., 445, 455.

35. Vespers for the Nativity, 254. It is maybe also not coincidental that Christ is called the "sun" (and not just the "son") throughout many liturgies, festal and otherwise.

36. Lity for Nativity, 263.

37. Ode 3 at Matins for the feast of the Ascension (330, 331).

38. Proclus of Constantinople affirms this in a homily on ascension: "The nature of creation is distributed in heaven and on earth, / but the grace of today, having bridged the division of these things, / does not permit me to see the division. / For who would in future say that heaven is separated from things on earth . . ." Homily 21.1, in *Homilies on the Life of Christ*, trans. J. H. Barkhuizen (Brisbane: Centre for Early Christian Studies, 2001).

39. Joseph Ratzinger, *The Spirit of the Liturgy*, trans. J. Saward (San Francisco: Ignatius Press, 2000), 71.

40. Clayton Schmit, *Too Deep for Words: A Theology of Liturgical Expression* (Louisville: Westminster John Knox Press, 2002), 19.

41. Limouris, *Church, Kingdom*, 45.

42. Schmemann in Fisch, *Liturgy and Tradition*, 58.

43. Lathrop wants to connect this cosmological dimension with current cosmology so as to result in a changed worldview: "The argument of this book is that the strong central symbols of Christian liturgy can stand in lively and helpful dialogue with the needs for a current cosmology. Indeed, when those symbols are celebrated in a strong assembly with a clear open door . . . they can have a surprising cosmological resonance. Assembly gathered, the great bath enacted or remembered, Scripture read and preached and sung, many things prayed for, the holy meal held, assembly and resources sent—these things can propose, reinforce, and, most importantly, radically and continually reorient our worldview" (Lathrop, *Holy Ground*, 15). Later he claims more specifically that baptism has "implications for cosmology" (ibid., 112). He also rhetorically implies that this ought to have concrete implications for how we treat the earth: "If the Christian assembly gathers in the presence of this same God, the God celebrated in this story, does that assembly similarly deal so gently with the earth as God does with the bush? Does the assembly carry itself so harmlessly to the location of its meeting? Do we take off our shoes? The question is deeper yet: does that assembly invite us to see the place on which we meet—and the earth around the meeting—as holy ground? Do the stories we tell, the meals we eat, the rituals we keep, engage us in caring for the earth with which we live? Or not? Do they rather support us in the contrary practice, in our own unlimited use of what lies around us, without concern for the consequences? With these inquiries, we come to the most obviously urgent of the cosmological questions before us" (ibid., 125).

44. *Being and Time*, §§22–24. (Something similar is obviously true for the experience of time, inasmuch as an anxiously anticipated event can feel much closer than the next moment.) Phenomenologists have thought much about the relationship between space and time. Husserl occasionally connects them, arguing that the way in which we experience the duration of time is not unlike our experience of the extension of space. Even when trying to distinguish them strictly, as Heidegger for instance seeks to do, there are clearly some parallels and connections between the two. In the *Zollikon Seminars*, for example, Heidegger begins with a discussion of space—in order to get to a discussion of the body—but then interrupts this with a discussion of time, before returning to space and corporeality more fully. Clearly the analysis of time is taken to illuminate also something about space. See also *Being and Time*, §70. For a discussion of the role of space in Heidegger, see Didier Franck, *Heidegger et le problème de l'espace* (Paris: Minuit, 1986).

45. In this respect it is interesting that the Lucernare (mentioned also by Egeria) is one of the oldest liturgical occasions and its "evening song" to the setting of the sun the oldest Christian hymn for which we have evidence.

46. English translation in: Heidegger, *Basic Writings*, ed. David Farrell Krell (San Francisco: HarperCollins, 1993), 343–63.

47. Ibid., 350.

48. He explicates this in terms of the function of "mortals" to "save" the earth, "receive" the sky, "await" the divinities, and "initiate their own essential being" as mortals (ibid., 352). Heidegger points out that nearness and remoteness are never just interval or extension or if so they would be immensely impoverished (ibid., 357).

49. Lacoste, *Experience and the Absolute*, 21.

50. Lacoste uses strong language: "Just as Dasein was without God in the world, mortals live without God in the 'Fourfold,' and it is by no means certain that the God for which they wait is worthy of the name" (ibid., 18). Indeed, his main problem seems to be not with the human experience of place (e.g. as sacred), but with the consequence that it makes the transcendent (God) too immanent (cf. ibid., 35). A crucial part of his strong insistence on rupture, eschaton, and non-experience is his desire to protect God's transcendence and absoluteness and to avoid any "possession" of the divine.

51. Ibid., 25, 22.

52. The language of liminality is very popular in the theological literature on liturgy (as briefly discussed in the Introduction). Lathrop is much closer to Lacoste inasmuch as he consistently refuses any move to a more fully "realized" eschatology. Schmemann is much happier to claim that "heaven" really comes "to earth" or becomes present in liturgy and that we enter within it (or into "the kingdom"). One should also note that Heidegger's discussion of world (and space) in *Being and Time* is not as opposed to his conception of earth (and space) in the later essays as Lacoste claims. Lacoste's is a distinct interpretation, not merely an application of Heidegger.

53. *Experience and the Absolute*, 31, 32.

54. Ibid., 33, 37.

55. Steinbock has developed the Husserlian distinction between "home" world and "alien" world in his *Home and Beyond: Generative Phenomenology after Husserl* (Evanston, Ill.: Northwestern University Press, 1995).

56. See Janet Donohoe, *Remembering Places: A Phenomenological Study of the Relationship between Memory and Place* (Lanham, Md.: Lexington Books, 2014), 25.

57. Gorman speaks of this as common to all ritual spaces (*Ideology of Ritual*, 209).

58. Houtman contends that "what is common to all sacred space is again [like time] its fragmentary nature: it is set apart from space that is not sacred,

whether this 'other' space is neutral or profane. Thus, boundaries and boundary markers are necessary and essential characteristics of any space that is holy." He also points out that "the development from holy place to a cult site venerated by many believers could take several centuries and shows a consistent pattern." Schwartz argues in the same collection: "The *sine qua non* for a location to be considered sacred is the abiding presence of the God of Israel there" (*Sanctity of Time and Space*, 2, 5, 11).

59. For a phenomenological account of liminal spaces—borders, boundaries, edges, surfaces, limits, and so forth—see Edward S. Casey, *The World on Edge* (Bloomington: Indiana University Press, 2017).

60. Even our accounts of the parousia, or paradise, are always deeply informed by our experience of this here and now. Descriptions of "paradise," whether liturgical or not, are usually heavily influenced by the author's concrete spatial and geographical experience (cf. the text by Baun mentioned earlier).

61. "Openness" would be more something like "Offenheit" in German, which he does use in other contexts in his later work.

62. Indeed, Marion's notion of receptivity might be more appropriate here.

63. Cf. Henry Maguire, *The Icons of their Bodies: Saints and their Images in Byzantium* (Princeton: Princeton University Press, 1996).

64. Edward S. Casey stresses this point in his *Getting Back into Place: Toward a Renewed Understanding of the Place-World* (Bloomington: Indiana University Press, 2009). See especially Part II: The Body in Place (41–105).

3. Corporeality

1. Jean-Marie Gueullette, *La Beauté d'un geste* (Paris: Cerf, 2014), 60–61.

2. From the Prayers of Preparation for Communion.

3. An entire issue of *Concilium* is devoted to this topic. *Liturgy and the Body*, ed. Louis-Marie Chauvet and François Kabasele Lumbala, *Concilium* 1995/3 (London: SCM Press; Maryknoll: Orbis Books, 1995). The collection also includes some contributions on liturgical space, the senses, memory, and symbolism.

4. Mitchell, *Meeting Mystery*, 32. Irwin also points to this repeatedly in *Sacraments*, 217, 232–33.

5. Mitchell, *Meeting Mystery*, 94.

6. Margaret Scott, *The Eucharist and Social Justice* (New York: Paulist Press, 2008), 87.

7. Chauvet, *Symbol and Sacrament*, 141.

8. Ibid., 155.

9. Ibid., 355. This involves for him a constant interplay between body and cosmos (ibid., 357).

10. Ibid., 369. He reiterates similar points in his *The Sacraments: The Word of God at the Mercy of the Body* (Collegeville, Minn.: Liturgical Press, 2001). He

also makes the three-fold distinction of bodies there, although he calls them body of desire, of tradition, and of nature instead (114).

11. Pfattreicher, *Liturgical Spirituality*, 9. Saliers similarly says: "In corporate worship, Christians engage in activities which articulate and shape how they are to be disposed toward the world. Those who say they love God but who are *not* disposed to love and serve the neighbor are misunderstanding the words and actions of worship" (in Anderson, *Liturgy and the Moral Self*, 18).

12. Anderson, *Christian Identity*, 81. See also Bruce T. Morrill, ed., *Bodies of Worship: Explorations in Theory and Practice* (Collegeville, Minn.: Liturgical Press, 1999). Stephen Buckland highlights the relation between memory and embodiment: "All of these practices shape the body in the most literal sense: dispositions to smile or frown carve lines upon the face, muscles in tongues and limbs develop knacks of speaking and walking, different tasks produce callouses in different places, mould spines in different ways. . . . Through such habitual bodily practices, the experiences of previous generations are 'sedimented' in bodies. Through such practices, a body 're-members' its identity. That is to say, it discovers and reinvents, enforces and reinforces its identity, and in this way gives 'life' to its members—or takes life away; life, that is, 'as it is lived' by members of the myriad interlocking, overlapping, multi-layered, and conflicting groupings that constitute a human community. Postures and gestures characteristic of a class, of a whole people, are inherited; family traits are passed on—familiar and yet individual" (in Chauvet, *Liturgy and the Body*, 50–51).

13. Mitchell, *Meeting Mystery*, 149.

14. Hughes, *Worship as Meaning*, 284. See also Antonio Donghi, *Words and Gestures in the Liturgy*, trans. W. McDonough et al (Collegeville, Minn.: Liturgical Press, 2009). Flanagan similarly says: "The music, the speech, the stylised gestures, and the white robes of the actors, all denote a condensed expression of what is to be revealed, but which lies presently concealed in symbols" (*Sociology and Liturgy*, 75). Chauvet's work discusses liturgical and sacramental symbolism extensively.

15. Randi Rashkover, *Liturgy, Time, and the Politics of Redemption* (Grand Rapids, Mich.: Eerdmans, 2006), 20.

16. Saliers, *Worship as Theology*, 163–64.

17. For a detailed exploration not only of Husserl's concepts of *Körper* and *Leib*, but also for what this means for inter-subjectivity, i.e. my encounter with the body or flesh of the other, see Didier Franck, *Flesh and Body: On the Phenomenology of Husserl*, trans. Joseph Rivera and Scott Davidson (London: Bloomsbury, 2014). This treatment of Husserl has had tremendous influence on French thinking about this issue since its publication. See also Natalie Depraz, *Transcendance et incarnation. Le statut de l'intersubjéctivité comme altérité à soi chez Husserl* (Paris: Vrin, 1995) and her *Lucidité du corps. De l'empirisme transcendental en phénoménologie* (Dordrecht: Kluwer Academic Publishers, 2001).

18. Lévinas translates it as "mon propre corps organique" in his original translation of Husserl's *Cartesian Meditations*. Ricoeur was the first to render it as "chair" in his early introduction to Husserl's phenomenology. (I owe this information to Emmanuel Falque and Richard Kearney respectively.) For a detailed consideration of *Körper* and *Leib* and the viability of their various French translations, see Natalie Depraz's entry "Leib/Körper/Fleisch" in the *Dictionary of Untranslatables: A Philosophical Lexicon*, ed. Barbara Cassin (Princeton: Princeton University Press, 2014), 561–65.

19. In that respect, things are easier for the German phenomenologists. Edith Stein, Gerda Walther, and Hedwig Conrad-Martius all operate with five terms rather than two: *Körper, Leib, Seele, Gemüt,* and *Geist*. For a more detailed exploration, see my "Körper, Leib, Gemüt, Seele, Geist: Conceptions of the Self in Early Phenomenology," *Gerda Walther's Phenomenology of Sociality, Psychology, and Religion*, ed. Antonio Calcagno (New York: Springer, 2019), 85–99.

20. For his awareness of the theological tradition, see his essay "Faith and Good Faith," where he makes the famous claim that "the incarnation changes everything." Merleau-Ponty, *Sense and Non-Sense*, trans. Hubert L. Dreyfus and Patricia Allen Dreyfus (Evanston, Ill.: Northwestern University Press, 1964), 174. This claim means for him that God now becomes exterior and is not merely interior. This transforms faith into something more fragile, finite, and ambiguous because it always lives in the tension between the absolute interior and the more concrete exterior. The essay is about the church's or Christianity's social and political engagement in conversation with Daniélou. God as Father is the conservative element; the incarnation refers to the revolutionary one.

21. *Befindlichkeit* is translated as *l'affection* into French, although English uses state-of-mind (Macquarrie and Robinson), attunement (Stambaugh), or disposedness (Dahlstrom). Of these, affectivity seems by far the best translation, partly because Heidegger himself uses *Affektion* in a couple instances.

22. Heidegger, *Zollikon Seminars*, see especially the sessions in May 1965.

23. *Phenomenology of Perception*, 147, 151, respectively.

24. See his *Incarnation* and *Material Phenomenology*, trans. Scott Davidson (New York: Fordham University Press, 2008).

25. See especially *In Excess*, 82–103.

26. *The Erotic Phenomenon*, trans. Stephen Lewis (Chicago: University of Chicago Press, 2007), 106–50.

27. Ibid., 151–222.

28. See his discussion of Henry in *Le combat amoureux*, 197–238.

29. See *The Wedding Feast*, 218–29.

30. Marion has recently challenged this interpretation of Descartes in his *On Descartes' Passive Thought: The Myth of Cartesian Dualism* (Chicago: University of Chicago Press, 2018).

31. We think of the body today almost entirely in Cartesian and Galilean terms, as an object in space that has a certain extension and weight, which can be measured and described, a thing of the senses, separate from the thinking mind that might be lodged within it, but is something qualitatively different. Although our society is obsessed with the "look" of bodies (preferably athletic, healthy, and young) and seeks to indulge its desires at all points (fueled by media, technology, and advertising), it also has a deep (Cartesian) distrust of the body, especially when it fails us and reveals our finitude by becoming frail, by aging, and by dying. And our fascination with technology is increasingly moving us into a virtual world that is still in some sense physical and material (not only by the huge data centers in which the memory of the ephemeral "clouds" are stored, but also more immediately by the way in which it involves constant touching of screens and "gadgets"), but not fully corporeal and certainly not fleshly. Affectivity has been moved into a virtual space that is no longer embodied or enfleshed. Not only have space and body become separated, but also flesh and affectivity.

32. Merleau-Ponty says: "Sacramental words and gestures are not simply the embodiment of some thought. Like tangible things, they are themselves the carriers of their meaning, which is inseparable from its material form. They do not evoke the idea of God: they are the vehicle of his presence and action. In the last analysis the soul is so little to be separated from the body that it will carry a radiant double of its temporal body into eternity" (*Sense and Non-Sense*, 175).

33. This is precisely one of the aspects to which Peter Brown points in his argument that early Christianity broke down social barriers and that poverty was a much more important issue in the early centuries than sexuality. *The Body and Society* (London: Faber & Faber, 1989).

34. Steinbock's thoroughly phenomenological discussion of pride and humility as "moral emotions" enables a phenomenological use of these terms without immediate suspicion of recourse to theology. See his analyses of pride and humility in *Moral Emotions*, Chapters 1 and 7, respectively.

35. Varghese points to the link between genuflection, fasting, and repentance: "The general rule is that the genuflection is observed on a fasting day. Thus we can note that there is a link between genuflection and fasting; both are expressions of repentance. The Eucharistic celebration, the preparation rites and the pre-anaphora include genuflections, also symbolizing penitence" (*West Syrian*, 115).

36. Saliers claims that "participation in the liturgy requires our humanity at full stretch" (*Worship as Theology*, 28).

37. *Lenten Triodion*, trans. Kallistos Ware and Mother Mary (South Canaan, Pa.: St. Tikhon's Seminary Press, 2002), 187.

38. Ibid., 370.

39. Ibid., 379.

40. *Lenten Triodion*, 392. Or: "O Saviour, heal the putrefaction of my humbled soul, for Thou are the one Physician; apply plaster, and pour in oil and wine—works of repentance, and compunctions with tears" (ibid., 408). Similar statements are repeated frequently both in the Canon and throughout the Lenten liturgies. Illness of soul and body are always held together here; the wounds of one affect the other. Sin is interpreted as disintegration and pollution (both internal and external, self-caused and inflicted), repentance as the pathway to purification, wholeness, and health.

41. Second Ode, *Lenten Triodion*, 384.

42. For example, many of the Cappadocian poverty sermons chide the wealthy for their unjust practices and attribute drought or flood to their greed and mistreatment of the poor. See Holman, *Hungry Are Dying*.

43. In that respect, it is interesting that most ordination ceremonies involve some measure of being vested by others and a hierarchical liturgy always involves the bishop being dressed by others in the midst of the community. He does not put on any of his own garments, but all are put on him by others.

44. Lacoste, *Experience and the Absolute*, 40. ("Dasein exists in the world without God," 41.)

45. Ibid., 41. (The English translation renders *surcroît* as "surplus" rather than "excess" and *donation divine* as "divine donation" rather than employing the language of givenness.)

46. Ibid., 42, trans. lightly modified.

47. Ibid., 44.

48. Ibid., 37.

49. Ibid., 37–38. Lacoste suggests that this is an anticipation of the eschatological resurrection of the flesh: "For what is in question in the liturgical 'dance' is this: the body symbolically allows worldly or earthly logic to take leave of its inscription in place. We can leave aside the question of a possible eschatological destiny of the flesh, and refrain from asking whether the liturgical dance imitates in advance the definitive presence of man risen before God . . . But implicit in the liturgical 'dance' is the possibility of being symbolically absent from world and earth, not so as to give the impression of death, but to make manifest a dimension of life that is neither worldly nor earthly" (ibid., 38–39).

50. Indeed, he says in this context that our "being-before-God" "does violence" to our "being-in-the-world" (ibid., 48).

51. Marion, *God Without Being*, trans. Thomas A. Carlson (Chicago: University of Chicago Press, 1991), 7–24. See also his *Idol and Distance*, trans. Thomas A. Carlson (New York: Fordham University Press, 2001).

52. This is one of the (many) reasons why photography or filming within liturgy contradicts the very essence of what liturgy is about and is utterly antithetical

to what it claims to be doing. It is not a spectacle to be contemplated or a form of self-exhibition.

53. This "failure" should not, however, be immediately attributed to the "fact" that we have not yet reached the eschaton.

54. For example: "The time for combat is at hand and has begun already; let all of us set forth eagerly upon the course of the Fast, offering our virtues as gifts to the Lord" (Monday of the First Week, *Lenten Triodion*, 191); "O ye faithful, let us take upon ourselves great labours in this season of abstinence" (Aposticha, Fourth Sunday, *Lenten Triodion*, 368).

55. Cf. Natalie Depraz, *Le corps glorieux. Phénoménologie pratique de la* Philocalie *des pères du désert et des pères de l'église* (Leuven: Peeters, 2008).

4. Sensoriality

1. Cited in Mango, *Art of the Byzantine Empire*, 92.

2. As pointed out also by Béatrice Caseau, "Christian Bodies: The Senses and Early Byzantine Christianity," in *Desire and Denial in Byzantium*, ed. Liz James (Aldershot, UK: Ashgate, 1999), 103–4.

3. Liz James actually argues that it was the sense most privileged by the Byzantines: "In Christian Byzantium, with its privileging of the sense of sight, both before and after the eight century, religious images had to exist. The nature of vision, *phantasia* and memory made them inevitable. The rest, as we see during Iconoclasm, was negotiation" (in Nesbitt, *Experiencing Byzantium*, 67).

4. On the topic of vestments, see Warren T. Woodfin, *The Embodied Icon: Liturgical Vestments and Sacramental Power in Byzantium* (Oxford: Oxford University Press, 2012). It is striking that Woodfin heavily employs the language of mimesis throughout his treatment.

5. See Liz James, *Light and Colour in Byzantine Art* (Oxford: Clarendon Press, 1991); Leslie Brubaker, *Vision and Meaning in Ninth-Century Byzantium* (Cambridge: Cambridge University Press, 1999); Clemena Antonova, *Space, Time, and Presence in the Icon: Seeing the World with the Eyes of God* (Farnham, UK: Ashgate, 2010); Claire Nesbitt, "Shaping the Sacred: Light and the Experience of Worship in Middle Byzantine Churches," *Byzantine and Modern Greek Studies* 36, no. 2 (2012): 139–60; Glenn Peers, *Sacred Shock: Framing Visual Experience in Byzantium* (University Park: Pennsylvania State University Press, 2004); Pentcheva, *Sensual Icon* and "Hagia Sophia and Multisensory Aesthetics."

6. See Andrew Louth, "Light, Vision and Religious Experience in Byzantium," in *The Presence of Light: Divine Radiance and Religious Experience*, ed. Matthew Kapstein (Chicago: University of Chicago Press, 2004), 85–103, and Liz James, "Senses and Sensibility in Byzantium," *Art History* 27, no. 4 (2004): 522–37. This distinction should also guard us against extrapolating too freely

from our contemporary experience to what or how earlier centuries might have experienced.

7. Liz James describes the effect of *ekphrasis* as follows: "the speaker did not necessarily use words to conjure an impression. Rather, words were used to evoke and stimulate memories and to bring to life the images already stored in the listener's mind/memory. By summoning up such mental images, the orator called up the emotions and thoughts associated with the sights and memories. In this way, phantasia was constructed as mimetic imagination. To be able to imagine, the audience had to already have knowledge of the pre-existing reality that it could re-visualize. Thus imagination was also bounded by accepted truths and value. For evocations to be effective, they had to correspond to specific experiences, shared values, cultural norms which could be recognized by the audience and shared by the speaker." Liz James, "Art and Lies: Text, image and imagination in the medieval world," in *Icon and Word*, eds. Antony Eastmond and Liz James (Farnham, UK: Ashgate, 2003), 59–71 (citation on 62). See also: Liz James and Ruth Webb, "Ekphrasis and Art in Byzantium," *Art History* 14 (1991): 1–17; Ruth Webb, "The aesthetics of sacred space: narrative, metaphor, and motion in *ekphraseis* of church building," *Dumbarton Oaks Papers* 53 (1999): 57–94; Brubaker, *Talking about the Great Church*; Schibille, *Hagia Sophia*.

8. Heather Hunter-Crawley comments on the way light operated in Syrian churches: "A silver cross displayed in this context would wax and wane in brightness (both according to light levels and the viewer's position in relation to the object), and reveal subtle changes in colour and tone. The experience of the light effects of these crosses would have been dynamic—moving, changing, revealing, and then concealing—and like divinity itself, the effect could not be completely contained or controlled (candles might substitute sunlight, yet levels of sunlight depend on atmospheric conditions), but the impact could be awe-inspiring and mystifying. Through this a Christian might sensually experience in a moment what Scripture and sermon would take thousands of words to communicate— the mysterious and ineffable nature of the infinite and living God" (in Nesbitt, *Experiencing Byzantium*, 183).

9. James claims that this constitutes a fundamental change in imagery and visual imagination vis-à-vis the ancient world. She argues: "The dimensions of this revolution are staggering. In effect, a highly nuanced visual language that had been developed over the course of a thousand years to express man's sense of cosmic order, to deal with the forces beyond his control, to carry his aspirations and frustrations, to organize the seasons of his life and the patterns of his social intercourse, was suddenly discarded. . . . In their place a new language of images was laboriously composed, selected, assembled, rehearsed, and refined. . . . The new images should not be thought of as simply filling up the voids left by the

overthrow of the old, but as actively competing with the old images" (*Light and Colour*, 6, 8).

10. Rico Franses, "When all that is Gold does not Glitter: On the strange history of looking at Byzantine art" (*Icon and Word*, 13–23).

11. For the fullest account of this, see Pentcheva's description of visual and acoustic experience of Hagia Sophia in "Hagia Sophia and Multisensory Aesthetics." She frequently uses phenomenological terminology in her description and sees herself as providing a phenomenological account, albeit not in a philosophical sense. Franses also comments on the interplay of visibility and invisibility: "The shift that takes place, evident in scene after scene in the Renaissance, is one away from anything in the visual field that is not absolutely clear and easy to see. Whatever does not reveal itself fully and distinctly to vision, the vague, obscure, and indiscernible, is refused. It is almost as though vision takes on a new arrogance, a heightened sense of its own importance, a sense of what it can do, and decides that it will not tolerate anything over which it does not have total dominion. . . . Byzantine vision, by contrast, as the golden images demonstrate when the reflection-absorption binary is active, is indeed tolerant of uncertainty, obscurity, and things that escape it, it is not as demanding that everything be revealed to it" (in *Icon and Word*, 20). From this he draws (somewhat questionable) theological conclusions: "Yet the case to be made for Byzantine vision is infinitely stronger in that it can more easily tolerate uncertainty and obscurity. The obscurity in the pictures is hardly deployed there simply because the period vision can tolerate it. Byzantine theology is full of the idea that there is much in the workings of Christianity that escapes human understanding" (ibid., 20).

12. On the use of the dialogue style in patristic homiletics and poetry, see Mary Cunningham, "Dramatic device or didactic tool? The function of dialogue in Byzantine preaching," in *Rhetoric in Byzantium*, ed. Elizabeth Jeffreys (Aldershot, UK: Ashgate, 2003), 101–13; Sebastian Brock, "Dialogue hymns of the Syriac Churches," *Sobornost* 5, no. 2 (1983): 35–45; Brock, "Dramatic Dialogue Poems," in *IV Symposium Syriacum. Literary Genres in Syriac Literature*, ed. H. J. W. Drijvers, R. Lavenant, C. Molenberg, and G. J. Reinink (Rome: Pontificum Institutum studiorum Orientalum, 1987), 135–47; Brock, "Syriac Dispute Poems: The Various Types," in *Dispute Poems and Dialogues* (Leuven: Orientalia Lovaniensia Analecta 42, 1991), 109–19; M. Hoffmann, *Der Dialog bei den christlichen Schriftstellern der ersten vier Jahrhunderte* (Berlin: Akademie Verlag, 1966); Bernd Reiner Voss, *Der Dialog in der frühchristlichen Literatur* (Munich: W. Fink, 1970). Cunningham argues that such dialogue is primarily a means to give the preacher authority and to impose such authority on the congregation. That seems far from obvious to me and I do not think it is the primary purpose of these dialogues.

13. The dialogue style was a popular form in Syriac hymnody especially and probably precedes its liturgical use. See several of the articles collected in Sebastian Brock, *Studies in Syriac Christianity: History, Literature and Theology* (Aldershot, UK: Ashgate/Variorum, 1992) and his *Fire from Heaven: Studies in Syriac Theology and Liturgy* (Aldershot, UK: Ashgate/Variorum, 2006). I have engaged the Syriac hymnody and especially its dialogue feature more fully in my "Performing Anatheism: Dialogic Hospitality in Syriac Liturgical Poetry," *The Art of Anatheism*, ed. Richard Kearney and Matthew Clemente (London: Rowman & Littlefield, 2017), 175–95.

14. A particularly popular version that entered the liturgical cycle permanently is the dialogue between Mary and the angel at the annunciation. Mary is explicitly praised for arguing with the angel and posited as a contrast to Eve who simply gives in to the serpent without argument. Not only is Mary affirmed to be right in questioning the angel to ensure he is really a messenger from God, but she is applauded for her rationality. For example: *Bride of Light: Hymns on Mary from the Syriac Churches*, trans. and ed. Sebastian Brock (Kerala, India: St. Ephrem Ecumenical Research Institute, 1994); two hymns for Annunciation in his translated collection *Treasure-house of Mysteries: Explorations of the Sacred Text through Poetry in the Syriac Tradition* (Yonkers, N.Y.: St. Vladimir's Seminary Press, 2012), 135–43, 241–44. Homilies also often employed such dialogue features. See *Wider Than Heaven: Eight-Century Homilies on the Mother of God*, trans. Mary B. Cunningham (Crestwood, N.Y.: St. Vladimir's Seminary Press, 2008) and Jacob of Serug, *On the Mother of God*, trans. Mary Hansbury (Crestwood, N.Y.: St. Vladimir's Seminary Press, 1998).

15. Pentcheva explores and reconstitutes the acoustics of Hagia Sophia in her "Hagia Sophia and Multisensory Aesthetics" and the larger project associated with it. Probably the most extensive work has been done by Alexander Lingas who employs the term "soundscape" to explore the sonal architecture of Byzantine liturgy. See, for example, his essay "From Earth to Heaven: The Changing Musical Soundscape of Byzantine Liturgy," in Nesbitt, *Experiencing Byzantium*, 311–58. For other discussions of music, not all of which focus on Byzantine music, see: Everett Ferguson, "Toward a Patristic Theology of Music," *Studia Patristica* 24 (1993): 266–83; Calvin Stapert, *A New Song for an Old World: Musical Thought in the Early Church* (Grand Rapids, Mich.: Eerdmans, 2007); Jeremy Begbie, *Resounding Truth: Christian Wisdom in the World of Music* (Grand Rapids, Mich.: Eerdmans, 2007); Alexander Lingis, *Sunday Matins in the Byzantine Cathedral Rite: Music and Liturgy* (Farnham, UK: Ashgate, forthcoming).

16. Susan Ashbrook Harvey, *Scenting Salvation: Ancient Christianity and the Olfactory Imagination* (Berkeley: University of California Press, 2006). She ultimately argues that the olfactory imagination functioned as a form of knowledge in ancient Christianity. She contends that already Dionysius the Areopagite

(often dismissed as overly Platonic) in his commentary on the liturgy gives "extraordinary prominence" to "the olfactory aspects of liturgical practice" and insists "on the significance of sensory experience as an epistemological tool." Dionysius dwells "at length on olfactory experience as revelatory of divine truth and as vehicle for religious knowledge" (ibid., 136, 138).

17. Hence the scandal when Father Zosima starts smelling after his death in Dostoevsky's *The Brothers Karamazov*. Harvey shows, however, that these associations are often ambiguous, as stench can also be a tool for sanctity in some cases (*Scenting Salvation*, 201–6).

18. *Scenting Salvation*, 181.

19. Harvey has shown this in a different sense for the way in which liturgical poetry presents Mary's "housekeeping," her preparation of her body for the reception of the divine, which includes perfume and fragrance in the preparation. Susan Ashbrook Harvey, "Interior Decorating: Jacob of Serug on Mary's Preparation for the Incarnation," *Studia Patristica* XLI (2006): 23–28.

20. "And while the moisture remains on your lips, touching it with your hands, sanctify your eyes, forehead, and your other senses." Cyril of Jerusalem, *Lectures on the Christian Sacraments*, trans. Maxwell E. Johnson (Yonkers, N.Y.: St. Vladimir's Seminary Press, 2017), V.22, 135. Lathrop comments on this same passage when he argues that in Jerusalem "receiving communion itself was to be an 'orientation' of the senses toward a world held in the extravagant mercy of God" (in Anderson, *Liturgy and the Moral Self*, 42). This is examined in more detail by Georgia Frank, "'Taste and See': The Eucharist and the Eyes of Faith in the Fourth Century," *Church History* 70, no. 4 (2001): 619–43. See also Heather Hunter-Crawley, "Embodying the Divine: The Sensational Experience of the Sixth-Century Eucharist," in J. Day, ed. *Making Senses of the Past: Toward a Sensory Archaeology* (Carbondale, Ill.: Illinois University Press, 2013), 160–76. For an examination of early eucharistic texts more broadly, see Paul F. Bradshaw, ed., *Essays on Early Eastern Eucharistic Prayers* (Collegeville, Minn.: Liturgical Press, 1997).

21. Irwin, *Text and Context*, 220, 219. For another discussion of such embodiment, see Patrick W. Collins, *Bodying Forth: Aesthetic Liturgy* (New York: Paulist Press, 1992).

22. Saliers, *Worship as Theology*, 159, 162. He also comments that "the remembrance of the words is carried and prompted by the melody and sometimes the harmonic and rhythmic elements," hence creating "dissonance for worshiping assemblies when familiar texts are set to new tunes" (ibid., 161). Flanagan is quite critical of the way technology has changed our relationship to sacred music: "No longer does one have to wait to hear a Haydn mass. One can play it with ease, instantly and anywhere, on a CD player, or on a video, in a way that makes no demands that might unsettle with a reciprocal gaze. We do

not permit the sacred object to ask a question. . . . A gin and tonic can be had while stretched out on the sofa, giving the Sanctus an uplifting effect. One can recline secure in the knowledge that no manners are violated in this civil right to private listening to sacred music with no holy strings attached. . . . Technology ruptures the relationships liturgies can make by civilising that which is sacerdotal." Thus, "for them, penitential pronouncements convey pleasure not the pain of pious yearning. The secular appropriation of sacred music, where it is converted into a commodity amongst others, disables the capacity to hear anew its message when heard in a holy place" (*Sociology and Liturgy*, 333).

23. Ibid., 76.

24. "As a specific way of thinking, sacramental thinking is universal. In other words, all things, not just some things, can be transformed into sacraments." Leonardo Boff, *Sacraments of Life, Life of Sacraments*, trans. J. Drury (Washington: Pastoral Press, 1987), 89. He gives as examples a cigarette butt, a family mug, homemade bread, and other such items.

25. Ibid.

26. Paul Janowiak, *The Holy Preaching: The Sacramentality of the Word in the Liturgical Assembly* (Collegeville, Minn.: Liturgical Press, 2000), 19.

27. Hughes, *Worship as Meaning*, 295. Similarly Ratzinger stresses that "not only do the human body and signs from the cosmos play an essential role in the liturgy but that the matter of this world is part of the liturgy" (*Spirit of the Liturgy*, 220).

28. For example, Lathrop says: "These things of the meeting are holy things: formative teaching together with the gracious bath; powerful words together with the meal of thanksgiving; all our days and yet the astonishing 'eighth day' to both the week and the year; our praise and thanksgiving, but also our lament; the assembled people together with their scheduled leadership, their priests and pastors. Here is the summary tradition of the ancients, the order of the church, the liturgical list offering our world a sanctuary of meaning" (*Holy Things*, 225).

29. Irwin, *Text and Context*, 153.

30. Saliers, *Worship as Theology*, 143.

31. Chauvet, *Symbol and Sacrament*, 398.

32. Lathrop, *Holy Things*, 164.

33. Ibid., 93.

34. Chauvet, *Symbol and Sacrament*, 552.

35. In *Creation and Liturgy*, ed. Ralph McMichael (Washington: Pastoral Press, 1993), 242–43.

36. Lathrop, *Holy Ground*, 3.

37. Varghese, *West Syrian*, 142. Limouris says in a very similar vein: "The life of the church celebrates and communicates this renewal and reconciliation and witnesses to its reality in and for the world. By taking elements from creation

and celebrating their being renewed and used by God to convey his saving presence through word and sacraments, the church witnesses to the restored relation between God and the cosmos as the new creation in Christ. This sacramental witness to Christ is an authentic and evangelical demonstration of the unity and renewal at the heart of the church. It proclaims the existence of the church as standing with the world. The church exists from God and for the world, to manifest this reality: God is with us and for the whole of humankind" (*Church, Kingdom*, 170).

38. Irwin claims: "An ethical response to liturgy necessarily leads to an environmental ethic. Put somewhat differently this is to assert that since the ecological crisis is often linked to the concern for justice, the liturgy as the locus for meeting the Just One becomes the logical and most traditional locus for grounding the justice of environmental ethics. Another way the liturgy offers the most useful avenue for environmental ethics concerns the way it articulates a theology and practice allied with the just distribution of the world's resources" (*Text and Context*, 339). See also Lawrence Mick, *Liturgy and Ecology in Dialogue* (Collegeville, Minn.: Liturgical Press, 1997).

39. Scott sees all kinds of implications: "The Eucharist is about inclusivity, and is both a protest and resistance to social exclusion. . . . The Eucharist challenges the agricultural subsidies and unfair trade practices of the richer nations. It is a statement about sweatshops and about land issues. It speaks to the exploitation of the planet. . . . Embedded in Eucharist are issues around discrimination, vulnerability, and violence" (*Eucharist*, ix). But this is not limited to Western liturgical scholars. The argument that lifting the bread and cup at the Eucharist has implications for the rest of creation is maybe the most popular Orthodox claim about how their tradition has ecological implications. For a critical examination of this ecological argument, see my "Grounding Ecological Action in Orthodox Theology and Liturgical Practice? A Call for Further Thinking," *Journal of Orthodox Christian Studies* 1, no. 1 (2018): 61–77.

40. See also his *La voix nue. Phénoménologie de la promesse* (Paris: Minuit, 1990); *Saint Augustin et les actes de paroles* (Paris: Presses Universitaires de France, 2002); *Symbolique du corps* (Paris: Presses Universitaires de France, 2005); *La joie spacieuse. Essai sur la dilatation* (Paris: Presses Universitaires de France, 2007). He also returns to the issue of response and responsibility in several other texts.

41. Chrétien, *Ark of Speech*, 129, trans. lightly modified. In another context he says: "What is beautiful is what calls out by manifesting itself and manifests itself by calling out" (*Call and Response*, 9).

42. *Ark of Speech*, 136, 144–47.

43. Speech "gives us a voice in the true sense: our voice is not abolished as our own voice by the act of resaying, since this silent voice requests ours in

response" (Chrétien, *Call and Response*, 28). Chrétien is not explicitly talking about liturgy (or even prayer) in this text, but makes broader claims about voice, speech, and beauty. We will return to his treatment more fully in the chapter on affectivity.

44. Probably the most extensive exploration of sensory experience in phenomenology is that of Merleau-Ponty in *The Phenomenology of Perception*. He provides detailed analyses of the experiences of the senses, often by examining the ways in which their functioning is affected by illness. He is primarily concerned with distinguishing a phenomenological from an intellectualist or rationalist account. I have therefore here chosen to focus on Marion's claims about the sensory experiences of aesthetic or religious phenomena instead of summarizing Merleau-Ponty's extensive discussion, which is less relevant to the topic at hand.

45. Marion, *The Visible and the Revealed* (New York: Fordham University Press, 2008), 119–44, especially 127–33.

46. *Believing in Order to See*, 111–15, 131–35.

47. For a fuller account, see my "Jean-Luc Marion's Spirituality of Adoration and its Implications for a Phenomenology of Religion," in *Breached Horizons: The Philosophy of Jean-Luc Marion*, ed. Steve Lofts and Antonio Calcagno (London: Rowman and Littlefield, 2018), 188–217, and the final chapter of *Degrees of Givenness*.

48. *Wedding Feast*, 218–29. See also his essay on the Eucharist in Kearney, *Carnal Hermeneutics*, 279–94.

49. Falque fully acknowledges that he is moving to theology here. Part of his argument concerns precisely a push for a combination of phenomenology and theology that would no longer draw (artificial?) distinctions between them. As may be obvious from my treatment, I am hesitant about this proposal.

50. Obviously, not all rites of anointing are solely about healing, although even in the chrismation in the context of baptism there may well be an element of that.

51. It is interesting that there is very little room for silence in Orthodox liturgy, unlike what is the case for some Western rites. Does the silence function in other ways? Is silence equivalent to the hiddenness of the "mystical" elements of the service, taking place in the altar area where we do not see what goes on? Is it a problem that choirs often attempt to cover up this silence and to entertain us with fancy arrangements? Costin Moisil twice points to the fact that Orthodox liturgy has no place for silence in his examination of the flexibility that chanters or choir directors must exercise in order to deal with the variable length of certain liturgical moments or actions, although he provides no rationale for, or commentary on, this fact. "Expecting the Unexpected: Tailoring Chants for the Liturgy of the Faithful," in *Creating Liturgically: Hymnography and Music*, ed.

Ivan Moody and Maria Takala-Roszczenko (Jyväskylä, Finland: International Society for Orthodox Church Music, 2017), 334, 340.

52. This may be why people often sway to the chanting of texts in many liturgical traditions. The rhythm of the chant is expressed corporeally.

53. This may say something about why today's homilies are not as vividly remembered as the poetic speeches apparently given by patristic homilists such as Proclus of Constantinople; their poetic elements may well have been an important mnemonic tool. See Barkhuizen's introduction to his translation of Proclus's homilies: Proclus, *Homilies*, 12–22. He concludes his survey of the various stylistic means of Proclus's homiletic rhetoric: "It is important to note that these and other stylistic features not only served merely as rhetorical embellishment of his homilies, but rather also as homiletic techniques to aid comprehension and further instruction . . . on the part of the audience" (22).

54. Indeed, many of the patristic writers were quite concerned with the strong impact of music on affect that could also have dangerous or subversive implications. Susan Ashbrook Harvey points out that the Syriac poet Jacob of Serug was worried about this and "fretted to his congregation about 'responses (or chorus, chants) which are not true; troublesome and confused sounds; melodies which attract children; ordered and cherished songs; skillful chants, lying canticles . . . Your ear is captivated by song.' The music of the theater told its stories in melodies and verses that lingered in the mind, hummed by children and adults alike. The dangers of the wrong music were real." "Liturgy and Ethics in Ancient Syriac Christianity," *Studies in Christian Ethics* 26 (2013): 314.

55. Julia Kristeva, *The Revolution in Poetic Language*, trans. Margaret Waller (New York: Columbia University Press, 1984). See also Dávid Pancza, "The Question of Rhythm in Middle Byzantine Chant," in Moody, *Creating Liturgically*, 542–63.

56. Similarly, liturgical music might be much closer to Lévinas's notion of the "saying" rather than the solidified "said" of philosophical discourse. Although liturgical music, at least in the Orthodox tradition, is far from impulsive and certainly has "solidified" over time, the way it functions phenomenologically is closer to the evoking of moods than it is to conveying abstract meaning.

57. Hemming claims "we do not speak in praying, we learn to hear" (*Worship as a Revelation*, 114).

58. Psalm 140 in the Orthodox numbering based on the Septuagint; Psalm 141 in Western numbering based on the Hebrew text.

59. See also Martimort, *Church at Prayer I*, Section II, chapter III. For a more philosophical approach, employing Chrétien, see Bruce Ellis Benson, *Liturgy as a Way of Life* (Grand Rapids, Mich.: Baker Academic, 2013).

60. See *Lenten Triodion*, 168–83. Constantin Andronikof criticizes this anthropomorphic language and judges it a low point of liturgy in *Le cycle Pascal. Le sens des fêtes II* (Paris: Éditions l'Age d'Homme, 1985), 109.

61. Chrétien, *Call and Response*, 5, 12.

62. Lacoste contends that liturgical chant is an effort of the body which sanctifies (*Présence et parousie*, 76). The chant gives words to all of creation (ibid., 78). Chrétien also claims this in *The Ark of Speech*.

63. Marion, *God Without Being*, 17–18.

64. Patricia Cox Miller works this out in great detail in her *The Corporeal Imagination: Signifying the Holy in Late Ancient Christianity* (Philadelphia: University of Pennsylvania Press, 2009). There are several popular stories of a sick person sleeping in a church or praying and a saint exiting his or her icon to administer a healing touch. Cox Miller discusses some of these in her book. See also Bissera V. Pentcheva, "Miraculous Icons: Medium, Imagination, and Presence," in Brubaker, *Cult of the Mother of God*, and Eastmond and James, *Icon and Word*.

65. For example, Symeon the New Theologian exhorts his monks who were suspicious of the use of too much incense in liturgy: "These aromatics, put together by human hands and perfuming your senses with the fragrance of scented oils, depict, and, as it were, suggest your own creation by the art of their making. Because just as the perfumer's hands fashion the blended perfumes from different essences and the product is one essence out of many, so, too, did God's hands fashion you, who are cleverly composed and combined with the intelligible elements of the spiritual perfume, that is to say, with the gifts of the life-creating and all-efficacious Spirit. You, too, must give off the fragrance of his knowledge and wisdom, so that those who listen to the words of your teaching may smell his sweetness with the senses of the soul and be glad with spiritual joy" (Symeon, Discourse XIV, cited in *Scenting Salvation*, 144).

66. The association between incense and prayer is also frequent in earlier sacrificial imagery and not particular to Orthodox or more broadly Christian liturgy. For a broader exploration of fragrance and flavor in Byzantine experience, see Andrew Dalby, *Flavours of Byzantium* (Totnes, UK: Prospect, 2008).

67. *Call and Response*, 13.

68. See especially *Being Given*, §13, 119–31.

69. Or if an experience is not utterly overwhelming or excessive does that mean that we have failed in some way and are not able to bear their weight because of our sinfulness, as Marion frequently suggests?

70. One should also note that the patristic authors frequently share the ancient suspicions (expressed most fully by Plato) about drama and excessive spectacle as "mere appearance" that leads astray from the true reality.

71. *Experience and the Absolute*, 103.

72. Ibid., 105.

73. Ibid.

74. Lacoste, "Liturgy and Coaffection," 93–105. See also the third chapter of *L'Intuition sacramentelle* (which gives the book its title), 59–95.

75. "Liturgy and Coaffection," 97.

76. Chauvet agrees with this, but is critical of it: "The objects or materials used in ritual are equally separated from their usual utilitarian purposes: a golden chalice is used for drinking, exactly like a glass; but it is of such another order that at the extreme, its form and gleaming decorative ornaments scarcely allow its original purpose to show. In the same way our hosts have been so removed from their status as ordinary bread that . . . they remind us of bread only with great difficulty" (*Symbol and Sacrament*, 330).

77. Lacoste, *Experience and the Absolute*, 175.

78. Ibid. This obviously does not address the question of the incongruence between a vow of poverty and the lavish decoration and expensive implements of many churches even in monastic settings that required significant resources and expenditure. It is telling that Lacoste's examples are almost always singular and excessive in some form: the ascetic, the holy fool, the mystic, and others.

79. Lacoste acknowledges this in a (somewhat dismissive) reference to the "cult" of liturgy (which he clearly does not consider "illuminating").

80. See George Galavaris, *Bread and the Liturgy: The Symbolism of Early Christian and Byzantine Bread Stamps* (Madison: University of Wisconsin Press, 1970); Eastmond and James, *Icon and Word*; Liz James, ed., *Art and Text in Byzantine Culture* (Cambridge: Cambridge University Press, 2007). See also, in a different sense, Cox Miller, *The Corporeal Imagination*.

81. Lacoste does speak of reception in this context.

82. This obviously cannot be a full phenomenology of the Eucharist, which would require a separate treatment, but only a brief account of how the eucharistic gifts appear or manifest in their sensory presence as elements experienced within the larger liturgical world.

83. Saliers stresses this dimension of gratitude in response to the gifts: "Here is the thankful response to what God has already given. Even in the recital of the 'words of institution' there is thanksgiving, and again in the very act of presenting the bread and the cup in oblation, thanks is rendered. The language *and* the gesture of grateful response coinhere, that is, form an indissoluble unity" (*Worship as Theology*, 94).

84. The presanctified bread set aside for the liturgy of the presanctified gifts obviously constitutes a special case, but even there the bread is ultimately meant to be consumed in its entirety. The same is true of the "reserved Eucharist" that is taken to people who are sick and cannot attend liturgy.

5. Affectivity

1. Proclus, *Homilies on the Life of Christ*, 2.1, 71.

2. See also: James Hinterberger, "Emotions in Byzantium," in *A Companion to Byzantium*, ed. Liz James (Chichester, UK: Wiley-Blackwell, 2010), 123–34.

3. For a succinct discussion of this ascetic and liturgical ambivalence about the body and the passions, see John Behr, *The Mystery of Christ* (Crestwood, N.Y.: St. Vladimir's Seminary Press, 2006), 146–66.

4. *Lenten Triodion*, 279.

5. Ibid., 358, 361.

6. Ibid., 447.

7. Also: "A storm of passions besets me, O compassionate Lord. / I have darkened the beauty of my soul with passionate pleasures, and my whole mind I have reduced wholly to mud. / I am clad in a coat that is spotted and shamefully bloodstained by the flow of my passionate and pleasure-loving life." Great Canon, Ode 2 (*Lenten Triodion*, 381–82, with different translation).

8. *Lenten Triodion*, 349.

9. See Hannah Hunt, *Joy-Bearing Grief: Tears of Contrition in the Writings of the Early Syrian and Byzantine Fathers* (Leiden: Brill, 2004).

10. *Lenten Triodion*, 378, 395. Mary of Egypt is lauded for having "shed streams of tears, to quench the burning of the passions" and requested to "grant the grace of these thy tears to me also, thy servant" (ibid., 398).

11. Ode 8 (ibid., 408).

12. Schmemann strongly stresses the element of joy in liturgy, even in the liturgies of Great Lent. This is a constant theme in his work.

13. For a discussion of this in the Great Canon, see: Getcha, "Le Grand Canon pénitentiel de saint André de Crète. Une lecture typologique de l'histoire du salut," in *La liturgie, interprète de l'Écriture* (Rome: Edizioni Liturgiche, 2003), 105–20. He contends that biblical history becomes ours in the Canon and that we are to imitate the examples provided. Andrew Mellas examines the role of emotion in the Great Canon specifically in his "Feeling Liturgically: Reflections on Byzantine Hymnography and Compunction," in Moody, *Creating Liturgically*, 392–413.

14. Aristotle, *Poetics* 4 (1448b), 11 (1452b), 14 (1453b).

15. He identifies seven functions: "to integrate external sources of anxiety into the human order; to speak to the unconscious through symbol; to give life sense and value; to facilitate the expression and catharsis of feelings in individuals and groups; to help address the unsettledness and unpredictability of life; to reveal and enact the power and permanence of a group; to mark the cycles and passages of human life" (Anderson, *Christian Identity*, 62).

16. Guardini, *Spirit of the Liturgy*, 26.

17. Don E. Saliers, *Worship and Spirituality* (Philadelphia: Westminster Press, 1984), 47.

18. Morrill, *Eucharist*, 37.

19. Wainwright, *Worship with One Accord*, 212.

20. Senn, *New Creation*, 23.

21. Mellas, "Feeling Liturgically," in Moody, *Creating Liturgically*, 413.

22. Ibid.

23. Janowiak, *Standing Together*, 45.

24. Flanagan, *Sociology and Liturgy*, 44.

25. Janowiak, *Standing Together*, 157.

26. He calls this his "central thesis" (Saliers in Anderson, *Liturgy and the Moral Self*, 17). He also contends that "every act of liturgy is an act of resistance against *no* future, against hopeless, loveless, unjust, and faithless worlds" (Saliers, *Worship as Theology*, 105).

27. Mitchell, *Meeting Mystery*, 44.

28. Hughes, *Worship as Meaning*, 301.

29. Chauvet, *Symbol and Sacrament*, 371.

30. This is not the case for Henry whose discussion of self-affectivity often mentions joy and pain, but primarily uses them as examples to establish his larger phenomenological claims about auto-affection rather than providing a specific analysis of them as particular affects or emotions.

31. *Being and Time*, §29. Heidegger provides further discussions of affect in other places. I focus on the account of *Befindlichkeit* because it has been by far the most influential, especially on the French phenomenologists.

32. "Wie befinden Sie sich?" is a very polite way of asking someone how they are doing or feeling.

33. "Although liturgical inexperience need not give rise to boredom, boredom is a constant and useful reminder to us that nonexperience is essential to the liturgical play—and that it can be intolerable to us" (Lacoste, *Experience and the Absolute*, 149).

34. Lacoste, "Liturgy and Coaffection," 100.

35. Ibid., 100–1.

36. Ibid., 101.

37. Ibid., 101–2.

38. Ibid., 102.

39. "As for the liturgy, it is inaugurated by a distancing, that is by a critique of sensibility in its 'religious' use as 'feeling,' and what counts for the divine presence counts for the presence of the Other. . . . An affectivity that does not serve the manifestation of the world, but that of the neighbor and of God: the liturgical logic of presentiment tells us that this is not unthinkable. But for that to become reality, this world must pass . . . or at least it must be bracketed" (ibid., 103).

40. Lacoste, *L'Intuition sacramentelle*, 91. He distinguishes such a "sacramental" experience from a "religious" experience or an experience of the sacred (which he judges a "degenerate" experience that is only "pseudo-sacramental").

41. Steinbock distinguishes between feelings and feeling states because manifold—even contradictory—feelings can be present in a particular feeling state, thus capturing a distinction between a feeling or mood and its underlying basis.

Befindlichkeit serves a similar function for Heidegger in the sense that it underlies particular moods or tonalities, although it is more like a general disposition
of being attuned or finding oneself always already in a mood rather than a particular state corresponding to a specific feeling or mood.

42. Steinbock, *Moral Emotions*, 14.

43. Ibid., 263.

44. Ibid., 264.

45. Ibid., 267; emphasis his. Also: "But these movements and interrelations
are intrinsic to the experiences themselves, and are not something imposed on
the outside or linked coincidentally, as if we were constructing an idea of the
person or theorizing what it means to be a virtuous human being" (ibid., 267).
He thinks of them as "founding" emotions that have moral weight, as well as
social, political, economic, and ecological significance (ibid., 277).

46. *Moral Emotions*, 14, 15. The examination of the particular moral emotions he discusses always points to the ways in which it opens such an interpersonal sphere or shuts it down, how it directs us toward others or closes us in
upon ourselves.

47. Ibid., 238.

48. Saliers speaks of music as a kind of language: "A third hidden language
is that of sound and silence. Music is but the extension of speech. The silences
between words are as important as the sounds themselves, for both together
create the primary acoustical image with which we pray. Music and silence must
surround the reading and hearing of the church's corporate memories contained
in the Scriptures. The art forms of music—congregational, choral, and instru-
mental—grow naturally out of this fundamental perception. Singing is an
extension of speaking; music is the language of the soul becoming audible"
(Saliers, *Worship and Spirituality*, 53).

49. Karim says: "For Instance, the canon of the Nativity is composed in the
first mode, which is very pleasant and joyful. The second mode, which invokes
humbleness, is used for the canon of Epiphany as the Lord condescended to be
baptized by a servant. The canon of the Annunciation is composed in the fourth
mode, which invokes fear, since the Virgin was frightened when learning what
was to happen to her" (in Best, *Worship Today*, 16).

50. Besides the texts by Lingis mentioned in the previous chapter, see also:
James W. Mackinnon, ed., *Music in Early Christian Literature* (Cambridge: Cambridge University Press, 1989); Egon Wellesz, *A History of Byzantine Music and
Hymnography* (Oxford: Clarendon Press, 1961); Nina Maria Wanek, ed., *Psaltike: Neue Studien zur byzantinischen Musik* (Vienna: Praesens Byzantinistik,
2011); Moody, *Creating Liturgically*.

51. For example, Leontius of Constantinople, *Fourteen Homilies*, trans.
Pauline Allen (Brisbane: Australian Association for Byzantine Studies, 1991),
Homily VIII.3, 106. At the same time, he encourages them to "wear clothing

appropriate to the feast" insofar as they can afford it but not going beyond their means (Homily IX.4, 114).

52. For example, Chrysostom exhorts his audience: "The person fasting ought most of all to keep anger in check, learn the lessons of mildness and kindness, have a contrite heart, banish the flood of unworthy passions, . . . avoid becoming enthralled by money, be lavish in almsgiving, drive all ill-will to one's neighbor from the soul." *Homilies on Genesis* 8.14, trans. Robert Hill (Washington: Catholic University of America Press, 1990), 113. In general, Chrysostom misses no occasion to point to any possible lesson to be drawn from a biblical character for its moral implications.

53. Aposticha for Monday of First Week, *Lenten Triodion*, 198.

54. For example: "I mourn and weep when I ponder death and see our beauty made in the image of God laid in the grave, disfigured, dishonored, and lacking form. O wonder! What is this mystery that comes to pass for us? Why should we be given over to corruption? And why should we be wedded to death? Truly, as it is written, it is by the command of God Who gives the departed rest." "What distress does the soul have as it departs from the body? How many tears does it shed? And no one has mercy on it. It directs its eyes to the angels to whom it entreats in vain. Extending hands to men, it has no one to help. Therefore, my beloved brethren, having considered the shortness of this life, let us ask repose with Christ for the departed, and for our souls great mercy." "As you see me set before you mute and without breath, weep for me, my brethren, family, and all who know me, for I spoke with you only yesterday, and suddenly the fearful hour of death came upon me. Come, all those who love me and give me the last kiss, for never again shall I journey or talk with you until the end of time." (All citations from the Orthodox funeral liturgy.) See also, Alexander Schmemann, *The Liturgy of Death* (Yonkers, N.Y.: St. Vladimir's Seminary Press, 2016). It should be said, though, that Schmemann judges these texts "of gloom and darkness" a later aberration (112–13) and thinks the fundamental Christian message is that of triumph over death (157–63).

55. See also Cuneo's reflection on the Orthodox funeral rites in *Ritualized Faith*, 204–18.

56. Cuneo, *Ritualized Faith*, 84. It is obviously a question whether the music as originally composed was meant to strike its listeners as beautiful or was instead experienced as (solely) evoking sorrow, especially when using the forms of lament common in the culture. Does a recognition of "beauty" require that the music be experienced as a "performance" in the sense of contemplation rather than participation? In either case, Cuneo is certainly right that immersion and reenactment, especially in regard to their emotive elements, are complex in a variety of ways.

57. The whole issue of beauty and its function in liturgy, although extremely important, is not something I can explore within the bounds of this discussion.

58. In the patristic literature this is especially evident in the Syriac hymns, which deliberately imaginatively envision the emotional lives of various biblical characters and elaborate on the story in such a way as to allow various members of the prospective liturgical audiences to identify with the characters more fully (see my "Performing Anatheism"). Maybe it would be useful to retrieve some of these hymns for use liturgically today?

59. The term "philanthropos" is probably the most frequent term employed for God in the liturgy.

60. For an account of this in the tradition, see: Michael Philip Penn, *Kissing Christians: Ritual and Community in the Late Ancient Church* (Philadelphia: University of Pennsylvania Press, 2005).

61. Cuneo suggests that the primary point of liturgical singing is to create a unity conducive to peace. See *Ritualized Faith*, 126–44. While I am not convinced that all liturgical music has the same goal, I am in full agreement with him that this belongs "to the unduly neglected category of *ordinary religious experience*" (ibid., 144, emphasis his).

62. All the phrases in this paragraph are from the Divine Liturgy (the standard eucharistic service).

63. "Likewise, when it comes to the experience of illness, Americans largely consider sickness shameful and, therefore, a condition preferably kept quiet and managed in private. Illness and mortal decline may carry senses of failure, with the financial, personal, and social burdens that so often accompany sickness only adding to the sense of shame." Morrill, *Divine Worship and Human Healing: Liturgical Theology at the Margins of Life and Death* (Collegeville, Minn.: Liturgical Press, 2009), 32. This sense must have been even far stronger in a culture that not only was not as aware of infection and contagion and did not necessarily understand the transmission of disease, but at the same time placed high emphasis on directing the "humors" of the body and "caring for the soul" through the training of the body.

64. This is obviously not to equate physical illness with sin—although both say something about human finitude—but merely to point to their similar phenomenological structure of immanence and even isolation.

65. Indeed, several scholars focus the mimetic function of liturgy on Christ. Senn says: "So the whole liturgy became a kind of dramatic reenactment of the Christ event, especially of his passion. Everything done in the liturgy reminded the assembly of some aspect of the life of Christ. . . . Merely attending the liturgy was an act of sanctification, whether one received communion or not, because it was a way of participating in the saving mystery of Christ" (Senn, *The People's Work*, 87).

66. See also Bissera Pentcheva on "The Performative Icon" in which she treats "performance" as "mimesis" and argues that it is particularly present in icons. Pentcheva, "The Performative Icon," *Art Bulletin* 88, no. 4 (2006): 631–55.

67. For example: "The righteous man shows mercy all day long; his delight is in the Lord, and walking in the light he shall not stumble. All this was written for our admonition, that we should fast and do good" (Fifth Sunday in Lent, Matins, *Lenten Triodion*, 461).

68. Some of the saints are actually hilariously unique individuals whose personality breaks through some of the "neat" histories the tradition tries to construct around them. The goal of imitation does not constitute a complete denial of individuality or all covering over of particular characteristics. It is imitation within and as a self, not a complete erasure of self, despite all the exhortation to self-denial. For an account of recent research in Byzantine hagiography, see Antonio Rigo, Michele Trizio, and Eleftherios Despotakis, eds., *Byzantine Hagiography: Texts, Themes, and Projects* (Turnhout, Belgium: Brepols, 2018).

69. Saliers says: "If Christian liturgy is to be the ongoing prayer of Jesus Christ in and through his body in the world, then all human vulnerabilities, complexities, and our primordial creaturely need to acknowledge the source and summit of human existence—all are brought to praise and thanksgiving 'In, with, and through Jesus Christ in the unity of the Holy Spirit'" (*Worship as Theology*, 105).

70. John Chrysostom, *On Wealth and Poverty*, trans. Catharine P. Roth (Crestwood, N.Y.: St. Vladimir's Seminary Press, 1984), 31.

6. Community

1. Dalmais reminds us: "As used originally in the Greek cities, 'liturgy' could mean any 'public service,' but especially services that were costly and were accepted as done in the name of the city because they were linked to its most vital interests. In a culture permeated by religious values (as most of the traditional cultures were), 'liturgy' thus understood was predicated first and foremost of actions expressing the city's relations to the world of divine powers on which it acknowledged itself to be dependent. 'Liturgy' referred, therefore, not to cultic actions of individuals or private groups but only to those of the organized community, that is, the entire people, who realized that they shared a single destiny and a collective memory. In other words, liturgy belonged to what has sometimes been called a 'perfect [or: complete] society.' This is why the name can and even ought to be reserved (as it is in official documents) for the exercise of a worship that is public in the fullest sense, that is, a worship actually offered in the name of the community, which acknowledges it as its own" (in Martimort, *Church at Prayer I*, 233).

2. For twentieth-century accounts of Orthodox ecclesiology, see: Nicholas Afansiev, *The Church of the Holy Spirit*, trans. Vitaly Permiakov (Notre Dame, Ind.: University of Notre Dame Press, 2007); John D. Zizioulas, *Eucharist, Bishop, Church: The Unity of the Church in the Divine Eucharist and the Bishop During the First Three Centuries* (Boston: Holy Cross Orthodox Press, 2001).

Schmemann also argues vigorously against any conception of liturgy as a purely private experience. For example, *The Eucharist: Sacrament of the Kingdom* (Crestwood, N.Y.: St. Vladimir's Seminary Press, 1987), 81–99, 229–45; he also notes the interdiction "against one priest serving more than one eucharist on the same altar" per day (ibid., 95).

3. Irwin, *Sacraments*, 218.

4. Baldovin, *Urban Character*, 260.

5. Ibid., 261, 264.

6. Baldovin, *Worship*, 62.

7. In Anderson, *Liturgy and the Moral Self*, 29.

8. Saliers, *Worship as Theology*, 133.

9. Ibid., 134.

10. Ibid., 135.

11. Lathrop, *Holy Things*, 128. Scott also stresses: "We participate in the corporate life of the Body of Christ as community, as a local parish and as the universal Church. The Eucharist is a real, social, historical, and relational reality. It is about participation, communion, and dialogue; about building up of community and creating real human fellowship" (*Eucharist*, 87). See also, Mark Searle, ed. *Liturgy and Social Justice* (Collegeville, Minn.: Liturgical Press, 1980); Mary Bellman, "Corporate Worship as Hospitality," *Liturgical Ministry* 11 (2002): 174–81; Frank Coady, "Hospitality in the Liturgy," *Liturgical Ministry* 11 (2002): 182–86.

12. Varghese, *West Syrian*, 144.

13. Mitchell, *Liturgy and the Social Sciences* (Collegeville, Minn.: Liturgical Press, 1999), 15.

14. Mitchell, *Meeting Mystery*, 32.

15. Anderson, *Christian Identity*, 192.

16. Janowiak, *Standing Together*, 18.

17. Ibid., 31.

18. Ibid., 34.

19. In Best, *Worship Today*, 40.

20. Wainwright, *Worship with one Accord*, 24.

21. Anderson, *Christian Identity*, 194.

22. In Anderson, *Liturgy and the Moral Self*, xi.

23. Morrill, *Human Healing*, 129.

24. Lathrop, *Holy Things*, 212.

25. "We live in a world—at least this is true of assimilated, English-speaking North Americans—where a basic, gut-level commitment to common values and a common world view has broken down. Such a world has a great deal of trouble focusing on common symbols; this in turn weakens the liturgy which is rooted in the celebration of such symbols in ritual action. In other words, liturgy

requires a passionate, even if implicit, commitment to a common view of the world. This does not imply that every liturgical experience is exclusively communal; there are times when individuals experience something completely different from the rest of the community depending on their mood or circumstance. However, today's problem is that we tend to bring fundamentally individualized experience and expectations to liturgical life" (Baldovin, *Worship*, 63).

26. Ibid., 68.

27. Ibid., 196.

28. Pickstock, *After Writing*, 171.

29. Hemming, *Worship as a Revelation*, 24–42.

30. Guardini, *Spirit of the Liturgy*, 42.

31. Cf. Max Scheler, *The Nature of Sympathy* (London: Routledge, 2008); Edith Stein, *On the Problem of Empathy*, trans. Waltraut Stein (Washington: ICS Publishers, 1989).

32. See *Being and Time*, §26.

33. *Being and Time*, §27.

34. *Being and Time*, §47.

35. Merleau-Ponty, *Phenomenology of Perception*, Part II, Chapter 4 and the beginning of Part III.

36. Ibid., 372–73.

37. Merleau-Ponty claims that we always see the consciousness of another only across a physical body, just as we see society and politics only in and across a concrete "social body." He goes on to affirm that "our bodies bear witness to what we are; body and spirit express each other and cannot be separated" (*Sense and Non-Sense*, 173). (In this respect, it is interesting that he then goes on to speak of good and evil as being purely in the mind. Surely they also become embodied?)

38. Heidegger speaks of the possibility of "Fürsorge" (solicitude), Merleau-Ponty as "inter-lacing," Lévinas of "substitution." Yet in the phenomenological treatments the accounts of alterity are rarely linked very fully with the phenomenological accounts of the body. Marion explores the question to some extent when he discusses erotic flesh, where two bodies bear on each other and give each other mutual flesh in their exposure to each other. Lévinas speaks of the caress as touch of the other. But overall bodies tend to remain separate for phenomenology. They do not become incarnate in each other. Yet in some ways, all of our bodies *do* become incarnate in each other. There is no human body that was not first of all flesh of another flesh. And even after the forceful ejection from the womb, the infant body has to be touched and held or it dies. No human body can do without loving touch. Untouched bodies shrivel. We experience our bodies in the world as seen and heard by others. To some extent, we see ourselves only through each other. In aging and illness, our bodies again become dependent on other bodies, maybe revealing more fully what has been true all along, that our bodies cannot be without others.

39. See especially the essay "Pathos-With" in his *Material Phenomenology*, 101–34.

40. Levinas, *Totality and Infinity: An Essay on Exteriority*, trans. Alphonso Lingis (Pittsburgh: Duquesne University Press, 1969), 21–30 and *Otherwise than Being or Beyond Essence*, trans. Alphonso Lingis (Pittsburgh: Duquesne University Press, 1998), 99–129. See also his *Time and the Other*, trans. Richard A. Cohen (Pittsburgh: Duquesne University Press, 1987); *God, Death, and Time*, trans. Bettina Bergo (Stanford: Stanford University Press, 2000); *Of God Who Comes to Mind*, trans. Bettina Bergo (Stanford: Stanford University Press, 1998).

41. For the first full exposition, see *Totality and Infinity*, 187–247.

42. This sentiment is already previewed to some extent in the early *On Escape*, trans. Bettina Bergo (Stanford: Stanford University Press, 2003).

43. Most fully in Part V of *Being Given*.

44. See his essay "From the Other to the Individual," trans. Arianne Conty, *Levinas Studies: An Annual Review* (Pittsburgh: Duquesne University Press, 2005), 99–117.

45. *In the Self's Place: The Approach of Saint Augustine*, trans. Jeffrey Kosky (Stanford: Stanford University Press, 2012), 283.

46. Ibid., 285.

47. "Just as and because God is seen always already as a gift giving and giver without any condition, even that of its reception by some receiver outside God (and who, in all cases, could by definition never receive it as and as much as it gives itself—namely, with an excess lacking all measure), so, too, and consequently I find myself, me, always already given (gifted with and recipient of myself), even before having received reception of it. I have originally the rank of gifted [*adonné*], given to oneself before being able to receive even one's proper self. In the self's place, I receive reception of me from elsewhere than myself. The aporia of the self, therefore, never disappears—it is received as the horizon of my advance toward the immemorial" (ibid., 288).

48. "And as I am (myself, ego) that which I seek (the *self's* place), since I am what I love, it follows that I will never cease coming to the *self's* place, to the degree that I bury myself in the incomprehensible into whose image I understand myself. There where I find God, all the more as I continue to seek him, I find myself all the more myself as I never cease to seek that of which I bear the image. In the self's place there is not a shape of consciousness, nor a type of *subjectum*, but that unto which the self is like and refers" (ibid., 312). These are the final lines of the book.

49. Lacoste, *Recherches sur la Parole*, 267.

50. For Falque, see the final part of his *God, the Flesh, and the Other: From Irenaeus to Duns Scotus*, trans. William Christian Hackett (Evanston, Ill.: Northwestern University Press, 2015). The issue of haecceity underlies the entire

discussion of alterity in Part III, but is explicitly addressed on pages 264–77. He ultimately agrees with Marion that only love can fully individuate us.

51. Falque, in his much more explicitly theological phenomenology, combines his notion of the flesh, marriage, and the Eucharist into a reading of sacramental experience as "incorporation" or even "inter-corporation." In the eucharistic experience, we become one flesh with God, are fully incorporated into the divine. He also develops this notion in the direction of eros/marriage and the suffering flesh of the dying body, suggesting that all three share certain structures in common. But even here the incorporation begins from the self; it is the person at prayer or in eucharistic participation who is incorporated into Christ. His extensive analyses of suffering, death, birth, resurrection, and so forth always assume a singular self or occasionally two singular selves. Although it is, like Marion's, a receptive self (occasionally considerably more active than Marion's; Falque is quite critical of the increasing emphasis on passivity in the French tradition), it is not a plural or communal self.

52. Even in Henry, the "son within the Son" is always singular. The account of community is the logical outflow of his claims about our living from and within the divine life; it is not the starting point. Some thinkers on occasion raise the possibility of a "third," another "other," as in Lévinas's account of justice or Marion's account of the third as the child issuing from the erotic experience and ultimately as God who loves me first.

53. At the same time there is a strong fear of a loss of individuality or selfhood in an indistinct communal (or even "communist") mass of anonymity. (Henry is criticized for this and it is the claim he tries to refute consistently, albeit not always successfully.)

54. This is obviously not a statement about scientific historical or archeological antiquity, but about how it is phenomenologically experienced. Liturgical texts were composed at a specific point in time and practices emerged in particular contexts, even if these origins cannot always be traced easily. Yet they are experienced as in some way "always already having been" and as participating in time "immemorial" (cf. the chapter on temporality).

55. Phrases from the Orthodox funeral liturgy.

56. That is not to say that ethnic communities are always inhospitable; they can also be immensely generous and hospitable. At the same time, one should admit that particular liturgical communities have been rather less than welcoming over the centuries and that certain liturgical occasions (such as Holy Friday) have even permitted outright hostility to certain groups, especially to Jews. Yet it is the very same service that speaks of Christ explicitly as a stranger ("Give me this Stranger, who from his youth has been received as a stranger in this world. Give me this Stranger, who has no place to lay his head . . . Give me this Stranger, the refuge of the poor and weary . . .") and enjoins hospitality to

strangers more broadly. The particular aberrations and misuses of liturgy must be honestly acknowledged and dealt with, but those concrete instances do not deny the basic structures of liturgy, which point in a different direction.

57. Saints and their relics "came to be seen as conduits of spiritual power" (Cox Miller, *Corporeal Imagination*, 36). This also explains why cities often fought over the relics of the saints or even stole them from each other.

58. This may well be why several thinkers in the Eastern tradition venture in the direction of apokatastasis, the redemption of all. It is somehow unthinkable that one could be saved without all the others. It is not just that God's mercy for individuals is so great that it undoes individual justice, as some of the contemporary thinkers seem to imply, but rather that there is no notion of isolated individuals in the patristic age that could be "saved" in isolation from others. We are all wrapped up with each other. (Indeed, theologically speaking, Christ's death on behalf of all makes no sense if people are only considered as isolated individuals. He would have died only for one other and not for all. Regardless of how exactly one thinks of humanity as connected in and via Christ, in the new Adam—or for that matter, in the "old" Adam—it has to be thought of as connected in some way or the Christian notion of redemption makes very little sense.)

59. In fact, as noted in the previous chapter, Cuneo thinks that such unity and peace is the primary goal of liturgical singing.

60. The sanctoral cycle, which cannot be examined here, does this even far more fully, especially in monastic experience. Every day of the year is devoted to several saints, their lives are read and contemplated and one is continually encouraged to pattern one's own life on theirs. The imitative structure of salvation may well be one of the main characteristics of Byzantine spirituality, which affected many other aspects of life. The Byzantines are often chided for not being more inventive or creative, for slavishly imitating patterns of the past. But this may be closely connected to a spirituality that eschewed invention as a mark of a focus on the self and instead favored imitation as a patterning on those superior to me (cf. Aristotle's *Poetics*).

61. Admittedly, many of the female characters fall into ancient stereotypes of women as either virgins or prostitutes. A discussion of the experiences of women and the role of gender in liturgy goes beyond the scope of this treatment. For a fuller examination of the topic, see: Teresa Berger, *Women's Ways of Worship: Gender Analysis and Liturgical History* (Collegeville, Minn.: Liturgical Press, 1999).

62. Of course that does not mean that this never happens: We do often merely observe. Liturgy probably always courts the danger of turning into mere spectacle.

63. Maybe the real problem with the use of "empathy" as access to the other in the phenomenological literature is not the notion of empathy or compassion

as such, but rather the fact that it proceeds from the subject and assumes the other as modeled on the self.

7. Intentionality

1. Stichera for "Lord, I call" at Vespers for the Sunday of Orthodoxy (Ware, *Lenten Triodion*, 300). Similar statements are made throughout the liturgies for this Sunday.

2. Irwin, *Sacraments*, 355.

3. Morrill, *Eucharist*, 35.

4. Dalmais in Martimort, *Church at Prayer I*, 230.

5. Anderson, *Christian Identity*, 45.

6. Taft, *Liturgy of the Hours*, 340.

7. Guardini, *Spirit of the Liturgy*, 19.

8. Hemming, *Worship as a Revelation*, 114; emphases his.

9. Ibid., 115.

10. Ibid., 116.

11. Ibid., 117.

12. Hemming, 163; emphasis his.

13. Ibid., 158; emphasis his.

14. Ibid., 165. But what phenomenological access could we possibly have to God's self-understanding?

15. Mitchell, *Meeting Mystery*, 59.

16. Wolterstorff, *Acting Liturgically*, 26, 27.

17. Ibid., 29.

18. Ibid., 118.

19. "When Christians participate in liturgical enactments so as thereby to worship God, they do so in the expectation and with the prayer that God will participate along with them in enacting the liturgy." He goes on to assume (rather than justify) that God is the liturgical agent and to "explore the various forms that God's agency takes in liturgical enactments," primarily (but not solely) God's speaking to us (ibid., 209). See Chapter 10 of the book.

20. Wolterstorff also includes a strong ethical element in his final two chapters, reflecting on love and justice, respectively (Chapters 12 and 13). For example: "if the liturgical assembly itself manifests justice, and if God's love of justice is clearly presented in the readings, sermons, and hymns, then the participants are formed into acting justly outside the assembly as well as within" (ibid., 273). He relies heavily on James Cone's theology for an articulation of what this means concretely.

21. Saliers, *Worship as Theology*, 27.

22. Dalmais, *Church at Prayer I*, 231.

23. See also: John J. Egan, "Liturgy and Justice: An Unfinished Agenda," *Origins* 13 (1983): 399–411; James Empereur and Christopher Kiesling, *The Liturgy That Does Justice* (Collegeville, Minn.: Liturgical Press, 1990).

24. Morrill, *Eucharist*, 11. In a different context, he articulates more explicitly "the *meaning* of what we do in sacramental rites and what that *means* in relation to ethical behavior and socio-political engagement" in conversation with the theology of Edward Schillebeeckx. "Liturgy, Ethics, and Politics: Constructive Inquiry into the Traditional Notion of Participation in Mystery," in *Meeting Mysteries, Understanding Liturgies: On Bridging the Gap between Liturgy and Systematic Theology*, ed. Joris Geldhof (Leuven: Peeters, 2015), 187.

25. Robert Sokolowski, *Eucharistic Presence: A Study in the Theology of Disclosure* (Washington: Catholic University of America Press, 1994), 217.

26. Ibid., 213.

27. Chauvet, *Symbol and Sacrament*, 316.

28. Ibid., 329.

29. Ibid., 339.

30. Chauvet, *Sacraments*, 87.

31. Hughes, *Worship as Meaning*, 252. Yet he is also critical of the opposite tendency: "Rather than deprecating the conventional forms, the ritual practices and the designated places through which, or in which, people have traditionally encountered God, instead of demolishing churches and replacing them with multi-purpose 'service centres', instead of transforming priestly ministry into vaguely religious forms of therapy or management styles of leadership, Protestant leaders might have done better in looking for the ways of *creating sanctuary* for people overwhelmed by ordinariness, in trying to *generate sacral spaces* as genuine alternatives to mundanity" (ibid.).

32. Dietrich von Hildebrand is quite emphatic that it is the former not the latter: "The divine Office is recited primarily because all praise and glorification is due to God, the fullness of all holiness and majesty, and not because it will bring about a transformation of ourselves. The Liturgy is not primarily intended as a means of sanctification or an ascetic exercise. Its primary intention is to praise and glorify God, to respond fittingly to Him." *Liturgy and Personality* (Baltimore: Helicon Press, 1960), 4.

33. Husserl, *Ideas I*, §58.

34. See especially the lecture "Phenomenology and Theology."

35. Lacoste, *La phénoménalité de Dieu. Neuf études* (Paris: Cerf, 2008).

36. "The Voice without Name: Homage to Levinas," in *The Face of Other and the Trace of God: Essays on the Philosophy of Emmanuel Levinas*, ed. Jeffrey Bloechl (New York: Fordham University Press, 2000), 224–42. He makes the same claim in the essay mentioned earlier, "From the Other to the Individual."

37. See his chapter on Lévinas in *Combat amoureux*, 113–36. Falque also reiterates Marion's critique about the lack of individuation in Lévinas.

38. "God and Philosophy," *Basic Philosophical Writings*, ed. Adriaan T. Peperzak, Simon Critchley, and Robert Bernasconi (Bloomington: Indiana University Press, 1996), 141. See also the slightly revised version in *Of God Who Comes to Mind*, and his lectures on "God and Onto-theo-logy" in *God, Death and Time*.

39. As we have seen earlier, he insists that this is about the possibility of an appearance or manifestation of the divine as a phenomenon, not about confirming any actual historical incidence of God's appearing. See *Being Given*, 367, note 90.

40. Marion, *Being Given*, 244; *Believing in Order to See*, 133–35.

41. For example, *Believing in Order to See*, 103–5, 108–11.

42. See *Being Given*, 234–47.

43. Marion, *Erotic Phenomenon*, 221–22.

44. Marion, *In the Self's Place*, 11–55.

45. See especially the first chapter of *Negative Certainties*.

46. Marion, *Being Given*, 264; trans. lightly modified. The language of "filter" or "prism" is employed on the next page. Following Lévinas, he calls this "counter-intentionality" rather than intentionality. The pole of intentionality is moved to the phenomenon that gives itself entirely from itself without any conditions, hence without phenomenological horizon and without constituting ego (ibid., 185–89, 199–221). See also, *In Excess*, 44–53.

47. Marion, *In Excess*, 50, 51.

48. Marion, *Believing in Order to See*, Chapter 8.

49. Marion, *God Without Being*, 139–58, and *Believing in Order to See*, 136–43.

50. Marion, *God Without Being*, 139–58. For an explicit critique of this, see the final chapter of my *Degrees of Givenness*, 170–92.

51. Marion, *In Excess*, 157.

52. Marion, *Erotic Phenomenon*, 146–50. See also the essay from *The Visible and the Revealed* mentioned earlier.

53. Marion, *In Excess*, 161–62.

54. Lacoste, *Recherches sur la Parole*, 164–80. Much of Lacoste's analysis in this book is concerned with (individual or monastic) practices of contemplation and prayer, especially the tradition of *lectio divina*. He is not primarily speaking of ecclesial liturgy, although he occasionally mentions it in examples.

55. Ibid., 209.

56. Ibid., 219–22.

57. Ibid., 280–85.

58. See Falque's discussion of this in *Combat amoureux*, 265–96.

59. Falque, *God, the Flesh, and the Other*, 21–112.

60. Kevin Hart, *Kingdoms of God* (Bloomington: Indiana University Press, 2014), 130.

61. Ibid.

62. Ibid., 136. He repeatedly distinguishes between a narrow (Husserlian) philosophical sense of phenomenology and a broader sense that allows for a "phenomenological theology" (ibid., 143)—I take it that he sees himself as providing such a phenomenological theology. He also stresses that "Christianity is finally not a matter of bringing God to presence in human consciousness but rather of allowing oneself to come into the presence of God, the two modes of 'presence' being quite different" (ibid., 147). While this is probably true *theologically*, precisely in the way in which Hart unfolds it here, *philosophically* it remains the case that "no phenomenology can neutrally identify God as triune—that is, no phenomenology within the limits of philosophy can have anything to say about the Trinity" (ibid., 176). A "phenomenology of the Christ" or "the true supreme phenomenology," for which Hart calls here (ibid., 178), is only possible as a theological project.

63. Ibid., 148.

64. See his "Ethics of the Spread Body," *Somatic Desire: Rethinking Corporeality in Contemporary Thought*, ed. Sarah Horton et al. (Lanham, Md.: Lexington Press, 2019), 91–116. There is a repeated slippage in Falque's work between affirming animality as our true fleshly humanity and seeking to transform it in a phenomenological manner that rises above animality to a fuller humanity, patterned on Christ, as "another way of being in the world." See, for one example, the last part of *Metamorphosis of Finitude*, 95–153.

65. Many of Chrétien's essays start in a more poetic, literary, or aesthetic context and then end on a theological, spiritual, or mystical note. To give just one example, the essay on "Body and Touch" ends: "When the entire body radiates and burns through this divine touch, it becomes song and word. Yet that which it sings with its entire being, collected whole and gathered up by the Other, is what it cannot say, what infinitely exceeds it—excess to which touch as such is destined, and which in the humblest sensation and least contact here below was already forever unsealed to us" (*Call and Response*, 131). (These are also the final lines of the book.)

66. "If God has created the world for us, we recreate the world for God. We carry each other within; we give birth to each other. And when we do, we cannot tell the dancer from the dance." Kearney, *The God Who May Be: A Hermeneutics of Religion* (Bloomington: Indiana University Press, 2001), 110. See also Kearney, *Anatheism*, 101–30.

67. John D. Caputo, *The Insistence of God* (Bloomington: Indiana University Press, 2013). See also his *The Weakness of God* (Bloomington: Indiana University Press, 2006), and *The Folly of God: A Theology of the Unconditional* (Salem, Ore.: Polebridge Press, 2016).

68. In that respect, it is somewhat ironic that Marion draws so heavily on theologians from the Eastern tradition (Dionysius, Gregory of Nyssa, Maximus,

and others) and yet is quite dismissive about contemporary Orthodoxy. See, for example, the interview in *Ruf und Gabe: Zum Verhältnis von Phänomenologie und Theologie*, ed. Josef Wohlmuth (Bonn: Borengässer, 2000). For an excellent secondary source on his treatment of the patristic tradition, see Tamsin Jones's *A Genealogy of Marion's Philosophy of Religion*. It is also noteworthy that the European country that has embraced his thought most enthusiastically is Orthodox Romania. More of his books are translated into Romanian than any other language besides English. See, for example, Nicolae Turcan, *Apologie după sfârșitul metafizicii: Teologie și fenomenologie la Jean-Luc Marion* (Bucharest: Editura Eikon, 2016).

69. This may also indicate that the question whether liturgy is primarily about redemption or primarily about fostering ethics or justice is a false dichotomy. It is in our directedness toward God in worship and veneration that we are transformed as persons and oriented toward others in compassion. The two are not in competition with each other and one does not exclude the other.

70. In this respect, Marion's distinction between "theological actuality" and "phenomenological possibility" actually makes good sense. Phenomenology makes no claim about God's existence or presence in liturgy, but examines the structures of human experience. What is problematic about the distinction is when "possible" phenomenological structures are posited as the only way in which a phenomenon of revelation *must* occur.

71. Liturgy does distinguish hermeneutically between divine and human other. While we are "with" the human other, we are "toward" God. Worship is offered only to God. We stand *together* before God and orient our worship *toward* the divine. We enter liturgy with the expectation to be reconciled with the human other and forgiven by the divine other, but even such forgiveness is always mediated by the human other (as in the rites of forgiveness or even the sacrament of confession).

72. Here, Marion is quite right that this is not about describing God in any sort of metaphysical sense. The language of praise or prayer offered in liturgy is not language that tries to define the divine or encapsulate God in a concept.

73. Cuneo claims that "the fundamental contribution of the liturgy, then, is to provide act-types and conceptions of God such that by performing those act-types under those conceptions one can engage God by doing such things as blessing, petitioning, and thanking God" (*Ritualized Faith*, 160). He identifies this as a kind of "ritual knowledge" that enables us to engage God rather than just formulate abstract beliefs about him.

74. It should be admitted that this has not always been the case (blessings for icons and vestments are actually quite late), but certainly is routinely the case now.

75. When no such expectation becomes visible, maybe that says something about a corresponding lack of experience and intentionality.

76. Indeed, this stress on mercy is very strong in the tradition, sometimes to the point that it is seen as opposed to justice. Isaac the Syrian insists that God's justice is like a speck of sand in comparison with the ocean of God's mercy, which is incomparably greater (Homily 50).

Conclusion

1. Anderson, *Christian Identity*, 28.

2. Ibid., 193.

3. This is constantly claimed in various forms by the Orthodox literature on ecology. For one example, see Patriarch Bartholomew, "Orthodox Liturgy and the Natural Environment," in *Encountering the Mystery: Understanding Orthodox Christianity Today* (New York: Doubleday, 2008), 98–100.

4. Taft, "What Does Liturgy Do?" 195, 210, 211, respectively.

5. Lathrop tries to maintain this tension constantly in his work on liturgy, frequently by repeating: "The holy things for the holy. Yet, only one is holy." For example: "The most significant iconoclasm, however, is found in the contained critique of the ordo, the perpetual dialogue of 'holy things, holy people' with 'one is holy'" (*Holy Things*, 158).

6. Kavanagh, *On Liturgical Theology*, 176.

7. Is there any way to formulate a "holistic" view of liturgy that does not become "fundamentalist" or "totalizing"? Can there really be an idea of "doing the world" that is not at the same time a claim to hegemony and a plea for hierarchy? What about the "exclusiveness" of the religious worldview that is always in competition with other visions, which seem inherently, by their very structure, incompatible? Yet, can we live our own vision in splendid isolation from others and without interacting with them? Neither seems entirely satisfying and both seem a fundamental denial of what liturgy means.

8. Lawrence A. Hoffman, *Beyond the Text: A Holistic Approach to Liturgy* (Bloomington: Indiana University Press, 1987).

9. For example, in the iconoclastic controversies in the seventh and eighth centuries, the fact that icons and vestments were *not* blessed was used as an argument by both sides.

10. In regard to liturgy maybe most strongly by Davies: "Because we live in a secular universe, the numinous [which he sees promoted by Byzantine liturgy that in his view borders on magic] is no longer a meaningful category. Because we live in a secular universe, the idea of two worlds has little or no relevance." Therefore worship is "not a drawing apart from the world, but is itself a worldly activity. It is not an entering into a sacred realm. It is therefore not a means of encountering an other-worldly reality, but is concerned with how the holiness of the common is made manifest." In fact, continuing to practice liturgy for him is a serious error: "Of course, when worship is divorced from everyday life, as exemplified by our inherited Christian forms which are no longer at home in a

secular universe, it ceases to be rooted in the world and a crisis of meaningless-ness is created." J. G. Davies, *Every Day God: Encountering the Holy in World and Worship* (London: SCM Press, 1973), 251, 256, 272. Many other scholars reject the sacred/secular distinction for other reasons, albeit not necessarily in terms of liturgical expression. These are, of course, real questions. If, in fact, the sacred is now meaningless to most people, then one wonders what the point of perform-ing liturgy is. Can we re-create the sacred? Can it be recovered? Or should we just cling to its remains? Can traditions that have died or are in the process of dying be resurrected? Can we endow them with "new" meaning or is that a denial of their identity and a merely arbitrary process of imposing meaning? Do "secular" people have a "hunger" for the "sacred" or is that just a myth invented by religious people who feel under attack from the culture around them? Many of these questions go beyond the scope of the present study, which tries to unfold the meaning of liturgy as practiced, with the assumption that it is indeed meaningful to the people who are engaged in it.

11. Nor should it be, because that would somehow imply that it has been completely misunderstood for the past 2,000 years and required phenomenology to show something no one had ever noticed before. Rather, to put it in maybe slightly too Heideggerian terms, phenomenology should at least on some level confirm some of our more inchoate intuitions about primordial reality.

12. Cf. Kearney's work in *Anatheism* or *Reimagining the Sacred*. This does not mean, however, as pointed out in the previous chapter, that all such distinctions should be collapsed or that we cannot make meaningful phenomenological dis-tinctions between a "within" and a "without" of liturgy or between the religious "sacred" and the "sacred" of the everyday.

BIBLIOGRAPHY

Afansiev, Nicholas. *The Church of the Holy Spirit.* Translated by Vitaly Permiakov. Notre Dame, Ind.: University of Notre Dame Press, 2007.

Akentiev, Constantin C., ed. *Liturgy, Architecture, and Art in the Byzantine World. Papers of the XVIII International Byzantine Congress and Other Essays Dedicated to the Memory of Fr. John Meyendorff.* St. Petersburg: Byzantinorossica, 1995.

Anatolios, Khaled. "Heaven and Earth in Byzantine Liturgy." *Antiphon: A Journal for Liturgical Renewal* 5, no. 3 (2000): 1–10.

Anderson, E. Byron. "Worship and Belief: Liturgical Practice as a Contextual Theology." *Worship* 75, no. 5 (2001): 432–52.

———. *Worship and Christian Identity: Practicing Ourselves.* Collegeville, Minn.: The Liturgical Press, 2003.

Anderson, E. Byron, and Bruce T. Morrill, eds. *Liturgy and the Moral Self: Humanity at Full Stretch Before God: Essays in Honor of Don E. Saliers.* Collegeville, Minn.: The Liturgical Press, 1998.

Andronikof, Constantin. *Des mystères sacramentels.* Paris: Cerf, 1998.

———. *Le cycle fixe. Le sens des fêtes I.* Paris: Cerf, 1970.

———. *Le cycle Pascal. Le sens des fêtes II.* Paris: Éditions l'Age d'Homme, 1985.

———. *Le sens de la liturgie.* Paris: Cerf, 1988.

———. "Le temps de la liturgie." In *Eschatologie et liturgie. Conférences Saint-Serge XXXIe Semaine d'Études Liturgiques 1984*, edited by A. M. Triacca and A. Pistoia. Rome: Edizioni Liturgiche, 1985.

Antonova, Clemena. *Space, Time, and Presence in the Icon: Seeing the World with the Eyes of God.* Farnham, UK: Ashgate, 2010.

Archatzikaki, Jacques. *Étude sur les principales fêtes chrétiennes dans l'ancienne Église d'Orient*. Geneva: Weber, 1904.

Arranz, Miguel. "Les grandes étapes de la liturgie byzantine: Palestine— Byzance—Russie. Essai d'aperçu historique." In *Liturgie de l'Église particulière, liturgie de l'Église universelle. Conférences Saint-Serge XXIIe Semaine d'Études Liturgiques 1975*. Rome: Edizioni Liturgiche, 1976.

Baldovin, John F. *Baptism, Eucharist, Ministry*. Geneva: World Council of Churches, 1982.

———. *Liturgy in Ancient Jerusalem*. Alcuin / GROW Liturgical Study 9 / Grove Liturgical Study 57. Bramcote, UK: Grove Books Limited, 1989.

———. *The Urban Character of Christian Worship: The Origins, Development and Meaning of Stational Liturgy*. Rome: Pontificum Institutum Studiorum Orientalium, 1987.

———. "The Uses of Liturgical History." *Worship* 82, no. 1 (2008): 2–18.

———. *Worship: City, Church, and Renewal*. Washington: Pastoral Press, 1991.

Bartholomew, Ecumenical Patriarch. *Encountering the Mystery: Understanding Orthodox Christianity Today*. New York: Doubleday, 2008.

Baumstark, Anton. *Comparative Liturgy*. Edited by F. L. Cross. Westminster, Md.: Newman Press, 1958.

Baun, Jane. *Tales from Another Byzantium: Celestial Journey and Local Community in the Medieval Greek Apocrypha*. Cambridge: Cambridge University Press, 2007.

Bebis, George S. "Worship in the Orthodox Church." *Greek Orthodox Theological Review* 22 (1977): 429–43.

Beckwith, Roger T. *Daily and Weekly Worship: From Jewish to Christian*. Nottingham, UK: Grove Books, 1987.

Begbie, Jeremy. *Resounding Truth: Christian Wisdom in the World of Music*. London: SPCK, 2008.

Behr, John. *The Mystery of Christ: Life in Death*. Crestwood, N.Y.: St. Vladimir's Seminary Press, 2006.

Bell, Catherine. *Ritual: Perspectives and Dimensions*. New York/Oxford: Oxford University Press, 1997.

———. *Ritual Theory, Ritual Practice*. Oxford: Oxford University Press, 1992.

Bellman, Mary L. "Corporate Worship as Hospitality." *Liturgical Ministry* 11 (2002): 174–81.

Bello, Angela Ales. *The Divine in Husserl and other Explorations*. Translated by Antonio Calcagno. Dordrecht: Springer, 2009.

———. *Husserl sul problema di Deo*. Rome: Studium, 1985.

Benson, Bruce Ellis. *Liturgy as a Way of Life*. Grand Rapids, Mich.: Baker Academic, 2013.

Berger, Teresa. "Liturgy—a forgotten subject-matter of theology?" *Studia Liturgica* 17 (1987): 10–18.

————. "Liturgy and Theology—An Ongoing Dialogue." *Studia Liturgica* 19 (1989): 14–16.

————. *Women's Ways of Worship: Gender Analysis and Liturgical History*. Collegeville, Minn.: Liturgical Press, 1999.

Berger, Teresa, and Bryan D. Spinks, eds. *Liturgy's Imagined Past/s: Methodologies and Materials in the Writing of Liturgical History Today*. Collegeville, Minn.: Liturgical Press, 2016.

Bertonière, Gabriel. *The Historical Development of the Easter Vigil and Related Services in the Greek Church*. Rome: Orientalia Christiana Analecta 193, 1972.

Best, Thomas F., and Dagmar Heller, eds. *Worship Today: Understanding, Practice, Ecumenical Implications*. Geneva: WCC Publications, 2004.

Bitton-Ashkeloni, Brouria. *Encountering the Sacred: The Debate on Christian Pilgrimage in Late Antiquity*. Transfiguration of the Classical Heritage 28. Berkeley: University of California Press, 2005.

Boff, Leonardo. *Sacraments of Life, Life of Sacraments: Story Theology*. Translated by J. Drury. Washington: Pastoral Press, 1987.

Bouyer, Louis. *Life and Liturgy*. London: Sheed and Ward, 1962.

————. *The Paschal Mystery: Meditations on the Last Three Days of Holy Week*. Translated by M. Benoit. Chicago: Henry Regnery, 1950.

Bradshaw, Paul F. *Daily Prayer in the Early Church*. New York: Oxford University Press, 1982.

————, ed. *Essays on Early Eastern Eucharistic Prayers*. Collegeville, Minn.: Liturgical Press, 1997.

————. "Liturgical Theology." *Studia Liturgica* 30, no. 1 (2000): 1–128.

————. *The Search for the Origins of Christian Worship: Sources and Methods for the Study of Early Liturgy*. Oxford: Oxford University Press, 2002.

Bradshaw, Paul F., and Lawrence A. Hoffman, eds. *The Making of Jewish and Christian Worship: Two Liturgical Traditions*. Notre Dame, Ind.: University of Notre Dame Press, 1991.

Bradshaw, Paul F., and Johnson E. Maxwell. *The Origins of Feasts, Fasts, and Seasons in Early Christianity*. Collegeville, Minn.: Liturgical Press, 2011.

Braga, Carlo, ed. *L'espace liturgique: ses éléments constitutifs et leurs sens. Conf. Saint-Serge (2005)*. Rome: Edizioni Liturgiche, 2006.

Brock, Sebastian, ed. and trans. *Bride of Light: Hymns on Mary from the Syriac Churches*. Kerala, India: St. Ephrem Ecumenical Research Institute, 1994.

————. "Dialogue Hymns of the Syriac Churches." *Sobornost* 5, no. 2 (1983): 35–45.

————. "Dramatic Dialogue Poems." In *IV Symposium Syriacum. Literary Genres in Syriac Literature*, edited by H. J. W. Drijvers, R. Lavenant, C. Molenberg, and G. J. Reinink, 135–47. Rome: 1987.

————. *Fire from Heaven: Studies in Syriac Theology and Liturgy*. Aldershot, UK: Ashgate/Variorum, 2006.

————. *Studies in Syriac Christianity: History, Literature and Theology*. Aldershot, UK: Ashgate/Variorum, 1992.

————. "Syriac Dispute Poems: The Various Types." In *Dispute Poems and Dialogues*, edited by G. J. Reinink and H. L. J. Vanstiphout, 109–19. Leuven: Orientalia Lovaniensia Analecta 42, 1991.

————. *Treasure-House of Mysteries: Explorations of the Sacred Text through Poetry in the Syriac Tradition*. Yonkers, N.Y.: St. Vladimir's Seminary Press, 2012.

Brown, Peter. *The Body and Society*. London: Faber & Faber, 1989.

Brubaker, Leslie. *Talking about the Great Church: Ekphrasis and the Narration of Hagia Sophia*. Prague: Byzantinoslavika, 2011.

————. *Vision and Meaning in Ninth-Century Byzantium: Image as Exegesis in the Homilies of Gregory of Nazianzus*. Cambridge: Cambridge University Press, 1999.

Brubaker, Leslie, and Mary B. Cunningham, eds. *The Cult of the Mother of God in Byzantium: Texts and Images*. Farnham, UK: Ashgate, 2011.

Buchwald, Hans. *Form, Style and Meaning in Byzantine Church Architecture*. Aldershot, UK: Ashgate, 1999.

Bulgakov, Sergius. *The Orthodox Church*. Translated by E. S. Cram. London: Centenary Press, 1935.

Butcher, Brian A. *Liturgical Theology After Schmemann: An Orthodox Reading of Paul Ricoeur*. New York: Fordham University Press, 2018.

Cabasilas, Nicholas. *A Commentary on the Divine Liturgy*. Translated by J. M. Hussey and P. A. McNulty. London: SPCK Press, 1960.

Calivas, Alkiviadis. *Essays in Theology and Liturgy*. Brookline, Mass.: Holy Cross Orthodox Press, 2003.

Cameron, Averil. *The Byzantines*. Oxford: Blackwell, 2006.

————. *Continuity and Change in Sixth-Century Byzantium*. London: Variorum, 1981.

Cameron, Averil, and Robert G. Howard, eds. *Doctrine and Debate in the East Christian World, 300–1500*. Farnham, UK: Ashgate, 2011.

Caputo, John D. *The Folly of God: A Theology of the Unconditional*. Salem, Ore.: Polebridge Press, 2016.

————. *The Insistence of God*. Bloomington: Indiana University Press, 2013.

————. *The Weakness of God*. Bloomington: Indiana University Press, 2006.

Carroll, Thomas K. and Thomas Halton. *Liturgical Practice in the Fathers*. Wilmington, Del.: Michael Glazier, 1988.

Casey, Edward S. *Getting Back into Place: Toward a Renewed Understanding of the Place-World*. Bloomington: Indiana University Press, 2009.

————. *The World on Edge*. Bloomington: Indiana University Press, 2017.

Cassin, Barbara, ed. *Dictionary of Untranslatables: A Philosophical Lexicon*. Princeton: Princeton University Press, 2014.

Cavanaugh, William T. *The Myth of Religious Violence: Secular Ideology and the Roots of Modern Conflict*. Oxford: Oxford University Press, 2009.

Chan, Simon. *Liturgical Theology: The Church as Worshiping Community*. Downers Grove, Ill.: InterVarsity, 2006.

Chauvet, Louis-Marie. *The Sacraments: The Word of God at the Mercy of the Body*. Collegeville, Minn.: Liturgical Press, 2001.

———. *Symbol and Sacrament: A Sacramental Reinterpretation of Christian Existence*. Collegeville, Minn.: Liturgical Press, 1995.

Chauvet, Louis-Marie, and François Kabasele Lumbala, eds. *Liturgy and the Body. Concilium*. London: SCM Press / Maryknoll, N.Y.: Orbis, 1995.

Chrétien, Jean-Louis. *The Ark of Speech*. Translated by Andrew Brown. London: Routledge, 2004.

———. *The Call and the Response*. Translated by Anne A. Davenport. New York: Fordham University Press, 2004.

———. *Hand to Hand: Listening to the Work of Art*. Translated by Stephen E. Lewis. New York: Fordham University Press, 2003.

———. *La joie spacieuse. Essai sur la dilatation*. Paris: Presses Universitaires de France, 2007.

———. *La voix nue. Phénoménologie de la promesse*. Paris: Minuit, 1990.

———. *Saint Augustin et les actes de paroles*. Paris: Presses Universitaires de France, 2002.

———. *Symbolique du corps*. Paris: Presses Universitaires de France, 2005.

———. *Under the Gaze of the Bible*. Translated by John Marson Dunaway. New York: Fordham University Press, 2015).

———. *The Unforgettable and the Unhoped for*. Translated by Jeffrey Bloechl. New York: Fordham University Press, 2002.

Chupungco, Anscar J. *The Cosmic Elements of Christian Passover*. Studia Anselmiana 72. Analecta Liturgica 3. Rome: Editrice Anselmiana, 1977.

———. *Cultural Adaptation of the Liturgy*. New York: Paulist Press, 1982.

———. *Liturgical Inculturation: Sacramentals, Religiosity, and Catechesis*. Collegeville, Minn.: Liturgical Press, 1992.

Coady, Frank. "Hospitality in the Liturgy." *Liturgical Ministry* 11 (2002): 182–86.

Collins, Patrick W. *Bodying Forth: Aesthetic Liturgy*. New York: Paulist Press, 1992.

Colwell, John E. *Promise and Presence: An Exploration of Sacramental Theology*. Waynesboro, Ga.: Paternoster, 2005.

Cooper, Adam G. *The Body in St. Maximus the Confessor*. Oxford: Oxford University Press, 2008.

Corbon, Jean. *The Wellspring of Worship*. Translated by Matthew J. O'Connell. New York: Paulist Press, 1988.

Cox Miller, Patricia. *The Corporeal Imagination: Signifying the Holy in Late Ancient Christianity.* Philadelphia: University of Pennsylvania Press, 2009.

Cuneo, Terence. *Ritualized Faith: Essays on the Philosophy of Liturgy.* Oxford: Oxford University Press, 2016.

Cunningham, Mary B. "Dramatic device or didactic tool? The function of dialogue in Byzantine preaching." In *Rhetoric in Byzantium: Papers from the Thirty-Fifth Spring Symposium of Byzantine Studies, Exeter College, University of Oxford, March 2001,* edited by Elizabeth Jeffreys, 101–13. Aldershot: Ashgate/Variorum, 2003.

———. *Gateway of Life: Orthodox Thinking on the Mother of God.* Yonkers, N.Y.: St. Vladimir's Seminary Press, 2015.

———, ed. and trans. *Wider Than Heaven: Eight-Century Homilies on the Mother of God.* Crestwood, N.Y.: St. Vladimir's Seminary Press, 2008.

Cunningham, Mary B., and Pauline Allen, eds. *Preacher and Audience: Studies in Early Christian and Byzantine Homiletics.* Leiden: Brill, 1998.

Cyril of Jerusalem, *Lectures on the Christian Sacraments.* Translated by Maxwell E. Johnson. Yonkers, N.Y.: St. Vladimir's Seminary Press, 2017.

Dalmais, Irenée Henri. "La liturgie comme lieu théologique." *La Maison Dieu* n. 78 (1964): 97–106.

Dalby, Andrew. *Flavours of Byzantium.* Totnes, UK: Prospect, 2008.

Dastur, Françoise. *Heidegger et la question du temps.* Paris: Presses Universitaires de France, 1990.

Davies, J. G. *Every Day God: Encountering the Holy in the World and Worship.* London: SCM Press, 1973.

Depraz, Natalie. *Le corps glorieux. Phénoménologie pratique de la* Philocalie *des pères du désert et des pères de l'église.* Leuven: Peeters, 2008.

———. *Lucidité du corps. De l'empirisme transcendental en phénoménologie.* Dordrecht: Kluwer Academic Publishers, 2001.

———. *Transcendance et incarnation. Le statut de l'intersubjéctivité comme altérité à soi chez Husserl.* Paris: Vrin, 1995.

Dix, Gregory, and Simon Jones. *The Shape of the Liturgy.* London: Continuum, 2005 [1945].

Doering, Lutz. *Schabbat: Sabbathalacha und -praxis im antiken Judentum und Urchristentum.* Tübingen: Mohr Siebeck, 1999.

Doig, Allan. *Liturgy and Architecture: From the Early Church to the Middle Ages.* Farnham, UK: Ashgate, 2008.

Donghi, Antonio. *Words and Gestures in the Liturgy.* Translated by W. McDonough, D. Serra, T. Bertagni. Collegeville, Minn.: The Liturgical Press, 2009.

Donohoe, Janet. *Remembering Places: A Phenomenological Study of the Relationship between Memory and Place.* Lanham, Md.: Lexington Books, 2014.

Dunn, Geoffrey D., and Wendy Mayer, eds. *Christians Shaping Identity from the Roman Empire to Byzantium: Studies Inspired by Pauline Allen*. Leiden: Brill, 2015.

Dunn-Wilson, David. *A Mirror for the Church: Preaching in the First Five Centuries*. Grand Rapids, Mich.: William B. Eerdmans, 2005.

Eastmond, Antony. *Art and Identity in Thirteenth-Century Byzantium*. Aldershot, UK: Ashgate, 2004.

Eastmond, Antony, and Liz James, eds. *Icon and Word: The Power of Images in Byzantium*. Farnham, UK: Ashgate, 2003.

Egan, John J. "Liturgy and Justice: An Unfinished Agenda." *Origins* 13 (1983): 399–411.

Ehrhard, Albert. *Überlieferung und Bestand der hagiographischen und homiletischen Literatur der griechischen Kirche*. 3 vols. Leipzig: J. C. Hinrichs, 1936–1939.

Empereur, James. *Models of Liturgical Theology*. Bramcote, UK: Grove Liturgical Publications, 1987.

———. *Worship: Exploring the Sacred*. Washington: The Pastoral Press, 1987.

Empereur, James L., and Christopher G. Kiesling. *The Liturgy That Does Justice*. Collegeville, Minn.: The Liturgical Press, 1990.

Fagerberg, David. *On Liturgical Asceticism*. Washington: Catholic University of America Press, 2013.

———. *Theologia Prima: What Is Liturgical Theology? A Study in Methodology*. Chicago: Hillenbrand Books, 2004 [1992].

Falque, Emmanuel. *Crossing the Rubicon: The Borderlands Between Philosophy and Theology*. Translated by Reuben Shank. New York: Fordham University Press, 2016.

———. *God, the Flesh, and the Other: From Irenaeus to Duns Scotus*. Translated by William Christian Hackett. Evanston, Ill.: Northwestern University Press, 2015.

———. *The Guide to Gethsemane: Anxiety, Suffering, Death*. Translated by George Hughes. New York: Fordham University Press, 2019.

———. *Le Combat amoureux. Disputes phénoménologiques et théologiques*. Paris: Hermann, 2014.

———. *The Metamorphosis of Finitude: An Essay on Birth and Resurrection*. Translated by Georges Hughes. New York: Fordham University Press, 2012.

———. "Toward an Ethics of the Spread Body." In *Somatic Desire: Rethinking Corporeality in Contemporary Thought*, edited by Sarah Horton et al., 91–116. Lanham, Md.: Lexington Press, 2019.

———. *The Wedding Feast of the Lamb: Eros, the Body, and the Eucharist*. Translated by George Hughes. New York: Fordham University Press, 2016.

Ferguson, Everett. *Toward a Patristic Theology of Music*. Leuven: Peeters, 1993.

Fisch, Thomas, ed. *Liturgy and Tradition: Theological Reflections of Alexander Schmemann.* Crestwood, N.Y.: St. Vladimir's Seminary Press, 1990.

Fisher, Eugene J., ed. *The Jewish Roots of Christian Liturgy.* New York: Paulist Press, 1990.

Flanagan, Kieran. *Sociology and Liturgy: Re-presentations of the Holy.* London: Macmillan, 1991.

Florensky, Pavel. *The Pillar and Ground of Truth.* Translated by Boris Jakim. Princeton: Princeton University Press, 1997.

Florovsky, George. *Bible, Church, Tradition: An Eastern Orthodox View.* Vol. 1 of *Collected Works.* Belmont, Mass.: Nordland Publishing, 1974.

Franck, Didier. *Flesh and Body: On the Phenomenology of Husserl.* Translated by Joseph Rivera and Scott Davidson. London: Bloomsbury, 2014.

———. *Heidegger et le christianisme. L'explication silencieuse.* Paris: Presses Universitaires de France, 2004.

———. *Heidegger et le problème de l'espace.* Paris: Minuit, 1986.

Frank, Georgia. "'Taste and See': The Eucharist and the Eyes of Faith in the Fourth Century." *Church History* 70, no. 4 (2001): 619–43.

Gadamer, Hans-Georg. *Truth and Method.* Translated by Joel Weinsheimer and Donald G. Marshall. New York: Continuum, 2004.

Galadza, Daniel. *Liturgy and Byzantinization in Jerusalem.* Oxford: Oxford University Press, 2018.

Galatariotou, Catia. "Travel and Perception in Byzantium." *Dumbarton Oaks Papers* 47 (1993): 221–41.

Galavaris, George. *Bread and the Liturgy: The Symbolism of Early Christian and Byzantine Bread Stamps.* Madison: University of Wisconsin Press, 1970.

Germanus of Constantinople. *On the Divine Liturgy.* Translated by Paul Meyendorff. Crestwood, N.Y.: St. Vladimir's Seminary Press, 1984.

Getcha, Job. "Le Grand Canon pénitentiel de saint André de Crète. Une lecture typologique de l'histoire du salut." In *La liturgie, interprète de l'Écriture. II. Dans les compositions liturgiques, prières et chants. Conférences Saint-Serge XLIXe Semaine d'Études Liturgiques 2002,* edited by C. Braga and A. Pistoia, 105–20. Rome: Edizioni Liturgiche, 2003.

———. *The Typikon Decoded: An Explanation of Byzantine Liturgical Practice.* Translated by Paul Meyendorff. Yonkers, N.Y.: St. Vladimir's Seminary Press, 2012.

Getcha, Job, and M. Stavrou, eds. *Le Feu sur la terre. Mélanges offerts au Père Boris Bobrinskoy pour son 80e anniversaire.* Paris: Presses Saint-Serge, 2005.

Gorman, Jr., Frank H. *The Ideology of Ritual: Space, Time and Status in the Priestly Theology.* Journal for the Study of the Old Testament, Supplement Series 91. Sheffield, UK: Sheffield Academic Press, 1990.

Grdzelidze, Tamara. "Liturgical Space in the Writings of Maximus the Confessor." *Studia Patristica* XXXVII (Leuven: Peeters, 2001): 499–504.

Greisch, Jean. *Le Buisson ardent et les lumières de la raison. L'invention de la philosophie de la religion.* 3 vols. Paris: Cerf, 2002–2004.

Groen, Bert, Steven Hawkes-Teeples, and Stefanos Alexopoulos, eds. *Inquiries into Eastern Christian Worship: Selected Papers of the Second International Congress of the Society of Oriental Liturgy, Rome, 17–21 September 2008.* Leuven: Peeters, 2012.

Grondin, Jean. *La philosophie de la religion.* Paris: Presses Universitaires de France, 2009.

Groppe, Elizabeth T. "Holy Things from a Holy People: Judaism and the Christian Liturgy." *Worship* 81, no. 5 (2007): 386–408.

Guardini, Romano. *The Spirit of the Liturgy.* Translated by Ada Lane. New York: Crossroad Publishing, 1998 [1930].

Gueullette, Jean-Marie. *La Beauté d'un geste.* Paris: Cerf, 2014.

Guthrie, Harvey H. *Theology as Thanksgiving: From Israel's Psalms to the Church's Eucharist.* New York: Seabury, 1981.

Hadot, Pierre. *Philosophy as a Way of Life: Spiritual Exercises from Socrates to Foucault.* Oxford: Blackwell, 2011.

———. *What Is Ancient Philosophy?* Cambridge, Mass.: Harvard University Press, 2004.

Hannick, Christopher. "Exégèse, typologie et rhétorique dans l'hymnographie byzantine." *Dumbarton Oaks Papers* 53 (1999): 207–18.

Hart, Kevin. *Kingdoms of God.* Bloomington: Indiana University Press, 2014.

Harvey, Susan Ashbrook. "Interior Decorating: Jacob of Serug on Mary's Preparation for the Incarnation." *Studia Patristica* XLI (2006): 23–28.

———. "Liturgy and Ethics in Ancient Syriac Christianity: Two Paradigms." *Studies in Christian Ethics* 26 (2013): 300–16.

———. *Scenting Salvation: Ancient Christianity and the Olfactory Imagination.* Berkeley: University of California Press, 2006.

Heidegger, Martin. *Basic Writings.* Edited by David Farrell Krell. San Francisco: HarperCollins, 1993.

———. *Gesamtausgabe 64: Der Begriff der Zeit.* Frankfurt/M: Vittorio Klostermann, 2004.

———. *The Hermeneutics of Facticity.* Translated by John van Buren. Bloomington: Indiana University Press, 1999.

———. "Phenomenology and Theology." In *The Religious,* edited by John D. Caputo, 49–65. Oxford: Blackwell, 2003.

———. *The Phenomenology of Religious Life.* Translated by Matthias Fritsch and Jennifer Gosetti-Ferencei. Bloomington: Indiana University Press, 2004.

———. *Sein und Zeit*. Tübingen: Max Niemeyer Verlag, 1993. Translated by John Macquarrie and Edward Robinson as *Being and Time*. New York: Harper, 2008.

———. *Zollikoner Seminare*. Edited by Medard Boss. Frankfurt/M: Vittorio Klostermann, 2006. Translated by Franz Mayr and Richard Askay as *Zollikon Seminars: Protocols—Conversations—Letters*. Evanston, Ill.: Northwestern University Press, 2001.

Hemming, Laurence Paul. *Heidegger's Atheism: The Refusal of a Theological Voice*. Notre Dame, Ind.: University of Notre Dame Press, 2002.

———. *Worship as a Revelation: The Past, Present and Future of Catholic Liturgy*. London: Burns and Oates, 2008.

Hénaff, Marcel. *The Price of Truth: Gift, Money, and Philosophy*. Translated by Jean-Louis Morhange. Stanford: Stanford University Press, 2010.

Henry, Michel. *I Am the Truth: Toward a Philosophy of Christianity*. Translated by Susan Emanuel. Stanford: Stanford University Press, 2003.

———. *Incarnation: A Philosophy of the Flesh*. Translated by Karl Hefty. Evanston, Ill.: Northwestern University Press, 2015.

———. *Material Phenomenology*. Translated by Scott Davidson. New York: Fordham University Press, 2008.

———. *Paroles du Christ*. Paris: Seuil, 2002.

Heschel, Abraham. *The Sabbath: Its Meaning for Modern Man*. New York: Farrar, Strauss and Giroux, 1951.

Hildebrand, Dietrich von. *Liturgy and Personality*. Baltimore: Helicon Press, 1960.

Hinterberger, James. "Emotions in Byzantium." In *A Companion to Byzantium*, edited by Liz James, 123–34. Chichester, UK: Wiley-Blackwell, 2010.

Hoffman, Lawrence A. *Beyond the Text: A Holistic Approach to Liturgy*. Bloomington: Indiana University Press, 1987.

Hoffmann, Manfred. *Der Dialog bei den christlichen Schriftstellern der ersten vier Jahrhunderte*. Texte und Untersuchungen 96. Berlin: Akademie Verlag, 1966.

Holman, Susan R. *The Hungry Are Dying: Beggars and Bishops in Roman Cappadocia*. Oxford: Oxford University Press, 2001.

Horner, Robyn. *Jean-Luc Marion: A* Theo-*logical Introduction*. Hants, UK: Ashgate, 2005.

Housset, Emmanuel. *Husserl et l'idée de Dieu*. Paris: Cerf, 2010.

Houtman, Alberdina, Marcel J. H. M. Poorthuis, and Joshua Schwartz, eds. *Sanctity of Time and Space in Tradition and Modernity*. Leiden: Brill, 1998.

Hughes, Graham. *Worship as Meaning: A Liturgical Theology for Late Modernity*. Cambridge: Cambridge University Press, 2003.

Huizinga, Johan. *Homo Ludens: A Study of the Play-Element in Culture*. Kettering, Ohio: Angelico Press, 2016 [1938].

Hunt, Edward David. *Holy Land Pilgrimage in the Later Roman Empire AD 312–460*. Oxford: Clarendon Press, 2002 [1982].

Hunt, Hannah. *Joy-Bearing Grief: Tears of Contrition in the Writings of the Early Syrian and Byzantine Fathers*. Leiden: Brill, 2004.

Hunter-Crawley, Heather. "Embodying the Divine: The Sensational Experience of the Sixth-Century Eucharist." In *Making Senses of the Past: Toward a Sensory Archaeology*, edited by J. Day, 160–76. Carbondale: Illinois University Press, 2013.

Husserl, Edmund. *Cartesian Meditations: An Introduction to Phenomenology*. Translated by Dorion Cairns. The Hague: Martinus Nijhoff, 1960.

———. *The Idea of Phenomenology*. Translated by L. Hardy. Dordrecht: Kluwer Academic Publishers, 2010.

———. *Ideas Pertaining to a Pure Phenomenology and to a Phenomenological Philosophy*. Translated by F. Kersten. The Hague: Martinus Nijhoff Publishers, 1982.

———. *On the Phenomenology of the Consciousness of Internal Time (1893–1917)*. Translated by John Barnett Brough. Dordrecht: Kluwer Academic Publishers, 1991.

Hussey, J. M., and Andrew Louth. *The Orthodox Church in the Byzantine Empire*. Oxford: Oxford University Press, 2010.

Irwin, Kevin W. *Context and Text: Method in Liturgical Theology*. Collegeville, Minn.: The Liturgical Press, 1994.

———. *The Sacraments: Historical Foundations and Liturgical Theology*. New York: Paulist Press, 2016.

Jacob of Serug. *On the Mother of God*. Translated by Mary Hansbury. Crestwood, N.Y.: St. Vladimir's Seminary Press, 1998.

James, Liz, ed. *Art and Text in Byzantine Culture*. Cambridge: Cambridge University Press, 2007.

———, ed. *A Companion to Byzantium*. Chichester, UK: Wiley-Blackwell, 2010.

———. *Desire and Denial in Byzantium*. Aldershot, UK: Ashgate, 1999.

———. *Light and Colour in Byzantine Art*. Oxford: Clarendon Press, 1991.

———. "Senses and Sensibility in Byzantium." *Art History* 27, no. 4 (2004): 522–37.

James, Liz, and Ruth Webb. "Ekphrasis and Art in Byzantium." *Art History* 14 (1991): 1–17.

Janowiak, Paul. *The Holy Preaching: The Sacramentality of the Word in the Liturgical Assembly*. Collegeville, Minn.: Liturgical Press, 2000.

———. *Standing Together in the Community of God: Liturgical Spirituality and the Presence of Christ*. Collegeville, Minn.: Liturgical Press, 2011.

Jasper, David, and R. C. D. Jaspers, eds. *Language and the Worship of the Church*. London: Macmillan, 1990.

John Chrysostom. *Homilies on Genesis*. Translated by Robert C. Hill. *The Fathers of the Church*, Vols. 74 and 82. Washington: Catholic University of America Press, 1986 and 1990.

————. *On Wealth and Poverty*. Translated by Catharine P. Roth. Crestwood, N.Y.: St. Vladimir's Seminary Press, 1984.

John of Damascus. *Three Treatises on the Divine Images*. Translated by Andrew Louth. Crestwood, N.Y.: St. Vladimir's Seminary Press, 2003.

Johnson, Luke Timothy. *The Revelatory Body: Theology as Inductive Art*. Grand Rapids, Mich.: William B. Eerdmans, 2015.

Johnson, Maxwell E., ed. *Between Memory and Hope: Readings on the Liturgical Year*. Collegeville, Minn.: The Liturgical Press, 2000.

Johnson, Maxwell E., and Edward L. Philipps, eds. *Studia Liturgica Diversa: Essays in Honor of Paul F. Bradshaw*. Portland, Ore.: Pastoral Press, 2004.

Jones, Tamsin. *A Genealogy of Marion's Philosophy of Religion: Apparent Darkness*. Bloomington: Indiana University Press, 2011.

Joubert, Jean-Marc. "La notion d'espace sacré: Une approche philosophique." In *L'espace liturgique: ses éléments constitutifs et leur sens. Conférences Saint-Serge LIIe Semaine d'Études Liturgiques 2005*, edited by C. Braga, 217–33. Rome: Edizioni Liturgiche, 2006.

Jungman, Josef A. *The Early Liturgy: To the Time of Gregory the Great*. Notre Dame, Ind.: University of Notre Dame Press, 1959.

Kavanagh, Aidan. *Elements of Rite: A Handbook of Liturgical Style*. New York: Pueblo Publishing, 1982.

————. *On Liturgical Theology: The Hale Memorial Lectures of Seabury-Western Theological Seminary, 1981*. Collegeville, Minn.: The Liturgical Press, 1984.

Kearney, Richard. *Anatheism: Returning to God After God*. New York: Columbia University Press, 2010.

————. "Epiphanies of the Everyday: Toward a Micro-Eschatology." In *After God: Richard Kearney and the Religious Turn in Continental Philosophy*, edited by John Panteleimon Manoussakis, 3–20. New York: Fordham University Press, 2006.

————. *The God Who May Be: A Hermeneutics of Religion*. Bloomington: Indiana University Press, 2001.

————. "Toward an Open Eucharist." In *Ritual Participation and Interreligious Dialogue*, edited by Marianne Moyaert and Joris Geldhof, 138–55. London: Bloomsbury Academic, 2016.

Kearney, Richard, and Brian Treanor, eds. *Carnal Hermeneutics*. New York: Fordham University Press, 2015.

Kearney, Richard, and Jens Zimmermann, eds. *Reimagining the Sacred: Richard Kearney Debates God*. New York: Columbia University Press, 2016.

Kelleher, Margaret Mary. "Hermeneutics in the Study of Liturgical Performance." *Worship* 67, no. 4 (1993): 292–318.

Kennedy, George A. *Classical Rhetoric and Its Christian and Secular Tradition from Ancient to Modern Times.* London: University of North Carolina Press, 1980.

———. *Greek Rhetoric under Christian Emperors.* Princeton: Princeton University Press, 1983.

Kennedy, Greg. *The Ontology of Trash.* Albany, N.Y.: SUNY Press, 2007.

Krautheimer, Richard. *Early Christian and Byzantine Architecture.* Baltimore: Penguin, 1986.

Kristeva, Julia. *The Revolution in Poetic Language.* Translated by Margaret Waller. New York: Columbia University Press, 1984.

Krueger, Derek. *Liturgical Subjects: Christian Ritual, Biblical Narrative, and the Formation of the Self in Byzantium.* Philadelphia: University of Pennsylvania Press, 2014.

Lacoste, Jean-Yves. *Experience and the Absolute: Disputed Questions on the Humanity of Man.* Translated by Mark Raftery-Skeban. New York: Fordham University Press, 2004.

———. *La phénoménalité de Dieu. Neuf études.* Paris: Cerf, 2008.

———. *L'intuition sacramentelle et autres essais.* Paris: Ad Solem, 2015.

———. "Liturgy and Coaffection." In *The Experience of God: A Postmodern Response*, edited by Kevin Hart and Barbara Wall, 93–103. New York: Fordham University Press, 2005.

———. *Note sur le temps. Essai sur les raisons de la mémoire et de l'espérance.* Paris: Presses Universitaires de France, 1990.

———. *Présence et parousie.* Paris: Ad Solem, 2006.

———. *Recherches sur la Parole.* Louvain-la-Neuve: Peeters, 2015.

Larin, Vassa. "'Active Participation' of the Faithful in Byzantine Liturgy." *St. Vladimir's Theological Quarterly* 57, no. 1 (2013): 67–88.

———. "Feasting and Fasting According to the Byzantine Typikon." *Worship* 83, no. 2 (2009): 133–48.

Lathrop, Gordon W. *Holy Ground: A Liturgical Cosmology.* Minneapolis: Fortress Press, 2003.

———. *Holy People: A Liturgical Ecclesiology.* Minneapolis: Fortress Press, 1999.

———. *Holy Things: A Liturgical Theology.* Minneapolis: Fortress Press, 1998 [1993].

Leontius of Constantinople. *Fourteen Homilies.* Translated by Pauline Allen. Brisbane: Australian Association for Byzantine Studies, 1991.

Levinas, Emmanuel. *Basic Philosophical Writings.* Edited by Adriaan T. Peperzak, Simon Critchley, and Robert Bernasconi. Bloomington: Indiana University Press, 1996.

———. *God, Death, and Time.* Translated by Bettina Bergo. Stanford: Stanford University Press, 2000.

————. *Nine Talmudic Readings*. Translated by Annette Aronowicz. Bloomington: Indiana University Press, 1990.

————. *Of God Who Comes to Mind*. Translated by Bettina Bergo. Stanford:
Stanford University Press, 1998.

————. *On Escape*. Translated by Bettina Bergo. Stanford: Stanford University
Press, 2003.

————. *Otherwise Than Being or Beyond Essence*. Translated by Alphonso Lingis.
Pittsburgh: Duquesne University Press, 1998.

————. *Time and the Other*. Translated by Richard A. Cohen. Pittsburgh:
Duquesne University Press, 1987.

————. *Totality and Infinity: An Essay on Exteriority*. Translated by Alphonso
Lingis. Pittsburgh: Duquesne University Press, 1969.

Limouris, Gennadios, ed. *Church, Kingdom, World: The Church as Mystery and
Prophetic Sign*. Faith and Order Paper No. 130. Geneva: WCC, 1986.

Lingis, Alexander. *Sunday Matins in the Byzantine Cathedral Rite: Music and Liturgy*. Farnham, UK: Ashgate, forthcoming.

Lossky, André. "Commémoration liturgique des séismes et confession de la toute-
puissance divine." In *Liturgie et cosmos. Conférences Saint-Serge XLIVe Semaine
d'Études liturgiques (1–4 juillet 1997)*, edited by A. M. Triacca and A. Pistoia,
131–51. Rome: C.L.V. Edizioni Liturgiche, 1998.

————. "Le Typicon byzantine: Une autorité dans la liturgie de l'Église?" In
*L'autorité de la liturgie. Conférences Saint-Serge LIIIe Semaine d'Études Litur-
giques 2006*, ed. C. Braga, 115–32. Rome: Edizioni Liturgiche, 2007.

Lossky, Vladimir. *The Mystical Theology of the Eastern Church*. Crestwood, N.Y.:
St. Vladimir's Seminary Press, 2002 [1957].

Louth, Andrew. "Light, Vision and Religious Experience in Byzantium." In *The
Presence of Light: Divine Radiance and Religious Experience*, edited by Matthew
Kapstein, 85–103. Chicago: University of Chicago Press, 2004.

————. "Space, Time and the Liturgy." In *Encounter Between Eastern Orthodoxy
and Radical Orthodoxy: Transfiguring the World through the Word*, edited by
A. Pabst and C. Schneider, 215–31. Farnham, UK: Ashgate, 2009.

————. "Theological Reflections on Pilgrimage." *ΠΡΛΤΙΚΑ ΙΒ ΕΠΙCΤΗΜΟΝΙ
ΚΟΥ CΥΜΠΟCΙΟΥ*, 97–102. Thessaloniki: University Studio Press, 2001.

Mackinlay, Shane. *Interpreting Excess: Jean-Luc Marion, Saturated Phenomena,
and Hermeneutics*. New York: Fordham University Press, 2010.

Mackinnon, James W., ed. *Music in Early Christian Literature*. Cambridge: Cambridge University Press, 1989.

Maguire, Henry. *Earth and Ocean: The Terrestrial World in Early Byzantine Art*.
University Park: Pennsylvania State University Press, 1987.

————. *The Icons of their Bodies: Saints and their Images in Byzantium*. Princeton:
Princeton University Press, 1996.

————. *Nectar and Illusion: Nature in Byzantine Art and Literature.* Oxford: Oxford University Press, 2012.

Mainstone, Rowland J. *Hagia Sophia: Architecture, Structure and Liturgy of Justinian's Great Church.* London: Thames & Hudson, 1997.

Mango, Cyril. *The Art of the Byzantine Empire 312–1453: Sources and Documents.* Toronto: University of Toronto Press, 1986.

————. *Byzantine Architecture.* New York: Abrams, 1976.

————. *Byzantium: The Empire of the New Rome.* New York: Charles Scribner's Sons, 1980.

Manoussakis, John Panteleimon. *The Ethics of Time: A Phenomenology and Hermeneutics of Change.* London: Bloomsbury, 2017.

————. *God After Metaphysics: A Theological Aesthetics.* Bloomington: Indiana University Press, 2007.

Marinis, Vasileios. *Architecture and Ritual in the Churches of Constantinople: Ninth to Fifteenth Centuries.* Cambridge: Cambridge University Press, 2014.

————. "Defining Liturgical Space." In *The Byzantine World*, edited by Paul Stephenson, 284–302. London: Routledge, 2010.

Marion, Jean-Luc. *Being Given: Toward a Phenomenology of Givenness.* Translated by Jeffrey L. Kosky. Stanford: Stanford University Press, 2002.

————. *Believing in Order to See.* New York: Fordham University Press, 2017.

————. *The Erotic Phenomenon.* Translated by Stephen Lewis. Chicago: University of Chicago Press, 2007.

————. "From the Other to the Individual." Translated by Arianne Conty. *Levinas Studies: An Annual Review*, 99–117. Pittsburgh: Duquesne University Press, 2005.

————. *Givenness and Revelation.* Translated by Stephen E. Lewis. Oxford: Oxford University Press, 2016.

————. *God Without Being.* Translated by Thomas A. Carlson. Chicago: University of Chicago Press, 1991.

————. *The Idol and Distance: Five Studies.* Translated by Thomas A. Carlson. New York: Fordham University Press, 2001.

————. *In Excess: Studies of Saturated Phenomena.* Translated by Robyn Horner and Vincent Carraud. New York: Fordham University Press, 2002.

————. *In the Self's Place: The Approach of Saint Augustine.* Translated by Jeffrey L. Kosky. Stanford: Stanford University Press, 2012.

————. *Negative Certainties.* Translated by Stephen E. Lewis. Chicago: University of Chicago Press, 2015.

————. *On Descartes' Passive Thought: The Myth of Cartesian Dualism.* Chicago: University of Chicago Press, 2018.

————. *Prolegomena to Charity.* Translated by Stephen E. Lewis. New York: Fordham University Press, 2002.

————. *Reduction and Givenness: Investigations of Husserl, Heidegger, and Phenomenology.* Translated by Thomas A. Carlson. Evanston, Ill.: Northwestern University Press, 1998.

————. *Reprise du donné.* Paris: Presses Universitaires de France, 2016.

————. *Ruf und Gabe: Zum Verhältnis von Phänomenologie und Theologie,* ed. Josef Wohlmuth. Bonn: Borengässer, 2000.

————. *The Visible and the Revealed.* New York: Fordham University Press, 2008.

————. "The Voice without Name: Homage to Levinas." In *The Face of Other and the Trace of God: Essays on the Philosophy of Emmanuel Levinas,* edited by Jeffrey Bloechl, 224–42. New York: Fordham University Press, 2000.

Martimort, Aimé G., ed. *The Church at Prayer I: Principles of the Liturgy.* Collegeville, Minn.: The Liturgical Press, 1987.

————. *The Church at Prayer II: The Eucharist.* Collegeville, Minn.: The Liturgical Press, 1987.

————. *The Church at Prayer III: The Sacraments.* Collegeville, Minn.: The Liturgical Press, 1987.

————. *The Church at Prayer IV: The Liturgy and Time.* Collegeville, Minn.: The Liturgical Press, 1986.

Mathews, Thomas F. *Byzantium: From Antiquity to the Renaissance.* New York: Harry N. Abrams, Inc., 1998.

————. *The Clash of Gods: A Reinterpretation of Early Christian Art.* Princeton: Princeton University Press, 1993.

————. *The Early Churches of Constantinople: Architecture and Liturgy.* University Park: Pennsylvania State University Press, 1971.

Maunder, Chris, ed. *The Origins of the Cult of the Virgin Mary.* London: Burns & Oates, 2008.

Maximus Confessor. "The Church's Mystagogy." In *Selected Writings.* Translated by George C. Berthold. New York: Paulist Press, 1985.

Mazza, Enrico. *Mystagogy: A Theology of Liturgy in the Patristic Age.* Translated by Matthew J. O'Connell. New York: Pueblo Publishing, 1989.

McCall, Richard D. *Do This: Liturgy as Performance.* Notre Dame, Ind.: University of Notre Dame Press, 2007.

McGowan, Andrew B. *Ancient Christian Worship: Early Church Practices in Social, Historical, and Theological Perspective.* Grand Rapids, Mich.: Baker Academic, 2014.

McKay, Heather A. *Sabbath and Synagogue: The Question of Sabbath Worship in Ancient Jerusalem.* Leiden: E. J. Brill, 1994.

McMichael, Ralph N., Jr., ed. *Creation and Liturgy: Studies in Honor of H. Boone Porter.* Washington: Pastoral Press, 1993.

McVey, Kathleen E. "The Domed Church as Microcosm: Literary Roots of an Architectural Symbol." *Dumbarton Oaks Papers* 37 (1983): 91–121.

Merleau-Ponty, Maurice. *Phenomenology of Perception*. Translated by Donald A. Landes. London: Routledge, 2012.

———. *Sense and Non-Sense*. Translated by Hubert L. Dreyfus and Patricia Allen Dreyfus. Evanston, Ill.: Northwestern University Press, 1964.

Meßner, Reinhard. *Einführung in die Liturgiewissenschaft*. Paderborn: Ferdinand Schöningh, 2001.

Meyendorff, John. *Byzantine Theology: Historical Trends and Doctrinal Themes*. New York: Fordham University Press, 1983 [1974].

Mick, Lawrence E. *Liturgy and Ecology in Dialogue*. Collegeville, Minn.: Liturgical Press, 1997.

Micks, Marianne H. *The Future Present: The Phenomenon of Christian Worship*. New York: The Seabury Press, 1970.

Mitchell, Nathan D. *Liturgy and the Social Sciences*. Collegeville, Minn.: Liturgical Press, 1999.

———. *Meeting Mystery: Liturgy, Worship, Sacraments*. Maryknoll, N.Y.: Orbis, 2006.

Moody Ivan, and Maria Takala-Roszczenko, eds. *Creating Liturgically: Hymnography and Music*. Jyväskylä, Finland: International Society for Orthodox Church Music, 2017.

Morrill, Bruce T. *Anamnesis as Dangerous Memory: Political and Liturgical Theology in Dialogue*. Collegeville, Minn.: Liturgical Press, 2000.

———. "The Beginning of the End: Eschatology in the Liturgical Year and Lectionary." *Liturgical Ministry* 12 (2003): 65–74.

———, ed. *Bodies of Worship: Explorations in Theory and Practice*. Collegeville, Minn.: Liturgical Press, 1999.

———. *Divine Worship and Human Healing: Liturgical Theology at the Margins of Life and Death*. Collegeville, Minn.: Liturgical Press, 2009.

———. *Encountering Christ in the Eucharist: The Paschal Mystery in People, Word, and Sacrament*. New York: Paulist Press, 2012.

———. "The Liturgical Is Political: A Narrative Theological Assessment of Alexander Schmemann's Work." *Questions Liturgiques/Studies in Liturgy* 98, nos. 1–2 (2017): 41–59.

———. "Liturgy, Ethics, and Politics: Constructive Inquiry into the Traditional Notion of Participation in Mystery." In *Meeting Mysteries, Understanding Liturgies: On Bridging the Gap between Liturgy and Systematic Theology*, edited by Joris Geldhof, 187–206. Leuven: Peeters, 2015.

Morris, Rosemary, ed. *Church and People in Byzantium*. Birmingham: Birmingham University Press, 1990.

Mueller-Jourdan, Pascal. *Typologie spatio-temporelle de l'Ecclesia byzantine. La Mystagogie de Maxime le Confesseur dans la culture philosophique de l'Antiquité tardive*. Leiden: Brill, 2005.

Mühlenberg, Ekkehard, and Johannes van Oort, eds. *Predigt in der Alten Kirche*.
    Kampen, Netherlands: Kok Pharos Publishing House, 1994.
Nesbitt, Claire. "Shaping the Sacred: Light and the Experience of Worship in
    Middle Byzantine Churches." *Byzantine and Modern Greek Studies* 36, no. 2
    (2012): 139–60.
Nesbitt, Claire, and Mark Jackson, eds. *Experiencing Byzantium. Papers from the
    44th Spring Symposium of Byzantine Studies, Newcastle and Durham, April
    2011*. Aldershot, UK: Ashgate, 2013.
Neunhauser, Burkhard. "Liturgiewissenschaft: Exakte Geschichtsforschung oder
    (und) Theologie der Liturgie." *Ecclesia Orans* 4 (1987): 7–102.
Nichols, Bridget. *Liturgical Hermeneutics: Interpreting Liturgical Rites in Perfor-
    mance*. Frankfurt/M: Peter Lang, 1994.
Opperwall, Daniel G. *A Layman in the Desert: Monastic Wisdom for a Life in the
    World*. Yonkers, N.Y.: St. Vladimir's Seminary Press, 2015.
Ossorguine, Nicolas. "Éléments cosmique de la mystagogie liturgique." In *Myst-
    agogie: Pensée liturgique d'aujourd'hui et liturgie ancienne. Conférences Saint-
    Serge XXXIXe Semaine d'Études Liturgiques 1992*, edited by A. M. Triacca and
    A. Pistoia, 243–51. Rome: Edizioni Liturgiche, 1993.
Ousterhout, Robert. "Holy Space: Architecture and the Liturgy." in *Heaven on
    Earth: Art and the Church in Byzantium*, ed. Linda Safran, 81–120. University
    Park: Pennsylvania State University Press, 1988.
Page, Gill. *Being "Byzantine": Greek Identity before the Ottomans*. Cambridge:
    Cambridge University Press, 2008.
Papaconstantinou, Arietta, and Alice-Mary Talbot, eds. *Becoming Byzantine:
    Children and Childhood in Byzantium*. Cambridge, Mass.: Harvard University
    Press, 2009.
Peers, Glenn. *Sacred Shock: Framing Visual Experience in Byzantium*. University
    Park: Pennsylvania State University Press, 2004.
Penn, Michael Philip. *Kissing Christians: Ritual and Community in the Late
    Ancient Church*. Philadelphia: University of Pennsylvania Press, 2005.
Pentcheva, Bissera. "Hagia Sophia and Multisensory Aesthetics." GESTA 50, no.
    2 (2011): 93–111.
———. "The Performative Icon." *Art Bulletin* 88, no. 4 (2006): 631–55.
———. *The Sensual Icon: Space, Ritual, and the Senses in Byzantium*. University
    Park: Pennsylvania State University Press, 2010.
Pentecostarion. Boston: Holy Transfiguration Monastery, 1990.
Pfattreicher, Philip H. *Liturgical Spirituality*. Valley Forge, Pa.: Trinity Press
    International, 1997.
Photios. *The Homilies of Photius Patriarch of Constantinople*. Translated by Cyril
    Mango. Cambridge, Mass.: Harvard University Press, 1958.
Pickstock, Catherine. *After Writing: On the Liturgical Consummation of Philoso-
    phy*. Oxford: Blackwell Publishers, 1998.

Pott, Thomas. *Byzantine Liturgical Reform: A Study of Liturgical Change in the Byzantine Tradition.* Translated by Paul Meyendorff. Crestwood, N.Y.: St. Vladimir's Seminary Press, 2010.

Power, David N. *Unsearchable Riches: The Symbolic Nature of Liturgy.* New York: Pueblo Publishing, 1984.

———. *Worship: Culture and Theology.* Washington: The Pastoral Press, 1990.

Proclus, Bishop of Constantinople. *Homilies on the Life of Christ.* Translated by Jan Harm Barkhuizen. Early Christian Studies 1. Brisbane: Australian Catholic University, 2001.

Procopius. *Buildings.* Translated by B. Dewing. Cambridge, Mass.: Harvard University Press, 1940.

Rashkover, Randi. *Liturgy, Time, and the Politics of Redemption.* Grand Rapids, Mich.: William B. Eerdmans, 2006.

Ratzinger, Joseph Cardinal. *Feast of Faith: Approaches to a Theology of the Liturgy.* Translated by G. Harrison. San Francisco: Ignatius Press, 1986.

———. *The Spirit of the Liturgy.* Translated by J. Saward. San Francisco: Ignatius Press, 2000.

Ray, Walter D. *Tasting Heaven on Earth: Worship in Sixth-Century Constantinople.* Grand Rapids, Mich.: William B. Eerdmans, 2012.

Rentel, Alexander. "Where Is God in the Liturgy?" *St. Vladimir's Theological Quarterly* 59, no. 2 (2015): 213–33.

Ricoeur, Paul. *Essays on Biblical Interpretation.* Edited by Lewis S. Mudge. Philadelphia: Fortress Press, 1980.

———. *Figuring the Sacred: Religion, Narrative, and Imagination.* Translated by David Pellauer. Edited by Mark I. Wallace. Minneapolis: Fortress Press, 1995.

———. *Freedom and Nature: The Voluntary and the Involuntary.* Translated by Erazim V. Kohák. Evanston, Ill.: Northwestern University Press, 2007 [1966].

———. *From Text to Action: Essays in Hermeneutics II.* Translated by Kathleen Blamey and John B. Thompson. Evanston, Ill.: Northwestern University Press, 2007 [1991].

———. *Interpretation Theory: Discourse and the Surplus of Meaning.* Fort Worth: Texas Christian University, 1976.

———. "Life in Quest of Narrative." In *On Paul Ricoeur: Narrative and Interpretation,* edited by David Wood, 20–33. London: Routledge, 1992.

———. *Oneself as Another.* Translated by Kathleen Blamey. Chicago: University of Chicago Press, 1992.

———. *The Symbolism of Evil.* Translated by Emerson Buchanan. Boston: Beacon Press, 1967.

———. *Time and Narrative.* Translated by Kathleen McLaughlin and David Pellauer. 3 vols. Chicago: University of Chicago Press, 1984–88.

Riesebrodt, Martin. *The Promise of Salvation: A Theory of Religion.* Translated by Steven Rendall. Chicago: University of Chicago Press, 2010.

Rigo, Antonio, Michele Trizio, and Eleftherios Despotakis, eds. *Byzantine Hagi-ography: Texts, Themes, and Projects*. Turnhout, Belgium: Brepols, 2018.

Riou, Alain. *Le monde et l'église selon saint Maxime le Confesseur*. Paris: Beauch-esne, 1973.

Rivera, Joseph. *The Contemplative Self after Michel Henry: A Phenomenological Theology*. Notre Dame, Ind.: Notre Dame University Press, 2015.

Rouwhorst, Gerard. "How Eschatological was early Christian Liturgy?" *Studia Patristica* XL (Leuven: Peeters, 2006): 93–108.

Saliers, Don E. *Worship as Theology: Foretaste of the Divine Glory*. Nashville: Abingdon Press, 1994.

———. *Worship Come to Its Senses*. Nashville: Abingdon Press, 1996.

Scheler, Max. *The Nature of Sympathy*. London: Routledge, 2008.

Schibille, Nadine. *Hagia Sophia and the Byzantine Aesthetic Experience*. Farnham, UK: Ashgate, 2014.

Schmemann, Alexander. *The Eucharist: Sacrament of the Kingdom*. Crestwood, N.Y.: St. Vladimir's Seminary Press, 1987.

———. *For the Life of the World: Sacraments and Orthodoxy*. Crestwood, N.Y.: St. Vladimir's Seminary Press, 1973.

———. *Great Lent: Journey to Pascha*. Crestwood, N.Y.: St. Vladimir's Seminary Press, 1996.

———. *Introduction to Liturgical Theology*. Crestwood, N.Y.: St. Vladimir's Seminary Press, 1986.

———. *The Liturgy of Death*. Yonkers, N.Y.: St. Vladimir's Seminary Press, 2016.

Schmit, Clayton J. *Too Deep for Words: A Theology of Liturgical Expression*. Louis-ville, K.Y.: Westminster John Knox Press, 2002.

Schrijvers, Joeri. *An Introduction to Jean-Yves Lacoste*. Farnham, UK: Ashgate, 2012.

Schulz, Hans-Joachim. *The Byzantine Liturgy: Symbolic Structure and Faith Expression*. Translated by Matthew J. O'Connell. New York: Pueblo, 1986.

Scott, Margaret. *The Eucharist and Social Justice*. New York: Paulist Press, 2008.

Searle, Mark, ed. *Liturgy and Social Justice*. Collegeville, Minn.: The Liturgical Press, 1980.

Senn, Frank C. *Christian Worship and Its Cultural Setting*. Philadelphia: Fortress Press, 1983.

———. *New Creation: A Liturgical Worldview*. Minneapolis: Fortress Press, 2000.

———. *The People's Work: A Social History of the Liturgy*. Minneapolis: Fortress Press, 2006.

Sheldrake, Philip. *Spaces for the Sacred: Place, Memory, and Identity*. Baltimore: Johns Hopkins University Press, 2001.

Shoemaker, Stephen J. *Ancient Traditions of the Virgin Mary's Dormition and Assumption*. Oxford: Oxford University Press, 2002.

Smith, James K. A. *Imagining the Kingdom: How Worship Works*. Grand Rapids, Mich.: Baker Academic, 2013.

Sokolowski, Robert. *Eucharistic Presence: A Study in the Theology of Disclosure*. Washington: Catholic University of America Press, 1994.

Stapert, Calvin. *A New Song for an Old World: Musical Thought in the Early Church*. Grand Rapids, Mich.: William B. Eerdmans, 2007.

Stein, Edith. *On the Problem of Empathy*. Translated by Waltraut Stein. Washington: ICS Publishers, 1989.

Steinbock, Anthony. *Home and Beyond: Generative Phenomenology after Husserl*. Evanston, Ill.: Northwestern University Press, 1995.

———. *Moral Emotions: Reclaiming the Evidence of the Heart*. Evanston, Ill.: Northwestern University Press, 2014.

———. *Phenomenology and Mysticism: The Verticality of Religious Experience*. Bloomington: Indiana University Press, 2007.

———. "The Poor Phenomenon: Marion and the Problem of Givenness." In *Words of Life: New Theological Turns in French Phenomenology*, edited by Bruce Ellis Benson and Norman Wirzba, 120–31. New York: Fordham University Press, 2010.

Strawley, J. H. *The Early Sources of the Liturgy*. Cambridge: Cambridge University Press, 1957.

Stringer, Martin D. *On the Perception of Worship: The Ethnography of Worship in Four Christian Congregations in Manchester*. Birmingham: Birmingham University Press, 1999.

———. *A Sociological History of Christian Worship*. Cambridge: Cambridge University Press, 2005.

———. "Text, Context and Performance: Hermeneutics and the Study of Worship." *Scottish Journal of Theology* 53 (2000): 365–79.

Symeon of Thessalonika. *The Liturgical Commentaries*. Translated by Steven Hawkes-Teeples. Toronto: Pontifical Institute of Mediaeval Studies, 2011.

Taft, Robert F. *Beyond East and West: Problems in Liturgical Understanding*. Washington: Pastoral Press, 1984.

———. *The Byzantine Rite: A Short History*. Collegeville, Minn.: Liturgical Press, 1992.

———. "Liturgy as Theology." *Worship* 56, no. 2 (1982): 113–17.

———. *Liturgy: Model of Prayer, Icon of Life*. Fairfax, Va.: Eastern Christian Publications, 2008.

———. "The Liturgy of the Great Church: An Initial Synthesis of the Structure and Interpretation on the Eve of Iconoclasm." *Dumbarton Oaks Papers* (1980–1981): 45–75.

———. *The Liturgy of the Hours in East and West: The Origins of the Divine Office and Its Meaning for Today*. Collegeville, Minn.: Liturgical Press, 1993 [1986].

———. *Through Their Own Eyes: Liturgy as the Byzantines Saw It.* Berkeley, Calif.: InterOrthodox Press, 2006.

———. "What Does Liturgy Do? Toward a Soteriology of Liturgical Celebration: Some Theses." *Worship* 66, no. 3 (1992): 194–211.

Talley, Thomas J. *The Origins of the Liturgical Year.* Collegeville, Minn.: Liturgical Press, 1991 [1986].

Tarasov, Oleg. *Icon and Devotion: Sacred Spaces in Imperial Russia.* London: Reaktion Books, 2002.

Temps et Liturgie. La Maison-Dieu Nr. 147. Paris: Cerf, 1981.

Theodoret of Cyrrhus. *A History of the Monks of Syria.* Kalamazoo: Cistercian Studies 88, 1985.

Tollefsen, Torstein Theodor. "The Mystery of Christ as a Key to the Cosmology of St. Maximus the Confessor." *Studia Patristica* XLII (Leuven: Peeters, 2006): 255–58.

Torevell, David. *Losing the Sacred: Ritual, Modernity and Liturgical Reform.* Edinburgh: T&T Clark, 2000.

Tracy, David. "Paul Ricoeur: Hermeneutics and the Dialectic of Religious Forms." In *Hermeneutics and the Philosophy of Religion: The Legacy of Paul Ricoeur,* edited by Ingolf U. Dalferth and Marlene A. Block, 11–34. Tübingen: Mohr Siebeck, 2015.

Triacca, A. M. and Pistoia, A., eds. *Liturgie et cosmos. Conférences Saint-Serge XLIVe Semaine d'Études liturgiques 1997.* Rome: C.L.U.-Edizioni Liturgiche, 1998.

Turcan, Nicolae. *Apologie după sfârșitul metafizicii: Teologie și fenomenologie la Jean-Luc Marion.* Bucharest: Editura Eikon, 2016.

Turner, Victor. *Celebration: Studies in Festivity and Ritual.* Washington: Smithsonian Institution Press, 1982.

———. *From Ritual to Theatre: The Human Seriousness of Play.* New York: Performing Arts Journal Publications, 1982.

———. *The Ritual Process: Structure and Anti-Structure.* London: Routledge, 1969.

Turner, Victor and Edith. *Image and Pilgrimage in Christian Culture: Anthropological Reflections.* New York: Columbia University Press, 1978.

Uthemann, Karl-Heinz. "Die Kunst der Beredsamkeit in der Spätantike: Pagane Redner und christliche Prediger." *Neues Handbuch der Literaturwissenschaften* 4 (1996): 327–76.

Vagaggini, Cyprian. *Theological Dimensions of the Liturgy: A General Treatise on the Theology of the Liturgy.* Collegeville, Minn.: The Liturgical Press, 1976.

Varghese, Baby. *West Syrian Liturgical Theology.* Aldershot, UK: Ashgate, 2004.

Vikan, Gary, ed. *Early Byzantine Pilgrimage Art.* Washington: Dumbarton Oaks Byzantine Collection Publications, 2010.

————, ed. *Sacred Images and Sacred Power in Byzantium*. Aldershot, UK: Ashgate, 2003.

Vogel, Dwight W. *Primary Sources of Liturgical Theology: A Reader*. Collegeville, Minn.: Liturgical Press, 2000.

Voss, Bernd R. *Der Dialog in der frühchristlichen Literatur*. Munich: Wilhelm Fink Verlag, 1970.

Wainwright, Geoffrey. *Doxology: The Praise of God in Worship, Doctrine and Life*. London: Epworth Press, 1980.

————. *Eucharist and Eschatology*. London: Epworth Press, 1971.

————. *Worship with One Accord: Where Liturgy and Ecumenism Embrace*. Oxford: Oxford University Press, 1997.

Wainwright, Geoffrey, and Karen B. Westerfield Tucker, eds. *The Oxford History of Christian Worship*. New York: Oxford University Press, 2005.

Walker, Peter W. L. *Holy City, Holy Places? Christian Attitudes to Jerusalem and the Holy Land in the Fourth Century*. Oxford: Clarendon Press, 1990.

Walker White, Andrew. *Performing Orthodox Ritual in Byzantium*. Cambridge: Cambridge University Press, 2015.

Wanek, Nina Maria, ed. *Psaltike: Neue Studien zur byzantinischen Musik*. Vienna: Praesens Byzantinistik, 2011.

Wardley, Kenneth Jason. *Praying to a French God: The Theology of Jean-Yves Lacoste*. Farnham, UK: Ashgate, 2014.

Ware, Kallistos. *The Orthodox Church*. New York: Penguin, 1963.

Ware, Kallistos, and Mother Mary, trans. *The Festal Menaion*. South Canaan, Pa.: St. Tikhon's Seminary Press, 1998.

————. *The Lenten Triodion*. South Canaan, Pa.: St. Tikhon's Seminary Press, 2002.

Webb, Ruth. "The Aesthetics of Sacred Space: Narrative, Metaphor, and Motion in *ekphraseis* of Church Buildings." *Dumbarton Oaks Papers* 53 (1999): 57–94.

————. *Ekphraseis, Imagination and Persuasion in Ancient Rhetorical Theory and Practice*. Farnham, UK: Ashgate, 2009.

Wellesz, Egon. *A History of Byzantine Music and Hymnography*. Oxford: Clarendon Press, 1961.

White, James F. *Documents of Christian Worship: Descriptive and Interpretive Sources*. Edinburgh: T&T Clark, 1992.

————. *Introduction to Christian Worship*. Nashville: Abingdon Press, 2000 [1990].

White, James, and Susan White. *Church Architecture: Building and Renovating for Christian Worship*. Nashville: Abingdon Press, 1988.

White, Susan J. *Christian Worship and Technological Change*. Nashville: Abingdon Press, 1994.

————. *A History of Women in Christian Worship.* London: SPCK, 2003.

————. *The Spirit of Worship: The Liturgical Tradition.* Maryknoll, N.Y.: Orbis; London: Darton, Longman and Todd, 2000.

Whitow, Mark. *The Making of Orthodox Byzantium, 600–1025.* London: Macmillan, 1996.

Wilkinson, John. *Egeria's Travels.* Westminster, UK: Aris & Phillips Ltd., 1999.

————. *From Synagogue to Church: The Traditional Design.* London: Routledge, 2002.

————. *Jerusalem Pilgrims before the Crusades.* Oxford: Aris and Philipps, 2011.

Winkler, Gabriele. *Studies in Early Christian Liturgy and Its Context.* Aldershot, UK: Ashgate, 1997.

Wolterstorff, Nicholas. *Acting Liturgically: Philosophical Reflections on Religious Practice.* Oxford: Oxford University Press, 2018.

Woodfin, Warren T. *The Embodied Icon: Liturgical Vestments and Sacramental Power in Byzantium.* Oxford: Oxford University Press, 2012.

Woolfenden, Gregory W. *Daily Liturgical Prayer: Origins and Theology.* Aldershot, UK: Ashgate, 2004.

Wybrew, Hugh. *The Orthodox Liturgy: The Development of the Eucharistic Liturgy in the Byzantine Rite.* Crestwood, N.Y.: St. Vladimir's Seminary Press, 1989.

Zimmerman, Joyce Ann. *Liturgy and Hermeneutics.* Collegeville, Minn.: Liturgical Press, 1999.

————. *Liturgy as Language of Faith: A Liturgical Methodology in the Mode of Paul Ricoeur's Textual Hermeneutics.* Lanham, Md.: University Press of America, 1988.

————. *Liturgy as Living Faith: A Liturgical Spirituality.* Scranton, Pa.: University of Scranton Press, 1993.

Zizioulas, John D. *Being as Communion: Studies in Personhood and the Church.* Crestwood, N.Y.: St. Vladimir's Seminary Press, 1985.

————. *Communion and Otherness: Further Studies in Personhood and the Church.* London: T&T Clark, 2006.

————. *Eucharist, Bishop, Church: The Unity of the Church in the Divine Eucharist and the Bishop During the First Three Centuries.* Boston: Holy Cross Orthodox Press, 2001.

INDEX

adoration, 83, 98, 109, 123, 157, 170, 179, 186, 253*n*47

affect/affectivity, xii, 10, 18, 19, 26, 27, 28–29, 39, 51, 54, 67, 70, 77, 79, 85, 87–88, 91, 92, 98, 111, 122, 125–47, 153, 159, 161, 163, 165, 166, 167, 181, 182, 186, 187, 189, 195, 197, 202, 203, 244*n*31, 253*n*43, 254*n*54, 258*nn*31,39; auto-affection/self-affectivity, 6, 15, 17, 86, 154, 199, 258*n*30; coaffection, 23, 131, 218*n*72, 243*n*21, 255*n*74, 256*n*76, 258*nn*34–39. See also *Befindlichkeit*; emotion

altar, 59, 60, 62, 65, 67, 71, 72, 74, 75, 81, 91, 96, 102, 103, 150, 253*n*51, 263*n*2; altar cloth, 120

alterity, 26, 28, 154–57, 164–65, 173–74, 192, 264*n*38, 266*n*50

anamnesis/anamnetic, 22, 35–37, 45, 169, 218*n*63, 226*n*20. See also memory

Anderson, E. Byron, 35, 83, 128, 149, 150, 169, 190, 217*n*61, 220*n*85, 225*n*15, 227*n*30, 230*n*75, 231*nn*81,83, 242*n*12, 257*n*15, 263*nn*7,15,21,22, 268*n*5, 273*nn*1–2

apophatic, 8, 173

appropriate/appropriation, 22, 43, 46, 50–55, 70, 78, 90, 91, 105, 120, 127–28, 141, 149, 162–65, 195, 231*n*81, 251*n*21. *See also* disappropriation

architecture, 1, 21, 27, 58, 59–63, 69, 77, 101, 105, 192, 201, 209*n*24, 232*n*2–33*n*4, 235*n*9, 236*n*21, 237*n*27, 249*n*15

Aristotle, 4, 51, 128, 230*n*73, 257*n*14, 267*n*60

ascetic/asceticism, 5, 6, 10, 25, 32, 48, 104, 126, 127, 136, 142, 143, 144, 160, 162, 179, 230*n*74, 231*n*78, 256*n*78, 257*n*3, 269*n*32

attunement, 130–31, 135, 138, 140, 243*n*21. See also *Befindlichkeit*; mood

authenticity, 53, 164, 192

awe, 92, 129, 133, 135–38, 140–41, 160, 172, 176, 182, 185, 196, 247*n*8. *See also* reverence; veneration

Baldovin, John, 61, 148, 150, 209*n*26, 216*n*48, 221*n*89–22*n*90, 229*n*67, 230*nn*71,75, 231*n*76, 235*nn*14–15, 236*nn*18–19, 263*nn*4–6, 264*nn*25–27

Christina M. Gschwandtner teaches Continental Philosophy of Religion at Fordham University. Her most recent books include *Degrees of Givenness: On Saturation in Jean-Luc Marion* (Indiana, 2014) and *Marion and Theology* (T&T Clark, 2016). She has also translated several French books and articles by various authors.

ORTHODOX CHRISTIANITY AND CONTEMPORARY THOUGHT

Aristotle Papanikolaou and Ashley M. Purpura, series editors

Christina M. Gschwandtner, *Welcoming Finitude: Toward a Phenomenology of Orthodox Liturgy.*

Pia Sophia Chaudhari, *Dynamis of Healing: Patristic Theology and the Psyche*

Brian A. Butcher, *Liturgical Theology after Schmemann: An Orthodox Reading of Paul Ricoeur.* Foreword by Andrew Louth.

Ashley M. Purpura, *God, Hierarchy, and Power: Orthodox Theologies of Authority from Byzantium.*

George E. Demacopoulos, *Colonizing Christianity: Greek and Latin Religious Identity in the Era of the Fourth Crusade.*

George E. Demacopoulos and Aristotle Papaniklaou (eds.), *Orthodox Constructions of the West.*

John Chryssavgis and Bruce V. Foltz (eds.), *Toward an Ecology of Transfiguration: Orthodox Christian Perspectives on Environment, Nature, and Creation.* Foreword by Bill McKibben. Prefatory Letter by Ecumenical Patriarch Bartholomew.

Aristotle Papanikolaou and George E. Demacopoulos (eds.), *Orthodox Readings of Augustine* [available 2020]

Lucian N. Leustean (ed.), *Orthodox Christianity and Nationalism in Nineteenth-Century Southeastern Europe.*

John Chryssavgis (ed.), *Dialogue of Love: Breaking the Silence of Centuries.* Contributions by Brian E. Daley, S.J., and Georges Florovsky.

George E. Demacopoulos and Aristotle Papaniklaou (eds.), *Christianity, Democracy, and the Shadow of Constantine.*

Aristotle Papaniklaou and George E. Democopoulos (eds.), *Fundamentalism or Tradition: Christianity after Secularism*

Georgia Frank, Andrew S. Jacobs, and Susan R. Holman (eds.), *The Garb of Being: Embodiment and the Pursuit of Holiness in Late Ancient Christianity*

Ecumenical Patriarch Bartholomew, *In the World, Yet Not of the World: Social and Global Initiatives of Ecumenical Patriarch Bartholomew.* Edited by John Chryssavgis. Foreword by Jose Manuel Barroso.

Ecumenical Patriarch Bartholomew, *Speaking the Truth in Love: Theological and Spiritual Exhortations of Ecumenical Patriarch Bartholomew.* Edited by John Chryssavgis. Foreword by Dr. Rowan Williams, Archbishop of Canterbury.

Ecumenical Patriarch Bartholomew, *On Earth as in Heaven: Ecological Vision and Initiatives of Ecumenical Patriarch Bartholomew.* Edited by John Chryssavgis. Foreword by His Royal Highness, the Duke of Edinburgh.

CPSIA information can be obtained
at www.ICGtesting.com
Printed in the USA
LVHW112128190919
631670LV00004B/32/P